POLICE LEADERSHIP
AND MANAGEMENT

POLICE LEADERSHIP AND MANAGEMENT

Editors

Margaret Mitchell
John Casey

THE FEDERATION PRESS
2007

Published in Sydney by

The Federation Press
PO Box 45, Annandale, NSW, 2038.
71 John St, Leichhardt, NSW, 2040.
Ph (02) 9552 2200. Fax (02) 9552 1681.
E-mail: info@federationpress.com.au
Website: http://www.federationpress.com.au

National Library of Australia
Cataloguing-in-Publication entry

Police leadership and management.

Bibliography.
Includes index.
ISBN 978 186287 649 1 (pbk.)

1. Police administration. 2. Leadership. 3. Police – Supervision of.
I. Mitchell, Margaret. II: Casey, John (John Peter). III. Title.

363.2068

 Text printed on
100% recycled paper

Typeset by The Federation Press, Leichhardt, NSW.
Printed by Southwood Press, Marrickville, NSW.

Contents

Acknowledgments

We would like to express our deep gratitude to each and every contributor to this volume, and to our peer reviewers. It has been a pleasure to work with you and bring this collection together. Your challenging and interesting perspectives from your areas of expertise will contribute to the further development of policing in this new 21st century. We also acknowledge the stimulation and insights provided by the many policing colleagues, both operational police and educators, with whom we have worked in several countries and jurisdictions over the years. You have taught us a lot about the characteristics of good leaders and managers. Thank you all. We thank Denise Cail for her careful proofreading and reference checking and in particular for the excellent way in which she dealt with our contributors. Sincere thanks go to Neil Radford for his meticulous work in preparing the Index for this book. We know and appreciate how much work this involves. We also thank Jenny Exall at Federation Press who saw this project through to its conclusion.

Margaret Mitchell
John Casey
July 2007

Contributors

Margaret Mitchell

Dr Margaret Mitchell is an Associate Professor and Director of the Sellenger Centre for Research in Law, Justice and Policing at Edith Cowan University, Perth. She was with the Australian Graduate School of Policing, Charles Sturt University, New South Wales from 1999 to 2005 where she taught post-graduate programs in police management. Before moving to Australia, she was Director of the Police Research Unit, at Glasgow Caledonian University, Scotland from 1992 until 1999. Her academic background is complemented by applied experience through a two-and-a-half-year secondment as Senior Policy Officer at NSW Police working on police reform following the Wood Royal Commission. Her previous books include *The Aftermath of Road Accidents* (1996, Routledge), which remains a pivotal collection on the subject, and *Remember Me: Constructing Immortality* (2007, Routledge).

John Casey

Dr John Casey is an Associate Professor in the School of Public Affairs, Baruch College, City University of New York, USA. He was a Senior Lecturer in management, leadership and governance at Charles Sturt University, New South Wales from 1999 to 2007. He was also a visiting lecturer in criminal justice at the University of Maine at Augusta, USA in 2006 and at the Universitat Autònoma de Barcelona, Spain in 2004 and 2006. From 1992 to 1998, he was the Executive Officer of the Masters in Public Management program at a three-university consortium in Barcelona and a consultant to the European Union working on public sector development in Eastern Europe. Previously, he was the Director of the Mayor's Office of Adult Literacy for the City of New York, USA and a social services manager in Sydney, Australia. He is currently writing a book on the international dimensions of policing.

Chris Cunneen

Dr Chris Cunneen holds the NewSouth Global Chair in Criminology at the University of New South Wales. Previously, he was the Director of the Institute of Criminology at Sydney Law School. Professor Cunneen has published widely in the area of juvenile justice, policing, and Indigenous issues including *Juvenile Justice. Youth and Crime in Australia* (2002, Oxford University Press), *Conflict, Politics and Crime* (2001, Allen & Unwin), *Faces of Hate* (1997, Federation Press) and *Indigenous People and the Law in Australia* (1995, Butterworths).

David Dixon

Dr David Dixon is Dean of the Faculty of Law at the University of New South Wales in Sydney. Professor Dixon's books include *Law in Policing: Legal Regulation and Police Practices* (1997, Clarendon Press), *A Culture of Corruption: Changing an Australian Police Service* (1999, Hawkins Press) and *Interrogating Images: Audio-visually Recorded Police Questioning of Suspects* (2007, Sydney Institute of Criminology). His recent and current research includes projects on police interrogation, international policy transfers in policing, questioning of suspects and police reform.

Scott Gardner

Dr Scott Gardner is an Associate Professor, and Director of Postgraduate and Professional Education at Murdoch University in Perth, Western Australia. His core research and teaching interests are organisational change, strategic management, and the role of professional knowledge in human resource management practices. He has over 15 years' experience in academia and consulting for government and the private sector, and worked with the Edith Cowan University/Western Australia Police partnership on the design and delivery of their officer development programs from 2003 until 2006.

John Gillespie

John Gillespie was a member of the Western Australia Police for over 30 years having served in many operational and administration/corporate positions. He is the recipient of a bravery medal and Commissioners Commendations, has higher educational qualifications in Police Management and Public Administration, and recently completed a Masters by Research. He is currently working in the Pacific Region as a Community Justice Adviser.

Tracey Green

Tracey Green is a former police officer from the UK where she spent 22 years mostly as a Detective working in drug operations and homicide investigation. She reached the rank of Detective Inspector before moving to Australia. She is now the Sub-Dean Policing and Director of the Centre for Investigative Studies and Crime Reduction at Charles Sturt University, New South Wales. Tracey's areas of interest include investigation, leadership, police negotiation and investigative interviewing.

Ellen Grote

Dr Ellen Grote is an applied linguist working on language and the law at the Sellenger Centre for Research in Law, Justice and Policing at Edith Cowan University in Perth, Western Australia. Her research interests include the use of language in law and justice interviews, with a particular focus on police investigative interviews. She also lectures in communication skills for justice practitioners and police.

Vincent Hughes

Dr Vincent Hughes is the Assistant Director of Professional Development at the Western Australia Police Academy. He has a good understanding of police management issues having spent 18 years in the *Garda Siochana* – Republic of Ireland Police Force. In addition he worked on organised crime syndicates as a Crime Analyst with both the Western Australia Police and the former National Crime Authority.

Paul Jackson

Dr Paul Jackson worked as an Information Systems Development Manager and Consultant in Australia and Germany for over 25 years. He now teaches Information Systems and Knowledge Management at Edith Cowan University in Perth, Western Australia. His particular research interest is investigating knowledge and information management from philosophical, social and cognitive perspectives to improve outcomes.

Stephen Jiggins

Dr Stephen Jiggins has held a range of senior public affairs appointments including Media Director for the Australian Federal Police from 1994 until 2002. In that role he was involved in media management for a range of complex and sensitive police operations including major transnational investigations. Dr Jiggins' doctoral thesis examined the relationship between police organisations and the print news media in Australia. He maintains an active interest in policing through his work on the Police Leadership program at Charles Sturt University, New South Wales.

Ian J Lanyon

Ian Lanyon is the Executive Director of the Australasian Police Professional Standards Council (APPSC). Ian is seconded from Victoria Police, where he is a Commissioned Officer having served since 1985 in areas including homicide, armed robbery, drugs, DNA and arson squads. In 1999 he was selected by the Commonwealth as a Station Leader and spent 14 months in Antarctica in charge of Davis Antarctic Station. Ian holds a Bachelor of Laws and a Bachelor of Policing.

Colleen Lewis

Dr Colleen Lewis is an Associate Professor and Head, School of Humanities, Communications and Social Sciences at Monash University, Victoria. Her major research interests include police accountability, police-government relations and civilian oversight models. She is the author of *Complaints Against Police: the Politics of Reform* (1999, Hawkins Press) and co-editor and contributor to the books *Counter Terrorism and the Post Democratic State* (2007 forthcoming with Jenny Hocking and Edward Elgar); *It's Time Again: Whitlam and Modern Labor* (2003 with Jenny Hocking, Circa Books); *Civilian Oversight of Police: Governance, Democracy and Human Rights* (2000 with Andrew

Goldsmith, Hart Publishing); *Unpeeling Tradition: Contemporary Policing* (1994 with Keith Bryett, Macmillan) and *Corporate Management in Australian Government* (1989 with Glyn Davis and Patrick Weller, Macmillan).

Lorraine Mazerolle

Dr Lorraine Mazerolle is a Professor in the School of Criminology and Criminal Justice at Griffith University, Brisbane. She is the recipient of many US and Australian research grants on policing, a Fellow of the Academy of Experimental Criminology and author (with Janet Ransley) of *Third Party Policing* (2006, Cambridge University Press), *Policing Places with Drug Problems* (1995, Sage Publications (as Lorraine Green)) and (with Jan Roehl) *Civil Remedies and Crime Prevention* (1998, Criminal Justice Press).

David Mutton

David Mutton coordinates the Master of Forensic Psychology degree at the University of Western Sydney, where he has been a full-time academic since 2001. From 1990 until 1995 he was the Senior Psychologist, and then in 1995 was appointed the Chief Psychologist, of the NSW Police. From 1980 until 1990 he was a Psychologist and Senior Psychologist in the NSW Department of Corrective Services. His main areas of research interests are regarding resilience and help-seeking in emergency services personnel.

Stephen Pierce

Stephen Pierce was a Visiting Fellow at the Australian Institute of Police Management from January 2005 to January 2007. He has a 29-year police career with Victoria Police and significant operational experience in the State Crime Squads particularly in Asian and organised crime. He received a number of community awards during this period. He also has recent experience as State Manager of the Crime Prevention Office. Stephen has a Masters of Business Administration (Deakin); Masters of Leadership and Management (Policing) (Charles Sturt); Grad Cert App Mgt (AIPM); Assoc Diploma Policing (Monash); and was a Williamson Fellow with Leadership Victoria in 2003.

Tim Prenzler

Dr Tim Prenzler is an Associate Professor and lectures in the School of Criminology and Criminal Justice at Griffith University in Brisbane. He teaches in the areas of crime prevention, security management, and ethics and accountability in criminal justice. His research interests include security industry regulation, police corruption prevention and gender in policing. He recently co-edited *An Introduction to Crime* (with Hennessey Hayes, 2007, Pearson Education), co-authored *The Law of Private Security in Australia* (with Rick Sarre, 2005, Thomson Lawbook Co) and co-edited *Police Reform: Building Integrity* (with Janet Ransley, 2002, Hawkins Press).

Janet Ransley

Dr Janet Ransley is a Senior Lecturer in the School of Criminology and Criminal Justice, Griffith University, Brisbane. She teaches in the areas of law, policy and white collar crime, and has research interests in the governance of policing, policing new and challenging problems, and court and tribunal processes. Recent publications include a book, *Third Party Policing* with Lorraine Mazerolle (2006, Cambridge University Press), an edited collection, *Police Reform: Building Integrity* with Tim Prenzler, (2002, Hawkins Press), and articles on court and inquiry practices, preventive detention and policing.

Glenn Ross

Glenn Ross has over 25 years' experience in the criminal justice systems in Victoria, New South Wales and Western Australia. He recently held the positions of Manager Research, Policy and Reform Unit of the Kennedy Royal Commission into Police Corruption in Western Australia, and Manager Corruption Prevention, Education and Research with the Corruption and Crime Commission of Western Australia and is undertaking a PhD at Edith Cowan University researching commissions of inquiry. Glenn is Adjunct Associate Professor with the Sellenger Centre in the School of Law and Justice at Edith Cowan University, Perth.

Rick Sarre

Dr Rick Sarre is Professor of Law and Justice at the School of Commerce, University of South Australia. Formerly he was Head of the School of Law and Legal Practice at the university. He is currently an Associate of the Australian Institute of Criminology, South Australian representative on the board of the Australian and New Zealand Society of Criminology, and a member of the Board of Directors of the International Police Executive Symposium. He has held Visiting Researcher positions at Graceland University (Iowa, USA) and Umeå University (Sweden).

Gary Shaw

Gary Shaw is a Detective Chief Inspector who has 29 years of police service with Northumbria Police in the UK, mostly in criminal investigation. He is currently on secondment to the National Centre for Policing Excellence (Operations) as the National Investigative Interviewing Coordinator. His current role is as an Operational Consultant to forces investigating major crime, formulating implementation plans around the ACPO National Interview Strategy.

Allan Sicard

Allan Sicard has been a member of NSW Police for 26 years, and has served in both country and metropolitan locations with the last posting as the Local Area Commander at Moree, a remote location in north-west New South

Wales. Allan spent 14 years as a Detective in high crime locations such as Blacktown and Bankstown and has also worked with Crime Agencies in organised Asian crime and with Internal Affairs in the Integrity Testing Unit. Allan is currently working on the creation of a Good Practice Unit with the Commissioner's Inspectorate. He has a Graduate Certificate in Public Administration (Policing) and has completed a Masters in Public Administration (Policing).

Patrick F Walsh

Patrick Walsh is Senior Lecturer in criminal intelligence and Course Co-ordinator of Post-Graduate Intelligence Studies at the Australian Graduate School of Policing, Charles Sturt University, New South Wales. His research interests include intelligence theory and practice, and transnational security. He has worked as an Intelligence Analyst in national security and law enforcement agencies.

Margaret Mitchell dedicates this book to Sir Willie Rae, QPM, Chief Constable of Strathclyde Police, with gratitude.

John Casey dedicates this book to his parents, Agatha and Stephen Casey. Thank you for the foresight and courage to flee your country of birth and for starting a new life with your family in Australia.

INTRODUCTION

POLICE LEADERSHIP AND MANAGEMENT

Margaret Mitchell and John Casey

This volume deals with the range and complexity of contemporary police leadership and management. The governance of contemporary police organisations requires leaders and managers, even at the local level, to work in and understand complex social, political and organisational environments. We invited contributors whom we believed would summarise and contextualise the essential issues for those working in leadership and management positions at every level in policing. This has produced an interesting and challenging collection that we hope will answer questions as well as raise questions about the changing landscapes of policing. Through the wide range of topics in this collection, we explore what is changing, what is known about the impact of these changes and what leaders and managers now need to do or anticipate as a consequence. By examining leadership and management in one volume, we see the two roles as naturally linked.

Operational policing is no longer the isolationist and militaristic activity it once was. Rather, contemporary policing embraces new models of 'partnership' and 'community' to manage crime and disorder. And, although command and control models are still important in many police operations, leading and managing police organisations increasingly depends on professional development and encouraging enthusiasm and innovation in police officers and staff. These themes of partnership and innovation are reflected in several of the contributions, and we see both as a fundamental characteristic of new policing. Our own fieldwork with supervisors has underlined the challenges managers face in maintaining the enthusiasm of probationers as the frustrations of the job are encountered. The new generation of police leaders and managers needs to shed some of the old models and have the confidence to understand when command and control is needed, to be open to ideas from outside policing, to encourage open communication and to devise ways to encourage innovation. For many this will involve a paradigm shift just as profound as the shift to New Public Management in the 1980s.

Police officers work with issues at all 'ends' of the justice system. They need to be many things to many people. They interact with the community – allowing small children to try on police hats for a photo – participate in consultative exercises, and are the community's 'eyes and ears' collecting local intelligence that may be of the gravest significance in investigating or anticipating organised crime or political violence. And all of this occurs within the framework of intense scrutiny from many levels of internal and external accountability. Their colleagues, each of whom at one stage of their career or another may end up as a rivals for promotion, create a working context that combines competition with the cohesiveness that characterises the social and psychological work environment of policing. Compared with many other public sector and private organisations, the sheer variety of police business is, arguably, of a different order. We see police leaders and managers as faced with very different challenges than those in other organisations, requiring special abilities to prioritise their work. It is important for police managers and leaders to have time to reflect, critically evaluate and synthesise all these issues, and to be supported in their capacity to do so.

Royal commissions and inquiries into policing in Australia and elsewhere in the world, the rise in the strength and scope of oversight agencies, the diversification of communities, the impact of fluctuations in the availability of narcotic drugs, greater use of social drugs and the rise of consumerism in every area of the public service have each placed pressures on setting organisational priorities. The escalation in international crime and threats to security has had a significant impact on strategic priorities and the evolution of new policing responses. We can see in jurisdictional mission statements, corporate plans, business plans and strategic directions a recognition of and attempt to bring some order to this wide range of demands and new directions for policing.

Given this breadth of police business how are we to understand policing, and the responsibilities of police managers and leaders? Our own chapter on the requirements of police leaders and managers opens the collection describing the range of ways in which the characteristics of good leaders and managers have been organised into taxonomies. We consider the substantial list of essential skills, knowledge and attitudes required by police managers and leaders at each level of the hierarchy of responsibility. This chapter serves to underline the range, scope and depth of leading and managing such complex organisations, and we have placed this chapter first to provide a framework within which to fit the detail of later chapters.

The volume is then organised according to three broad themes. The first part, on the new operational context of policing, embraces law, intelligence, investigations, and the changes in policing practices as a result of partnerships with agencies outside policing. The second part addresses internal staff development and performance management, external accountability and oversight, and the increasing importance of education in the practice of professional policing. The third part explores the demands placed on police organisations from the external social and political environment. Police relationships with Indigenous communities, the local community and the news media are discussed, as are the impact of trans-national crime and the role of police in international deployments. Interestingly, the contributors have put relatively little emphasis on the difference between jurisdictions, tending instead to treat policing in Australia almost as though it were a single entity. We see this largely as a result of globalisation and the fundamental similarity in the concerns and challenges facing many police jurisdictions.

This collection is aimed at every level of leader and manager in policing, and at the many students of policing and police management. It is also intended as a handbook for the increasing numbers of academics and practitioners conducting research on organisational and operational aspects of policing. We hope that *Police Leadership and Management* will assist all police and police scholars in their endeavours.

REQUIREMENTS OF POLICE MANAGERS AND LEADERS FROM SERGEANT TO COMMISSIONER

John Casey and Margaret Mitchell

Senior officers in Australian police agencies are responsible for complex organisations that function within an increasingly uncertain environment in which law and order politics have taken on an even greater salience (Edwards 2004; Findlay 2004). This chapter considers the skills, knowledge and attitudes required by police managers and leaders at each level of the hierarchy of responsibility. Each level of promotion provides new challenges for frontline officers moving into management roles as they begin to deal with more complex responsibilities, greater ambiguities, and the increased public exposure that goes with senior management and leadership in police organisations. The brief of police managers and more senior police officers can be particularly difficult due to a relative lack of comparable experience in other work settings, since they are likely to have spent their entire careers in one policing organisation. Moreover, these organisations have only recently sought to shake off a long tradition of command and control structures and, due to this working culture, aspiring managers and leaders may not have been overtly encouraged or rewarded for the skills needed to manage and lead large contemporary policing organisations (Murray 2002; Lee & Punch 2004).

Management and leadership are conceptually different, but senior officers need to be adept at both in order to effectively deliver the range of policing programs and strategies and to steer their organisations through the dual dynamics of close scrutiny and constant change that typify contemporary Australian policing. In an attempt to categorise the expectations of managers, individual jurisdictions have defined what officers at each level would be expected to do. In addition, as a foundation to allow more cross-jurisdictional permeability, the Australasian Police Professional Standards Council (APPSC) a coordinating entity created by the Australian and New

Zealand police agencies, has also developed a taxonomy of levels of management and leadership (APPSC 2006a; 2006d). To augment our understanding of police management and leadership in its wider context, we will also examine the Australian Public Service Integrated Leadership System (Australian Public Service Commission 2006), which provides a highly detailed taxonomy through which to understand the management and leadership capabilities expected at each level of responsibility in public organisations. But first we will look at the wider context of contemporary Australian policing, and the changes that have occurred in its functioning and culture which are of relevance to the work of its managers and leaders.

Australian police organisations

Police agencies in Australia are relatively large organisations when compared with other Australian government departments and police agencies overseas (see Table 1.1, below, Australian State and Territory police personnel and expenditure). Public order and public safety accounts for some 10 per cent of public spending in Australian States although the percentage allocated to policing varies between States. Typically public order and safety is the third largest expense after education and health, which each account for about 20 to 25 per cent (Australian Productivity Commission 2006). Australian police agencies are smaller than many overseas national and metropolitan agencies, for example the French *Gendarmerie* has 93,000 officers and the London Metropolitan Police has 30,000, although are considerably larger than most regional and local agencies in the US and UK where policing is based on small and overlapping territorial jurisdictions.

Table 1.1: Personnel and expenditures in Australian policing

	ACT*	NSW	NT	QLD	SA	TAS	VIC	WA
Total personnel including sworn and civilian staff	802	18,503	1340	11,950	4861	1504	13,035	6172
Total expenditure in $millions	92.6	1940.9	158.7	1053.3	480.8	138.8	1332.9	676.9

* Australian Capital Territory (ACT) local policing only; figure does not include Australian Federal Police which has approx 3500 staff (in national and international posts).

Source: Authors, based on figures from Australian Productivity Commission (2006) & AIC (2006)

Unlike other public and private organisations of a similar size, police agencies are still almost like 'artisan' entities (Lee & Punch 2004), relatively isolated from outside influences to the 'craft' of policing. Indeed the Royal Commission into whether there has been Corrupt or Criminal Conduct by any Western Australian Police Officer (Kennedy 2004) observed that policing operates in a 'vacuum ... cloistered from the wider public service'

(Vol II, p 170). While civilianisation of some positions has brought into the organisation staff with experience in other agencies and professions, more than 70 per cent of employees of police agencies are sworn officers, and the relatively few civilians generally occupy administrative positions.

Sworn officers enter as young recruits and then stay in one agency throughout their policing career. Despite efforts to create lateral entry systems between Australian jurisdictions it has not yet been achieved. The picture is, however, changing. In Western Australia for instance, there are multiple entry pathways to join the organisation, for example through the cadet program and, through the new University degree pathway created in partnership with Edith Cowan University. Further, during 2006, officers at different levels of seniority joined directly from a range of English, Scottish, Welsh and Irish police organisations and became sworn officers of Western Australia Police after 12 weeks of Academy training in State legislation and Western Australia Police systems and standard operating procedures. This same pathway into policing has been adopted in New Zealand and in South Australia. The recruitment and retention crisis in Australian policing which has affected some States more than others requires both lateral entry and lateral thinking to create solutions.

Commissioners can be appointed from other jurisdictions and, in recent years, some senior cross-jurisdictional appointments have been made, and some have also been appointed from overseas. The home page of the APPSC website prominently displays a link to an Australasian Police Vacancies webpage which promotes cross-jurisdiction mobility. This has not yet been embraced by jurisdictions and a search of the listings on the webpage reveal that all the managerial positions advertised since the page was launched in early 2004, are from either the Western Australia Police or the Australian Federal Police (APPSC 2006a). Even within one jurisdiction, it can be difficult for a sworn officer to occupy a civilian public service position within law enforcement, crime prevention or corruption investigation without resigning from their police rank and losing many of the acquired benefits. This relative lack of permeability of policing severely restricts the scope for exchange of ideas and experiences between police and other organisations, and curtails the opportunity for managers and would-be managers to learn in other work settings.

Despite their relative isolation, police agencies have been the focus of the same changes as have other public agencies, and the past 20 years has seen constant reform of the public sector. Public sector agencies have moved from a public *administration* framework, emphasising inputs and the correct implementation of rules using bureaucratic processes, to a *New Public Management* approach focusing on outputs and on the tacit contract between government and the public to provide efficient and effective services. More recently public sector reform has moved to a *governance* approach focusing on outcomes, accountabilities and on providing public goods through networks of public, non-profit and private sector organisations (Long 2003; Fleming & Rhodes 2004). Although policing in Australia has not experienced the same level of funding constraint or outsourcing as have most other public agencies, many of the fundamental organisational concepts of public sector reform have been adopted, as reflected in the emergence of new operating discourses such as the 'governance of security' (Wood & Dupont 2006).

Change in Australian policing has also been driven by cycles of scandals, investigating inquiries and commissions with substantial recommendations for reform. Major inquiries or royal commissions have taken place in at least one of the Australian States every five to eight years (McDonnell 2001). In fact the propensity for expensive and far-reaching royal commissions, not only in policing, could be thought of as a characteristic of the Australian political landscape. Each inquiry or commission has focused on policing in that one jurisdiction, however, the outcomes and recommendations have influenced and driven reform in other States. The Fitzgerald Inquiry in Queensland (1989), the Wood Royal Commission in New South Wales (1997) and the Kennedy Royal Commission in Western Australia (2004) have each made recommendations unique to their particular jurisdictions. They are, however, also based on general public sector reform frameworks and have relevance for organisational structures and operational directions throughout Australian police agencies. The royal commissions and inquiries are both a cause and a symptom of the greater external scrutiny, oversight and accountability that contemporary policing must respond to under contemporary governance regimes. They have also been instrumental in moving police management away from traditional command and control structures.

Each of these profound changes in the internal and, importantly, the external environment of policing in Australia have implications for the skills, knowledge and style of management and leadership that are appropriate to contemporary policing – as former New South Wales Commissioner, Peter Ryan called it, creating and managing an organisational context of 'dynamic stability'.

The skills and capacities required of police leaders and managers

[Senior staff in the public sector] require a mixture of technical and management expertise as well as leadership capabilities ... the precise balance will depend on the level of seniority (Australian Public Service Commission 2004, p 7).

The skills and capacities needed to manage agencies operating within new governance and accountability frameworks are very different than those required under the traditional command and control structures. There is now more of an emphasis on the social skills of communication, cooperation across the agency and externally, on the ability to motivate staff, on the critical thinking skills required for operating in a complex work environment, and on democratic styles of leadership that promote trust and consultation (Murray 2002; Lee & Punch 2004). New Public Management had tended to place primary emphasis on the more narrowly focused outputs management elements of senior police responsibilities (Long 2003), but the broader scope of governance has again brought to the foreground the need for operational leadership. Police managers and leaders at all levels are subject to far greater pressure to deliver high-level performance in a context of conflicting priorities, and one could argue that the stakes are particularly high for management and leadership in policing. Externally, the level of political and community concern over public order and crime ensures close and continual scrutiny of what the organisation is achieving. Dupont's (2006) observation that the role of police commissioners has evolved from that of 'caretakers' to 'innovators and change implementers' can be applied equally to all managerial ranks. As Edwards (2004) notes:

> At the same time as command has been devolved downwards so that local senior officers have far more responsibility for the manner of policing in their area, their actions are more tightly constrained than ever and inspectors and superintendents are subject to far more accountability procedures than even before (Edwards 2004, p 310).

In the following we will try to draw out the distinction between the roles, skills and capacities of managers and leaders. On the surface, managers and leaders share a goal of achieving the objectives of the organisation, although their primary focus will differ. Managers, it could be said, emphasise the efficient and effective allocation and control of resources – importantly human resources – to achieve objectives, while leaders have the capacity to influence others and to combine individuals and resources to determine strategic directions. Management is task-oriented and focuses more on administrating existing policies and procedures, while leadership is more people-oriented and seeks to innovate by developing the policies and procedures of the future and by motivating and inspiring staff (Macdonald 1995; Long 2003).

While management and leadership are different, most of those in positions of responsibility tend to possess a combination of the capabilities and expertise of both (National Institute for Governance 2003, p 4). We can conceive of a manager without leadership qualities – one who effectively organises resources to deliver determined outputs, but lacks the aptitude to lead others; and a leader without the capabilities of a good manager – the charismatic visionary who boldly moves the organisation in new directions, but is not a 'details person'. In practice it is unlikely that a good manager does not display leadership qualities and that a good leader does not have a mastery of managerial skills. Many authors emphasise the differences between management and leadership – and some even regard managers and leaders as separate individuals within an organisation – but in fact mastery of both facets is needed for a successful career in most organisations.

Both management and leadership have behavioural and functional dimensions: the behavioural dimension encompasses the innate and learned qualities of managers and leaders, while the functional dimension involves the technical skills and capabilities related to the tasks that must be performed at each level. Management theories tend to emphasise the functional dimension, and the focus has been on developing inventories of managers' responsibilities and roles that answer the question: what does a manager do? Adams and Beck (2001) in their study on the critical behaviours needed by police managers in Australia used the classification of managerial functions developed by Luthan (1995 in Adams and Beck 2001, p 2) and the definition of managerial roles developed by Mintzberg (1973 in Adams and Beck 2001, p 5) to construct a framework which describes the dimensions of police management behaviours. Table 1.2 compares the inventories of Adams and Beck, Luthan and Mintzberg.

Table 1.2: Comparison of Adams & Beck, Luthan and Mintzberg

Adams & Beck's Dimensions	Luthan's Managerial Behaviours	Mintzberg's Managerial Roles
Traditional Management	Planning; coordinating; decision-making; problem solving; controlling; monitoring	Resource allocator; entrepreneur; disturbance handler; monitor
Human Resources Management	Motivating; reinforcing; disciplining; managing conflict; staffing; training; developing	Leader
Routine Communication	Exchanging information; handling paperwork	Disseminator
Networking	Interacting with outsiders; socialising; politicking	Spokesman; negotiator; figurehead; liaison

Source: Authors, based on Adams and Beck (2001)

In contrast, leadership theories emphasise behavioural qualities and analyse how these qualities can be used to drive effective practice in an organisation. There has been an evolution from early theories that focused only on cataloguing the personality characteristics of leaders to current theories that emphasise the situational and contingency nature of leadership and how these impact on the behaviours required by leaders (Cacioppe 1998; Centrex 2006). Leadership theories can be classified as follows:

- **Trait theories** – lists trait or qualities associated with leadership. They describe the traits, some innate some learned, of those destined to lead.
- **Behaviourist theories** – translate traits into patterns of behaviour that are categorised as 'styles' (eg autocratic, delegative, and democratic).
- **Situational and Contingency theories** – leadership is specific to the situation in which it is exercised. Analysing situational variables, such as the competency of subordinates, the organisational culture, etc, can assist in predicting the most appropriate leadership style for a given circumstance.

Current contingency theories focus more on the outcomes of leadership. *Transactional* leadership seeks to ensure effective outcomes of current goals, by maximising efficiency and reinforcing the bottom line, while *transformational* leadership creates future visions and drives organisational change by releasing potential and transcending daily affairs (Cacioppe 1998; Densten 2003; Long 2003; Centrex 2006). Figure 1.1 shows the relationship between the different elements of leadership theories.

A comparison of Table 1.2 (page 9) and Figure 1.1, below, demonstrates that, despite the conceptual differences, there is considerable crossover between management and leadership theories. For example in Table 1.2, one of Mintzberg's managerial roles is that of leader, and some of the Luthan's managerial behaviours, such as motivating and politicking, are more commonly associated with leadership. It may be that the point of inflection between management and leadership is this shift from transactional to transformational leadership. While senior officers focus primarily on the transactional aspects of effectively administrating within the current parameters of the organisation, they are more managers than leaders, but when the focus shifts to the transformational and to the implementation of change, then an officer becomes more explicitly a leader. The need for more transformational leadership in policing has become a central theme of current police leadership dialogues, and the development of transformational culture is seen as crucial element in ensuring that policing continues to reform

Figure 1.1: The relationship between the elements of leadership theories

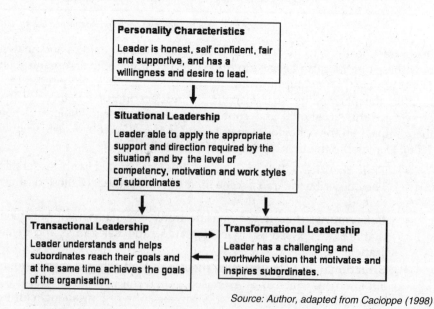

Source: Author, adapted from Cacioppe (1998)

itself in response to the changing social and political realities (Murray 2002; Negus 2002; Long 2003; Centrex 2006).

Both management *and* leadership capabilities, along with the requisite technical expertise, are necessary throughout an officer's career. However there are differing views as to how they relate to each other. One view is that as one rises up the hierarchy, the technical skills of the front-line officer gives way to a need for the managerial skills of middle ranking officers, which then give way to the need for leadership skills in senior officers. In contrast to this orderly sequence, is the recognition that leadership is necessary at all ranks and so officers need to demonstrate leadership early in their career. Equally, technical and managerial skills continue to be important at all levels of seniority. In fact, the Australian Public Service Integrated Leadership System (Australian Public Service Commission 2006) emphasises the integration of leadership and management at each of the professional level of Public Service (PS), the middle-management level of Executive Leaders (EL) and for roles in the Senior Executive Service (SES). Figure 1.2 (over the page) shows how the skills are combined at each level.

In the same vein, the model used by the English and Welsh police leadership program at Central Police Training and Development Authority (Centrex), is based on a concept of 'cradle-to-grave' leadership, on the basis that policing at all ranks confers a responsibility to lead. As one Director of Leadership at Centrex has stated:

> We need to accept the reality that senior ranks have significantly less direct contact with staff. The person who has the most contact may be a personnel manager, control room operator or perhaps the station sergeant. The positive implications from developing leadership skills in these colleagues would be dramatic (Police Professional 2005).

Leadership skills are therefore considered to be equally necessary early in early career while more responsibility with increasing rank requires management skills to complement them. Figure 1.3 (page 12) depicts how Centrex conceptualises the relationship between supervision, management and leadership.

The lack of a clear separation between manager and leader is particularly evident in the context of policing organisations, in which senior staff were themselves once frontline officers, and where middle and senior managers are likely to have spent their careers in one agency. Senior police officers are concurrently managers and leaders (and also administrators, supervisors, commanders, and executives). Densten (1999; 2003) from a leadership perspective and Adams and Beck (2001) from a managerial perspective analysed the work of senior police in Australian police agencies and, despite the different conceptual approach of the studies, they all ultimately emphasised the importance of similar leadership 'behaviours'. Adams and Beck (2001) focused on the behaviours required by managers and recommended that managers engage in 'directive leadership ... balanced by a willingness to include staff in the process and provide rewards for a job well done' (p 29), while Densten (2003) analysed leadership requirements at senior levels and concluded that there was a need for more transformational leadership that motivates staff and drives change.

Figure 1.2: Australian Public Service, Integrated Leadership System

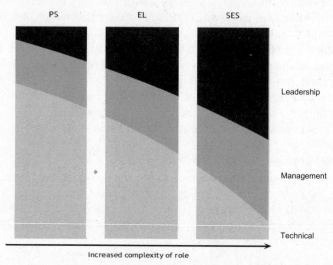

Source: *Australian Public Service Commission (2006)*

Figure 1.3: Centrex: relationship between supervision, management and leadership

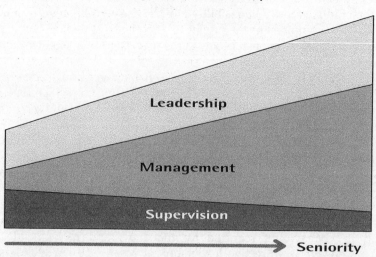

Source: *Centrex (2006, p 9)*

New rank, new responsibility

> Top quality leaders are crucial to any successful organisation. Leadership is particularly important in the police service, not only for chief constables and their senior teams, but also for junior officers, who have to act as leaders on a daily basis – either for their colleagues or for members of the public (Home Office 2001, p 124).

In addition to having to deal with more organisational responsibilities, as officers move into the most senior ranks they move into employment based on performance contracts. They are also subject to intense media scrutiny, criticism from police associations and their own officers, and may face the possible withdrawal of support by their own executive. Contracts are often not renewed, some senior officers are dismissed, and others are 'encouraged' to take early retirement. A recent study of Canadian senior police (Biro et al 2001) found that they had become more like executives of other organisations – having to balance competing interests, experiencing multi-layered accountability, being accountable for achieving value for money, politically astute, and prepared to manage under scrutiny. Many senior police comment on the steep learning curve when they begin any new more responsible, duties, and that they have to learn quickly on the job. They also comment that there is almost no available education or training that is able to fully prepare them for the pressure of achieving results in a climate of constant change (Macdonald 1995; Dupont 2006).

As we have seen, both management and leadership capabilities are required by police officers from very early on in their careers. As they rise up the ranks they are faced with more complex situations and decisions requiring enhanced knowledge and skills as well as different attitudes and approaches. Each police agency describes the roles and responsibilities, and the required skills of each level through specific position descriptions. To denote increasing levels of responsibility, police agencies in Australia use the traditional police ranks of Constable, Sergeant, Inspector, Superintendent and Commissioner (there is some variation between States in the use of these ranks), interspersed with some civilian public service positions. Only the Australian Federal Police eschews this rank structure, using the designation of Federal Agent for a wide range of operational positions. Table 1.3 (over the page) presents the Australasian Police Professional Standards Council generic designations compared with an example of rank role definition (based on various Victoria Police position descriptions and APPSC level descriptions) and illustrates how increasing responsibility at managerial levels is defined. The APPSC, in an attempt to allow comparability across ranks and jurisdictions, uses generic categories of practitioner, specialist, supervisor, manager and executive when developing competency standards and policies on qualifications.

Taking this taxonomic approach further, the Australian Public Service Commission has developed the Integrated Leadership System (ILS), referred to earlier, providing detailed descriptors of the different levels of responsibi-

Table 1.3: Roles of Supervisors, Managers and Executives

Level (APPSC)	Rank (Victoria Police)	Definition of role
Supervisor	Senior Sergeant	Manages personnel and prepares, promotes implements and evaluates local level action plans. Promotes and contributes to the corporate management planning process.
Manager	Inspector	Strategically manages, supports and co-ordinates the delivery of services with accountability for the effectiveness quality cost and standard of outputs. Performs a leadership role within the District/Regional portfolio to achieve cultural change
Manager – Executive	Superintendent	[Managerial roles as above] and participates in and provides informed contributions to the design and implementation of divisional and department- wide management plans. Represents the division or department by way of authoritative oral and written presentation
Executive	Assistant Commissioner, Deputy Commissioner Chief Commissioner	Leads the development and implementation of organisational polices, practices and services. Warrants the effective and efficient delivery of services. Leads and develops an effective team.

Source: Authors, based on various Victoria Police position descriptions and APPSC level descriptions

lity in the public service. As we have seen earlier, the ILS assumes a mix of technical, managerial and leadership 'components' in the work of senior staff grouped in five 'capability clusters' of the expertise required by staff at Executive Leader level and in the Senior Executive Service (Table 1.4, page 15). The ILS provides a detailed analysis of the new capabilities required and the increasing complexities of already acquired capabilities at each of five senior levels in the Australian Public Service: Executive Leader 1 and 2, and Senior Executive Service 1, 2 and 3.

The ILS describes that as a public servant rises through the levels of employment, greater complexity is encountered in four key aspects (APSC 2006, p 45) which most managers and leaders would recognise immediately:

- **Future focus** – Focus shifts from considering the longer-term implications of actions to developing a vision and direction for the future. This is most evident in the *Shapes strategic thinking* capability cluster.

Table 1.4: ILS clusters and corresponding capabilities

Cluster	Capabilities
Shapes strategic thinking	Inspires a sense of purpose and direction Focuses strategically Harnesses information and opportunities Shows judgment, intelligence and common sense
Achieves results	Builds organisational capability and responsiveness Marshals professional expertise Steers and implements change and deals with uncertainty Ensures closure and delivers on intended results
Cultivates productive working relationships	Nurtures internal and external relationships Facilitates cooperation and partnerships Values individual differences and diversity Guides, mentors and develops people
Exemplifies drive and integrity	Demonstrates public service professionalism and probity Engages with risk and shows personal courage Commits to action Displays resilience Demonstrates self awareness and commitment to personal development
Communicates with influence	Communicates clearly Listens, understands and adapts to audience Negotiates persuasively

Source: Author, based on Australian Public Service Commission (nd)

- **Breadth of contact** – Stakeholder interactions become more frequent and the range of stakeholders increases. This is most evident in the *Cultivates productive working relationships* capability cluster.
- **Breadth of impact** – Shift occurs from an impact on one's self and the team, to an impact on a business unit, the whole organisation and then an impact on the whole of government. This is most evident in the *Shapes strategic thinking* and the *Achieves results* capability clusters.
- **Breadth of responsibility** – Shift in responsibility that develops from individual and team outcomes to responsibility for achieving organisation wide outcomes. This is most evident in the *Achieves results* capability cluster.

While various police jurisdictions have statements of the capabilities required of senior ranks, so far there has been no direct comparison of Australian police ranks with their equivalents in the ILS. It is beyond the scope of this chapter to do that, but by comparing police and general public service wage structures it can be deduced that the Executive Leaders corresponds roughly to Senior Sergeant to Inspector ranks, and the Senior Executive Service corresponds to Superintendent rank and above. The English and Welsh police, through Centrex, have recently developed a Police Leadership Qualities Framework which in effect links police leadership with broader public sector leadership requirements. The objective of the Framework was to 'set out, for the first time, what the Police Service believes about leadership in terms of its constituent elements of styles, values, ethics, standards and competences' (Centrex 2006, p i). These elements are analysed at five levels: leading by example, leading others, leading teams, leading units and leading organisations.

The business of promotion

Much of what has been said in the previous sections has implied an individual's orderly progression up the ranks based on merit and on having demonstrated the capability, or at least the potential, to manage and lead. Being promoted implies that the person has displayed the necessary management and leadership qualities for success in meeting higher responsibilities. Sometimes this is demonstrated through 'acting up' in higher positions, such that most individuals who are promoted will have had some experience in the role before achieving it through application and promotion.

In police organisations where many have joined from school, there are additional problems associated with promotion, however, as officers must compete with people they have worked with and known for a long time. It is also, as many senior police note, 'lonely at the top'. The study by Biro et al (2001) of Canadian senior police, found a growing gap between operational police and senior police. Many commentators have described the cultural and conceptual divide between 'street cops' and 'management cops' first identified by Reuss-Ianni and Ianni in 1983 (Reuss-Ianni & Ianni 2005) and further described by Foster (2003) and Lee & Punch (2004). Sir John Stevens (quoted in Orr-Munro 2005, p 20) said:

> Officers and support staff will follow people who have got credibility and know what they are talking about. Do not underestimate leadership in this service. You only get good morale and proficiency when people think they are being led by those who know the business and have done the business.

In a survey by Rowe (2006) of police constables' opinions of senior officers, salient was the view that they [the senior officers] were 'divorced from the reality of police work and did not appreciate the difficulties faced by junior ranks'. Rowe also found that this problem seemed to be exacerbated in constables' minds by schemes such as 'accelerated promotion' on the basis that the promoted officers could not have developed the necessary experience in 'real' police work.

Officers need also, as they rise further up the hierarchy, to jettison previously acquired attitudes and behaviours as they now manage and supervise those with whom they previously were equals. Newly promoted officers need to resolve how to manage the divide between the two, and the social aspects of their rise in the context of a working environment where everyone 'knows you'. Given the emphasis on reform and change in Australian policing, it can be a real challenge for those being promoted to develop critical distance from the learning and socialisation of their earlier careers.

Promotion, however, is not always orderly and merit-based – there is also the element of luck and timing. Even a good promotion system is no guarantee of success and it is not always the best candidates who are promoted. It is sobering to recall that the Peter Principle states that managers in hierarchical organisations are promoted to their level of incompetence. An oft-quoted observation usually attributed to Groucho Marx may be relevant here: 'the secret of success is honesty and fair dealing ... if you can fake that, you've got it made'. Successful management and leadership is situational and contextual and an officer may display all the potential qualities for senior management duties only to then 'crash and burn' or prove to be a disaster for the organisation. Senior officers can succeed in one situation, yet fail in another apparently similar situation. Or they may simply have the misfortune to be presented with a series of insurmountable events and challenges beyond their control.

The senior executive positions to which officers aspire, and the entire context of promotion, have also become more complex because of changes in the demographic make-up of police organisations, and a major challenge facing police managers is that of working with diversity in all its forms. Gender and ethnic-racial balances dominate discussions about diversity, but there are other dimensions that must also be addressed. Civilianisation of some senior positions has meant that executive positions can become an arena for the tensions between sworn and civilian staff. Within the Australian Federal Police, for example, management responsibilities can alternate between sworn and civilian staff and civilians can expect to take on both operational duties and exercise a management function over sworn officers. Moreover recent changes in 'rank lock step' provisions in some States have meant that officers can now apply for positions which are more than one step up. Merit is increasingly as important as seniority and senior police generally no longer work only within the comfort zone of the cohort with whom they started their career. Additional dimensions of diversity in policing are the result of the participation of police in collaborative projects with other agencies, the role of volunteers and even ideological diversity as policing shakes off its reputation as a bastion of conservatism.

The UK Home Office has suggested that the quality of police leadership could be improved by giving officers with 'potential' the opportunity through secondment to work in public or private organisations, and in the voluntary sector (Home Office 2003). However, succession planning and providing opportunities to develop capable officers continues to be a challenge in the face of time pressures at work and cost which prevents officers from taking advantage of opportunities to develop their skills. Given the fact, alluded to previously, that most police stay in the one organisation and find it relatively difficult to move from one jurisdiction to another, or to move out of the organisation and return after experiencing another work context, opportunities to develop can only take a range of predictable forms. Officers are instead moved around the organisation, taking on new roles, projects and responsibilities sometimes with surprising frequency and suddenness in order to develop skills. If they have been in non-operational roles, or working on a special project, officers will invariably be placed again in an operational role to demonstrate their operational capabilities before being considered for promotion.

Higher education

Gradually, the impact of higher education is infiltrating the organisation and is being considered more in promotion decisions (see Lanyon and Pierce in this volume). Tertiary education for managers and leaders has been an expectation for a number of years in Australia. In 1993, the Australasian Police Ministers' Council entered into an agreement with Charles Sturt University to establish the Australian Graduate School of Police Management (now the Graduate School of Policing) at the former Australian Police Staff College at Manly, New South Wales, and in 1995, the Staff College became the Australian Institute of Police Management. Around the same time, a number of jurisdictions created their own leadership programs and secured certification agreements with several tertiary institutions. With the impetus of these initiatives, many senior officers now have graduate education, in management or other disciplines. In the UK too, in 2004, the Home Office proposed that officers who hoped to become superintendents should have a 'formal qualification' (Home Office 2003).

More junior officers are now undertaking study (not only in management subjects) and many now enter the organisation already with at least a TAFE qualification and increasingly a tertiary university degree. They also attend courses and seminars – and perform well – so can be more quickly considered for higher positions. Education and training for the development of managers and leaders continues to be a significant strategy. A current project of the APPSC is examining the appropriate education standards for the various levels within policing (APPSC 2006d). A preliminary proposal suggests that the appropriate level for supervisors would be a Graduate Certificate, for managers a Graduate Diploma and Masters for executives, but given that the considerable differences between jurisdictions it has not yet been adopted as a framework at the national level. The appointment of Dr Karl O'Callaghan in Western Australia, the first police commissioner with a doctorate degree, may be symbolic of the new educational standards in Australian policing.

But there continues to be considerable controversy about what sort of education and training will best prepare officers for management and leadership responsibilities. In the recent Report of the Kennedy Royal Commission in WA (Kennedy 2004) the main thrust of the education recommendations is that police management education should help break the isolation that often characterises policing. These recommendations echo those in earlier Australian police enquiries such as the NSW Wood Royal Commission (Wood 1997) and in overseas reports such as the UK Home Office's *Policing a New Century* (Home Office 2001). Essentially, all the reports state that police management education must become more outwardly focused, and the reports highlight the need for greater involvement of civilians in police education. Kennedy, for example, recommended that the position of the head of the Police Academy in WA be opened up to civilian appointment and more civilian educators appointed (Kennedy 2004).

Kennedy (2004) also directly enters into the pedagogical debate over whether to develop 'skilled technicians' or 'reflective practitioners'. He notes that the two approaches are not mutually exclusive, but that policing has traditionally placed a greater emphasis on skills training. Kennedy suggests that this now needs to be balanced with educational approaches that require officers to also reflect on the nature of their occupation, its place within society and the techniques for performing their work. Police managers should be in a position to contrast their own experiences with the practices of a wide range of agencies, and this can be achieved through both course content and by encouraging police to seek education outside the confines of the profession.

Despite the prevalence of such recommendations, there are continued tensions between education and training (Lee & Punch 2004). Australian police agencies have built alliances with universities and have funded external education by officers, but they have also built up their own internal capacities to provide leadership education in each jurisdiction. As a result police officers most often end up together in the same classroom with other police and are taught primarily by police, or former police now working in education institutions. This approach can often preclude contact with other professions and with the wider range of inputs recommended by the reports cited above. A challenge for the future will be to strike a workable balance, between the need to provide management and leadership education that is relevant and authentic to policing, and the need to stretch current organisational and cultural boundaries.

Conclusion

A decade ago, in Etter and Palmer's 1995 volume on police leadership in Australasia (Etter and Palmer 1995) the then New Zealand Police Commissioner concluded his chapter on the skills and qualities of future police leaders by stating:

> For many years it has been recognized that crime is no longer the province of the police alone. Harnessing and coordinating the goodwill for the public and developing partnerships … remains the best option as we strive to create safer communities. The individuals selected to lead … will be intelligent, articulate, creative, innovative, visionary … and employees will be empowered to make decision in an environment of teamwork and cooperation (MacDonald 1995, p 232).

The decade since then has shown that this vision of policing and of the leadership environment required to move it forward is not uncontested. The current heightened security climate has seen a swing back to a seemingly more hard-line combatitive approach from what some now deride as the 'softly-softly politically correct policing approach' (*Sydney Morning Herald* 2006). The representational evidence of this has been the May 2006 decision of the New South Wales Government to revive the name NSW Police *Force*, reversing a 15-year trend in which the concept of *Service* was foregrounded (the Queensland Police Service is now the only *service* left in Australia, with Western Australia recently changing from Western Australia Police Service ('WAPS') to simply Western Australia Police ('WAPol'). The service approach is now often portrayed as something imposed on police from outside by progressive and woolly-headed academics and politicians, yet an analysis of the statements of police leaders over the past decades, including John Avery's seminal *Police: Force or Service* (Avery 1981), shows that it has equally come from within policing and from internal police decisions about effective operational strategies.[1]

In his recent review of policing in Australia, Findlay (2004) noted the continued need for the improvement of the service function, but also noted that such initiatives are usually sacrificed in the name of tougher crime control programs. He warned that the outcome could be the 'reinvention of feudal police organisations' (p 172). It is worth speculating whether in fact it is possible to reinvent the feudal police organisations given the changes over the past decades and the subsequent new requirements expected of officers in managerial and leadership ranks. As officers may ascend the ranks from Sergeant to Commissioner in today's public sector climate, their prospects of success are directly linked to their capacity to understand and embrace the skills and capabilities needed to lead a 21st century law enforcement agency.

---

1   For example see Seltmann (2005).

PART I

THE CHANGING CONTEXTS OF OPERATIONAL POLICE WORK

The first part of Police Leadership and Management provides a range of perspectives on the new operational context of policing. These six chapters describe some of the major shifts taking place in policing, not least of which is the new spirit of partnership that characterises the way that crime and disorder is being prevented and managed. This is a profound shift having implications not only for an organisation's external relationships, but also for the underpinning philosophies and approaches of the police working culture representing a move away from operational 'silos'.

Janet Ransley and Lorraine Mazerolle repeat the evidence that traditional policing methods have been ineffective in controlling or preventing crime. Ransley and Mazerolle present a new model of 'third-party' policing in which the responsibility for crime and disorder is now shared with a range of government and non-government partners requiring a change in the management and deployment of police human resources and a shift to more open dealings with external partners. Tim Prenzler and Rick Sarre also discuss the concept of shared responsibility for crime management in the context of the working relationships between public and private law enforcement agencies. They argue that what might seem a logical cooperative relationship is fraught with difficulties due to legal and procedural problems and fundamentally different philosophies.

Police leaders and managers increasingly need to navigate the complexities of this relationship with a security industry that is increasing in scope and size. David Dixon's chapter considers the changes to the legal regulation of policing reflective of broader changes in social and governmental processes. He also examines fundamental changes currently underway which challenge the idea of the law as conservative and stable.

Change is also taking place in the management of the intelligence function due to the increasing focus on intelligence in many areas of tactical and strategic operational work. Patrick Walsh emphasises the need for managers to understand more fully how intelligence gathering and analysis can assist in strategic planning in all areas of policing. Improved investigations, and n particular improved investigative interviewing is also a cornerstone of police work. Tracey Green and Gary Shaw underline the importance of supervision and accountability in investigative interviewing and argue that all operational police must be able to conduct professional and ethical interviews that are admissible in court. As a salutary tale, the authors present examples of miscarriages of justice from the UK because of the poor quality of the collection of this essential evidence. Research on the cognitive interview by Ellen Grote and Margaret Mitchell concludes this chapter and indicates that correct procedures and practices need to be instilled in recruits and practitioners and reinforced through appropriate management and supervision. This chapter also argues that evidence from research can proactively assist police managers in policy and practice change, and in changing legislation to meet operational needs. The final chapter in this part includes commentary relevant to operational policing by Margaret Mitchell on evidence-based policy and procedures. The chapter argues that the contemporary emphasis on evidence- or intelligence-driven approaches to decision-making has caused a greater focus on research. A fundamental understanding of research and the ability to use research as a 'tool' to improve policing practice and evaluate outcomes in police management is an essential for leaders and managers.

2

CHANGING LAW, CHANGING POLICING

David Dixon

Law's conventional image is as a conservative force. As a formalised, authoritative exposition of particular social norms, it is associated with stability, certainty, and solidity. This chapter will argue that this image is increasingly outdated and inappropriate as regards law in policing. An accurate image of law in contemporary policing would have to include elements of instability, uncertainty and malleability. The chapter will consider first some significant changes in the legal regulation of policing which occurred in the final third of the past century, and then some fundamental changes which are currently underway. In both cases, policing is part of broader changes in social and governmental processes. Of course, real life does not fit into neat boxes of academic classification: trends and developments outlined here are not neatly linear, not least because of resistance to them, as the penultimate section will indicate.

Law permeates policing. To give just a few examples, public police institutions are legally structured by public law (Lewis, in this volume), while private security is subject to a growing body of law (Sarre & Prenzler 2005). Relations between police officers and police departments are governed by complex fields of employment and contract law. Disputes between officers and complainants are subject to private as well as public law (McCulloch & Palmer 2005). While police departments are replacing their traditionally massive sets of rules in the form of Commissioner's Instructions with more specific guidelines and codes of conduct (Dixon 1999b), they continue to be disciplined organisations which are structured around rules. Public accountability is maintained through a complex legal structure (Ross, in this volume). A significant part of police work involves drawing on legal resources to deal with disputes, enforcing law, preparing the early stages of the prosecution process, and giving evidence in court. Inevitably selective because of the constraints of length, this chapter will focus on issues illustrated by examples from the law relating to criminal investigation and public order maintenance.

Attitudes towards law

Police officers' attitudes towards law are characteristically ambivalent. On one side, there is the familiar grumbling about the way that the justice process interferes with police attempts to control crime (by, for example, alleged laxity in bail determinations or sentencing). Such tension between police and law is a natural part of an adversarial justice system in which the role of police extends beyond investigation into the prosecution process. Antagonism towards law has long been found in elements of police culture. A considerable body of research based on observation of police work presents evidence of beliefs that the job can't be done according to the rulebook and that policing skill is learnt through operational experience rather than formal, rule-based training (Dixon 1997, Ch 1). While presented as being derived from experience, such cultural beliefs are prone to slipping into myth. For example, the belief that the right to silence significantly impedes criminal investigation has been very widespread in policing, yet numerous empirical studies have demonstrated that few suspects exercise this right successfully, and that doing so does not usually increase the likelihood of their acquittal (Dixon 1997, Ch 6).

This hostility towards law has been tempered by other streams of talking and thinking in which law is vital to policing. A central tenet of the 'professional' model which emerged from policing in the USA in the mid-20th century was a conception of policing as an essentially legal function. As a way of distancing their organisations from the corruption of city politics, police reconceived themselves as autonomous professionals whose loyalty was to the law, not to politicians. In England, the legal mythology of the 'office of constable' was developed, claiming for police a special (if nebulous) place under the rule of law. Complementing this legalism was the presentation of police departments as rational bureaucracies, in which policies set by police managers were transmitted into police practice via rules. This 'legal bureaucratic' approach became standard.

The importance of law was recognised in very different fashion by a wave of academic and policy-focused writing which criticised both the narrow focus of 'culturalist' accounts and the unreality of legal bureaucratic accounts (Dixon 1997, Ch 1). They demonstrated that law provides the structures within which police cultures operated. Such critiques drew attention back to the law, not as a vague legitimating force but as a combination of various types of rules, with some of them providing the wide discretion enjoyed by street-level practitioners (Smith & Gray 1985). Law was reconceived as a powerful legitimating ideology facilitating police work (McBarnet 1981).

A highly influential way of thinking about law in policing stems from Packer's celebrated dichotomy of due process and crime control in criminal justice (1968, Ch 8). One product of these competing value systems is the police ambivalence about law noted above. Packer's dichotomy emerges very frequently in public discourse about policing in the form of the metaphor of 'balance'. The notional ideal is an even balance between due process and crime control, notably with police powers and suspects' rights weighed off against each other. The balance is usually said to be between the civil liberties of suspects and society's right to protect itself. In cruder references, the term 'suspects' is replaced with 'offenders' or 'criminals', which, leaping to the conclusion that the justice process is intended to decide upon, ends any useful discussion. Debate about criminal justice usually takes the form of complaints that either police powers or suspects' rights have grown, upsetting the balance, and that legal change is needed to re-set it.

As a metaphor, 'balance' in criminal justice has had remarkable influence on policy-making. At times, it seems that the metaphor takes the place of substantial thinking about issues. An unfortunate example was the tendency of the Royal Commission on Criminal Justice (in England and Wales, 1991-1993) to refer to 'the "balance" favouring one solution rather than another as if this were some ineffable mystery that requires no supporting explanation about how the conclusion was reached' (Ashworth 1994, p 294). As Zedner suggests, 'Typically, conflicting interests are said to be 'balanced' as if there were a self-evident weighting of or priority among them. Yet, rarely are the particular interests spelt out, priorities made explicit, or the process by which a weighting is achieved made clear' (2005a, p 511). Research shows that the complex relationship between police powers and suspects' rights cannot be captured by a simple metaphor of balance. Its central weakness is that its binary nature does not take account of the fact that there is a communal, and not just an individual, interest in the protection of rights. This is not merely a matter of principle – ie that a democratic society deserving the name should treat people in a certain way. There is also an instrumental interest: if failure to provide suspects with substantial rights leads to a wrongful conviction, then those who are really guilty escape justice (usually forever, because the investigation has been misdirected for so long). This is a glaring but often ignored lesson of the miscarriage of justice cases which have shamed the criminal justice systems of Anglophone countries in recent decades. This failure to appreciate 'the double-sided nature of miscarriages of justice ... serves to perpetuate a ... misleading dichotomy between 'soft' and 'tough' measures, between effective crime control and civil liberties' (Hogg 1995, p 314).

This balance metaphor, which has been the 'scourge of many debates about criminal justice policy' (Ashworth 1994, p 292) is particularly problematic in the contemporary context of concern about terrorism. When the balance is 'between the security interests of the majority and the civil liberties of that tiny minority of persons who find themselves subject to state investigation', giving priority to the former is almost automatic (Zedner 2005a, p 513). In this self-interested utilitarianism, 'The only balance in question is the balance between the majority's security and *other* people's rights' (Dworkin 2003). When those others are racial, ethnic or religious minorities, the outcome can be deeply problematic. Critics of such developments argue that we should see the communal as well as the individual character of rights, empathise with the potential subjects of control by imagining us in their place, and be aware of the tendency of exceptional powers to become nor-malised, applying to all (Zedner 2005a, pp 513-515). Zedner makes a strong case for principles of 'parsimony, proportionality, certainty, transparency, and accountability' (2005a, p 531).

The authorise and regulate strategy

Until the final third of the 20th century, the marginality of law was a notable feature of everyday police practice in Australia and England. Such legal regulation as there was came from common law administered by the courts. Police forces were disciplined organisations, but such discipline came princi-pally from internal police management rather than external law. Formal police powers were very limited. In carrying out their key tasks of controlling crime and maintaining order, officers could draw upon broad offences (parti-cularly, in Australia, public order offences related to drunkenness). Notional-ly, the criminal process was dominated by magistrates and judges. People who were arrested were to be brought before a magistrate without delay. Magistrates issued warrants providing authority to arrest and search. The judges instructed police on how to carry out their duties by issuing various versions of the Judges' Rules. By the mid-20th century at the latest, the law had become anachronistic in crucial areas, failing for example to acknow-ledge the crucial shift of responsibility in the investigative stages of the criminal justice process from magistrates to police which had occurred a cen-tury before. The judges' rules were written in a way that demonstrated the authors' very limited understanding of police practices (Dixon 1997).

As Karl Alderson has demonstrated in a definitive history of police powers in post-war New South Wales (2002), this relationship between law and policing is primarily to be explained as the product of a distinctive set of beliefs about policing in England which were carried over to Australia. Origi-nating in the particular condition under which reform of policing in early and mid-19th century England had been possible, the ideas of the police officer as a 'citizen in uniform' and as the holder of the ancient office of cons-table were crucial (Reiner 2000). Taken together, these distanced the police from the rest of the State and emphasised their connection with the com-munity and (at a largely rhetorical level) with the law. In 1929, the Royal Commission on Police Powers and Procedure (RCPPP) (in England and Wales) reported that:

> The Police ... have never been recognised, either in law or in tradition, as a force distinct from the general body of citizens ... [T]he principle remains that a Policeman ... is only 'a person paid to perform, as a matter of duty, acts which if he were so minded he might have done voluntarily'. Indeed, a policeman possesses few powers not enjoyed by the ordinary citizen, and public opinion, as expressed in Parliament and elsewhere, has shown great jealousy of any attempt to give increased authority to the Police (RCPPP 1929, p 6).

In 1962, another English Royal Commission endorsed 'the principle that police powers are mostly grounded in the common law and differ little from those of ordinary citizens' (1962, p 11).

The potent myth about the English tradition overlay a reality in which, to do their job, police had to do more than the law allowed. In the absence of clear legal powers to do what was expected of them (notably, stop and search suspects and question suspects in custody before charging them), police had either to exploit legal loopholes (such as producing time for custodial interrogation by arresting suspects when the courts were closed) or to evade the law by relying on the suspect's notional consent to being searched or 'helping with inquiries' at the station. Another alternative was to search or detain unlawfully, relying on the courts' persistent unwillingness to exclude unlawfully obtained evidence.

Policing was practicable largely because the courts abstained from active supervision of police practices. This was particularly significant in Australia, where the courts were, notionally, the primary means of controlling police practices. Despite conventional grumbling from police about lack of support from the courts, empirical studies demonstrate just how limited judicial intervention was (for example, Presser 2001). Notably, the common law prohibition of detention for questioning before charge was reduced to rhetoric by the courts' toleration of police evasion of the law. External factors played their part too: so long as there was no great public concern about crime, the popular press took a civil libertarian line, opposing the extension of formal police powers (Alderson 2002, p 61). As Alderson concludes, in the years between 1945 and 1968:

> Dominant ways of thinking ... emphasised faith in police, belief in an ideal of police/community cooperation, and a playing down of the importance, and desirability, of formal legal powers. It also emphasised faith in the courts as the best forum for redressing injustice, controlling police misconduct and upholding citizens' rights (Alderson 2002, p 83).

In summary, the defining characteristic of this period in law-policing relations was legalistic rhetoric which masked an essentially permissive policing environment. According to an authoritative Australian survey in the mid-1960s:

> Little interest has been shown in this country ... in reassessing the adequacy of police powers ... Understandably the police themselves are rather reluctant to press claims for additional power for fear that their intentions might be misconstrued or that their representations might focus attention on existing practices of questionable legality. Only on rare occasions is the legality of police actions challenged in the courts, but there must be many occasions on which police officers ... feel it necessary in the interests of law enforcement to adopt measures which technically are not within the scope of their authority (Campbell & Whitmore 1966, p 32).

The final third of the 20th century saw the development of a new and distinctive approach to police powers in Britain and Australia. At the turn of the 20th century, the law of criminal investigation was becoming an inc-reasingly complex structure of laws, subsidiary rules and codes of practice. They provided clear authorisation to police to intrude on individual liberty in various ways – including stop/search, search of premises, and detention for investigative purposes. As explained above, police had routinely done these things before the new laws, exploiting the gaps and uncertainties in the common law and local legislation, and relying on their targets' ignorance of or inability to enforce their rights. What was new was that police now had clear authorisation for such practices.

However, the new laws did not merely legalise what police had always done or provide new powers. In defining police powers, the law both clari-fied them and set their limits. For example, if the police were authorised to detain suspects between arrest and charge, such detention was made subject to specific time limits. In addition, new powers were complemented by rights for suspects which were to be shifted from the airy rhetoric of judicial neglect to specific rules on, for example, access to legal advice. Indeed, while, legal police powers were substantially extended during this period, '[p]rovi-sion for provision, most of the criminal investigation legislation enacted has been about regulating the conduct of law enforcement officers and restricting the availability and use of powers' (Alderson 2002, p 8). The manner in which powers and rights are exercised was made subject to extensive administrative control with requirements of record-making, managerial supervision, and external review. Often seen at the time as merely an extension of police powers, the strategy should be understood as being to 'authorise and regulate' (Alder-son 2002).

Why did such regulatory developments occur? Their origin is to be found in a series of related social and political developments in Anglophone societies from the mid-1960s. Increasing levels of recorded crime and public concern about crime pushed policing into the political arena, provoking demands for increased police powers. At the same time, the growth of social liberalism led to pressure for protection of civil liberties and suspects' rights. A symbiotic relationship developed: proposals and demands from one side provoked contrary responses from the other. Notably in England in the 1970s, senior officers had entered public debate arguing that the law had to recognise their need for formal powers to do what they had long done infor-mally (Dixon 1999b, pp 44-45).

There was also a broader social and political context. At one level, the 'authorise and regulate' strategy was a product of a general shift towards for-malisation and extension of regulation in and by contemporary states. Equally, there were changes in the status of the objects of police attention: social democratisation in the mid-20th century meant that 'informality' in dealing with suspects became less appropriate. Suspects were no longer merely 'police property' (Reiner 2000) but citizens whose alleged offences did not set them outside the political community. They were therefore to be treated according to liberal democratic principles. These were best expound-ed by the Royal Commission on Criminal Procedure (in England and Wales) which provided a 'framework of first principles' – fairness, openness, accountability, and efficiency (RCCP 1981, p 126). This is a distinctively liberal democratic form of governance: while the need for State action is accepted, interventions into the life of any citizen required legal authority and justification which had to respect the citizen's liberties. Criminal justice has been constructed around a group of concepts, values and purposes which originate in liberal democratic politics. These include: the primacy of the individual and the individual's rights, the need for guilt to be proved by the prosecution beyond reasonable doubt, due process, a need for certainty, reactive response as the key role of policing agencies, punishment based on desert, and processes providing fairness and justice.

While Australia was ahead of Britain in conducting an inquiry committed to authorisation and regulation – the ALRC's influential second report on criminal investigation appeared in 1975 – it took longer than England and Wales to legislate. The Royal Commission on Criminal Procedure was followed by legislation in England and Wales, principally the *Police and Criminal Evidence Act 1984* (PACE). But it was not until 1991 that the Australian Commonwealth finally reformed Federal investigative law, while NSW took even longer: its *Crimes Amendment (Detention after Arrest) Act 1997* was eventually followed by a consolidating measure, the *Law Enforcement (Powers and Responsibilities) Act* in 2002. By this time, the social and political forces underlying the 'authorise and regulate' strategy had lost their momentum.

From 'authorise and regulate' to the politics of risk

In retrospect, the 'authorise and regulate' strategy has to be seen as the governing style suited to a particular, brief moment in the trajectory of social/liberal democracy, one in which the metaphor of balance was appropriate. There was real commitment to the objective of providing both for the police to have the powers that they need to do their job, and for suspects to have substantial rights. In England and Wales, there was also a considerable commitment of resources to make rights more than rhetoric, notably via the provision of funding for legal advice to suspects in police stations. Its culmination came with the establishment of the Royal Commission on Criminal Justice in 1991: the belated acknowledgement that the criminal justice process had convicted the wrong people in a long series of cases was expected by many to lead to significant reform which would give greater substance to measures protecting rights. However, by the time the Royal Commission reported in 1993, times were decisively changing. Far from a reconstitution of criminal justice around liberal principle, this Commission paid homage to the new gods of efficiency and effectiveness.

Key elements of the 'authorise and regulate' strategy have weakened. The distinctive liberal caution about extending police powers has evaporated (see below). 'Bureaucracy' is a term of abuse, a source of red tape to be cut. This tendency found notable expression in England and Wales with the Blair Government's breezy and worryingly ill-informed review of PACE (Home

Office/Cabinet Office 2002). This is just one example of much more general change in criminal justice. While here is a real and obvious danger in over-stating the generality, linearity and unity of such change, strong patterns and trends can be discerned

The central concepts of liberal democratic criminal justice are devalued in the new criminal justice. The key concern is now the minimisation of risk and the security of the group. Flexibility replaces certainty a virtue. Compliance and efficiency are more important than individual punishment or due process, There is less interest in understanding crime's causation than in accepting crime as normal, a choice to be controlled and insured against, in which 'attempts to cure or punish appear less logical than do moves to manage crime and minimize its costs' (Zedner 2005b, p 284). The State's responsibility for crime control is 'contracted out to private providers wielding State franchises, delegated to individuals and communities, or completely overtaken by the growing private security industry' (Zedner 2005b, p 284). Policing intervenes proactively, preventing and pre-empting problems rather than retrospectively solving them. Simply to say that all this goes against basic principle is rather like complaining that a game of chess isn't being played according to the rules of draughts. The game has changed, allowing those in government to dismiss the standard civil libertarian response to new police powers as anachronistic and irrelevant. While these developments have been underway for some time, they accelerated quickly after the terrorist attacks of 11 September 2001 or '9/11'. Parliaments are now in a constant cycle of extending anti-terrorism legislation in ways that routinely deviate from liberal democratic principles in the name of necessity.

The politics of law and order

In a development closely related to those outlined in the previous section, criminal justice generally, and policing specifically, have shifted from the margin of political priority to its centre (Garland 2001). Unfortunately, this emphasis on the significance of law and order is not matched by care or seriousness in its treatment. Even politicians who bow to the fashion for evidence-based policy are apparently happy to legislate without, or contrary to, the findings of any research base. Australia, and New South Wales in particular, suffers from a virulent form of this infection. Spurred on and harassed by media commentators whose influence is bizarrely disproportionate to their knowledge, governments legislate at the drop of a cliché. Powers are showered on police whether they need them or not (and no time is spent investigating whether they are needed and how they relate to police practice) and whether or not they will be useful. The rhetoric of war is *de rigeur*: insistence that wars are being fought against drugs and terrorism justifies the apparently endless expansion of police powers.

Such legislation has a crucial symbolic dimension: its specific provisions are less important than the message that the public's fears of crime and insecurity are taken seriously even though (in a classic example of amplification)

such fears can be increased rather than allayed by the reaction. Politicians must be seen to be doing something, and passing a law is a particularly effective way of being seen to act – even if appearance and reality do not correspond. Action must be swift: so when the NSW government legislated in 1998 in response to incidents of assaults with knives, the Police Minister commented approvingly 'This is instant law, this is a quick as instant coffee' (Dixon 1999c, p 164). Moral panics used to involve lengthy processes of amplification through the media, professionals and 'experts' before the law was changed (Cohen 1972). Now, the process is shortcut: almost before the broken glass had been cleared from the streets of Cronulla and Maroubra after the disorders of late 2005, the NSW Parliament had been recalled and, in a single day, the *Law Enforcement Legislation Amendment (Public Safety) Act 2005* had been introduced, 'debated' and passed into law. Maximum penalties were increased, access to bail was reduced, a new offence was created, and police powers to stop and search, close down areas, and control alcohol consumption were provided. The Premier told Parliament:

> I have recalled Parliament for one simple reason: new powers to uphold public order. And we are here to make sure that the police get the powers the need. Louts and criminals have effectively declared war on our society and we are not going to let them undermine our way of life (*Hansard*, Legislative Assembly, 15 December 2005, p 20621).

As if trying to exemplify the process of 'normalisation' of exceptional powers described by academic critics (Hillyard 1994), the second target of the new law (which had been introduced in response to inter-racial crime against a background of concerns about terrorism) was an Aboriginal housing estate in Dubbo.

During the 'authorise and regulate' strategy which was discussed above, police had to lobby for powers. Now, such lobbying is barely necessary: legislatures now shower police with gifts. As NSW Premier, Bob Carr provided notable examples:

> If police can identify another power they need to protect order and public safety, they will get it.
>
> If the police commissioner ever comes to me and says 'I need additional powers to arrest drug dealers', it goes without saying he gets them from the Carr Government (quoted Dixon 1999c, p 166).

Such statements express a relationship between government and police which is quite different from that conventionally associated with a liberal democracy, in which some healthy tension exists between the powers that the police want and the powers that they have.

Looking forward – new conceptions of law

As noted above, there is a temptation to present the drift from liberal criminal justice towards late-modern, risk-averse law and order in over-dramatic, linear fashion. In this section three significant exceptions and challenges to the dominant tendency provide an opportunity to look forward to more constructive relations between law and policing. These are developments in restorative justice, the rise of human rights, and a renewed emphasis on the interdependence of legality and efficiency.

Restorative justice

The significance of restorative justice for policing is analysed in more depth elsewhere in this volume. It is enough for present purposes to note that restorative justice provides a radical alternative to conventional criminal justice. For useful reviews of restorative justice in policing, see Skogan and Frydl (2004, pp 305-307) and Hoyle and Young (2003). The influence of restorative justice has allowed some idiosyncratic sections of the policing process to grow against the prevailing wind. While young people are often the targets of the law and order and risk-based initiatives discussed above, a significant exception is provided by the *Young Offenders Act* (NSW). Using familiar tools of authorisation and regulation, this legislation was designed to engage police in a constructive, diversionary process in which cautions are preferred to arrest (Chan 2005).

A related development is the growth of policing services designed to suit the very particular and complex problems of Indigenous communities. Research by Harry Blagg and his colleagues has demonstrated limits and possibilities of the emerging practice of using alternatives to conventional policing in Aboriginal communities (Blagg & Valuri 2004; see also Cunneen in this volume).

Human rights

The most important development in law for policing has yet to impact in any significant way on Australia: but any discussion looking forward must take account of the rise of human rights. After Britain incorporated the European Convention on Human Rights into domestic law via the *Human Rights Act 1998*, Australia is now the only large jurisdiction in the common law world which lacks significant domestic human rights protection. Being left behind by legally conservative and insular England should, in itself, be grounds for concern. While there is considerable activity at local level (with the ACT's *Human Rights Act 2004* and Victoria's implementation in 2007 of a Charter of Human Rights and Responsibilities (and consideration of a similar measure in New South Wales), the (Liberal/National) Commonwealth Government's opposition to incorporating human rights seems unshakable. Nonetheless, it seems likely that, later rather than sooner, Australian law will change. The longer that change is delayed, the greater will be the cost of isolating Australian law from the mainstream development of the common law (Charlesworth et al, 2003).

Police officers should not be concerned about the implications of incorporating human rights. The international agreements which provide their basis are, by nature, conservative and minimalist documents. Most rights are qualified and subject to the power of derogation: notably, these allow the exceptional powers created under anti-terrorism statutes to be enacted. The likely method of incorporating human rights is by means of ordinary legislation (itself subject to parliamentary supremacy and subsequent legislation) rather than entrenched constitutional change. While being incorporated, they may be further limited: a notable example is the way that the draft Victorian Charter greatly reduces the worth of the International Covenant on Civil and Political Rights to legal counsel by omitting the State's responsibility to pay for such counsel for indigent defendants. As for the impact of human rights, policing in Britain has not ground to a rights-enmeshed halt since the *Human Rights Act* came into force.

While the direct effects of incorporating rights may not be dramatic, it would be wrong to understate the indirect effects. Informed commentators on Britain and Canada point to the entwined changes in process and culture which have flowed from incorporating rights. In terms of process, legal change has to include consideration of the human rights implications of legislative proposals. At minimum, this should provide for more consideration and discussion than Bills receive under the current system. A recent problematic example in New South Wales was the *Crimes (Serious Sexual Offenders) Act 2006* which provides for preventive detention in prison for people who, although they have completed their sentence, are deemed too dangerous to release. No Bill was available for public comment or debate before the NSW Legislative Assembly 'debated' and passed this after no more than half an hour (*Hansard*, 29 March 2006). Eyes set on a forthcoming State election, the NSW Government was not interested in considering either the damage such legislation does to conceptions of punishment or the judicial process or other, more effective and principled, means of dealing with persistent sex offenders.

In terms of culture, the requirement to consider rights has had a significant impact on judicial methodology in England:

> From the bland view of democracy as requiring deference to legislators, courts have begun to see human rights as constitutive of democracy rather than ranged against it. With this has come the emergence of equality as a central democratic principle ... Other values are still in their infancy, foremost amongst them that of dignity (Fredman 2006, p 53).

Such change may flow down through other sectors of the criminal justice process. This can provide a crucial vehicle for making police officers see law as being made up not just of rules, but of principles. As Neyroud explains, the *Human Rights Act* 'brought both a new language to policing and a new decision-making calculus' (2003, p 585). Discretionary decisions must refer to the principle of proportionality, balancing 'the means proposed against the outcome intended and to ensure that any action is proportionate to the legitimate aim pursued' (Neyroud 2003, p 585). In place of simplistic appeals to 'balance', a 'rights-based' approach necessitates a fundamental reconsideration of the principles and fundamental purposes of criminal justice (Ashworth 1994, pp 292-296).

Western governments pose two significant threats to the rights approach. One is simply to insist that national security requires the suspension of
even the most basic rights. The other comes when they purport to speak
'rights talk', for example, countering suspects' rights with the communal
'right to security' (Zedner 2005a).

Legality and efficiency

A notable contemporary development is the appreciation that legitimacy is
crucial to efficiency, in the sense that that effective crime control can only be
accomplished by police who use their powers in ways which secure the approval of the communities in which they operate.

In England and Australia, a crucial source for this is Lord Scarman's
report on the Brixton Disorders (1981), which provided authoritative impetus
to the rise of community policing, Lord Scarman provided a classic restate-
ment of the relationship between law and policing. In Scarman's approach,
police could no longer simply invoke the law to justify their actions. If the
enforcement of law would lead to disruption of public peace, then the appropriate use of discretion would put preserving the peace above enforcing
law. All too often caricatured as justifying 'no-go' zones and improper toleration of illegal activities in minority communities, Scarman's approach provided overdue recognition of the significance, difficulty and complexity of
the police role. Scarman argued that police could only get the balance
between law enforcement and maintenance of public peace right if their discretionary decision-making was informed by contact and consultation with
the communities they police. While this led to a series of community consultative activities characterised by disappointment and frustration on both
sides, the fundamental message of Scarman's report remained valid: enforcing law is not a trumping argument.

The message of the Scarman report became all the more relevant after
another inquiry once again exposed deep problems in relations between
police and minority communities in Britain. The Macpherson Report (1999)
identified stop and search as a major source of problems. A subsequent program of research by the Home Office concluded strongly that the legitimacy
of stops and searches depended upon three elements: public trust and confidence, legality, and effectiveness. 'These three principles, far from being in
opposition, are largely consistent. The program's recommendations do not
involve trade-offs between them but reinforce one another. For example,
interventions to improve the effectiveness of searches are likely ... to
improve public confidence. Similarly, there is a close link between the legality of searches, and their effectiveness against crime and acceptability to the
public' (Miller, Quinton & Bland 2000, p 1). Far from legality and efficiency
being counterposed (as the balance metaphor implies), this research on stop
and search showed that they are interdependent.

It is notable that in a parallel but apparently quite separate stream of
theorising and policy analysis, similar conclusions are reached by a major

review conducted for the National Research Council in the US (Skogan & Frydl 2004, Ch 8). This confluence is not coincidental: the reports by Scarman, Macpherson and the National Research Council's stem from fundamentally similar problems in relations between police and minority communities.

A conceptual foundation from which these British and American reports could be developed (and applied to Australia) can be found in the increasingly influential work of Tom Tyler on procedural justice. Tyler's empirical work demonstrates the crucial importance of the manner in which police officers exercise their powers (Tyler 1989). In an important corrective to the dominant tendency to insist on the instrumental effectiveness of crime control policing in building public support, Tyler shows that how police are seen is as important as what they do. Public cooperation with and support for police depends not just on belief that police are effective in controlling crime, but also on perceptions of how police go about their work. Working within the law is vital: legality is a precondition for legitimacy. This is equally true for the general public, for those people who call for police assistance, and for those whom the police stop, search, and arrest (Skogan & Frydl 2004, pp 292-293). Contrary to many assumptions, outcomes of encounters are less important for those involved than their experience of 'procedural justice – an evaluation of the fairness of the manner in which their problem or dispute was handled' (Skogan & Frydl 2004, p 301). Such perceptions are particularly significant in minority communities which are most likely to experience police crime control activity. As Tyler and Fagan (2005) argue:

> The public cooperates with the police when they view them as legitimate authorities who are entitled to be obeyed. Such legitimacy judgments, in turn, are shaped by public views about procedural justice – the fairness of the processes the police use when dealing with members of the public (2005, pp 36-37).

Once again, the old contrast between due process and crime control, between rights and powers proves to be misleading: efficiency and legitimacy are not on opposing scales of a balance, but are interdependent. It is good to see this acknowledged in Directions in Australasian Policing: the introduction notes that 'To be effective police must enjoy the confidence, trust, cooperation and active support of the community' (APMC 2005, p 1). Unfortunately however the body of the document treats efficiency and legitimacy as separate matters: crime reduction is considered in 'Direction 1: Innovation in policing', while 'the proper exercise of authority and discretion' is considered separately under 'Direction 3: Professionalism and accountability'. This unhelpfully conforms to the conventional approach in which crime fighting is prioritised, while the manner in which power is exercised is considered as relevant only to control of misconduct. This misses the point that legitimacy is crucial, not just a desirable but secondary consideration. As Scarman (1981) argued, such trust, cooperation and active support must be generated from the way in which police officers interact with people and the way in which police departments are open to public consultation and accountability. The distance from community which was characteristic of the mid-20th century contort model of police professionalism and of more recent crime control focused policing is precisely the opposite of what is likely to produce the best results.

While police routinely insist on their commitment to 'community', the trends analysed earlier in this paper are incongruent. Community policing is now out of favour. While the rhetoric of community is maintained, community safety through crime reduction is now its context. For example, potential recruits to NSW Police are told that they 'will be helping to keep the community free from violence, crime and fear ... Your role as a police officer is to keep the streets safe, enforce the law and prevent crime'. The idea of policing as broader community service is downplayed. In a deeply symbolic change, NSW Police is to replace 'Service' with 'Force' in its title.

The need to give priority to legitimacy is particularly significant in responses to terrorism. The Australian Government's own review of anti-terrorism legislation has recently given a sharp warning about 'a considerable increase in fear, a growing sense of alienation and an increase in distrust of authority' among Muslim and Arab Australians and expressed 'serious concerns about the way in which the legislation is perceived by these communities (Commonwealth of Australia 2006, p 5). The London bombings of July 2005 illustrate starkly the costs of alienating minority communities and expose the fallacy of treating efficiency and legitimacy as if they sit at opposite ends of a balance.

Conclusion

The purpose of this brief chapter was to indicate that law in policing is a more complex, significant, changeable and changing concern than conventional accounts suggest. Policing and law are both changing both under the pressure of internal dynamics and in response to developments in their social and political contexts.

THIRD PARTY AND PARTNERSHIP POLICING

Janet Ransley and Lorraine Mazerolle

In this chapter we explore a major shift in the way policing work has been conceptualised and affected in contemporary times. Police now share the policing function with a range of other State and non-State third parties or partners. We argue that this shift has been caused by a broad transformation in the forms and techniques of social governance that has changed the way we think about crime, crime control and policing. Coupled with this change has been research showing that traditional policing methods were not effective in controlling or preventing crime. We survey these changes before moving on to examine their impact on policing, and the creation of new forms and techniques of crime control and prevention. The chapter finishes with a discussion of the implications for managers of this transformation to what we call third party, or partnership, policing.

Trends in governance, crime and policing

Until quite recently, the dominant notion of what constitutes both crime and the role of police was relatively straightforward. Crime was seen as essentially a legal problem, to be controlled, corrected and prevented through the application of law to individual offenders. Components of the public or State criminal justice system (police, courts, prosecutors, corrections) were responsible for this process. Policing was performed by State-employed police whose primary responsibilities were to maintain order and respond to individual crimes (see other chapters in this volume).

In the 1990s it became increasingly apparent that this depiction of criminal justice was no longer accurate for Australia and similar countries. The main indicators of change include:

- The move to privatisation, not just of prisons, but also of police work as seen in the growth of private police and security firms (see

Sarre & Prenzler 2005; Prenzler 2000; Prenzler and Sarre in this volume). Current estimates are that there are at least twice as many private investigators as public police in Australia (Prenzler & King 2002), and this does not take into account other forms of private police such as fraud investigators and controllers employed by financial institutions, retailers and audit firms.

- The establishment by governments of a myriad of enforcement and investigative agencies with specific responsibilities and often far greater powers than public police. Examples include crime and corruption commissions (eg Crime and Misconduct Commission (Qld), Independent Commission Against Corruption (NSW)), and white collar crime agencies (eg Australian Securities and Investment Commission). Such bodies can enforce cooperation, compel the answering of self-incriminating questions, and use other methods usually not available to police in investigating crime. In addition to agencies with specific crime functions, numerous regulatory bodies have some law enforcement functions, such as to investigate and prosecute non-compliance with workplace health and safety, environmental, building, planning, or tax laws.

- The adoption of crime prevention as a key local government responsibility. While crime and police have traditionally been the concerns of State governments, with a limited role for federal agencies under commonwealth law, many local councils now receive direct federal funding and employ crime prevention officers, install CCTV and employ private operators to conduct patrols and maintain security in problem areas (AIC 2004).

- The development of new legislative schemes directed at crime prevention and control, but delivered mainly through non-police agencies. For example, some States have responded to juvenile crime by increased penalties and enforcement of truancy provisions in education laws, to try and enforce parental responsibility. In Britain, new anti-social behaviour laws make local councils, schools and police jointly responsible for preventing crime problems in their areas (see Mazerolle & Ransley 2006a).

The overall effect of these changes is that much of the work of crime control and prevention now takes place outside the criminal justice system, performed by non-State agencies, using non-traditional methods. This goes beyond the privatisation of policing and prisons to what David Garland (1996, 1997) calls the 'responsibilisation' of crime control and prevention. By this he means that rather than being seen as a solely State function as it was for much of the 20th century, responsibility for safety and security is now also seen as a community and individual responsibility. This has not been an isolated trend, seen only in criminal justice. We have argued elsewhere (Mazerolle & Ransley 2004, 2006a, 2006b) that it is the governance of society itself that was transformed in the second half of the 20th century, from a model of

State control and intervention to a neo-liberal model based on notions of individual autonomy and government through networks or nodes. In this new model, the role of State agencies is not to do everything themselves, but to build communities, networks and partnerships to identify needs and risks, and deliver services.

The impact of these trends on policing has been to change the focus from State responsibility for preventing and correcting criminal behaviour to a system of crime control and prevention networks. Public police form one node of these networks, with private police or security firms, regulatory agencies, communities, business owners, schools and parents as other nodes. These networks may exist within legislated networks, but they are often episodic and ad hoc. Policing is now provided by these networks of de-centred service providers who focus on risk identification and minimisation. Loader's (2000) conceptual model of this process focuses on various levels of policing including:

- *by government*, through police, other law enforcement agencies, local government services such as CCTV, city patrols and guards;
- *through government*, where security services and technologies are purchased from private providers;
- *above government*, from the increasing number of trans-jurisdictional policies, agreements, obligations and services;
- *beyond government*, where communities or businesses provide their own security services; and
- *below government*, or local, neighbourhood initiatives, whether State-sponsored or not.

In addition to the transformation of policing, the conceptualisation of crime has also changed. Crime is now assessed in economic terms such as risk, choice and probability, rather than simply as a problem of individual offenders and offences (Garland 1996). That is, crime is seen as being controlled and prevented at least as much through limiting risks and opportunities, as through the detection, investigation, prosecution and correction of individual offenders. Feeley and Simon (1994) describe this new way of looking at offenders as 'actuarial justice'. By this they mean that the traditional concern with individual guilt and correction has been replaced with identifying dangerous groups to be managed to reduce their opportunity to prevent crime. This management process occurs through better surveillance (eg CCTV), incapacitation (eg through preventive detention), the development of offender profiles (such as drug couriers and terrorists), the identification of target 'risky groups' (eg repeat offenders, young people, homeless and mentally ill people) and risky places (eg hot spots, bars, parks).

So, fundamental change has occurred on three fronts. First, there is now a much broader governmental, community and individual responsibility for the performance of crime control and prevention rather than simply relying on public police. Second, the object of policing attention has changed from a focus on individual offenders, to attempts to identify and predict risky groups likely to be involved in offending. And third, policing strategies have changed to suit the new function and focus, as described in the next section.

Changes in policing strategies

The changes in societal context discussed above have far reaching implications for the organisation of police work. Police no longer, if they ever did, have a monopoly over responding to and preventing crime, but are expected to work in partnership with a range of other institutions, agencies and individuals. Generally, there is no clear framework for these types of partnerships (an exception is the *Crime and Disorder Act 1998* (UK)), but rather a set of 'top-down' expectations that police will work cooperatively with a range of partners to identify and respond to crime in ways that will vary from community to community and problem to problem. Ericson and Haggarty (1997) describe the contemporary police role as that of brokers for these partnerships – coordinating, providing information and resources, and responding to the risks. Risks are identified through the analysis of statistical data and technologies like COMPSTAT, for which police are responsible. The emphasis for much police work is now on:

* networks and partnerships rather than centralised police control of crime problems;
* individual communities and sub-communities and their problems rather than generalised crime scares;
* proactive problem solving rather than short term containment in response to complaints;
* identification and management of risks, based on statistical data, intelligence and other forms of information, rather than a traditional reaction to individual offences; and
* a general convergence of policing goals and strategies with those of other State and non-State agencies.

Apart from the social changes we have described, changes to police practices have also been driven by the organisational context, and by research about the effectiveness of various approaches to policing. Police work has typically been divided into two components: reactive and proactive strategies (Cordner 1979). Traditional, reactive policing is general and unfocused, and involves officers responding to calls for service. Proactive police work involves self-initiated activities focused on problem solving to minimise the occurrence or recurrence of particular crime problems.

By the early 1990s there was ample scientific evidence to show that traditional, reactive strategies had no impact on reducing or preventing crime – this applied to strategies including increased patrol intensity, improved response times, and increased numbers and presence of officers (see Weisburd & Eck 2004; Skogan 2004). Instead, there was a growing body of evidence suggesting that a focused, problem and partnership-driven approach to policing could be effective at reducing crime problems. Evidence of successful strategies summarised by Weisburd and Eck (2004) include foot patrol, directed patrols in crime hot spots, specific deterrence for some categories of offenders, proactive arrests for traffic offenders and disorderly conduct, drug market crackdowns, drink driving blitzes and aspects of problem-orientated and community policing (see Mazerolle & Ransley 2006a).

Weisburd and Eck (2004) recently developed a conceptual model describing a typology of policing approaches, ranged along two dimensions. The first dimension relates to 'level of focus' and contrasts unfocused tactics (general patrols) with those that are highly focused (eg targeting hotspots, repeat offenders, victims and calls for service). The traditional model of policing is unfocused, while new approaches tend to be strategically focused at reducing specific problems in small places or among small groups (of victims or offenders) with high concentrations of crime. The empirical evidence suggests that highly focused activities have more impact on reducing crime and disorder problems (Weisburd & Eck 2004; Mazerolle & Ransley 2006a; Mazerolle, Soole & Rombouts 2006).

The second conceptual dimension is the degree to which strategies involve mostly a law enforcement approach, or a wide range of intervention approaches involving partnerships. Some partnerships are generally focused, as in community policing. In community policing, police form partnerships with a wide array of agencies and entities to solve generic, as opposed to specific, problems across a community. Problem-orientated approaches, by contrast, are more targeted, involving the building of partnerships around clearly defined, specific problems, whether problem people (victims, offenders or callers), or places (hot spots). Again, there is growing evidence to show that while both types of partnership-orientated strategy have some success, those that are highly focused on particular problems have most impact on reducing crime and disorder (Mazerolle, Soole & Rombouts 2006).

In summary, the research evidence suggests that policing is most effective when it adopts a partnership approach to implementing a broad range of responses, rather than simply relying on traditional law enforcement techniques. Added benefits can be gained when these partnerships are highly focused and respond to particular problems of crime and disorder. Our thesis is that recent changes to contemporary policing are driven by:

(a)   the social transformations we described earlier;

(b)   research on what strategies work to reduce crime (Weisburd & Eck 2004);

(c)   growing public policy awareness that traditional strategies fail to control crime problems (Bayley 1994);

(d)   top-down pressure on police to be effective or risk reductions in levels of funding; and

(e)   pressure on police to form partnerships with government agencies, local governments and service providers which have their own powers of social control (eg regulators and service providers such as child protection agencies).

Third party policing (Mazerolle & Ransley 2006a), as described further below, is in our view the end result of these wider changes – a new form of policing that exemplifies and captures the dynamics of this new era of crime control.

Third party policing

The defining features of third party policing are that police form partnerships with a range of State and non-State agencies and individuals, and use non-traditional legal levers to control and prevent crime. From this common ground, however, third party policing exists in many forms. Some police agencies use third parties to solve ongoing problems within the context of their problem-oriented policing program.[1] In other police agencies third party policing might exist as an especially designed, stand-alone-policing program using a one-size-fits-all third party solution (eg Oakland's Beat Health Program, see Mazerolle & Ransley 2006a). In some jurisdictions, forms of third party policing are now mandated by governments, such as the crime and disorder reduction partnerships established under Britain's *Crime and Disorder Act 1998* (see Loader 2000).

In most police agencies, however, third party policing is implemented in very unconscious, episodic ways during routine patrol work. Where a local shop has a problem with loiterers selling drugs near its premises, rather than focus on traditional enforcement action, the shop owner may be encouraged by police to install better lighting or employ private security patrols to deter the problem. Similarly, police might join with liquor licensing authorities to encourage bar and nightclub operators to adopt better policies on serving alcohol to intoxicated and underage patrons, to deal with a night-time disorder problem in nearby streets. Frequent calls for service from a particular property could prompt police to cooperate with building inspectors or rental agents to target the source of the problem. By forcing a physical upgrading of the property, or the eviction of problem tenants, a source of neighbourhood crime may be diminished.

The common features in these responses are that police form networks with third parties to take advantage of legal powers and levers not otherwise available to them (eg engaging private security, licensing laws, building codes or tenancy agreements). Someone with power to act on the crime problem is given an incentive to do so, either voluntarily (eg to improve shop custom) or with the express or implied threat of coercion (eg penalties under licensing or building laws, contract termination). For police, their tools and strategies are extended beyond the usual criminal justice responses (criminal prosecutions, cautions etc) to include a range of civil penalties and

---

1   About one third of problem-orientated policing approaches use some type of third party policing response – see Mazerolle and Ransley (2006a).

pressures that do not attract the protections afforded to criminal justice actions, such as the need to identify particular offenders, and evidence to satisfy a criminal standard of proof.

In many cases, police are under pressure from public and private entities to 'do something, now' about crime problems. Recent transformations in regulation have also created new crime control opportunities: for example, in the past, regulator and local government powers were often weak or underused and there was little incentive for police to partner with them to reduce crime. Now, it is convenient and mutually beneficial for both parties to come together to solve a problem. Police provide around the clock service, and have powers of arrest not usually available to non-police agents. Non-police third parties have available to them powers (eg confiscation, licence revocation, closure of premises) that are more easily enforced, with lower burdens of proof, than required under criminal law. In short, the new age crime control landscape provides natural, mutually-beneficial opportunities for forging partnerships that were absent or at best unarticulated in the past. We describe the key dimensions of third party policing below, before moving on in the next section to discuss some of the implications for police managers.

Purpose of action

There are two primary purposes of third party policing activities: crime prevention or crime control. In crime prevention, the police seek to anticipate crime problems and reduce the probability of an escalation of the underlying conditions that may cause crime problems to develop. Third party policing that has crime prevention as its purpose of action operates to control those underlying criminogenic influences that may (or may not) lead to future crime problems. By contrast, third party policing that seeks to control existing crime problems explicitly aims to alter the routine behaviours of those parties that the police believe might have some influence over the crime problem. The apparent influence of third parties might be conscious or unconscious, it might be explicit or implicit, and it might be planned or unplanned.

Initiators of third party policing

While police are often the initiators, there are a variety of agencies and individuals that can initiate third party policing activities, including prosecutors, individual citizens, community groups, and law enforcement agents in regulatory agencies. Police identification of situations for third party policing often stems from, or coincides with, a community identification of the same problem.

Focal point

The focal point of third party policing can be people, places or situations (see Mazerolle, Roehl & Kadleck 1998). Sometimes third party policing efforts are directed specifically at categories of people such as young people, gang members or drug dealers. To address some types of crime problems, the focal point of third party policing efforts might be directed against specific places, often places that have been defined by police as hot spots of crime. Drug dealing corners, parks where young people hang-out, and public malls are typically the focal point of third party policing activities that address specific places as opposed to certain categories of people.

Situations can also give rise to criminogenic activity. Examples of criminogenic situations include bus stop placements that facilitate strong-arm robberies, late opening hours of bars that lead to bar room brawls, and the general availability of spray paint in hardware stores operating in high-risk communities. Police use the principles of situational crime prevention (see Clarke 1992) to encourage or coerce third party partners to change the locations of bus stops, reduce opening hours of problematic bars and restrict the sale of spray paint to minors.

Types of problems

Third party policing can, in theory, be directed against a broad range of crime and quality of life problems (see Finn & Hylto 1994). However, most examples and evaluations of third party policing comprise police efforts to control drug problems (see Eck & Wardell 1998; Green 1996; Mazerolle, Roehl & Kadleck 1998) and disorderly behaviour (see Mazerolle & Ransley 2006a).

Ultimate targets

The ultimate targets of third party policing efforts are people involved in deviant behaviour. In theory, the ultimate targets of third party policing could include those persons engaged in any type of criminal behaviour including domestic violence, white-collar offending, street crime and drug dealing. In practice, however, the ultimate targets of third party policing are typically those offenders that are vulnerable, disadvantaged and/or marginalised. Young people (see White 1998), gang members, drug dealers (Green 1996), vandals, and petty criminals typically feature as the ultimate targets of third party policing.

Third parties and partners

A key, defining feature of third party policing is the presence of some type of third person or partner used by police to prevent or control crime. The list of potential third parties is extensive and can include property owners, parents, bar owners, shop owners, local and State governments, insurance companies, business owners, inspectors, and private security guards. Partners are often stakeholders or regulators identified by police as being useful levers in controlling a crime problem.

Legal basis

A key defining feature of third party policing is that there is some sort of legal basis (statutes, delegated or subordinate legislation or regulations, contractual relationships, torts laws) that shapes police efforts to engage a third party to take on a crime prevention or crime control role. The most common legal basis of third party policing includes local, State, and federal statutes (including municipal ordinances and town by laws), health and safety codes, uniform building standards, and drug nuisance abatement laws, and liquor licensing. The legal basis does not necessarily need to be directly related to crime prevention or crime control. Indeed, most third party policing practices use laws and regulations that were not designed with crime control or crime prevention in mind (eg Health and Safety codes, Building Standards).

Types of sanctions and penalties

The civil sanctions and remedies available under third party policing schemes vary greatly including court-ordered repairs of properties, fines, forfeiture of property or forced sales to meet fines and penalties, eviction, padlocking or temporary closure of a rented residential or commercial property, licence restrictions and/or suspensions, movement restrictions, lost income from restricted hours and ultimately arrest and incarceration (see Mazerolle & Ransley 2006a; Mazerolle, Roehl & Kadleck 1998). Often, several civil remedies and sanctions may be initiated simultaneously to solve one problem.

Tools and techniques

Police operate on a continuum to engage third parties in their crime prevention or crime control activities. At one end of the spectrum, police can approach third parties and ask them to cooperate. They might consult with members of the community as well as local property owners and ask about ways to control an existing crime problem or to help alter underlying conditions that might lead to future crime problems. Alternatively cooperation with police may be compelled. This may involve police encouraging a building inspector to issue notices to repair to a property owner, accompanied by the threat of prosecution and ultimately court-forced compliance by the third party (in this case, the building inspector).

Types of implementation

There are many different ways that police implement third party policing practices including within the context of problem-oriented policing or situational crime prevention programs. Problem-oriented policing provides the management infrastructure (see Goldstein 1990) and step-wise approach to solving a crime problem (Eck & Spelman 1987) and situational crime prevention offers the police an appreciation for situational opportunities that might be exploited using third party policing tactics (Clarke 1992).

The most common manifestation of third party policing, however, is the ad hoc utilisation of third party principles initiated in an unconscious manner by patrol officers who are simply trying to find a way to solve a problem. For these police there is no script to follow, no policy that they are working within, and generally very little accountability for their actions. The police are working within the law, but using the law with little regard to the possible negative side-effects.

Implications for police managers and leaders

We argue that third party policing is not so much a strategy that police should consider, but that increasingly they will have no option but to adopt third party approaches to crime control. Global transformations in governance and regulation, increased powers to non-police entities, plurality of the enforcement function in contemporary society, pressure from non-police entities to forge partnerships and the naturally occurring, mutual benefits derived from partnerships are all factors that we argue will create overwhelming incentives and pressure on police to adopt the principles of policing via third parties. This section considers the implications for managers and leaders of this new form of policing.

The main issue is how third party policing can best be articulated and managed within individual agencies. As discussed above, there is no one size fits all answer to this question. In some cases, third party policing will be applied within the boundaries of a formal problem-solving approach, so that a particular problem will be identified, and a solution involving third parties will be developed and applied. Elsewhere, a situational approach may lead to the involvement of third parties, or governments may mandate network approaches. In many cases, as discussed, third parties will be involved in an ad hoc way at the initiative of local officers on the spot. Different approaches will suit different problems, but one of the challenges for managers is to understand the evidence on what works, to recognise good practice when it occurs, and to assess its potential for transfer and adaptation to other problems. If third parties can be used to reduce crime problems in one area, what is their potential for doing so elsewhere? What changes are needed to adapt to local circumstances? A major problem for managers is that to date little has been written about these issues. Because third party policing has arisen in a largely episodic and unplanned way, its implementation and management are under-researched. We have suggested a comprehensive agenda to develop understanding and knowledge in the area (see Mazerolle & Ransley 2006a, pp 203-226), but in the interim, the approach will continue to develop to meet policy imperatives imposed from above and beyond police agencies.

Another challenge for police leaders is in managing the potential side effects of third party policing, and in ensuring accountability for its outcomes. Possible negative side effects of third party policing fall into three main groups – adverse social consequences arising from police coopting other organisations and individuals to deal with crime, the possibility that third party policing only displaces crime into other areas or times, and the impact of third party policing on legal rights, civil liberties and laws.

Dealing first with possible adverse social consequences, third party policing can be seen as too reactive, dealing with the consequences and not the causes of serious social problems. Not only does this misuse resources, but it may also have a net-widening effect, drawing into the criminal justice system more and more of the socially disadvantaged, simply because they live in or are otherwise associated with a risky area or group. The counter-acting argument is that marginalised groups are also victimised by the effects of crime in their neighbourhoods, and third party policing by addressing these effects can actually help to improve their quality of life. This improvement comes not just from the closing down of crack houses and targeting of alcohol-fuelled violence, but from the flow-on effects of better housing and more peaceful schools caused by the stricter enforcement of regulatory codes. Socially marginalised groups can also be victimised by a denial of the benefits of third party policing activities, caused by the disproportionate allocation of policing and resources to one particular area or problem, at the expense of others. How police choose to target their third party policing activities could act to entrench or alleviate inequalities in the distribution of criminal justice and regulatory resources.

In addition to adversely affecting or re-victimising the ultimate targets of third party policing, there can also be negative consequences for police partners. Individuals, such as landlords and business owners, may find themselves increasingly the burden-bearers for crime control, and there can also be adverse effects from third party policing on regulators coopted by police. Third party policing can be an intrusion into the routine activities of regulatory agencies. The normal regulatory model may be suspended in favour of a more enforcement-oriented approach, disturbing the presumptively cordial relationship between regulator and regulated. Third party policing also skews the resource allocation of the regulatory agencies, albeit temporarily, and often does so without any foreseeable reciprocation.

While the adverse social consequences it can cause comprise the first group of possible negative side effects of third party policing, the second group is concerned with the extent to which these interventions may lead to problems being displaced to nearby places (spatial displacement) or to some other time (temporal displacement), being committed in another way (tactical displacement), or being transformed into some other kind of offence (target displacement) (Cornish & Clarke 1987). These negative displacement effects happen when a police intervention reduces a crime problem at one place, or in one particular situation, but fails to protect other nearby places or situations from offenders who are not discouraged or deterred from committing a crime. However, recent interventions that have directly measured the wider spatial effect of crime opportunity-reducing measures have shown that reductions in crime can be achieved with little displacement (Clarke 1992). The key issue here, as with avoiding adverse social consequences of third party policing interventions, is for careful consideration to be given to these factors before engaging in the intervention.

Apart from adverse social consequences and displacement, the third set of possible negative side effects from third party policing relates to its impact on legal rights and laws. The broadest issue here is concern with the cooption of civil law for criminal justice purposes. Civil laws generally rely on a lower standard of proof in establishing breaches, do not assume that targets are legally represented, and use a different system of sanctions and penalties. Traditionally those penalties did not involve the threatened loss of personal liberty through imprisonment, and therefore a lower standard of protection seemed justified. Some contemporary civil laws, however, have closed this traditional divide – not just by allowing for jail sentences for serious breaches (in Australia for example, under environmental protection and corporate regulation), but also such severe penalties as the loss of a licence to pursue an occupation, and the confiscation of possessions. Criticisms arise when these serious sanctions are sought not necessarily to further the aims of the regulatory scheme the civil law relates to, but as a way around the problems and protections developed in the criminal law.

So, we suggest there are three main types of negative side effects from third party policing (adverse social consequences, displacement, and impact on legal rights and laws) and each of these needs to be managed through careful police planning and usage. The issue of accountability is central to this, but many traditional assumptions about the role and nature of police accountability are threatened or weakened by developments such as private and pluralised policing, partnerships and risk assessment. The monopoly on police use of force is being broken, as coercive powers are extended to other agencies and officials. Legal and institutional mechanisms directed at controlling and making accountable police uses of power do not necessarily affect other providers of policing functions, particularly those that are not State agencies. Similarly, while third party policing holds promise of improved efficiency and effectiveness, how are managers to be held accountable for individual projects and their expenditure and outcomes, particularly when some of the resources are actually coopted from other agencies and individuals? Where agencies are mandated, or choose, to work together towards crime prevention and control, who bears ultimate responsibility for the success or failure of their decisions?

Much of the concern with accountability derives from the breadth and flexibility of police discretion in these areas – the discretion to enter into third party policing arrangements, to decide where to target them, against which targets, for the benefit of which groups, and using which legal or regulatory levers. This discretion is responsible for much of the usefulness of third party policing, enabling local level police to identify local problems and targets and develop community-based solutions, so accountability should not be directed at removing or stifling discretion. Instead, what is essential is as much transparency and openness as possible in these processes, and in the exercise of police discretion. It is important that there is some formalised means of community input into these processes and openness to scrutiny through public complaints mechanisms and other mainstream police accountability devices.

The major accountability implication for third party policing is the need for proper consideration of other agencies and of the individuals involved as proximate and ultimate targets. Police coordinating these types of interventions need to consider the full scope of which agencies might be involved in reaching a solution for the particular crime problem at hand, and considering those methods which least contribute to re-victimising the already socially disadvantaged, or spreading the adverse consequences beyond immediate targets. For example, are there housing agencies that can be involved to help relocate tenants from premises shut down for building code violations as part of a crack down on drugs, or are people simply left to fend for themselves?

Mazerolle and Prenzler (2004) suggest a checklist to be used by police planning third party policing interventions, to ensure the use of their discretion in an ethical and accountable way. The checklist covers such issues as the inclusion in the planning group of all possible stakeholders, the prioritising of negotiation and persuasion over threats, assessment of the impacts of the intervention including displacement and re-victimisation, consideration of whether benefits outweigh harms, notice to affected third parties, and weight given to concerns of fairness, equity, dignity and respect. The central issue for accountability is that there is a proper documenting of both the intervention and its planning, so that oversight can occur where necessary. It is also essential that such interventions are properly evaluated, so that the true benefits of coercive measures can be assessed and tested against the detriments.

Conclusion

In this chapter we have argued that there has been a fundamental shift in contemporary understandings of both crime and policing. This shift, along with research about what works in policing, has led to a new focus on police forming partnerships with other State and non-State agencies and individuals, to control and prevent crime. We have sketched the framework of third party policing, a strategy designed to develop and use police partnerships to deal with crime problems. Third party policing offers much promise as a contemporary response to crime, but there is a need for police leaders and managers to take a strong role in the design and implementation of approaches so as to minimise negative side effects, and maximise accountability.

4

PRIVATE POLICE: PARTNERS OR RIVALS?

Tim Prenzler and Rick Sarre

The question of how *public* law enforcement agencies should relate to *private* law enforcement agencies presents a growing challenge to policymakers and police managers. Given that private security is now roughly equal in size to police, according to some indicators, it would seem logical that the two should work closely together in pursuit of the common goal of crime reduction. However, the issues are much more complex than this simple statement of principle allows. The two sectors operate on fundamentally different philosophies, and cooperation needs to be carefully planned to ensure that public interest principles prevail over those of private profit.

The Australian security industry

There are different ways of measuring public and private policing in Australia. Unfortunately, none of them is perfect. Nonetheless, by overlapping several measures one can build a useful picture of the relative size of each sector. The census is a major source and the category 'guards and security officers', introduced in 1986, provides a core group to match against the category of 'police'. In the 15 years between the first count and the most recent in 2001, police numbers remained ahead of guards, but guards increased by 52.1 per cent compared to a 19.5 per cent increase in police numbers (see Figure 4.1, opposite).

A much wider range of security occupations became available in a consistent form for the two census years 1996 to 2001. These are compared both with police and the Australian population in Table 4.1 (opposite). The results show that the Australian population increased by 6.0 per cent, police numbers increased by 6.5 per cent and security providers increased by 31.1 per cent. Overall, these figures show a ratio of security providers to police of 1.2 to 1.0 in 2001.

Figure 4.1: Police officers, guards and security officers, Australian Census, 1986-2001

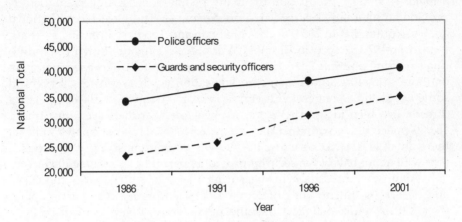

Source: Australian Bureau of Statistics (see Prenzler 2005)

Table 4.1: Security providers, Australian Census, 1996-2001

	1996	2001	% Change
Private Investigator	917	1228	+33.9
Security Adviser	595	793	+33.2
Locksmith	1493	1882	+26.0
Insurance Investigator	397	470	+18.3
Debt Collector	5931	9654	+62.7
Bailiff or Sheriff	581	637	+9.6
Security Officer	27,432	33,903	+23.5
Armoured Car Escort	51	102	+100.0
Guards and Security Officers (not elsewhere classified)	264	739	+179.9
TOTAL	**37,661**	**49,408**	**+31.1**
Police	37,993	40,492	+6.5
Population	17,892,423	18,972,350	+6.0

Source: Australian Bureau of Statistics (see Prenzler 2005)

As indicated, however, there are problems with these measures. For one, the census only reports persons' main occupations. Security work appears to be a major secondary occupation for many people. Licence figures, therefore, provide an alternative perspective on personnel. The most recent national analysis found that in 2003, under core State and Territory licensing systems, there were 97,182 security licences. Various adjustments down for individuals holding multiple licences and adjustments up for unlicensed operators or those operating under non-core legislation (such as process servers in some jurisdictions) suggested a very approximate figure of 100,000 persons directly involved in security work. In the same year there were just under 45,000 police officers in Australia (Prenzler 2005). These estimates indicate there are at least twice as many individuals working in security than police (but with about half of the security providers part-time) (Prenzler 2005).

Another complication in measuring the industry is that both census and licence figures do not differentiate between private and public operatives. Other sources suggest that the public sector component of security personnel in countries like Australia may be as high as 25 per cent (Prenzler 2005). A recent study that differentiated between police and private sector expenditures in Australia showed a 50/50 split (Mayhew 2003). At the same time, to be fair, it can also be argued that expenditures and personnel in anti-corruption agencies, fair trading and other public law enforcement agencies should be added to the public policing sector, as should unsworn personnel in police departments. This would likely tip the scales back to the public sector.

Putting all of these elements together is difficult. It could, for example, be argued that, regardless of money and expenditure, police retain primacy because police provide not only unofficial backup for private security providers, but offer a universal emergency service, and do most of the work in bringing offenders to justice. Others argue that private security has primacy because guards and consultants are focused on prevention, and because public sector policing services draw heavily on equipment supplied by private providers (Pastor 2003, p 44). Overall, a fair observation would be that the private sector makes up a substantial component of law enforcement and crime prevention services in Australia. Although their functions are not identical with police, private security should at least be considered as equal partners in the fight against crime. Additionally, the fact that the private sector is growing at a rate faster than the population and the police has extremely important implications for the public interest and accountability more generally.

Scandal and reform in private security

The 1980s and 1990s saw an expansion of the security industry but also a number of exposés of malpractice in areas such as assaults, fraud in alarm and patrol services, insider crime, and poor competency standards. These triggered an enlargement of State-based licensing systems, primarily through mandated training and the creation and application of disqualifying offences. The reforms appeared to usher in a period of stability. However, in 2003-2005, a series of fresh scandals over security officer conduct, along with revelations of deficient security standards in key areas, precipitated major reviews and modification of regulatory systems (Prenzler 2006).

Moves for a second round of reform came from within, as well as from outside, the industry. A major external factor was the continued menace of terrorism, combined with the growth of private/public security partnerships in critical sites such as airports (Wheeler 2005). There was a growing recognition of the central role of private security in public safety but also of the fact that security work holds a risk profile for misconduct and corruption similar to the high-risk profile of public policing. Tough oversight and a professionalisation process were needed to meet the security challenges of the 21st century. Overall, there was an accelerating convergence of public and private policing functions and standards, although the fact remained that the regulatory controls on security lagged well behind those of police.

Private and public policing

Despite the growth of private security, policing has been largely protected from the deliberate privatisation policies of the 1980s and 1990s. The figures cited above show police numbers increasing at a rate slightly higher than increases in the general population (ie, no 'downsizing'), and there has been little evidence of outsourcing of police work. The main factor behind the growth in private security has been market demand – driven in part by the steep rises in crime from the 1970s to the 1990s – as well as the firming of a shift in consciousness away from reliance on police to a mentality of 'self-protection' (Sarre & Prenzler 2005).

While the privatisation of policing by market forces appears to be the dominant mode of change, there is evidence of some facilitation of privatisation by governments and also cases of contracting out. Privatisation of security has not, of course, required legislative amendments. Private providers draw substantive authority from the law enforcement and self-defence powers of citizens and, in particular, from the rights of property owners to control entry to premises and protect property. Nonetheless, some special provisions aid private security – elements of weapons legislation for example – and some recent developments in the law have enlarged the scope of private operators – such as legal access to confidential information and stronger crowd control powers at designated sites (Sarre & Prenzler 2005). Governments have also outsourced some policing activities, most notably in the areas of open mall CCTV systems, traffic control at roadworks, and in specialist areas such as welfare fraud detection (King & Prenzler 2003). Surprisingly, perhaps, governments have also entered the market themselves, through the contract arm of the Australian Protective Service, for example, and the South Australian Police 'Police Security Services Branch

(PSSB)'. Australian police forces also engage in forms of commercial activity and partly-commercialised aid through consultancies and overseas missions.

Overlapping these trends are calls for greater cooperation and public-private partnerships. A key turning point in philosophy was marked by an address by former AFP Commissioner Peter McAulay to the 1994 Police Commissioners' conference. McAulay declared that the mutual exclusivity of private and public policing needed to come to an end. Since both services have common goals, he argued, a formal relationship was needed (see Golsby & O'Brien 1996). One of the first Australian studies of the issues concluded that:

> [There has been] a concern by some police that their role and functions were being eroded by the growth of private security. However, this view has matured over a period of time and police are now recognising that there are opportunities for the police and private security industry to work together (Golsby & O'Brien 1996, p 15).

One practical example of such cooperation is in the area of local government sponsored 'open street' CCTV systems that rely on coordinated responses between monitoring personnel and police. A recent Australian study found that the number of installations had increased from 12 in 1996 to 33 in 2002. Of the 33, 13 (or 40 per cent) were monitored by private security personnel (Wilson & Sutton 2003, p 92). The earlier survey by Golsby and O'Brien found cooperation was rated as good or very good by 52 per cent of police and 67 per cent of private security respondents. However, only a small number of police were positive about divesting functions to the private sector, and then only in areas such as operating speed cameras. About half the police saw 'reporting problems whilst on patrol' as a key area for cooperation but, surprisingly, neither group appeared interested in a shared communications system.

Internationally, the 1996 Atlanta Olympic Games was something of a test case for cooperative security on a large scale. There were, however, a number of criticisms of the operation, including poor communication and inadequate personnel standards (Forst & Manning 1999, p 35). However, the 2000 Sydney Olympics provided a high point in the effective deployment of mixed-source security services. Overall command was held by the NSW Police Service, with 4000 security officers working a combined total of 27,000 shifts with police and security volunteers over a two-week period. Coverage went beyond Olympic venues to 600 non-competition sites around the country (Sarre & Prenzler 2005, p 195). This achievement was mirrored more recently in the security success of the 2005 Melbourne Commonwealth Games.

The need for basic labour-intensive 'front-line' measures against terrorism in mass transit centres and other critical locations has been a major factor behind the development of public-private arrangements. The relatively cheaper rates associated with security personnel is crucial to their deployment, and the contracting in of personnel through private firms provides considerable flexibility. However, terrorism is not a sole consideration. In

2004 NSW Police Commissioner Ken Moroney recommended closer co-operation between police and security providers, emphasising that private security is 'an important part of providing [a] law enforcement approach, not only in the terrorism context but in the prevention of crime generally' (Petersen 2004, p 11). This principle of the two sectors working together for general crime prevention is embodied in the new Security Industry Authority in the UK, but premised on improved private sector professionalism. The Authority is explicit about its role in both underwriting basic levels of competency and conduct in the industry, and facilitating public/private cooperation. The 2004 annual report states:

> One of the reasons we came into being was to contribute as effectively as possible to a fundamental Government objective – reducing crime and the fear of crime ... But there is still a long way to go before the private security industry is viewed with trust by the general public, *as a partner by other law enforcement authorities*, and as making a real contribution to the fight against crime (SIA 2004, p 2, emphasis added).

A Law Commission of Canada (2002) Discussion Paper even floated the idea of shared training involving a switch from 'police colleges to policing colleges' as a way of equalising standards.

Partners or rivals?

One issue that has tended to be neglected in the current enthusiasm for public-private partnerships is that the two groups operate on fundamentally opposing principles. Public police have a duty to serve the public equally, whereas private providers are, for the most part, obliged only to their employer or principal. The latter can be a government agency, and contractual arrangements can require police-like duties to the public, but the basis of engagement remains selective. This has been highlighted in the media who have reported cases where private guards have refused to come to the aid of citizens endangered outside the guards' proprietorial zone (Sarre & Prenzler 2005, p 201). The absence of 'good Samaritan' legislation in Australia in circumstances of criminal activity underpins the limited responsibilities of security officers vis-a-vis police.

But of particular practical interest to police is the question of how these differing principles, and other differences in methods and skills, should inform how they relate to the private sector. Historically, police appear to have held largely antagonistic and dismissive attitudes towards their counterparts in the private sector (Shearing, Stenning & Addario 1985). In fact, they would probably have rejected the concept of 'counterparts'. An early report by the [US] Private Security Advisory Council (1977) suggested that cooperation was not feasible given the following factors:

- lack of mutual respect;
- negative stereotypes;
- status differentials;

- lack of communication;
- lack of standards in the private sector; and
- mutual perceptions of corruption.

Table 4.2 lists key opposing aspects of the two sectors. The primary differential, arguably, concerns police obligations to the public and private security obligations to the client. This plays out in a number of ways. Primarily, police are expected to respond to all calls for assistance (on a triage basis) and to bring offenders to justice after crimes have been committed. This includes calls from private security firms acting on behalf of their clients and taking over in a private arrest situation. Private security personnel, on the other hand, are free to focus on primary prevention of crime with no obligation to respond to calls for assistance that lie outside their contractual obligations. Although there are obligations to report more serious crimes, the initiation of a prosecution is also essentially discretionary.

Table 4.2: Competing principles of public policing and private security

Public	Private
taxpayer-funded	profit-driven
public interest	client interest
equal service	selective service
heavily regulated	less regulated
centralised, bureaucratic	fragmented, diverse
focused on law enforcement	focused on crime/loss prevention
offender-oriented	protection-oriented
reactive	proactive
public space	private space
specific powers	citizen powers
intensive training	limited training
limited discretion	wide discretion

Source: Sarre & Prenzler (2005, p 195)

Can, or should, these differences be overcome? The variety of possible types of relationship is, in fact, more complex than the simple opposition – partners or rivals – used in the title of this chapter. Model building can help in mapping out the options. Clifford Shearing (1992) was amongst the first to describe police/security relationships with the aid of theoretical models, suggesting three primary types covering 'State-centred', *'laissez-faire'* and 'pluralist' approaches. Sarre and Prenzler (2000) developed an eight-part model from the work of Shearing, as well as Johnston (1992). The eight-part model – or eight *models* – is summarised below:

1. The *property* model assumes that one sector works on private property and the other on public property. Public police work the roads, footpaths, parks and public squares of modern societies. Private security personnel work in corporate spaces and provide security technology for private residences, offices and factories. While limited forms of interface and overlap occur, the general private/public divide provides a defining boundary.

2. The *division of labour* model assumes that public police control crime primarily through the deterrent and incapacitative effects of arrest and prosecution, while the main contribution of private police is through a preventive presence.

3. In the *competing forces* model, the two sectors are assumed to have roughly similar capacities to respond to crime. Theoretically, there is very little standing in the way of the private sector providing most police functions. The two therefore compete for market share.

4. The *supplementary service* model assumes the essential character of the two sectors is the same, but their powers differ in crucial ways. While they both operate in the same crime control market, the public sector has precedence because of its greater authority (to deploy warrants for example and arrest for lower order offences). The private sector can only supplement the essential public service work of police.

5. The *ad hoc partnership* model assumes that the two sectors can combine if and when needed, regardless of differences in jurisdiction, powers and tasks. When a crisis or event is over, the formal relationships become redundant and the sectors diverge again.

6. The *combined forces* model assumes symbiotic cooperation and complementarity between the sectors. It optimistically asserts that the relationship is most often complementary, not adversarial, and that close permanent arrangements can be developed both at executive and operational levels to maximise the synergetic effects of cooperation.

7. An *unholy alliance* describes cooperation in terms of mutual corruption. Public and private forces, because of their functions, are likely to face intense temptation to breach procedural rules and compromise legal rights, and even to trade in illicit preferential treatment.

8. The *regulated intersections model* describes cooperation that is, for the most part, limited and closely regulated. Where interactions are inevitable, or deemed beneficial on a public interest test, they

are controlled by standardised procedures and subject to over-sight.

The way forward

The first seven models outlined above were all argued to be unsatisfactory at crucial points (Sarre & Prenzler 2000). Some closed down the possibility of mutual benefits completely. Others misrepresented the degree of overlap, or potential overlap, in many functions. The most optimistic model – combined forces – was considered to put too many egalitarian public policing prin-ciples at risk. The preferred model – regulated intersections – attempts to synthesise the best of the others. It recognises that the great bulk of police and security work is likely to continue to occur without direct interactions. Current trends are unlikely to alter this significantly. Nonetheless, inter-actions are inevitable and therefore need to be controlled. There is also a case for deliberately enlarging the scope of interactions within the public interest provisions of the police mission. Private providers are largely free to make their own decisions about cooperation but police need to set limits and stan-dards at the highest levels of policy decision-making and through the development of procedures; with a 'watching brief' over practice to ensure, for example, that some firms and their clients are not benefiting unfairly from police support. At the same time, cooperation 'on the ground' is likely to be enhanced by regular meetings at district and regional levels where local issues – such as specific crime problems or alarm response issues – can be addressed at operational levels.

Some of these recommendations have been developed in more detail in a 2005 US Department of Justice report, *Engaging the Private Sector to Promote Homeland Security: Law Enforcement-Private Security Relationships* (NIJ 2005). The report strongly endorsed the nine guidelines for anti-terrorist public-private operational collaboration originally set out by the Department of Homeland Security (DHS). These arguably have application to the wider crime problem (DHS 2003, pp 6-10):[1]

- Recognise the need for prevention.
- Establish a system, centre, or task force to serve as a clearinghouse for all potentially relevant domestically generated terrorism infor-mation.
- Ensure timely interpretation and assessment of information.
- Prepare Memorandums of Understanding (MOUs) and formal co-ordination agreements between public and private agencies. MOUs should describe mechanisms for exchanging information about vul-nerabilities and risks, coordination of responses, and processes to facilitate information sharing and multi-jurisdictional pre-emption of terrorist acts.

---

1   See <www.ojp.usdoj.gov>.

- Use community policing initiatives, strategies, and tactics to identify suspicious activities related to terrorism.
- Explicitly develop 'social capital' through collaboration among the private sector, law enforcement, and other partners so that data, information, assistance, and 'best practices' may be shared and collaborative processes developed.
- Coordinate federal, State, and local information, plans, and actions for assessments, prevention procedures, infrastructure protection, and funding priorities to address prevention.
- Establish a regional prevention information command centre and coordinate the flow of information regarding infrastructure.
- Include prevention and collaboration measures in exercises.

Overall, there appears to be a strong case for a sustained effort to develop optimal relationships, given the size of the crime problem and the many points of overlap in public and private policing. However, one of the problems for determining best-practice is the lack of adequately documented cases. For example, readers will be aware of the now commonplace deployment of larger numbers of security personnel at sporting events, with smaller numbers of police in more of a reserve role (Warren 1998). This would seem sensible and largely effective, but a research program on police-security relations would provide more objective data and better policy inputs in this area. Similarly, information-sharing shows considerable promise, if the risks can be controlled – particularly information about criminal identities and criminal *modus operandi*. One exception to the lack of research in this area is a recent Spanish study that examined the practical application of the regulated intersections model. Government intervention was focused on both minimising illegalities and maximising the benefits of formal communication. The study found that police and private security could productively work together on a routine basis in relation to procedures such as licence checks on suspect vehicles, information about suspect persons, recovery of stolen vehicles, back-up assistance to private security providers, and intelligence about organised crime. To avoid *ad hoc* interactions, information was successfully channelled through a coordination room (Gimenez-Salinas 2004).[2]

An associated issue concerns private security powers and responsibilities. As private security comes to be seen as a resource for public benefits, aligned to government policy, there is a stronger case for allowing licensed security providers to take on police-like powers. This is evident in the 'special constable' provisions often granted to private contractors for special events that involve large crowd-control functions. Powers like these, above those of ordinary citizens, could be a standard part of the licensing system. Inquiry agents engaged in debt collection and issuing summonses have argued that this 'commercial work' has a major public interest benefit that

---

2   For examples of diverse types of formal partnerships, although with limited evaluation, see NIJ (2005) at <www.ncjrs.gov>.

should entitle them to access a wider range of confidential databases for legitimate purposes, the right to demand answers from those they legitimately detain, and the capacity to apply for search warrants. These 'legitimate purposes' include finding the location of people who are trying to avoid the law, and locating evidence or identifying assets that may be subject to legal process. A question remains: is this the type of sharing of powers that police would support, and, if so, under what conditions?

The question of enhanced regulation leads to the final question of the police role in regulation of the industry. It could be argued that police regulating private security (as occurs in New South Wales, Victoria and Western Australia) is not an appropriate part of either a combined forces or regulated intersections model. Police are not regulators of business. This is not their area of traditional expertise or proper field of action. True, weapons licensing and criminal history checks are probably best left in expert police hands, but the day-to-day work of processing licences, monitoring conduct and developing professionalism would seem to be more appropriately placed within a fair trading or business and consumer affairs-style department. This would also help place security on a more independent standing, more appropriate to a partnership role with police.

Conclusion

The trend towards privatisation of security is now firmly entrenched around the world. A rapidly growing market for security services has allowed private suppliers to challenge, if not eclipse, government police services in terms of numbers and expenditures. Governments and police leaders therefore need to ensure that laws, regulations and procedures match the changing realities of policing, so that they do not remain framed in terms of a concept of policing (essentially public policing) that is no longer valid. Caution needs to be exercised, however, in rushing to expand significantly public-private cooperation in policing, given the fundamentally conflicting philosophical bases of their operations. There do, however, appear to be sufficient cases of successful cooperation where mutual benefits have occurred – especially from a public benefit perspective – to support further enlarging cooperative arrangements, subject to the constraints, reviewed above, of a regulated intersections approach.

5

MANAGING INTELLIGENCE: INNOVATION AND IMPLICATIONS FOR MANAGEMENT

Patrick F Walsh

As discussed elsewhere in this volume several factors have impacted on the business of policing and the skills now required by those who lead or manage it. Many of these external and internal drivers – globalisation, the changing nature of organised crime, terrorism, police corruption commissions, new managerialism and technology – have also caused changes to the management and development of specific policing disciplines, including intelligence.

This chapter argues that in order to respond to this changing operating environment the intelligence leader and manager need to equip themselves with a range of general and specialised management skills. Largely absent in the growing literature on intelligence, theory and practice in the policing context (see for example, Ratcliffe 2004; Maguire & John 2006) is a discussion of the specialised skills and attributes required to deal with the challenges of leading or managing an intelligence function. Management capabilities and attributes required by all police leaders and managers are discussed elsewhere in this volume, so discussion of such attributes will be limited to three areas in this chapter: strategic planning, performance management and organisational change.

Following this, the chapter concludes with a brief summation of the key challenges for intelligence management in the future, the greatest of which will be to develop effective intelligence doctrines that are relevant and useful for their agencies. For the next decade this will require managers with specific transformational leadership attributes.

General skills for the intelligence leader and manager

To put the discussion below in context, it is useful first to define the terms leader and manager. For the purpose of this chapter, and using the definitions by Robbins et al (2006, pp 9, 568):

> [L]eadership is the process of influencing a group towards the achieve-
> ment of goals, and management is the process of coordinating work acti-
> vities so that they are completed efficiently and effectively with and
> through other people.

While this definition implies that leadership and management are not the
same in many policing agencies, an individual will be required to perform
aspects of both roles. The rationale is that in most Australasian law enforcement agencies, the intelligence function and how it impacts on organisational
outcomes is still evolving, so the discipline has much to benefit from individuals who possess both leadership and management skills at each level of
responsibility. What, then, are the main leadership and management skills in
which an intelligence manager needs to have a solid grounding?

Strategic management

As suggested by Etter and Palmer (1995) and other more general works (eg
Mintzberg 1994) the police leader and manager has been working with good
strategic planning principles in their agencies. However, given the increased
complexity and accountability of the current environment, leaders and
managers of the intelligence function along with other specialised program
managers, require a more sophisticated approach and demonstrable proficiency in strategic management. This move towards a more formalised approach to strategic management will strengthen as intelligence products and
practices become more integrated into the agency's decision-making. As a
result, intelligence managers need to assess more accurately how their own
unit business planning can best support agency-wide strategic planning. Too
frequently in the past, the planning and management of intelligence products
have been dislocated from the wider strategic organisational goal-setting in
many Australasian law enforcement agencies.

Determining the level of involvement an intelligence manager will have
in the higher-end strategic planning of an agency will obviously vary
between organisations. Much will be determined by how close, in organisational terms, the intelligence manager is to the executive with responsibility
for the intelligence portfolio. However, even middle ranking and lower team
management intelligence positions with more operational responsibilities
will require a good grounding in strategic management. In practical terms,
this means that even team level managers will need to become more adept at
business planning to ensure unit objectives and outputs are integrated with
agency objectives.

Performance management

Developing skills in strategic management and planning also involves an
ability to understand how to measure outputs. Police leadership and
management in the 1990s became increasingly defined by measuring
performance by outputs, particularly measuring them quantitatively. As

Long suggests, during this time was a shift to 'New Public Management' or a 'performance culture' in the US and the UK, describing it as a culture characterised by setting targets and performance indicators, identifying core competencies and the redesignation of clients as customers (2003, p 632).

There are now many quantitative and qualitative methods used to measure performance. Probably the most well known quantitative performance measure is that derived from the approach COMPSTAT developed by the New York Police Department. COMPSTAT relies on the frequent delivery of accurate statistics to assess crime and police operational response (Cope 2003, p 341; Walsh & Vito 2004). In the Australasian police context many agencies have adopted similar quantitative and qualitative performance indicators, for example, Victoria Police uses a COMPSTAT approach, NSW Police uses Operation and Crime Review panels which are based on the COMPSTAT approach (Chilvers & Weatherburn 2004). The Australian Federal Police uses a *business activity analysis* process where the performance indicators of every section, including the intelligence function, are reviewed.

As also discussed by Mitchell (in this volume), the use of such approaches to measure performance is likely to increase at all organisational levels in a context of greater accountability and the continuing devolution of police responsibility. All commanders and unit managers, including those working in the intelligence function will need to be able to use these methodologies more strategically in order to evaluate their practice. In addition to being able to apply performance management tools to their own work and the work of others, intelligence managers in the future may be required to take on a larger role in monitoring the performance of the tools themselves and should be in a good position to take on this role. As custodians of much of the data and intelligence used to generate such reports, they ought to be able to assess trends and articulate any limitations in the quality and analysis of information used.

Organisational change

Another important issue related to managing the strategic objectives of law enforcement agencies and assessing performance is the requirement by leaders and managers to engineer organisational change. Police leaders and managers need to be able to work within, and design, appropriate organisational structures that can respond flexibly to the evolving operating environment. As raised by a number of authors in this volume, most Australasian law enforcement agencies have undergone significant organisational restructures over the past two decades. One of the most profound has been a move away from the traditional centralised military command structures to more decentralised models. This has meant a greater devolution of operational responsibility and the localisation of relevant expertise and specialist resources. Internal review processes, the evolution of new crime types and the growing complexity of all crime have each impacted on the way law enforcement agencies are now structured to deliver their services.

The impact the increased fluidity of organised crime groups, the criminal exploitation of technology and the role of police in counter-terrorism will also continue to require change in organisational structure and function. In addition, there is little doubt that debates about the relationships between crime, police numbers and police expenditure will continue to dominate managerial ideas about performance and organisational design (Neyroud & Beckley 2001, cited in Long 2003, p 642). However, in the future, effective organisational change will need to be informed not only by traditional rational-calculative models, but also by how leaders and managers can learn more strategically from the push and pull of internal and external factors (Long 2003, p 642). Proactive policing of future threats and opportunities will also depend on the effective management of information and knowledge about them to produce organisational learning (Senge 2003).

Over the past decade, changes in the organisational structure of most Australasian law enforcement agencies have already had a significant impact in how the intelligence function is now managed (Walsh 2005). However, as potential key brokers for organisational knowledge, intelligence leaders and managers must also become facilitators for organisational learning and redesigning in the future. In many agencies this will require bringing intelligence leaders closer to the central decision-making processes in order for the agency to learn, adapt and evolve to meet new challenges.

Specialised skills for the intelligence leader and manager

In the intelligence profession any specialised skills an individual may possess are driven by the context within which they work and are largely dependent on the scope of business, their level of decision-making and whether the manager is working within a sub-specialty of intelligence.

A useful discussion of specialised skills is possible, by exploring them in the context of the common leadership and management challenges confronting most leaders and managers in law enforcement intelligence environments. These common challenges relate to building and managing viable intelligence doctrines in Australasian law enforcement agencies. Hence, discussion in this remaining section will focus on a thematic discussion of skills and how they relate to managing contemporary issues in law enforcement intelligence doctrines.

At the broadest conceptual level, managing an intelligence function in contemporary law enforcement means being able to work with a range of interrelated doctrinal issues relating to how intelligence is processed and produced. Intelligence doctrine refers to the total of structures, systems and processes that underpin the tasking, collection, analysis and dissemination of intelligence. In particular, the development of good intelligence processes in law enforcement depends on effective leadership and management in three broad doctrinal areas: tasking and coordination; collection and analysis; and evaluation.

Improving leadership and management capabilities in these critical areas of intelligence doctrine will also be important in the future to all police agencies in achieving broader strategic and common directions, such as those articulated by the Australasian Police Ministers' Council, *Directions in Australasian Policing: 2005-2008* (APMC 2005). In particular, this document's guidance on enhancing policing innovation, cooperation and coordination places a heavy emphasis on the role of intelligence in enhancing performance in these areas, so it is important that those who aspire to leadership and management roles in the intelligence discipline acquire relevant core competencies and capabilities in these areas. The specific content and practice of competencies will change according to the management conditions in different agencies. However, as argued below, there are some fundamental intelligence principles and specialised competencies that all leaders and managers of intelligence should possess.

Tasking and coordination issues

The starting point in specialist intelligence management training is the ability to understand and manage better tasking and coordination of intelligence within the agency. This is a fundamental technical competency for all intelligence managers, and at the micro level specifically means the ability to identify client(s) or stakeholders and how best to manage the relationship between them and intelligence service providers (Nicholl 2004).

At first glance this seems straightforward for anyone with well-developed managerial skills. However, in the current environment, effective oversight of the tasking, use and coordination of intelligence is challenging, given that in many agencies the processes underpinning these activities are still developing. Further, as the past decade has demonstrated, externally driven changes in the operating environment will require leaders and managers of intelligence that can not only be 'project champions' for continued internal reform, but also be individuals who can quickly adapt intelligence tasking and coordination processes in support of evolving corporate objectives.

As discussed earlier, most Australasian law enforcement agencies over the past decade have moved away from the traditional centralised 'military command' organisational structure. This change has had profound implications for how intelligence is now being tasked and coordinated. Walsh (2005) in his review of intelligence-led policing in Australian law enforcement, provides an overview on the impact that changes in organisational models have had on tasking and coordination of intelligence in four Australasian law enforcement agencies: the Australian Federal Police (AFP), the Australian Crime Commission (ACC), Victoria Police and NSW Police.

In simple terms, the move to a more centralised/decentralised model has meant that intelligence is no longer seen as a specialist police resource exclusively controlled by executive management in headquarters. Intelligence in most agencies now is organised along centralised and decentralised lines. It is centralised in terms that there is usually some executive or functional control at Head Office (determining how intelligence as a discipline is coordinated), and then there is also the decentralised (regional and local) aspects of how intelligence is organised in police agencies today. The tasking and coordination of the intelligence function along with other specialist areas, is now managed at the regional and local levels according to priorities that are set at those levels. While this has created efficiencies and has empowered non-executive intelligence managers to apply resources more flexibly to local problems, it has also resulted in unevenness in some agencies in how intelligence functions are tasked and coordinated (Walsh 2005, p 23).

Many Australasian law enforcement agencies, particularly over the past decade, have attempted to resolve current deficiencies in how intelligence is tasked and coordinated. Internally driven change in the intelligence field in the AFP, Victoria Police and NSW Police has been significant. These agencies have debated organisational restructuring of intelligence functions and how they might best support operational and strategic priority setting.

Additionally, the creation of the ACC in 2003 represents a new way for an agency to task and coordinate intelligence in a national law enforcement agency using a national criminal intelligence priorities (NCIPs) framework. The ACC was established on 1 January 2003. It is the product of three former agencies: the National Crime Authority, the Australian Bureau of Criminal Intelligence and the Office of Strategic Crime Assessments. Other external factors that have influenced internal organisational changes in intelligence in Australasian law enforcement agencies have included an embrace by many of them of the discourse and practice of UK intelligence models such as *intelligence-led policing* and the *National Intelligence Model*. Intelligence-led policing is a hotly contested concept within the policing literature. For some it is not really a new model of policing but uses evidence and intelligence to do police work more smartly (Tilley 2003). For others (Walsh 2005), it is at least in part about a tighter integration of intelligence at all levels of decision-making. The NIM was developed in the UK National Criminal Intelligence Service (NCIS) in 2000 to provide the intellectual backbone and blueprint for an intelligence-led policing approach to policing in the UK. It is currently being rolled out in all 43 police services in England and Wales and is also being implemented in Scotland.

This is not the place for a detailed discussion of the two models, and much has been written about each including the rhetoric, practice and evidence of whether they do lead to better policing outcomes (see, for example, Ratcliffe 2002; Tilley 2003; Maguire & John 2006; Walsh 2005).

However, leaving aside debates surrounding the efficacy of these models, their emphasis on a new managerial approach to policing and intelligence in particular has influenced greatly the development of new tasking and coordination processes in many Australasian law enforcement agencies.

For example, in 2004 Victoria Police launched its new intelligence process called the Victoria Police Intelligence Model (VPIM), whose principles, including those related to the tasking and coordination of intelligence, were influenced heavily by the UK National Intelligence Model (Walsh 2005).

There have also been a number of other external drivers for change in tasking and coordinating in law enforcement agencies. For the AFP, an increasing focus on international policing and counter-terrorism has put new demands on the way its intelligence is tasked and coordinated. Similarly the Sydney 2000 Olympics and planning for the 2006 Commonwealth Games in Melbourne provided further catalysts for improvements in the way intelligence is tasked and coordinated in those agencies.

However it is clear that deficiencies remain in the way intelligence is tasked and coordinated in many law enforcement agencies, resulting in intelligence not fully supporting decision-making processes at all levels within agencies. Despite agencies establishing tasking and coordination groups and other forums at local regional and central levels, to better integrate intelligence into decision-making processes, many of these new measures are still works in progress.

One of the biggest problems in how intelligence is tasked and coordinated, which was also identified by Etter and Palmer (1995, p 14) a decade ago, is that there needs to be a stronger link between organisational planning and strategic intelligence. In modern law enforcement there remains an unavoidable tension between the pressure to deal with the here and now while attempting to position the agency to respond to threats coming across the horizon in the next five years. The fast reactive daily tempo of tasking and coordinating intelligence support, to more immediate tactical or operational objectives, has impacted on the ability of many agencies' intelligence functions to adequately service senior decision-makers and their government masters with higher-end strategic intelligence support.

While it is true that in a competitive information environment, heads of agencies have different ways of setting and managing strategic priorities, a lack of strategic intelligence support is a bit like flying blind. It is competitive as a result of police leaders and managers having other sources of information in which to make strategic, operational and tactical business decisions. Intelligence is just one information feed and other areas include policy areas in policing and government sources of information. Sustained corporate leadership is required to build an effective strategic intelligence capability. It will most likely fall to the corporate leader of the agency's intelligence function to drive this change. While better strategic intelligence support for executive decision-making will require sound leadership skills, reform at this level is also dependent on improved management in the tasking and coordination of intelligence at the operational and tactical levels.

Managers of intelligence functions at these levels will need a greater understanding of intelligence than their predecessors on how best to harness its capabilities in support of organisational priorities. Finally, improving how intelligence is tasked and coordinated in support of decision-making will require its leaders and managers to address lingering cultural barriers and misunderstandings about the value of intelligence products to organisational outcomes (Walsh 2005).

Intelligence collection

While sound management of intelligence tasking and coordination is critical to providing the right service to a client at the right time, the content of what is provided to them is a product of how the intelligence is collected and analysed. Intelligence collection and analysis are the vital steps of any intelligence process and so the effective management of all the human and technological resources that are involved in these two steps is also critical.

Intelligence collection, regardless of the level at which it takes place, should be seen as an entire agency planning activity. Regardless of whether the end goal is to collect intelligence that meets all the agency's strategic objectives or only those required to support the goals of one operation, similar collection planning and management implications are involved. It is clear that fundamental planning issues at any level need to be addressed including:

- what to collect?
- why?
- who has the information? and
- what is the reliability of the intelligence? (Higgins 2004).

This is straightforward, but the greater challenges for leaders and managers of intelligence will be to improve the quality of collection methodologies and systems that currently exist. While each agency has their own unique problems with intelligence collection there are three common issues that need further attention from all managers.

First, in the authors' own experience of working in two federal law enforcement agencies and through regular discussions with managers and intelligence analysts, there is still a lack of integration and coordination of collection efforts at all levels of decision-making. On a human level, this means frequently that officers not directly involved in the intelligence function, fail to understand that the intelligence they collect, could be relevant to others working in other parts of the organisation. This problem is complex and itself is the product of the absence of, or an ineffective, collection system, or old information management practices where officers store intelligence either in their heads or specific case files rather than in systems which allow others to use it.

Secondly, good intelligence collection practice has been hampered by the fact that a multitude of databases are in use in most Australasian agencies (for the collection and analysis of intelligence). It has only been in recent years that efforts have been made to make it easier for personnel to access and link intelligence which might be relevant to decision-making. Thirdly, with perhaps the partial exception of efforts being made by the ACC, more needs to be done to develop risk and threat assessment models for law enforcement agencies. It is clear from research and theoretical literature that measuring risk, threat and harm are still difficult methodologically (Vander Beken 2004). It is also clear that intelligence collection strategies can be driven from other processes, including strategic management, performance measurement and political. However, resources are limited so more thought by intelligence managers will need to go into strengthening risk, threat and harm assessment models.

It is not suggested here that Australasian law enforcement agencies are not enhancing their intelligence collection systems and methodologies and Walsh (2005) documents many recent improvements in four Australasian law enforcement agencies. The establishment of the ACC's national criminal intelligence priorities framework is an example. There is also growing evidence of support by agency heads underpinning improvements in collection systems. For example, addressing an intelligence conference in 2004, Commissioner Keelty made it clear that all AFP members should now see themselves as intelligence collectors (Keelty 2004).

Advancements have also been made over the past five years to improve information technology and information management systems essential to fostering good practice intelligence collection. However, in the next decade, being a leader or manager of intelligence a law enforcement agency will require sustained attention to improving collection methodologies and systems. In some agencies, managing this important part of the intelligence portfolio will also mean an ability to be a change agent to ensure that a corporate repository of intelligence will develop and can be reliably and rapidly called upon in support of objectives.

Intelligence analysis

It is clear that well-managed collection systems are essential to law enforcement agencies in order to potentially position themselves to respond to their changing operating environment. However, merely collecting intelligence is obviously insufficient alone if it is not used effectively to interpret, understand and predict changes in this environment. This is where the importance of a highly developed intelligence analytical capability comes in. Without well-trained analysts underpinned by good processes, decision-makers are unable to take advantage of intelligence assessments for the purposes of interpreting and changing the criminal environment. Hence, the role of the intelligence leader and manager in developing and maintaining high standards of analytical service will continue to be critical.

The context in which intelligence analysis occurs in Australasian law enforcement agencies has changed over the past decade. There is no doubt that the new police performance culture, increased technology, terrorism and organised crime, in particular, have placed more demands on intelligence analysis services as have internal organisational intelligence reviews, and new models of intelligence practice such as intelligence-led policing and the UK National Intelligence Model.

Intelligence-led policing and the idea of proactively using intelligence analytical techniques are gaining traction amongst many intelligence practitioners in Australasian law enforcement agencies. However, in practice, analysis could be more influential (Walsh 2005; Cope 2004).

Intelligence analysis incorporates a range of theoretical perspectives and is practiced in different contexts such as tactical, operational and strategic, therefore it is difficult to generalise about this disparate body of knowledge. However, regardless of whether one is talking about crime mapping, target profiling or strategic analysis tools, there are common issues blocking the best use of analysis in order to assist decision-making. Collectively these are linked to deficiencies in other areas of intelligence doctrine in law enforcement agencies, but specifically relate to poor quality data and intelligence, analytical 'tradecraft' and training issues, and organisational culture issues.

Cope's qualitative study of two police forces in the UK highlighted some of the problems related to data quality, training and related cultural issues (Cope 2004). Similarly, Walsh in his 2005 survey of intelligence-led policing in four Australasian law enforcement agencies, found the same issues impacted on the generation of good analysis and its integration into decision-making. For example, the problem of poor data sets, particularly in the analysis of high volume crimes is well known by analysts working in Australia and the UK.

At times, poor quality and incomplete data have been compounded by a less than strategic acquisition by agencies of databases and software programs. Access to good quality data and intelligence has also been a problem for strategic analysis, particularly when other staff or the collection system has not recorded relevant information. All of the above contribute to scepticism by decision-makers and other non-intelligence staff within law enforcement agencies about the reliability and relevance of analysis.

The impact of the products of intelligence analysis in Australasian law enforcement agencies has also been compromised by poor tradecraft and training issues. Tradecraft refers to the analysts' competencies and capabilities in creating an intelligence product that meets or anticipates the decision-maker's needs. It refers not only to the range of skills and experience in specific analytical techniques, but also to more generic advanced skills in critical thinking, research methodology and statistical modelling, amongst others.

While most Australasian law enforcement agencies have offered some analytical training to their intelligence officers, curricula have not always been at the standard required or have remained relevant to changes in organisational priorities. An obvious weakness in analytical training has been in strategic intelligence analysis. This situation is improving with agencies such as the AFP and Victoria Police investing more resources in strategic intelligence training. There are also now more specialised intelligence courses being offered internally and increasing collaboration with external education providers such as the National Strategic Intelligence Course (NSIC), which is run by Charles Sturt University in collaboration with the ACC and AFP (Walsh & Ratcliffe 2005), and with other tertiary providers such as Edith Cowan University and Macquarie University.

Another weakness in analytical training relates to an inability to equip analysts with advanced critical thinking and alternate analytical cognitive tools to challenge their conventional views about current or events likely to occur in the future. Both the 9/11 Commission and Flood Report identified these as important weaknesses in analytical standards (9/11 Commission Report 2004; Flood Report 2004).[1]

The uptake of analysis to support decision-making has also been challenged by views on the worth of intelligence analysis. There are residual negative attitudes even from some managers about the 'worth' of intelligence analysis.

Poor organisational cultural attitudes about intelligence are not always based on hostile views. In many cases, these attitudes relate to misunderstandings by non-intelligence personnel about analysis and its methodologies. As Cope usefully points out, police officers understand crime by gathering the facts at a scene, knowledge is experiential and contextual whereas analysts often requires a synthesis of data out of context (Cope 2004, p 199).

From a managers' perspective, the current problems in analytical doctrine are not easily resolvable in the next few years. There is evidence that some Australasian law enforcement agencies are improving their ability to extract data across one or more of their systems (Walsh 2005). However, the traditional hierarchical and 'siloing' approach to information still continues and is not conducive to rigorous analysis or decision-making.

It will be in the interest of intelligence managers to initiate discussions and projects to explore other organisational models for intelligence that encourage a more rapid and less hierarchical way to share data (Sheptycki 2004, p 22). Additionally, law enforcement agencies collect a plethora of data but more data does not necessarily better data. In the future, leaders and managers of intelligence will need to steer discussion not only about what systems should be purchased but also discussion about improving methodologies for the collection and analysis of data.

Perhaps quicker inroads can be made in training deficiencies. In the language of the UK NIM, an essential part of a new manager' brief will be to lead, coordinate and supervise improvements in the agency's knowledge products. Knowledge products include the agency's rules and protocols for doing the business of intelligence at all levels. They are all the rules of the 'trade'; and include competencies/training for practitioners, tradecraft, sharing intelligence and informant handling, data protection guidelines and

---

1   On analytical biases and mindsets, see Heur (1999) or for using alternate analysis to contest mindset, see George (2004).

codes of practice. In particular, an increased specialisation in policing will require leaders and managers of intelligence to take on a more proactive project management role in improving intelligence staff training at all levels. As the operating environment becomes more complex, fundamental questions about future training requirements need to be asked more regularly and strategically than they have in the past. Despite an increasing body of literature on police training in such areas of leadership and management there is little publicly known about intelligence analytical training standards in Australasia that future leaders/managers or researchers can draw from in designing or evaluating intelligence education. In 2006, the author and a colleague from Charles Sturt University were successful in receiving University grant funding to do some research that would examine these issues. A key objective of this research will be to provide the first national picture of the law enforcement intelligence profession's understandings of intelligence analysis and training.

Managers working in intelligence functions will need to audit for particular abilities, skills and knowledge (competencies), they require staff working at various levels of analysis (eg descriptive, exploratory or estimative intelligence) to possess (Moore et al 2005). *Descriptive analysis* refers to the simplest form of analysis. It is event-driven and is closely linked to a particular information source. *Explanatory analysis* results from inferences, including observations about patterns or changes in observed behaviour. Whereas, *estimative analysis* is the most complex form of analysis and has a predictive quality. What is the enemy likely to do in the future? See Moore et al (2005, p 214). The AFP has started to benchmark levels of intelligence training to particular practitioner levels, but more work in general needs to be done by agencies to match tasks to skill sets, as well as to provide career paths for intelligence staff.

Further, there also needs to be more management training opportunities at all levels for those wishing to become intelligence managers. It is not uncommon for future leaders and managers of intelligence in Australasian law enforcement agencies to learn skills on the job. However, the current intelligence reform agenda in many agencies requires personnel who can identify good practice, as well as have the ability to manage it effectively. Tertiary and industry courses are now starting to address some of the training requirements of intelligence managers. For example, Charles Sturt University offers a subject in its Graduate Diploma (Criminal Intelligence) award on intelligence management. From an industry perspective, the AFP delivered in 2006 its first Leadership in Criminal Intelligence Program to develop intelligence management skill sets for its staff and representatives from other agencies. Both initiatives are encouraging steps forward.

Intelligence evaluation

Evaluation is another area that is presenting problems for those managing Australasian law enforcement intelligence agencies. It is an area where there has been limited substantive reflection on practice or research. Similar to other doctrinal issues discussed earlier, evaluating intelligence needs to occur both at the process and product level. Currently there are weaknesses in both areas in most Australasian law enforcement agencies.

A priority area for the manager in evaluating intelligence processes, relates to improving systems for measuring and assessing the performance and skills, required by intelligence analysts. As law enforcement environments become more complex, there need to be more effective mechanisms in Australasian law enforcement agencies to measure performance, and better ways to assess what different skills may be required by intelligence analysts in the future. A starting point in managing for a better evaluation system of analysts is to assess current analyst competencies against the level of analysis.

Obviously different competencies are required for a person working in an intelligence support role (eg team work, communication and pattern recognition skills) compared to a strategic analyst (eg critical reasoning, advanced research and sophisticated knowledge of targets). As a first step in evaluating analytical performance, managers of intelligence in the future will need to clearly articulate competencies against the level of analysis that a position is expected to undertake (Moore et al 2005). While improving systems for evaluating analytical performance and assessing skill sets is a priority, managers will also need to link changes here to better evaluation in other areas, including tasking and coordination, collection and analysis.

Improvements can also be made in the ways intelligence products are evaluated. The most important of these is that a product is applicable to the client's decision-making. Timeliness, accuracy, objectivity, relevance and value-adding are other important considerations. In some Australasian law enforcement agencies similar product evaluation approaches are used by national security agencies, including attaching short satisfaction surveys to intelligence products. While this kind of qualitative data can be useful, in the author's experience they are not, if at all, filled out in a timely and satisfactory manner, and are rarely completed by those clients whose feedback would be most useful. Additional methods will need to be explored to evaluate that clients are receiving useful quality products. Finally, effective management of intelligence systems will need to adopt a more evidence based approach in assessing how intelligence impacts on all levels of decision-making. An increasing volume of research in the intelligence-led policing field suggests that intelligence in some operational contexts may help reduce crime (Ratcliffe 2003). However, more work needs to be done to understand the nexus between crime, intelligence and decision-makers and how intelligence impacts on crime. In particular, evaluating the role of strategic analysis in reducing the various economic, political and social harms of crime will present the greatest challenge for researchers and managers alike.

Conclusion

It is clear that within a decade since Etter and Palmer (1995) described the policing leadership and management environment in Australasia that much has changed in law enforcement intelligence. Over the past five years in particular, the rhetoric of intelligence-led policing and implementing change in relevant areas of intelligence doctrine to make it a reality has occurred in many agencies.

However, intelligence as a discipline in Australasian policing is now at crossroads. More needs to be done on a number of fronts if intelligence practice is to improve and become truly integrated into decision-making. Overall, the responsibility for this lies with the heads of agencies. Nevertheless, a better dividend from intelligence must be driven by good leaders and managers with the relevant specialists skills who will need to draw on a wide set of management and leadership skills and experience. However, there are specific technical skills and attributes too that will be required. Herman (1996, pp 333-334), reflecting on the skills required by managers working in national security agencies, suggested that ideal managers would include outstanding bureaucrats, entrepreneurs and scholars. This seems true also for their law enforcement colleagues, although perhaps in the current evolving discipline of law enforcement intelligence, leaders and mangers of intelligence should set their aspirations higher. In the current environment they should not just lead the intelligence reform agenda, but use knowledge gained there to help their organisation define new directions based on agreed principles and values.

6

EVIDENCE-BASED POLICY AND PRACTICE IN POLICE MANAGEMENT

Margaret Mitchell

It is fair to say that police organisations, traditionally, have not seen research as an important foundation of operational or strategic management decisions. Laycock (2001) made this same observation five years ago, but there are signs that things are changing. There has been a shift in thinking about evidence- or intelligence-driven approaches to policing and police management decisions requiring a greater focus on research data, which has come about because many aspects of the managerial and operational context of policing has changed.

In the operational context, police organisations have always been numerate in the sense that crime rates, arrest rates and clear up rates have been measured. However, further analysis of these data – to establish the potential causes of changes in crime rates in a particular area (for example, a particular person having been imprisoned and therefore not out in the community) or the relationship between different crimes (for example, the relationship between burglary and drug availability) – has not been carried out routinely. Nor, in the police organisational context, were either individual performance or organisational performance typically measured with any degree of commitment, objectivity or regularity. Within the community, even expensive programs such as CCTV placement may not have been properly evaluated, possibly because the impetus behind their implementation may be political or a reaction to a high profile crime, which *requires* that the program 'succeed'.

A new culture of measurement and analysis in police organisations

I will now consider what has changed in the external context of policing that has necessitated more research, measurement and analysis in a range of organisational and operational contexts. The changes in the external environment seem to have created a new culture of measurement and analysis, and an associated imperative to use existing research or conduct new research – activities that have been relegated traditionally to 'special departments' or 'special projects' and marginalised away from the central management of the organisation.

The public sector reforms and the New Public Management of the 1980s affected policing organisations as much as they did other parts of the public sector. The New Public Management 'movement' has been defined by Skelley (2002) in his critique as 'wedded to substituting business management and market mechanisms, "good things", for "evil and failing" government Bureaucracy'. The new approach was intended to increase accountability by measuring individual and organisational performance. In the late 20th and early 21st century of Australian policing, this approach was augmented by the recommendations of several inquiries and royal commissions into police behaviour and misconduct which each emphasised accountability and the measurement of performance.[1] In Australia and the US, as elsewhere, the need to demonstrate accountability and performance measurement has more recently been driven by the focus on corporate governance in all public sector organisations. The resulting greater prominence of police governance and management also stimulated interest about the measurement of policing performance; the community and stakeholders wanting to see value for money, amongst other outcomes.

Other obvious influences have generated more attention on measurement, data and information to assist appropriate decisions and deductions in operational settings. Outstanding amongst these is the official inquiry into the events of 11 September 2001 or '9/11' (9/11 Commission Report 2004) and the demand from the community about what information or intelligence was available to the authorities before it occurred. Much was in fact known, as we now understand. The Executive Summary of the 9/11 Commission Report states: 'The 9/11 attacks were a shock, but they should not have come as a surprise. Islamist extremists had given plenty of warning that they meant to kill Americans indiscriminately and in large numbers' (p 2). Elsewhere the Report recounts:

> During the Spring and Summer of 2001, U.S. intelligence agencies received a stream of warnings that al Qaeda planned, as one report put it, 'something very, very big'. Director of Central Intelligence George Tenet told us [US Intelligence agencies] 'The system was blinking red' (p 6).

That the knowledge was not analysed appropriately and put to good use was described in these terms: 'We believe the 9/11 attacks revealed four kinds of failures: in imagination, policy, capabilities and management' (p 339). This event raised awareness worldwide about what intelligence is, and how it can or should be used and it forced the central importance of data collection,

---

1   For example, see the *Final Report of the Royal Commission into the New South Wales Police Service* (Wood 1997).

analysis and interpretation into the consciousness of police worldwide, and into Australian police organisations at every level. The US Department of Justice (2005) concluded in their document on intelligence-led policing, *New Realities: Law Enforcement in the Post 9/11 Era* that:

> Information sharing must become a policy, not an informal practice. Most importantly, intelligence must be contingent on quality analysis of data. The development of analytical techniques, training and technical assistance needs to be supported (p vii).

As a result, fundamental intelligence practices such as collecting data, analysing it in order to see patterns in the data, and using data as the basis of prediction have moved into general policing from the sometimes rather marginalised confines of specialised or covert policing activities.

The inquiry following 11 September 2001 added to the culture change towards evidence-based policing and data based strategic management commenced by the use of COMPSTAT ('computerised statistics') models (Bratton & Knobler 1998). This approach is based on practical questions such as how crime data, demographic data and other intelligence can best be used to inform strategic operational planning at a local and regional level. Walsh (2001) saw it as paradigm shift amongst several forms of 'operational experimentation' that challenged the way police organisations should be managed. He defines COMPSTAT in this way:

> COMPSTAT is a goal-oriented strategic management process that uses computer technology, operational strategy and managerial accountability to structure the manner in which a police department provides crime-control services (p 347).

Bratton and Knobler (1998, p 224) identified four underlying characteristics of COMPSTAT, namely:

- accurate and timely intelligence;
- rapid deployment of personnel and resources;
- effective tactics; and
- relentless follow up and assessment.

The basic model was adopted in several policing jurisdictions, including in Australia. Chilvers and Weatherburn (2004) found that the use of the NSW Police version of COMPSTAT – the NSW Police Operation and Crime Review Panels ('OCRs') – that were developed under ex-Commissioner Peter Ryan, produced a reduction in crime. The reductions were in four offence categories: break and enter; armed robbery; motor vehicle theft; and sexual assault, although Chilvers and Weatherburn (2004) could not establish the precise cause of the reduction whether it was through 'deterrence' or 'incapacitation'. Walsh (2001) saw it as too early to assess whether COMPSTAT is effective, however, in the context of the current discussion, Walsh saw a clear advantage in that it required police organisations to:

> actively engage in their external environment in a structured and meaningful way [and that] this requires training officers in information

gathering techniques beyond that demanded by current police report taking (p 357).

Through COMPSTAT, not only the measurement of crime data and intelligence but, more importantly, its interpretation and meaning permeated police organisations, requiring senior managers and the leaders of police organisations to engage in understanding the meaning of data and analysis.

A further influence that has created a culture of measurement and research has been the rise of 'intelligence-led policing'. The term is now in common use and is defined by Ratcliffe (2003) as 'the application of criminal intelligence analysis as a rigorous decision making tool to facilitate crime reduction and prevention through effective policing strategies'. This is tied with the shift in policing underpinning the UK National Intelligence Model (Maguire & John 2006), through which strategic assessments, tactical assessments, target profiles and problem profiles are generated and used. As Maguire and John (2006, p 73) describe, these products are the result of:

> nine analytical techniques (results analysis, crime pattern analysis, market profile, demographic/social trend analysis, criminal business profiles, network analysis, risk analysis, target profile analysis, operational intelligence assessment).

They see these components of the National Intelligence Model, as 'an aid to better management of police business as a whole'. The prominence of analytic methods and strategic use of the products of the intelligence model have contributed to an improved understanding of research and analysis. As Cope (2003) emphasises however, having better information does not *necessarily* lead to greater use of data since there are still 'cultural barriers to the integration of analysis', specifically how this differs from action-oriented police work (p 357).

In the same way that good intelligence gathering and analysis practice involves collection of data, making sense of it, and coming up with best guesses, so too managers should use the data available to them, to strategically manage a work context that is often in a state of flux. Given the potential of a new culture of measurement and analysis, as conceptualised in this chapter, the following presents some practical ways in which research can be used as part of the day-to-day work of police managers and provide some examples of applied research. To apply research approaches to police work, police managers need to read published research that has been conducted in other settings and draw out the potential relevance to the local area, to manage research projects to effect organisational change and to participate in collaborative research with other agencies and with the local community.

1. Using published research

Police managers can make use of the burgeoning research on policing and police management, and critically evaluate the quality and the implications of this wealth of research to understand its significance for local conditions. Reports of applied research are available from many sources including the several research facilities dedicated to examining justice, crime and policing issues, such as the Australian Institute of Criminology in Canberra. Reports of applied research can also be obtained through the Police Foundation in Washington DC, the Home Office in London and the Federal Bureau of Investigation in the US. The UK Home Office is a prolific publisher of research reports and policy statements, and many of the concepts and results of research find their way into Australian policing policy and practice. These resources provide excellent sources of research on the challenges facing police organisations and provide the opportunity to compare different practices across the world. Other sources are dedicated to the practical application of research in public policy areas from which ideas for policy practice can be drawn, for example, Davies, Nutley and others operate the *Research Unit for Research Utilisation* (RURU) which aims to:

> facilitate the production and use of practical knowledge that will assist in enhancing the role of evidence in public policy and public services [and] develop a resource concerned with examining and improving the utilisation of evidence across the key public policy and public services areas [including] criminal justice.[2]

All published research is not *necessarily* useful or of high quality and needs to be read critically for two reasons. First, to ensure an understanding of how the author arrived at his or her conclusions from the research question and the method employed and from this whether the conclusions are valid. Secondly, in order to ascertain if, or how, the method used in the study or the study's policy implications can be usefully applied to the local area. Some indicators of good published research can help to separate it from poorly conducted research and/or unsubstantiated opinion (see Figure 6.1, over the page). Questions you should ask yourself when reading an article or a report in order to:

- assess research, for example, on innovative strategies. Evaluate the claims made in reports;
- assess the value and relevance of the research for the local operational context; and
- summarise the research and its local relevance to provide internal briefings.

Research reports from high quality institutions such as the Australian Institute of Criminology have been through a process of 'peer review' and are conducted by trained researchers. The same is usually the case with articles in good journals. As a rule of thumb, research that has been peer-reviewed is more likely to be dependable than one that has not. Peer review means that two to three people who have expertise in the area have read the article and have attested to its rigour. Examples of journals where police managers will obtain a great deal of worthwhile research are, the *Australian and New Zealand Journal of Criminology, Police Practice and Research: An International Journal of*

---

2   See <www.st-andrews.ac.uk/~ruru/role_and_rationale.htm>.

Figure 6.1: Reading a research report

- What is the practical or other context of this work?

- What is the research aim – ie what is the intention of the work?

- What is/are the research question(s) – ie is there a particular statement which sets out what the researcher is asking?

- How did the researcher go about answering the question and achieving the aims of the work – ie what method was used?

- What data were used – ie did the researcher examine existing records, review existing literature as the main data for the study, collect new information from people or from another source?

- What did they do with these data? How did they analyse the data or information?

- What claims do they make in their conclusions – ie how relevant are they to the stated aim(s) and question(s)?

- Most importantly: after looking at the method are you convinced that the methods used have actually demonstrated the results properly – or are there some leaps of logic?

Source: Author

Police Management and Strategies, or *Current Issues in Criminal Justice.* Readers who would like to know more about assessing the quality of evidence in evidence-based policy and practice should also see Pawson (2006).

2. Productive partnering with external researchers

If original new research needs to be done, police managers can work in partnership with researchers outside the organisation. It can be argued that part of the social responsibility of tertiary education institutions is to contribute to policy and practice change in policing and other public policy areas (Mitchell & Jennett 2007). However, there has existed a philosophical divide between academic researchers and the practitioners whose practices are the focus of the research. Because of the divide academics interested in policing practice typically have worked outside policing organisations adopting the stance of outsiders 'looking in' (Mitchell & Jennett 2007). Often their research was criticised or marginalised on the basis that, as outsiders, they did not understand the culture of police nor the practical constraints of police work. Certainly, abstract ideas or models provided by academics that do not provide immediate practical and applied guidance about specific problems are not seen as useful (Jennett, Elliot & Robinson 2003).

Productive partnering with tertiary institutions or research facilities

An evidence-based approach can be developed by working with external partners (other than engaging academics or consultants from outside the organisation) in a more distant relationship. In Australia, examples of police-academic research partnerships can be found at Edith Cowan University, Charles Sturt University, University of Tasmania, Griffith University, Macquarie University, Monash University, Flinders University, and the University of Western Australia. This is not an exhaustive list but it does indicate the level of interest in policing by academics who have entered into close, cooperative and mutually respectful, productive partnerships with police organisations. These partnerships can create research outcomes that are both of practical benefit and are also academically rigorous. Other examples are the study of police probationers in New South Wales by Janet Chan, Chris Devery and Sally Doran (2003), or the extensive study of investigative interviewing by John Clarke and Rebecca Milne in the UK (2001).

3. Using operational data collected by the organisation for research

Questions about best or good practice have stimulated an interest in what works in policing. Sherman (1998) coined the term 'evidence-based policing' to describe the process whereby research evidence underpins practice and Bayley's book, *What Works in Policing* (1997) placed 'what works' into the police lexicon. For contemporary police managers or administrators to establish what works, they need to be able to assess and compare those practices. Original research is often required to inform managers' decisions about applying programs or practices imported from another area, or even another country, and in assessing whether they will fit with the unique characteristics of a particular local command. The fact is, however, that an organisation's business needs to keep going and so the opportunity to conduct comparison studies or even full evaluations of programs can place extra burdens on the organisation. Those conducting research need to work around the imperatives of the business of the organisation in encouraging research and reflection. The burden of research can be lessened, however, by building research into day-to-day work and making it part of the normal routine of work. Data that are collected in the normal course of work can easily be used to underpin on-going evaluation.

Police managers and other staff need to be able to conduct research, or at least understand what is required to carry out research. The ability to understand or carry out quantitative and qualitative research in order to compare, correlate or quantify is required to undertake the following common projects.

Table 6.1: Examples of generic applied research projects

Conduct environmental scans of local conditions and local issues using information that is being collected in the normal course of work, or collect information where it is lacking.
Collect information as a basis for organisational and operational planning using information collected in the normal course of work, or collect new information where it is lacking.
Evaluate programs and projects, and use the correct research methods to evaluate outcomes.
Identify and apply good practice from other national and international jurisdictions and devise methods to implement good practice adapted for local conditions.
Compare productivity and performance data across jurisdictions and between jurisdictions and over time.
Analyse crime and performance data collected by local police offices or across jurisdictions.
Survey community attitudes to crime and policing.
Devise methods to create local or large scale organisational change and evaluate progress.
Summarise how a project was carried out and its results for internal briefings, or for local media release.

Source: Author

4. Practitioner research and 'action research'

The practitioner-researcher approach (Robson 2002, p 219) also presents a way of making research an everyday activity, so that the police officers themselves, at whatever level they are in the organisation, do the research and so are the 'producers' and 'consumers' of research (Jennet, Elliot & Robinson 2003). Successful implementation and evaluation can be enhanced if staff feel a sense of ownership over the implementation of new policy and practice (Mitchell & Jennett 2007; Jennett, Elliot & Robinson 2003). The important feature of this approach that makes it appropriate for police officers is that people learn actively when carrying out a task (Nutley, Walter & Davis 2002) and 'learning on the job' is the mode of learning preferred by police officers (Mitchell, Munro, Thomson & Jackson 1997). The practitioner-researcher model also means that managers and leaders benefit from the knowledge, insights and explanations of staff who deal daily with the issues and problems being researched. Action research is based on a model of iterative and reflective stages (Figure 6.2, opposite).

Figure 6.2: Stages of action research

1.	*Define the inquiry.* What is the issue of concern? What research question are we asking? Who will be involved? Where and when will it happen?
2.	*Describe the situation.* What are we required to do here? What are we trying to do here? What thinking underpins what we are doing?
3.	*Collect evaluative data and analyse it.* What is happening in this situation now as understood by the various participants? Using research methods, how can we find out about it?
4.	*Review the data and look for contradictions.* What contradictions are there between what we would like to happen and what seems to happen?
5.	*Tackle a contradiction by introducing change.* By reflecting critically and creatively on the contradictions, what change can we introduce which we think is likely to be beneficial?
6.	*Monitor the change.* What happens day-by-day when the change is introduced?
7.	*Analyse evaluative data about the change.* What is happening in the situation now — as understood by the various participants — as a result of the changes introduced? Using research methods, what can we find out about it?
8.	*Review the change and decide what to do next.* Was the change worthwhile? Are we going to continue it in the future? What are we going to do next? Is the change sufficient?

Source: Robson (2002, p 218). Reproduced with permission

While action research is an ideal model for the implementation of change in an organisation, it is also applicable when evaluating crime prevention or other programs in the community in which police are involved. Such community projects are intended to engage the community. Stakeholders and community members want to participate in projects with outcomes that affect them, and seek 'results' as quickly as possible. It is an ideal approach for 'whole of government' community development, community safety and crime prevention projects which are an important element in the business of a local area command. As Robson (2002, p 219) has said: 'Notwithstanding the obvious benefits that skills and experience bring, the underlying common sense core to the practice of social research ... is not difficult to grasp'.

Examples of published research

Presented below are examples of various types of research as illustrations. We can see from these that the results may assist problem solving and planning in a manager's own local area or division. A number of the following examples analyse data that are being collected by the organisation as a matter of course. Having knowledge of the data can inform managers where data collection is duplicated, where there are gaps and, importantly, how the data collected by the organisation (with appropriate ethical clearance) may be used for original research.

The first example (below) which was conducted through the Australasian Centre for Policing Research uses original questionnaire data by external researchers and concerns an issue of importance to strategic planning in human resources. Police organisations need to know who is resigning, why they are resigning and if there are any issues within the control of the organisation that are influencing their decision. If these matters are known based on research they can be addressed earlier and interventions designed to try to do something before losing experienced staff. It is obvious how the results of this research can be applied to a manager's own local area, and to the wider organisation.

The next example (Example 2, opposite), through the Australian Institute of Criminology, combined two existing data sets obtained from two State organisations in Queensland – the police service and the Department of Families and analysed it longitudinally. The results provided evidence for

Example 1

> **Lynch, J and Tuckey, M (2004)** *Understanding voluntary turnover: An examination of resignations in Australasian police organisations,* **Australasian Centre for Policing Research, Report Series No 143.1, South Australia.**
>
> Lynch and Tuckey analysed questionnaire data collected from 277 ex-police officers from Western Australia, South Australia and Victoria to find out why they had left policing. Five main reasons for resignation were found: *quality of life* was affected by the lack of time they spent with partners and families, social life was limited, job was stressful and they felt pressured in their role as a police officer; *lack of flexibility* due to shift work and rosters affected their ability to take care of family responsibilities and to care for their young children; generally *poor management* and a lack of support from management; *career concerns* regarding a lack of promotion and career opportunities; and *poor resources* reflected in low staff numbers and poor quality equipment.

potential change in legislation, policy and police procedures. Assuming that other relevant influences were controlled, for example the seriousness of the offence, the research demonstrated that cautioning by police appeared to be associated with lower rates of re-offending in juveniles. This suggests that cautioning juveniles for their first criminal activity, rather than arresting them, may be a more cost efficient method to deter juveniles from reoffending.

Example 2

> **Dennison, S, Stewart, A, and Hurren, E (2006) 'Police cautioning in Queensland: The impact on juvenile offending pathways',** *Trends and Issues in Crime and Criminal Justice*, **Report No 306, Australian Institute of Criminology, Canberra.**
>
> Dennison, Stewart and Hurren analysed juvenile offending data obtained from the Queensland Police Service and the Queensland Department of Families. Of the children born in 1983 and 1984, 14,572 juveniles (ages 10-16) had been cautioned by police. Follow-up found that of those who had received a caution, 69 per cent had no further contact with the juvenile justice system and 31 per cent had received subsequent cautions or appeared in court. They found that young people brought before court as a result of their first encounter with the police were more likely to re-offend in a shorter period of time, compared to juveniles receiving a caution for their first offence.

The third example (over the page) also through the Australian Institute of Criminology also used data being collected by Queensland Police Service (QPS) to assess the impact of the 'COMPSTAT type' reviews being conducted in QPS. These Operational Performance Reviews were built around identified 'hotspots' of criminal activity to guide adequate police resources in the 'hotspot' areas to reduce criminal behaviour. The implementation of operational performance reviews was found to be linked to a decrease in reported crime and the savings accrued through reduced crime compared with the operational costs of conducting operational performance reviews was found to be significant. This research contributes to the examination of the effectiveness of operational performance reviews as a regular feature of police strategic planning.

The fourth example (over the page) is a study by Sallybanks (2005) conducted by the Australian Institute of Criminology which demonstrates how existing data that has been collected for operational reasons can be used for original evaluative research. The results of this analysis can assist police management to develop appropriate preventative policies and procedures.

Example 3

Mazerolle, L, Rombouts, S, and McBroom, J (2006) 'The impact of Operational Performance Reviews on reported crime in Queensland', *Trends and Issues in Crime & Criminal Justice*, Report No 313, pp 1-6, Australian Institute of Criminology, Canberra.

Mazerolle, Rombouts and McBroom analysed crime statistics across 29 police districts in Queensland. Thirteen different crime types were identified and a range of 60 offences were divided into appropriate categories. Crime data were collected for 295 police divisions. Operational Performance Reviews were introduced in the Queensland Police Service in 2001. Criminal activity before the introduction of Operational Performance Reviews (1995-2001) was compared with criminal activity after the implementation of OPR (2001-2004). The total number of reported criminal activities was compared to the projected number of criminal activities and there was found to be a significant decrease in criminal activities reported.

Example 4

Sallybanks, J (2005) *Monitoring injuries in police custody: A feasibility and utility study.* Technical and Background Paper, Report No 15, Australian Institute of Criminology, Canberra.

Between 2001 and 2003 data from the New South Wales Computerised Operational Policing System (COPS) was analysed, with regards to injuries involving individuals detained by police. Any cases involving self-harm or injury, were extracted from COPS. By analysing the data, the following risk factors for detainees at risk of self harm or injury were determined: the majority involved males between the ages of 21 and 30 years of age; 19 per cent were of Aboriginal appearance; the majority were unemployed; over 75 per cent of detainees were affected by alcohol and over 30 per cent affected by drugs. Eighty-one per cent of injuries involved the detainees harming themselves; police cells, docks and vehicles were the most common places for injuries to occur; and over 40 per cent occurred between midnight and six o'clock in the morning.

Example 5

Australian Government (2007), *City of Gosnells STR8 Talking Community Safety Project, 2007-2010*, **National Community Crime Prevention Programme, Canberra.**

The project aims to build and strengthen relationships between youth and police by developing initiatives to reduce antisocial behaviour in two suburbs. Police statistics are used to identify types of crimes and age of offenders to target the programs. The project will deliver innovative/educational programs to the youth of those areas, addressing antisocial youth behaviour issues, through consultation and involvement with young people in the area. This innovative long-term approach to crime prevention may assist in the development and improvement of good relationships between young people and the police, and may lead to improved job satisfaction for police officers.

The final example (Example 5, above) is a crime prevention project in Perth, Western Australia which will be evaluated systematically but solely by community participants under the guidance of a university partner. The project will be evaluated at very regular intervals during the three years of its life, with the local youth and other members of the community each participating in the research and feeding back the outcomes, with the potential that certain strategies and programs will be replaced by others as the evaluation progresses. Over the course of the three years of the project, the results of the ongoing action research will inform subsequent iterations of the crime prevention programs.

Conclusion

Cope (2003) in her chapter on the use of crime data analysis in police organisations to direct police activity commented on the disjunction frequently found in police organisations between analysts and operational police (p 357). She also argued that there may not yet be an understanding of the value of analysis as a strategic tool beyond 'descriptive, retrospective information about crime' (p 358). She said:

> While recent developments have reinforced that importance to police forces of having an analytical capability, there remains insufficient understanding within the police service of why analysis is desirable and possible (p 358).

It seems that the disinclination to conduct new research on policing by police organisations that prevailed up until the 1990s resulted in a managerial culture unaccustomed to using research and evidence to inform decision-making, managers preferring their own considerable experience and intuition to guide decisions. As we have seen, however, several changes in the external and internal environments of policing have required a greater emphasis on intelligence-led and evidence-informed policing. Even without carrying out new research in their own jurisdiction, or local area command, police managers can access the wealth of existing research that can be applied to the local area.

The environment of policing is of course a changing policy and practice landscape, with profound changes every half decade or so. As an outstanding example, only a few years ago the possibility of urban terrorism was the concern of only a few countries seemingly very remote from Australia. Now, police managers and leaders include preventative and protective plans in their strategic planning, and local area commanders know that they need to work with staff and communities to raise awareness and to gather information on potential terrorist threats where possible. Police organisations need also to work cooperatively with other justice and intelligence agencies to ensure that information and intelligence is collected, analysed and – most importantly – understood. While many would regard the leap from world terrorism to the ability of police leaders and managers to understand, direct and utilise research, there is no question that policing organisations in Australia and New Zealand must become far more 'numerate' and analytical at every level – both organisationally and operationally. Research literacy and practitioner research can assist appropriate and measured responses to the dynamic environment of policing.

In all that has been suggested in this chapter, I have been conscious of the need when evaluating practices and innovations to ensure minimal disruption of police business and maximum participation by those whom the research is about, and who will be affected by it. Inevitably there will be more use of evidence-based approaches and a higher level of research literacy. This will be in part due to the larger numbers of university graduates and postgraduates in police organisations, as well as the shift to tertiary qualifications as an entry into the police who study subjects with an empirical or 'evidence-based' underpinning. Investment in research, and explicit organisational mechanisms to bring research closer together with policy and practice development, need to be implemented. Without specific commitment by organisations, evidence-based policies and practices will not result (Nutley 2003), and Edwards (2004) has argued for a commitment to designing learning organisations in which research is a central capacity required to build internal capacity. This, she believes, is necessary to narrow the divide between research and public policy, to encourage capacity in strategic partners, and to encourage understanding by agency leadership of the use of research for policy development (Edwards 2004, p 12).[3]

---

3   Website resources used in this chapter have included the UK Home Office <www.home.of
     fice.gov.uk/rds>, the Australian Institute of Criminology <www.aic.gov.au>, the Re-
     search Unit for Research Utilisation <www.st-andrews.ac.uk/ruru> and the Police Foun-
     dation <www.policefoundation.org>.

7

SUPERVISION AND MANAGEMENT OF INVESTIGATIVE INTERVIEWING: LEARNING FROM THE UK EXPERIENCE

Tracey Green and Gary Shaw

Imagine the situation in which an officer, due to give evidence in a criminal court, is first questioned over his or her level of training in investigative interviewing, and then about the supervision mechanisms that are in place while they conduct interviews. This is the level of scrutiny over investigative interviewing, and the importance that has been placed on these skills for the past 10 years in the United Kingdom. Every police officer, whether a detective or not, is required to demonstrate his or her knowledge and ability to conduct an investigative interview before being allowed to interview a witness, victim or suspect. While this is not yet the case in Australia, we will examine why this level of concern and scrutiny developed in the UK, and what policies and legislation was put in place as a result, and discuss the likelihood of a similar situation in Australia.

The core of policing remains the prevention, detection and reduction of crime and the protection of the public. At its heart is the investigative function. If the 'aim of an interview is to ascertain the truth of the matter under investigation' (Ord, Shaw & Green 2004, p 8), then fundamental to that aim is the quality of evidence and intelligence obtained from interviews with victims, witnesses and suspects. We argue that the ability to conduct professional and ethical interviews that are admissible in court is an essential skill for all operational police. As Burbeck (2003) notes, it is the gateway to the criminal justice system and the importance of getting it right first and every time cannot be over-emphasised.

With the increasing capacity of forensic science and DNA analysis, technological advances in surveillance equipment, telephone intercepts, listening devices and a greater dependence on these forms of evidence, it could be that the traditional skills of the investigator are being forgotten. This chapter focuses on the central importance of investigative interviewing skills and the role of leadership and supervision in maintaining these skills. Poor leadership and management of the investigative interview process may result in miscarriages of justice through wrongful convictions or a failure of the prosecution.

Police conduct in investigative interviewing and changes to this aspect of the justice system in the UK over the past twenty to thirty years will be examined to assist in benchmarking the current state of its development in Australian policing and the likely future direction of investigative interviewing practice. Police interviewing policies, practices and procedures in Australia have not yet been subject to the same court scrutiny as they have been in the UK, but this may be only a matter of time.

'Old school' interviewing

Twenty to 30 years ago in the UK, as in the US and Australia, the process of interviewing was very much a police 'trade secret'. What occurred in interview rooms largely remained there, with a written statement or transcript of the interview being the only record. This was the situation whether questioning suspects, witnesses or victims. At the time, the status of the police officer was such that the record of interview was rarely scrutinised, and management and supervision of interviews focused only on the result. A structured, well-written witness statement and a suspect's confession were seen as successful performance indicators (rather than any real concern about the techniques employed in the interview room used to obtain the result). Hopkins (cited in Schollum 2005), commenting on the interviewing behaviour of police in the 1930s in the US, said:

> Our police, with no legal sanction whatever, employ duress, threat, bullying, a vast amount of moderate physical abuse and a certain degree of outright torture; and their inquisitions customarily begin with the demand: 'If you know what's good for you, you'll confess'. (Hopkins cited in Leo 1992, p 35)

The situation was largely tolerated and in some circles even endorsed due to the pressure on the police for results (Morgan & Stephenson 1994). This was seen as far back as the 'Jack the Ripper' investigations in London in the 1880s, when police were under enormous pressure to remove the threat to public safety and obtain a confession with little regard to the ethics of how the confession was obtained (Gudjonsson 1992; Kassin & Gudjonsson 2004).

Miscarriages of justice in the UK

Similar pressure to remove threats to public safety was evident in the UK during the 1970s following several attacks on random civilian targets in England, attributed to the Provisional Irish Republican Army (IRA). The targeting of civilians by the IRA made the community fearful and demanding, invoking a 'means to an end' response by police. The pressure to find and bring to justice the people responsible for these acts of terrorism was enormous. In order to arrest and prosecute those responsible, the police may have believed that they were justified in applying whatever means they saw fit. This included tampering with evidence, persuasion, bribery, threats and violence to 'get their man' (Maguire 2003). Due process was seen as an inconvenient hurdle to the successful prosecution. As we now know, the haste to bring about convictions led to several infamous miscarriages of justice, which have shaped police practices and, in particular, the way in which interviews are conducted. Pivotal cases which caused these changes in practice in the UK will be described here.

In 1975 three Irish men and one 17-year-old English woman (Gerard Conlon, Patrick Armstrong, Paul Hill and Carole Richardson), who became known as the 'Guildford Four', were jailed for the bombing of two public houses in Guildford, England. These attacks killed seven civilians, and injured many more (Lutz, Ulmschneider & Lutz 2002). The prosecution relied heavily on written confessional evidence, appearing on several occasions (before the court) during the initial period of interrogation with visible injury. The accused made claims of assault, bullying and torture and consistently denied the written confessions. One of the accused, Gerry Conlon, said he confessed after the police had indulged in torture, squeezing his testicles, hitting him in the kidneys, slapping his face and threatening his family (Kennedy 1989). All four accused were convicted.

Fourteen years later in October 1989, the convictions were overturned, when the confessional evidence, on which the prosecution had relied so heavily, was found to be unreliable. The UK Home Secretary at the time, Douglas Hurd, ordered a judicial inquiry into the case as well as an official criminal investigation into the conduct of the officers involved:

> The investigation into the case, considered to be the biggest miscarriage of justice in Britain, was carried out by Avon and Somerset Police. They found serious flaws in the way Surrey police noted the confessions of the four. The confession of Patrick Armstrong was central to the investigation and the inquiry concluded the notes taken were not written up immediately and officers may have colluded in the wording of the statements (BBC News, 1989).

This case was pivotal in drawing attention to police interview and interrogation techniques.

The suspects in the equally famous case of the 'Birmingham Six' (Hugh Callaghan, Patrick Hill, Robert Hunter, Noel McIlkenny, William Power and John Walker) and the 'Maguire Seven' each made similar claims of the use of threats, violence and torture by interviewing officers (Lutz, Ulmschneider & Lutz 2002). In 1974 six men were convicted of bombing a tavern in Birmingham based mainly on forensic evidence that they had handled explosives. Similarly members of the Maguire family were convicted of handling explosives for the IRA. All were convicted, but the convictions were later overturned. A deciding factor in their acquittal was doubt surrounding the reliability of forensic evidence, although the allegations of abuse during interviews with police were a strong element of the defence. There is little doubt that, once armed with the forensic information provided by experts, investigative interviewers adopted 'abusive or deceptive means in the inter-rogation of the suspects' to obtain confession (Miller 2004, p 32). Forensic analysis of police notes and statement documents conducted during a later police inquiry indicated that statements made by the Birmingham Six had been altered at a later date by investigating officers (Schollum 2005). The Royal Commission on Criminal Procedure (1981) introduced the *Police and Criminal Evidence Act 1984* (Pearse & Gudjonsson 1996), which included com-pulsory audio recording of suspect interviews, in an attempt to end the use of coercive tactics.

The question arises as to how such poor police interview practices could have taken place and what role managers and supervisors had had in the investigation process. The explanation is that, frequently, senior officers undertook the interviews in high profile cases. Often very experienced, but out of touch and out of practice senior officers conducted interviews with high profile suspects, under immense pressure from their own supervisors, their peers, and the public to obtain a confession. Well into the 1990s it was common practice in the UK for senior investigating officers to conduct what were called *prime suspect* interviews. In fact there were few cases in which the senior officer would give up the chance to 'get the cough' (obtain a con-fession) from a suspect in a serious offence.

This is what took place in the case of *R v Heron*[1] in 1993. Nikki Allen, a seven-year-old girl from Sunderland in the North East of England, was murdered close to her home. The case attracted much media attention and, not surprisingly, the community demanded a result from police. George Heron, a local man was arrested on suspicion of the murder and interviewed by the two senior detectives on the case. During one of the five interviews by the senior detectives, Heron was told: 'you know … that we would not be speaking to you unless you were a major, major suspect in this investigation, don't you!' (*R v Heron* 1993). Heron admitted to the murder of Nikki Allen but, despite the fact that both he and his legal representative stated at the end of the final interview that they were 'very pleased with the way that [the case] has been dealt with', only the final interview tape was deemed to be admissible by the court. Justice Mitchell, presiding, stated that the inter-views were repetitive, suggestive, and oppressive, and that the officers tended to pass comment rather than question Heron. The senior officers who conducted the interviews with Heron did not conduct suspect interviews regularly nor were they conversant with the changes that had been brought about by the *Police and Criminal Evidence Act 1984*. In his review of the evi-dence, Justice Mitchell stated:

> [Investigators] may be persistent, searching and robust in their questioning. If they do not believe what they are being told then they are entitled to say so. Persistence must not however, develop into bullying,

---

1   Unreported, Crown Court, Leeds, Mitchell J, No T931928, 1 November 1993.

robustness must not develop into insulting or gratuitously demeaning questions, nor must robustness be regarded as an acceptable label for, what in truth, is no more than a repetitive verbal pounding, alleging the certainty of a suspect's guilt (*R v Heron*).

Heron was acquitted. Rather than conduct the interviews themselves, the role of the senior officers should have been to display leadership by selecting the most appropriate officers for the job. Had they done so, Heron's acquittal, its impact on Nikki Allen's family, and damage to the credibility of the police service could have been avoided. The need for leadership in investigation extends also to the management and supervision of interviewers to ensure that 'the goal of interviewing [remains] to collect truthful data to be used for informed decision-making and just action-taking' (Yeschke 2003, p 49). Certainly, the practice of senior officers taking the lead in interviewing in a major investigation was ill advised. Heron was eventually found liable in a civil case brought by Nikki Allen's parents.

R v Heron (1993) proved to be a turning point in the development of policy and practice on the admissibility of suspect interview evidence in the UK. Although compulsory audio tape recording had been introduced in the *Police and Criminal Evidence Act* in 1984, formal training had extended little beyond how to turn the equipment on and how to seal the tapes at the end of the interview. Before this, officers believed that courts would be forgiving of the methods they used in interviews in serious cases, on an unspoken understanding that both they and the court were fighting for the common good of securing a conviction. That is, they believed that noble cause corruption (Maguire 2003) would be tolerated. However there was growing public disquiet about the conduct of interviews in major crime investigations, and almost every criminal case before the courts had a trial within a trial (*voir dire*) about the admissibility of the suspect interview itself.

The *Criminal Procedure and Investigations Act* (1996) introduced the requirement of full disclosure by the prosecution of all material involved in a case, without parallel requirement for disclosure by the defence counsel. Amendments to the police caution were later introduced in an attempt to redress this imbalance – notifying the suspect that 'it may harm your defence if you do not mention when questioned something which you later rely on in court'.

The development of a professional model

In 1992 a steering group was set up by the UK Home Office, comprising experienced detectives, academics, representatives from the Home office and the Crown Prosecution Service (Baldwin 1993). They found:

> the main weaknesses [in interviewing] were a lack of preparation, general ineptitude, poor technique, an assumption of guilt, unduly repetitive, persistent or laboured questioning, a failure to establish the relevant facts and the exertion of too much pressure (Baldwin 1992, p 34).

It was further found that any confession or admission of any sort would be deemed inadmissible if it had been obtained by any form of oppression including repetitive persuasive questioning and comment. The following recommendations were made:

- All investigating officers should receive formal training on investigative interviewing;
- All senior officers should receive management of interview training;
- Senior officers should not generally conduct suspect interviews.

(Home Office Circular No 22, 1992)

The steering group tasked with assessing the problems and making appropriate recommendations had focused initially on interviewing suspects, but soon realised that the standard of victim and witness interviewing also needed to be of a high quality in order to support an effective interview of the suspect. The group also designed seven principles of investigative interviewing aimed at a more effective and ethical alternative to persuasive interviewing techniques (Home Office Circular No 22, 1992).

Principles of investigative interviewing

1. The role of investigative interviewing is to obtain accurate and reliable information from suspects, witnesses or victims in order to discover the truth about matters under investigation.

2. Investigative interviewing should be approached with an open mind. Information obtained from the person who is being interviewed should always be tested against what the interviewing officer already knows or what can reasonably be established.

3. When questioning anyone a police officer must act fairly in the circumstances of each individual case.

4. The police interviewer is not bound to accept the first answer given. Questioning is not unfair merely because it is persistent.

5. Even when the right of silence is exercised by a suspect the police still have a right to put questions.

6. When conducting an interview, police officers are free to ask questions in order to establish the truth except for interviews with child victims of sexual or violent abuse which are to be used in criminal proceedings they are not constrained by the rules applied to lawyers in court.

7. Vulnerable people, whether victims, witnesses or suspects must be treated with particular consideration at all times (Home Office Circular No 22, 1992).

The PEACE model

The steering group also developed the PEACE model of interviewing, an acronym reflecting the different stages of an interview:

- Planning and Preparation
- Engage and Explain
- Account
- Closure
- Evaluation

The PEACE model provided a framework for a more considered and structured approach to conducting all police interviews, whether with a suspect, victim or witness. It is based on sound theory and research and promotes the use of the core investigative skills of planning and preparation, questioning, listening and rapport building under the umbrella of 'cognitive interviewing' and conversation management techniques. Teaching, supervising and enforcing the use of appropriate investigative interviewing techniques can result in less time being spent in court contesting the admissibility of interview evidence.

Evaluations of the PEACE model have been positive, indicating that officers using the 'tool kit' of interviewing skills get better results. For example, Gudjonsson (1992) found that detectives trained in cognitive interviewing extracted 50 per cent more information from witnesses in serious crime cases. Similarly, Brock, Fisher and Cutler (1999) found that 70 per cent more correct facts were recalled than was the case through the standard interview.

The PEACE model was implemented nationally in the UK in 1993 with a comprehensive training program aimed at practitioners with two to six years of service. In 1997, recruits were included, and some police forces added specialist interviewing courses to enhance the standard training already provided. During the implementation of PEACE, it became apparent that supervisors also required training in how to support and assess their staff. One-week training courses were initiated to introduce senior staff to the model and the techniques. The adoption of the seven principles of ethical interviewing described above and the subsequent training was intended to provide a sound base of professionalism in investigative interviewing.

However, a review conducted in 2001 (Clarke & Milne) found that efforts to educate those involved in investigative interviewing on ethical and legal practices in interviewing was not as effective as it should have been (Clarke & Milne 2001; Yeschke 2003). Clarke and Milne (2001) found that although the interviewing ability of officers who had been trained in PEACE techniques had improved and that there had been a cultural shift and improvement in the ethos and ethical approach to interviewing, there was still a tendency for officers to cut corners and conduct 'question and answer' style-interviews, losing the opportunity to elicit detail and to guard against suggestion. Interviewing was still often inconsistent and counterproductive with many 'steadfastly clinging to the question-and-answer routine that was described as the standard police interview back in 1992 before the advent of PEACE' (Clarke & Milne 2001, p 113).

Effective supervision is the key to the successful use of the PEACE model (Clarke & Milne 2001; Baldwin 1992). Work by Shaw (2001), Shepherd (1991), and Burbeck (2001) shows that lack of effective supervision of monitoring and supervising or assessing the interviews conducted by their staff undermined the success of PEACE. Janet Stockdale (1993) also found in her study of the management and supervision of police interviews that 'many supervisors lacked credibility in the eyes of junior officers and the skills necessary for effective supervision and quality control of interviews' (p 6). Much of the blame for the apparent lack of adoption of the PEACE model by operational officers was also placed on the style and delivery of training packages (Clarke & Milne 2001). The model had been represented as an inflexible program or routine which, if adopted in its entirety for every interview, would take too much time and often be inappropriate. As a result it was argued that the model would be better represented as a 'flexible set of tools' as advocated by the National Crime Faculty in 1998 (Clarke & Milne 2001; Ord & Shaw 1999; Ord, Shaw & Green 2004).

The professionalisation of investigation

The UK Association of Chief Police Officers (ACPO) in 2003 approved the five-tier Investigative Interview Strategy designed by Centrex (Table 7.1, opposite). The main purpose of developing such a strategy and making it a national policy was to provide a framework for developing skills and to ensure the appropriate deployment of interviewers. The benefits were to:

- provide a structure for building skills;
- provide an audit capability of officers' skills;
- help identify training needs; and
- allow supervisors the opportunity to match the skill of the interviewer to the task at hand.

The five tiers are outlined in Table 7.1 (opposite).

The key elements for forces implementing the interview strategy are seen as training, workplace assessment and policy. Training programs have been designed and delivered to form the basis for each tier, but there is also greater awareness of the importance of an assessment of competency in the workplace to help maintain a level of credible professionalism. The creation of policies around the implementation of the five tiers is also essential to maximise effectiveness. To support this, the UK has a National Investigative Interviewing Strategic Steering Group chaired by a Chief Officer. A national infrastructure exists, with a National Interview Coordinator leading a team of Regional Coordinators. In addition, each force has an 'interview champion' to assist in policy and operational issues. This formalised infrastructure is essential in ensuring that best practice is maintained and developed. The

Table 7.1: Investigative interview strategy

1. Foundation – Interviewers in volume crime cases including theft, criminal damage etc, and basic skills taught during foundation training. This training can also serve as a refresher for those officers returning to operational work.

2. Investigator – Interviewers in serious crime cases including robbery, aggravated burglary and deception. Usually detective-designated officers.

3. Specialist Interviewer – Interviewers in major crime cases including murder/manslaughter, child sexual abuse, serious sexual assault, terrorism, fatal road traffic accidents and complex volume and serious crime cases. These interviewers could include experienced designated detectives or crash investigation officers.

4. Interview Supervisor – Supervisors ensuring quality assurance interviews are conducted. This is critical to the success of the implementation of the tiers and provides a robust and professional approach to management. It aims to train managers and those whose role provides an overview to identify good practice and areas for improvement. Good practice should be promulgated and development need addressed.

5. Interview Advisor/Manager – This tier is aimed at those providing management for specialist interviewers. It provides an expert consultancy role to the organisation on matters relating to interview policy.

Source: ACPO 2003

development of investigative interviewing is at the heart of the program to create a competent investigative workforce.

Interestingly, while the introduction of specialist interviewers (Tier 3) was initially envisaged as a short-term solution to help establish appropriate levels of skill and competence in serious cases, (ie the cases that could impact most on public confidence if mishandled) the benefit of selecting the 'right person for the job' – the investigator with the most appropriate skill set – has been recognised. These highly skilled officers now offer leadership and advice to less experienced staff, and help develop investigative strategies which are proving to be highly successful in the serious and serial crime arena.

The five-tier approach classifies the range of expertise to be assessed. A tier-four assessor (interview supervisor) should always be competent to the level that he or she is assessing, and this is considered when conducting checks and quality control. The importance of quality control was shown in one study, which estimated that 'ten per cent of the interviews assessed may have breached the *Police and Criminal Evidence Act*' (ACPO 2003, p 64). It is therefore recommended that when reviewing performance a range of interviews be randomly selected. Identifying such cases before they reach court not only saves time, money and embarrassment to the police service, but also helps identify the training and developmental needs of the individuals concerned.

The Australian context

In Australia the principles are firmly embedded in our own court rules on the admissibility of confessional evidence. There is no absolute rule that an interview should be rejected that has been conducted in the face of an objection by a suspect, or has been continued in circumstances where he or she indicates that they do not wish to continue. Rather, it is a question of degree as to whether such persistence renders the record of interview inadmissible and prejudicial to the accused.

The PEACE model has been embraced by many policing jurisdictions worldwide, including in some parts of Australia, Canada, New Zealand, and Europe (Schollum 2005). Queensland, Western Australia, New South Wales and Victoria have introduced some form of training on this model, aimed in particular at the recruit level and at detectives.

While much of the research originates from the UK, inflexible training, lack of supervision and a lack of support to junior officers also have the potential to impede the implementation of a professional interviewing model in Australia. Indeed, despite the evidence, the same mistakes may be made. The interviewing models are often delivered in an inflexible manner; senior officers continue to be unfamiliar with the techniques; and there is a lack of both 'buy-in' from supervisory officers and support offered to junior investigators. If it is generally accepted that both formal and informal interviewing of members of the community is an integral skill for any police officer, then this skill should be monitored and regularly assessed, as should be other core policing requirements:

> The PEACE model is definitely good practice, a view that has recently been endorsed again by ACPO council. Police managers of all grades should therefore promote, inspire and support the use of PEACE in line with protocol and the strive for excellence (Shaw 2002, p 2).

The PEACE model promotes good investigative techniques, eliciting more information from witnesses, victims and suspects, and allows a more effective investigative approach. Certainly the effectiveness of this was one of the drivers for the development of the model and its adoption in the UK, in an effort to address the reduced conviction rates and in response to a renewed focus on the care of victims emphasised by the recommendations of the Stephen Lawrence Inquiry[2] (MacPherson 1999). According to Shaw (2003), over the past 20 years the rate of conviction in England has halved from 18 to 9 per cent and 46 per cent of contested cases are acquitted. The use of effective professional interviews means that investigations can be better directed and lead to a greater chance of a successful prosecution. Time, money and resources can be saved by supplying reliable accurate information for a prosecution, and public confidence in police can grow as the credibility of investigation is demonstrated.

Similar issues are pertinent in Australia. While reported crime has decreased over the past two years, clear up rates remain low. In New South Wales, 22 per cent of offences were cleared between January 2003 and September 2005 across all crime categories. For volume crimes such as break and enter, theft of or from a motor vehicle, and theft from a person, this cleared rate fell to 5 per cent across the above time period (Moffatt, Goh & Poynton 2005). Moreover, the recent phenomenon of costs being awarded against police, where a prosecution fails, has proven to be a significant cost burden for Victoria Police and may be a more effective driver for change than the protection of suspects' rights. Each of these underlines the need for robust and effective investigation.

Research conducted over 15 years ago indicated that police had improved their techniques and attitudes towards suspects, adopting a more ethical approach which appreciates the rights of the suspect (Shepherd 1991). Nevertheless, the interviewing practice extended to victims and witnesses may still be poor, with routine interviews with victims and witnesses being little more than the collection of a quick statement. This can result in information being missed, which becomes obvious when the evidence is introduced in court. One study found that an average of 16 elements of evidentially valid information presented by interviewees was omitted from statements (ACPO 2003). Apart from the loss of any evidentiary benefit – the publication of such lapses in investigative professionalism are an embarrassment to police organisations. The use of a formalised and structured investigative interview model limits the loss of this information. Moreover, the implementation of a supervisory structure such as the UK's five-tier approach can reinforce the appropriate use of formalised and structured interviews. The experience of police colleagues in the UK offers an opportunity to ensure good practice in investigative interviewing in Australia from the outset, instead of awaiting examples of miscarriages of justice to drive 'knee-jerk' reform.

Conclusion

The art of conversation and eliciting information has been replaced by an over-reliance on forensic evidence. The demands of modern policing have

---

2   MacPherson Report (The inquiry into the police handling of the Stephen Lawrence murder).

removed some officers from their communities and with little opportunity to 'just talk' with people. Changes in legislation have reduced the detention time for suspects, with the result of less time to interview suspects. Effectively supervised ethical investigations must be at the heart of good policing, and police managers need to be able to withstand scrutiny of their decision-making. Investigation leaders should set the standards and framework within which their team should operate.

Criminal cases are reliant on evidence from a witness, victim or suspect which, if not accurately obtained, will jeopardise the investigation and any subsequent hearing (Baldwin 1993; Milne & Bull 1999; Shaw 2002). Officers have often been left to learn from practical experience, observing their more experienced colleagues and learning on the job. Obviously this is a risk and poor practice since poor technique and unethical behaviour can influence inexperienced officers leading to a lack of professionalism, missed opportunities and irreparable damage to an investigation (Shepherd 1993). The PEACE model has the potential to increase conviction rates, decrease complaints against police, increase public satisfaction with police, decrease court costs, avoid crises and improve professionalism. Its value has been demonstrated and its implementation requires effective leadership for it to be implemented fully in Australia.

Investigative interviewing with witnesses: a research note from Western Australia

Ellen Grote and Margaret Mitchell

Several conclusions can be drawn from this chapter by Green and Shaw – primarily the importance of appropriate training, comprehension of the process, using (cognitive and conversation management) interviewing strategies associated with the PEACE model and the reinforcement of good practice by supervisors in the field. This research note briefly describes some recent research projects undertaken in collaboration with the Western Australia Police (WAPol) and the Western Australian Police Academy, on specific aspects of investigative interviewing. This research note and chapter seven underline the fact that police techniques – in this case interviewing – are in a constant state of change. Research can assist the process of positive change, and police supervisors and managers need to be actively involved, not only in supervising staff, but also in encouraging research on practices. In this way, police managers can be proactive in policy and practice change, as well as in changing legislation so that it is relevant to operational needs. Their views can lead to change in important areas.

As made clear in this chapter from the experience of the UK police and their presentation of evidence in court, interviews with persons of interest are fraught with difficulties. However, as Kebell and Milne (1998) have said, interviews with *witnesses* are recognised by police to be the cornerstone of criminal investigations and prosecutions. Despite the fact that witness statements guide the direction of the inquiry and assist in identifying defendants and the offences to be charged (Heaton-Armstrong 1995; Heaton-Armstrong & Wolchover 1992; Kebell & Milne 1998; Milne & Shaw 1999), interviews with witnesses tend to receive less attention in both research and training (Bull 2006; Griffiths, Retford & Milne 2006).

The cognitive interview is part of the PEACE training package, adopted by WAPol and other Australian police agencies including New South Wales. As outlined earlier, the PEACE acronym refers to the five steps of investigative interviewing: 'Planning and Preparation; Engage and Explain; Account; Closure; and Evaluation' (Gudjonsson 2003; Milne & Bull 1999; Milne & Shaw 1999; Stacey & Mullan 1997). The *account* component of the model provides two alternatives:

1.   the *cognitive interview* for witnesses; and
2.   the *conversation management* strategy generally used for interviews with suspects or hostile witnesses.

Unlike the interviewing methods used in the United States, the PEACE model is based on, and informed by, extensive psychological research.[3]

In Western Australia, as in many jurisdictions, the recording of interviews with suspects is routine, but in recent years audio- or video-taping

---

3   See Schollum (2005) for a review.

witness interviews has been recommended in the research literature (eg Clarke & Milne 2001; Heaton-Armstrong 1995; Heaton-Armstrong & Wolchover 1992; Kebell and Milne 1998; Milne and Shaw 1999; Shuy 1998). Research in language and law (or forensic linguistics) recognises that writing a witness statement is an extremely complex *literacy event* (Rock 2001). It requires the use of five literacy skills – speaking, listening, writing, reading and viewing – often simultaneously. In contrast to the witness's statement being recorded, statements taken using the traditional 'pen-and-paper' approach rely solely on the skills of the interviewer to document and preserve the witness's first official verbal account of an incident. Taping can prevent the loss of potentially critical details, enable others to review witness interviews to extract additional evidence and – importantly in this context – provide a means of supervising witness interviewing practices. Witness interviews are recorded by many police departments across England and Wales, at least for complex cases (Heaton-Armstrong 1995; Heaton-Armstrong & Wolchover 1992) although not by Australian jurisdictions.

The research reported here is a controlled study of recruits conducting investigative interviews comparing the process and results of interviewing witnesses using the 'pen-and-paper' approach with a 'video-assisted' method. The research was conducted from a linguistic analysis perspective, since language is the medium through which the model is implemented in practice, so the novel aspect of the study examined recruits' language while learning and implementing the PEACE model's *cognitive interview* framework. While the PEACE model has undergone review and enhancement, the *actual language* used to implement the model has not been previously examined. A specific aim of the study was to find out the extent to which video recording the witness interview, and writing the witness statement from that, could reduce the cognitive demand of the interviewing process, and result in a more detailed and 'nuanced' witness statement.

Data Collection

Five sets of data were collected:

1. Field notes taken during the PEACE model training sessions;
2. Training materials;
3. Thirty-two DVD video recordings of the recruits' interviews with witnesses (actors);
4. Sixty-four witness statements, 32 written using the traditional 'pen-and-paper' approach and 32 using the 'video-assisted' method; and
5. Debriefing interviews in which the recruits rated and commented on the two methods as well as the cognitive interview model itself.

To obtain the witness statements written using the two methods, the recruits were assigned partners by the trainers. On the first day, half of the recruits (Partners A) were video-recorded while conducting 20-minute interviews with actors playing the role of a witness/victim of a burglary, and other half (Partners B) were given the DVD recordings of their partners' interviews. In this way, to write the witness statements, one group (A) used their hand-written notes taken during the live interview, while the other group (B) used notes taken while viewing the DVD recorded interviews. The video could be rewound and paused as needed while taking notes, but participants were limited to 30 minutes for scheduling reasons. On Day Two Partners A and B reversed their roles for a robbery scenario.

Propositional analysis, an approach used in both linguistic and psychological research (Kintsch 1974; Stubbs 1983), was implemented so that each proposition or clause was deconstructed into meaningful concepts, which were then counted. The witness statements were compared using this method. The recruits' use of language in their cognitive interviews and witness statements were the focus of *discourse analysis.*

Results

The propositional analysis of the witness statements indicated no significant differences in the number of meaningful facts between the two methods of interviewing. This was attributed to the scripted nature of the scenarios. The scenarios were relatively simple, containing a finite number of details that could be retrieved for inclusion in the statements. While the study did not show that the video-assisted approach helped capture more details, it did suggest differences in the individual skills of the recruits as they adapted their literacy skills (for example listening, speaking, reading, writing and viewing) to the specialised task of investigative interviewing. Of interest was the fact that seven recruits achieved higher scores than their partners regardless of the method used – suggesting that they were simply better at the practice. Further research would be needed to verify this, but the possibly unsurprising variation in individual skills provides even more support that witness interviews should be recorded (although in a practical sense this would make the process more time-consuming). In a real-world situation in which witness interviews take place without audio or video recording the interview, details would be lost.

We also debriefed the recruits. While there was no difference in the number of facts recorded, the recruits subjectively rated using the video more favourably with regard to the ease (vs difficulty), accuracy (vs inaccuracy) and enjoyment (vs frustration) of the task. The overall percentage ratings (74 per cent, 94 per cent and 81 per cent respectively) suggest that the recruits saw the task as cognitively less demanding, and believed the statement would be more accurate when they were able to use a video-recording.

The recruits' use of language raised a number of concerns. These included writing the witness's account in a non-chronological sequence; using long paragraphs and sentences, obscuring important details; and using 'police jargon' (even at the recruit stage) instead of the witness's own words. In the cognitive interviews, the recruits used few open questions; narrowed the scope of open questions with additional utterances before the witness could respond; co-constructed the witness's account by relying on information obtained before the formal interview; and interrupted free recalls with probing questions. These findings support the view expressed by Green and Shaw (in this chapter) regarding the need for scrutiny of witness interviews by supervisors. The study shows that language use in investigative interview training and subsequent practice needs attention, and officers should be encouraged to actively reflect on their use of oral language in interviews and written language in witness statements. The results of this study assist WAPol in very practical ways to make investigative interviewing practices more effective, transparent and accessible for evaluation and provide a detailed analysis of the *process* of interviewing. However, recording actual witness interviews would enable supervisors to monitor interviewing practices and provide opportunities for officers to examine their own use of language. After all, the final component of the PEACE model is *evaluation*.

The research partnership between Edith Cowan University and the WA Police Academy will continue in other projects: we are currently following up the cohort of recruits who participated in this study to discover the extent to which they apply the PEACE model training received at the Academy a year after they have been working with the 'community of practice' (Wenger 1998) of their respective police stations. Another study is examining the degree to which police officers with five or more years' experience apply the cognitive interview and conversation management frameworks in simulated test interviews. A third more comprehensive study will review the actual interviewing practices of front-line police officers and detectives to examine the extent to which the PEACE model is used currently in metropolitan and rural regions, and the level of supervision and support received from senior officers with respect to investigative interviewing. Interviews with Western Australian magistrates, judges, WA Department of Public Prosecution and defence lawyers will also be sought regarding the products of investigative interviews, ie, Records of Interviews (video recordings of suspect interviews and witness statements). Moreover, for the first time in Australia, the recording of interviews with witnesses will be trialled for research purposes.[4]

---

4   The authors may be contacted with regard to the results of these current studies, or for the full report of the research summarised in this note. Email: <e.grote@ecu.edu.au>.

PART II

DEVELOPING THE PROFESSION
OF POLICING

The seven chapters in this substantial section address a wide range of issues we see as having a significant impact on the increasing development of the human resource of contemporary police organisations. Ian Lanyon's chapter opens Part II with the history and development of the 'professionalisation' movement in policing. This movement is predicated substantially on higher levels of tertiary education (in addition to training) for all officers and on postgraduate management education for leaders and managers. Lanyon argues that promoting the professional status of police – and all that this entails – is now necessary to meet the current and future demands and expectations placed on policing practitioners. Stephen Pierce provides an excellent overview of leadership and management education programs. As Pierce points out the requirement for relevant and sophisticated police management education is a consequence of the need for leaders to be able to juggle a range of competing demands in a context of scarce resources. This necessitates not only in-service education of those taking on management roles but also creative partnerships with external providers such as universities and in other ways, such as secondments to develop police leaders.

A key component of these competing demands is the significant matter of police oversight which is a feature of police governance in many countries. Colleen Lewis's chapter is the first of two dealing with this subject. Lewis describes the conditions under which reform in policing was required, for example, the code of silence, and insular under-resourced organisations. She argues that reform in organisations like policing depends on significant change in the working culture, but it also depends on appropriate and strong leadership. Glenn Ross then goes on to examine accountability in more detail exploring the many implications of the term including the essential feature of maintaining the confidence of the community over whom police exercise their authority. A fundamental building block of cultural change is the desire to share information within the organisation and with other external organisations. Vincent Hughes and Paul Jacksons' chapter on information sharing in police organisations outlines the resistance to sharing information and the reasons for this. A theme which has been reflected in several of the chapters, namely a command and control approach, is also introduced by Hughes and

Jackson as one of the major reasons why officers and staff are unwilling to share information. Cultural change to facilitate information sharing to the benefit of the organisation will depend largely on the ability of leaders to create organisational environments that promote more fluid communication.

Linked to the concepts of accountability is the concept of individual and organisational performance management. John Gillespie, Allan Sicard and Scott Gardner describe, from their different perspectives, the pressure for increased accountability commencing with New Public Management at the end of the past century. They describe the essential features of performance management and some of the difficulties in implementing appropriate and sustainable performance management.

David Mutton's chapter concludes Part II with the difficult issue of the stress experienced by middle-ranking managers who see organisational factors as a greater source of stress than the more obvious sources such as dealing with danger and violence. Mutton's chapter underlines the need to understand the sources of this type of occupational stress and to find ways to mitigate it. Many managers in policing do not have a formal qualification in management and in-service training is limited. Coupled with this is the practice in policing of moving staff into different positions, with surprising frequency, to solve a human relations problem and for professional development. This means that managers and those in leadership positions experience both the advantages and disadvantages of 'acting up' into higher positions and dealing with new challenges.

8

PROFESSIONALISATION OF POLICING IN AUSTRALIA: THE IMPLICATIONS FOR POLICE MANAGERS

Ian J Lanyon

Historically, Australasian policing stems from UK organisations rooted in the 1830s when demands upon the police role were far from complex. The police replaced the military, however the military's organisational model was chosen to give structure to the police whilst providing the advantage of authoritarian management through which strict control could be exercised over subordinates (Rawlings 1995). Constables were thereby limited in the amount of discretion they exercised and there was little or no need for education, knowledge and skills resulting in their artisan status (Dale 1994).

Over time the police role has evolved and the environment in which police are required to practice requires the ability to exercise sound judgment and technical knowledge in a broad range of complex situations. Police have considerable discretion in the application of laws and procedure, which must be ethically applied in a vigilant and litigious society. The artisan status of police is no longer appropriate and professionalisation of police is now necessary to assist in meeting the current and future sophisticated demands and expectations upon our policing practitioners from all areas, but particularly the community.

While some argue that professionalisation is a natural evolutionary process, others assert that full professionalisation will only really be achieved through the reorganisation and radical restructuring of police organisations from the existing militaristic model. They argue that a new model conducive to the professional police practitioner is required, where control is through professional freedom (Maravelias 2003).

From at least 1990, when the Australasian Police Ministers Council (APMC) adopted the Statement of Police Education Needs, the leaders of policing have aspired to attaining 'full professional status' with this goal being reiterated in successive editions of the overarching policing strategy

'Directions in Australasian Policing' as produced on behalf of APMC on the advice of all Australasian Police Commissioners (APPSC 2001; APMC 2005). A major issue for police managers and executives is now being able to continue the work to date, and finally achieve full professionalisation of policing. This chapter attempts to map the journey thus far.

Defining professionalisation

Perhaps any discussion of professionalisation might best commence with some clarification of terminology. Profession, professional, professionalism, professionalisation are all terms that are used freely and often interchangeably thereby muddying their traditional meanings. Many of those who provide a service in return for reward, ranging from real estate agents to beauticians, refer to themselves as 'professionals', however, when we talk of 'professions' we tend to associate the term with an occupational status as achieved by doctors, lawyers, architects and more recently nurses to name but a few. Whilst numerous studies have been undertaken and a vast amount of literature has been written, there is very little concurrence upon a single definition that encapsulates the notion or defines a profession. Perhaps the greatest discourse has occurred over a number of decades within the discipline of sociology. Barber (1963, p 671) notes that 'theoretical and methodological consensus is not yet so great among sociologists that there is any absolute agreement on the definition of 'the professions'. Dingwall (1976, p 331) agrees that the concept of profession 'is notorious for the diversity of its definitions and usage by sociologists'.

The 'taxonomic' approach

An approach to defining professions that has dominated (labelled as the 'taxonomic approach' by Klegon (1978)), involves utilising a checklist of particular attributes to distinguish professions from non-professions. Perhaps one of the best known among those who have adopted this approach is Ernest Greenwood whose classic work continues to be quoted by academics in this area. Greenwood (1957, p 45) asserted that professions have the following attributes: systematic body of theory; professional authority; community sanction; ethical codes and a professional culture. Moore (1976, pp 5-6) offered another set of defining attributes, namely: full-time occupation; commitment to a calling; identifying with their peers – often in formalised organisation; possession of esoteric but useful knowledge and skills – based on specialised training or education of exceptional duration and perhaps of exceptional difficulty; service orientation; and professional autonomy. Moore suggests however that these attributes are 'not of equal value, and can be regarded as points ... along a scale of professionalism'.

Like the US Police Executive Research Forum, Rohl (1990a) has suggested that Australasian police should adopt Witham's (1985) 'attribute' approach, defining a profession around eight characteristics, namely:

1.   Operates as an organised body of knowledge, constantly augmented and refined;

2.   Involves a lengthy training/education period;

3.   Operates so as to serve its clients best;

4.   Operates autonomously and exercises control over members;

5.   Develops a community of practitioners through professional standards;

6.   Enforces a code of ethics and behaviour;

7.   Establishes uniform standards of practice; and

8.   Provides full professional mobility.

Another popular method of defining a profession is to provide a narrative that includes many of the attributes, such as that provided by the Australian Council of Professions (Southwick 1997 in Australian Competition and Consumer Commission 2006) who defines a profession as:

> A disciplined group of individuals who adhere to high ethical standards and uphold themselves to, and are accepted by, the public as possessing special knowledge and skills in a widely recognised, organised body of learning derived from education and training at a high level, and who are prepared to exercise this knowledge and these skills in the interest of others. Inherent in this definition is the concept that the responsibility for the welfare, health and safety of the community shall take precedence over other considerations.

Significantly, the Australian Competition and Consumer Commission (2006), whilst noting, 'there is no agreed definition of a profession', has adopted this definition.

The strategies approach

The 'attribute' approach has since been widely criticised (for example Greenwood 1957; Goode 1960; Barber 1963) and deficiencies in such theories well documented (Johnson 1972; Roth 1974; Parry & Parry 1976; Saks 1983). The general criticism has been that such models 'failed to appreciate the dynamic, procedural nature of professionalisation' (Allen 1991, p 52).

Klegon (1978) offered a somewhat different approach by identifying two dynamics – internal and external. He states that whilst the internal relate to strategies used by the profession (codes of ethics etc), it is the external that have largely been neglected by previous studies and which relate to 'control to other institutional forces and arrangements of power'.

Allen, in her 1991 study, articulated Klegon's eight major strategies for professionalisation that then need to be located within four spheres of influence, namely: economic, political, social and intellectual thereby addressing the 'external dynamics'. These strategies are:

1.   *Formulation of a Code of Ethics:* Once formulated, this code must be promoted as a symbol of the desire of the profession to serve the public.

2. *Delineation of the Area of Expertise:* Exclusive domain of practice must be identified and protected from encroachment, the knowledge base of the profession validating the professional claim.

3. *Control of Education and Entry:* education should be university based and closely monitored by the professional association(s). Further education might be required before entrance to the Association(s).

4. *Definition of Competence Levels:* promotion of differing classification of membership with reward in prestige and status for those who attain higher levels of expertise.

5. *Determination of Standards:* Utilising their autonomy, the profession will determine their own standards of practice.

6. *Image Building:* public promotion of positive image of the profession and by convincing the public of its professionalism, the occupation will be rewarded with professional recognition and status.

7. *Professional Unification:* The profession must be united as factionalism undermines public confidence.

8. *Achieving a Relationship with the State:* A balanced relationship with the State is required and achieved through legislative recognition and registration. (Allen 1991, pp 53-54)

As will be seen, Australasian policing to date has tended to favour the Rohl (1990a) eight point 'attributes' as a guide for professionalisation, a position that has more recently been questioned and perhaps more emphasis needs to be given to the so-called Klegon approach.

The story thus far ...

Whilst it is acknowledged that each of the National Common Policing Services, particularly the Australian Centre of Policing Research (ACPR), Australian Institute of Police Management (AIPM) and the National Institute of Forensic Science (NIFS) have each had a significant role in the professionalisation of policing to date, this chapter will focus primarily upon the work undertaken by the Australasian Police Professional Standards Council (APPSC) which, since 2001 has been specifically tasked with 'advancing police professionalisation'.

APPSC is an incorporated association comprising the Commissioners of Police from Australia and New Zealand along with the Presidents of the Police Federation of Australia and the New Zealand Police Association. APPSC, under a number of names, has existed since 1993 and in order to appreciate the history of professionalisation of Australasian policing, it is necessary to revisit some of the key decisions made along the way.

A significant catalyst for change arguably commenced with the *Dawkins Green Paper* (Australia, Parliament 1987b) followed by the *Dawkins White Paper* (Australia, Parliament 1988a) As a result, sweeping changes occurred in Australian higher education arrangements such as the amalgamation of universities and colleges, and radical reforms to funding arrangements including the introduction of Higher Education Contributions Scheme (HECS). Vocational education and training was also modernised and competency based training was introduced. These changes, combined with outcomes and recommendations from royal commission inquiries and internal reviews inevitably saw pressure placed on Commissioners to consider how best to reform to their organisations and implement necessary change. Accordingly, the Commissioners Conference in July 1988, considered the impact of HECS and other reforms upon policing. Subsequently, at their meeting on 25 November 1988, the APMC agreed that, 'a statement on national police education needs to be developed taking into consideration the positions of all jurisdictions'.

In 1990 a Steering Committee comprising Mr JK Avery, AO QPM, then Commissioner of Police New South Wales, Mr MJ Palmer APM, then Commissioner of Police, Northern Territory and Mr AD Rose, then Secretary, Commonwealth Attorney-General's Department, was formed and in consultation with all commissioners the 'statement' was drafted. This statement was subsequently considered at the APMC meeting on the 8 March 1990, where the following resolutions were agreed:

- A critical reform confronting Australian policing is the attainment of full professional status.
- Full professional status will entail national educational standards, formal higher education qualifications, improved police practices, and the establishment of uniform anti-corruption strategies.
- It is essential that the community be served by a highly qualified and ethical police force in which the public have trust.
- Over the past decade there has been a fragmented and uncoordinated development of tertiary courses offered to police. It is important that this ad hoc approach is avoided and efforts be redirected towards establishing uniform national standards.
- The nature of much criminal activity is now so complex and sophisticated that without a qualitative approach to performance neither government nor the community can be assured of gaining an adequate return on their investment in policing.
- Truly efficient and effective policing will only be achieved when policing develops a professional culture underpinned by superior management practices and a commitment to corporate excellence.

At that meeting the APMC also agreed that a National Police Professionalism Implementation Advisory Committee (NPPIAC) be established with the aim of implementing a national strategy for police higher education by 1 March 1991.

The newly formed NPPIAC, under the chairmanship of Mr NR Newnham, APM, then Commissioner of Police, Queensland, consulted widely with all police jurisdictions, tertiary institutions and industrial associations and reported to the Commissioners at a number of meetings. Two Board of Control meetings were held at the Australian Police Staff College (APSC) in

Sydney in November 1990 and March 1991. At their meeting in Canberra on 10 April 1991 (APSC 1991a), The Board of Control of the APSC – comprising all of the Australian Police Commissioners – received a report from NPPIAC and noted that in accordance with the decision of APMC on 8 March 1990, all jurisdictions had agreed on a *Statement of Strategic Direction* to guide their implementation. This Statement was known colloquially as the '10 point plan' and is reproduced below.

Figure 8.1: Statement of Strategic Direction

Noting the commitment to the pursuit of police professionalism and the recognition of policing as a true profession, all Australian Commissioners of Police have agreed to developing a strategy embracing the following elements:

(a) Establishment of agreed core standards for recruits entering community-based policing.

(b) Development of a national common core component for community-based police recruit training and education purposes, supplemented according to jurisdictional needs.

(c) Review and enhancement, followed by publication and promotion, of the Australian National Police Code of Ethics.

(d) Appropriate police training courses having national (as opposed to jurisdiction-specific) relevance and significance in the profession to be monitored and accredited (see (i) below).

(e) Tertiary and other courses undertaken by police as part of their ongoing professional development to be endorsed and accredited where appropriate (see (i) below).

(f) The future development of a national rating system to be applied to the educational activities undertaken by police as part of their ongoing professional development, to enhance objective comparison of courses, qualifications and standards achieved.

(g) Conduct of a national needs and demand analysis of requirements for police tertiary education requirements, recognizing the various and changing positions in and between jurisdictions, for the purpose of providing Governments and tertiary institutions with the clearest possible indications of police profession's future higher education needs.

(h) Further development of nationally accredited in-service courses to meet the needs of jurisdictions and for specific professional development of members of the profession.

(i) The Education Advisory Board to the APSC, in its capacity as a national police education standards council, to monitor, accredit as necessary and endorse courses, as referred to in (d), (e) and (h) above, and to work closely with providers of tertiary education to maximize the credits towards general tertiary qualifications gained by those successfully completing national police professional development courses.

(j)   The APSC will pursue recognition and status as a tertiary institution, with formal post-graduate standing for its executive development programs.

Source: APSC 1991a

The Board acknowledged, in expressing its agreement to the *Statement of Strategic Direction*, that this strategy would be implemented and progressed over several years and that individual jurisdiction requirements and special concerns would be taken fully into account in the course of that progression. It was further recognised that the strategy would create an environment that would enhance professional mobility between jurisdictions.

At the 1991 Conference of Commissioners of Police of Australasia and the South West Pacific Region held in Adelaide, March 1991, the issue of national competency standards was considered.[1] A paper was tabled outlining the role of the then National Training Board (NTB) and whilst this paper was received as 'Information Only' it was evident that representatives of the National Training Board intended communicating with Australian Police Commissioners to discuss the future development of national competency standards for the nation's police forces.

At the APSC Board of Control meeting on 10 October 1991, a report prepared by Mr Cooper of the National Training Board was considered. The Board formed a recommendation for APSC to have a role in the development of national competency standards for police and referred the matter to the Police Commissioners Conference for adoption.

An extraordinary meeting of the Police Commissioners Conference held at the APSC on 11 October 1991 resolved that:

- national skills standards should be developed for police forces by 1993 on the basis of Operational (recruit, general policing, and specialist skills) Supervision, Management and Executive functions;
- a National Police Skills Standards Council should be established to function as the Competency Standards Body (CSB) for the industry to coordinate the development, monitoring, and review of national skills standards for Australian police agencies; (it was later decided to use the title National Police Education Standards Council (NPESC)); and
- skill standards for all police functions should be implemented progressively from January 1993 (APSC 1991b).

A key aspect of the discussions undertaken by Police Commissioners in October 1991 involved the proposed NPESC being formally recognised by the National Training Board as the Competency Standards Body for the police industry. Application was sought and granted for this to occur in December 1991.

---

1   This material first appeared in a document by the APPSC prepared by HR Winzler and updated by I Lanyon (Winzler and Lanyon 2006) and is used with the permission of APPSC.

A National Competency Standards Project was commenced in the same year to 'fulfil NPESC's role in the coordination, development, monitoring and review of national core competency standards'. At the same time, by resolution of PCC, the APSC became The Australian Institute of Police Management (AIPM) out of the recognition that although some progress had been made in the direction of police professionalism in the various forums of Commissioners, Ministers and NPPIAC conferences, no appropriate vehicle existed to implement all of NPPIAC's Statement of Strategic Direction.

Although the AIPM's charter included development of police professionalisation issues, over time commissioners formed the view that NPESC, as the nationally recognised standards body, would become the primary vehicle through which strategic directions should be progressed and that it should acquire a separate legal standing for that purpose.

As a result, on 4 June 1993, NPESC was formally established as an independent legal entity under the *Associations Incorporation Act 1984* (NSW), the Council comprising all Australian Police Commissioners, a representative of the then Police Federation of Australia and New Zealand (PFANZ) and the Executive Director of AIPM as 'a representative of higher education'.

In 1993 NPESC described its purpose to:

> Develop, establish, maintain and approve standards of professional competency or any other matter relating to the development of the police profession in Australia (Winzler & Lanyon 2006, p 6).

On 12 March 1998, NPESC became the Australasian Police Education Standards Council (APESC) as a consequence of New Zealand Police becoming a full member, and membership increased by the addition of the New Zealand Police Association. The Fiji Police, at their request, was later admitted as an associate member.

In July 2000, the Public Safety Industry Training Package was endorsed by the Australian National Training Authority which contained a number of police-specific qualifications, including the Diploma of Public Safety (Policing), and effectively brought to a close the competency project commenced in 1991.

In May 2001, the then Chair of APESC, Tasmania Police Commissioner R McCreadie, AO APM, proposed a review of APESC's role, purpose, future directions, structure and governance. The rationale being: 1) the considerable changes in key police training and education positions and 2) a holistic review of APESC future was required with regard to contemporary policing developments and the need to position Commissioners appropriately to progress full professionalisation. Terms of reference for the review were subsequently agreed upon and a working party was established.

As a result of the review, APESC was renamed to the Australasian Police Professional Standards Council (APPSC) and it was agreed that the direction towards a police profession should embrace the broad principles underpinning established professions. The review, whilst conceding the vast variation in definitions of a profession, favoured the view expressed by the NSW Police Service in their submission to the Wood Royal Commission on employment and promotion in which the distinguishing elements of a profession were simply:

- a distinct body of knowledge and practice;
- of ethical foundation;
- offers lengthy formal education; and
- has registration.

A platform for professionalisation

Following the review in 2001, APPSC established the Platform for Professionalisation Strategy 2002-2005, which essentially initiated seven national projects encompassing a range of issues deemed relevant to the professionalisation of policing, namely:

Project 1 – Ongoing developments of competencies

Established with the aim to provide on-going development of competencies, qualifications, training and assessment materials for qualifications in the VET Sector. Particularly identifying those specialist areas within policing that were not covered by the Public Safety Training Package.

Project 2 – An Australasian police qualifications framework

This project, utilising the career model of Police Practitioner; Supervisor; Manager; Executive and Specialist aims to recognise the skills and knowledge expressed in qualifications necessary in the police context whilst providing a mechanism to plan education directions. This project aimed to ultimately propose an Australasian Police Education Qualifications Framework incorporating skills-based vocational qualifications and higher education outcomes.

Project 3 – An Australasian police statement of ethics

The aim of this project is to establish an Australasian Statement of Ethics. Whilst recognising existing Codes of Conduct and Ethics in each Jurisdiction, the project will attempt to articulate a common Statement that will augment the existing standards to become the 'Masthead' of Australasian Policing. It is intended that the resultant Statement be published, advertised and promoted.

Project 4 – Minimum educational qualification for practitioners (constables)

Aimed at recognising that all jurisdictions now deliver the Diploma of Public Safety (Policing) or equivalent as the minimum qualification for confirmation of, or permanent appointment to, the office of constable.

Project 5 – Recruiting standards

The aim of this project is to establish sustainable and defensible requisite standards, aside from education, for entry to the profession of policing. These standards will encompass consideration of personal integrity, experience and behavioural, physical and psychological fitness for admission to the profession as well as the timing of such admission. Potential exclusionary factors such as court appearances, criminal and traffic history and/or convictions and medical history will also be addressed.

Project 6 – Professional mobility

Although Inter-Police Agency mobility has been examined for a number of years and has resulted in numerous reports, no actual model or mechanisms have been developed to enable implementation to be considered. The aim of this project is to identify a workable mobility model and enabling mechanisms for Inter-Police Agency mobility at rank/level/function.

Project 7 – Transition from VET to Higher Education

Most jurisdictions have individually addressed higher education requirements and a number have existing arrangements with vocational training providers and universities at various levels. The aim of this project is to canvas existing links in order to identify and develop a model framework for delivery and transition from vocational to higher education in recognition that the profession of policing requires both skills-based training and knowledge-based education. This project will consider issues including the consistency of advanced standing or credits from relevant courses in VET to higher education programs and consistencies of transition in the police qualifications framework.

The project teams comprise representatives from each Australasian police jurisdiction along with the Police Federation of Australia and the New Zealand Police Association. Since their inception in 2002, varying levels or progression and achievement have been made by each project, whilst the aims and scope of some projects have been amended to fit more comfortably into the current strategy.

The current strategy

In March 2005, the Police Commissioners Conference established a review to progress the professionalisation and future direction of Australasian policing arrangements. A steering committee comprising four commissioners and a representative from the Australian Government Attorney-General's Department was established to guide a working party comprising representatives from each of the Australian and New Zealand Police agencies. The terms of reference for the review, inter alia, to:

> consider the scope and functions of APPSC with a view to further develop a professionalisation strategy with details of key activities and milestones to be reached, in order to progress policing from an occupation to a profession. Also consider the role and function of a professional body for policing (such as ANZIP) and an appropriate structure and arrangements for such a body (Winzler & Lanyon 2006, p 11).

In their paper *Achieving Professionalisation of Australasian Policing* (2006) the working party, based on 'best practice, the Directions in Australasian Policing 2005-2008, previous reviews and research', identified six key objectives integral to the attainment of full professional status for policing, namely:

1.   Develop a definition of the profession of policing.
2.   Implement university-based education for policing.
3.   Develop a body of knowledge.
4.   Propose ongoing professional development.
5.   Develop registration and standards for policing.
6.   Establish a professional body for policing.

Using these six objectives the work-to-date can be reviewed.

1.   *Develop a definition of the profession of policing*

Cioccarelli (2003) noted that the 'occupational arena of policing is at risk from environing occupations, principally because policing is yet to clearly determine and articulate its fundamental and exclusive role in contemporary liberal democracy', he went on stating 'one of the hallmarks of established professions is that they clearly stake out, and rigorously defend, their occupational turf'.

It is clear that in order to establish policing as a profession, there must first be an agreed position of opinion. Such a definition would serve to establish eligibility for membership to the profession whilst distinguishing policing from other government and private sectors. Defining the exclusive domain of policing is however not straightforward, as consideration must be given to the role of individual practitioners, and the role, tasks and functions of police agencies along with the framework in which police operate. This framework is particularly broad and is set not only by legislation and the common law, but also by government imperatives and most importantly community demands and expectations.

In January 2006, APPSC established a project, the aim to 'develop a definition for the Australasian Policing Profession' (APPSC Project 1a, 2006). At the APPSC General Meeting in Adelaide on 4 May 2006, there was significant discussion between the commissioners as to the appropriateness of merely accepting the aforementioned 'attribute' models of other professions as suitable for Australasian policing. The commissioners resolved that the scope of this project be extended to not only define the exclusive domain of policing but also 'to exploration of various models for police professionalisation'.

2.   *Implement university-based education for policing*

Klockars (1985) said:

> If police are to be true professionals – that is, professionals in more than name only – our society allows one path to that status. It must begin with a long period of education in an accredited, academic professional school at the college or postgraduate level, include or continue through a period of supervised internship and conclude with the granting of a licence with-

117

out which one cannot practice that profession. No true profession – neither medicine nor law, engineering, accounting, teaching, social work, nursing or clinical psychology – has ever achieved genuine professional status in any other way (p 114).

The resolution of the Australian Police Ministers at their meeting on 8 March 1990 was that 'full professional status will entail national educational standards, formal higher education qualifications' and placed education as a focus of professionalisation of policing. The need for professionalisation and higher education for police has also been recommended by three separate Royal Commissions (Fitzgerald 1989, Wood 1997 and Kennedy 2004).

Obviously university education on its own will not establish policing as a profession, however it is clear that recognition of professional status within contemporary society requires a professional level of education, that is, education within the higher education sector. Every profession has a specific degree that educates new entrants on their profession and given the increasing complexity of policing in society and the substantial amount of knowledge required to support a professional police practitioner, there is ample argument to support attainment of a specific degree in policing as the foundational education requirement for police practitioners.

At their meeting on 20 April 2005, the commissioners sitting as APPSC agreed that:

1.   Council recognises a higher education degree in policing as a desirable professional qualification for Australasian practitioners; and

2.   each council member jurisdiction progress implementation as a requisite for practitioners at a time and in a manner appropriate to that jurisdiction.

Most Australasian police agencies are already well on the way to achieving this, many having established relationships with various universities and some already delivering their foundational training in the higher education sector. The process is also occurring informally with many practitioners throughout Australasia undertaking university studies of their own accord. With a number of universities offering undergraduate-level police-specific qualifications, it is envisaged that the outcomes of APPSC Project 7 – Transition from VET to Higher Education, will provide 'principles, guidelines and outcomes' for degrees in applied operational policing. Further, if agreement can be established as to these requirements there exists the opportunity for the policing profession to determine their own education and training leading to some consistency in the core components of a degree throughout Australasia. The police profession would then need to provide some ongoing quality assurance of the courses and qualifications offered to the profession.

3.   Develop a body of knowledge

There is agreement between most writers on police professionalisation that a body of knowledge is an essential component of a profession (for example Avery 1991, p 9; Brown 1988, p 40; Dale 1994, p 210; Rohl 1990, p 27, to name a few). Such a 'body of knowledge' would encapsulate research-based initiatives and policing-best-practice particularly in crime prevention, control and community safety. Whilst there has been a huge increase in university-based research, to date such research remains largely inaccessible, scattered around the country in separate and protected databases and libraries. As Darvall-Stevens (1994, p 51) points out, arguably what is absent from Australasian policing is a forum for discussion, debate and critique on a wide range of policing subjects to which practitioners can openly and freely contribute.

In November 2005, APPSC initiated a project, the aim of which is to establish an 'Australasian Police Knowledge Bank'. Recognising the need to be more than a mere repository of documents, an internet test site was established in early 2006 known as the 'Australasian Police KnowledgeNET'. Here, discussion forums, chat rooms, and research databases are developed and maintained. It is envisaged that this project will encourage participation by a number of universities and in time the site will become the central point of police research and dialogue; a site openly accessible by public safety practitioners who will be encouraged to contribute thereby capturing and building upon the distinct body of knowledge of the policing profession.

4. *Propose ongoing professional development*

As stated in the report *Achieving Professionalisation of Australasian Policing* (2006), all members of any profession have a continuing obligation, to both them and to the community, to participate in professional development that improves their ability to engage in their field of practice by extending their knowledge and skills in areas that are relevant to their current practice needs. Whilst some professions leave responsibility for this on-going professional development upon the individual, others have it regulated by the profession and a professional body, and/or have ongoing professional development as a requirement by legislation.

While all jurisdictions have a critical interest in maintaining the currency of member's knowledge and skills, and in most jurisdictions certain ongoing training and certification requirements, once a person has entered the profession, it is important that they commit to maintaining the highest professional standards, including maintaining a high degree of expert knowledge and skills relevant to policing.

In January 2006, APPSC initiated a project, 1c – Registration for the Policing Profession, which will include research and investigation of models for ongoing professional development of policing practitioners.

5. *Develop registration and standards for policing*

The issue of whether there ought to be mandatory registration for police in Australasia is a significant one. Often linked to initial education, ethics and codes of practice, standards of practice and continuing professional development, registration is a common attribute of a profession and provides a professional with a licence to practice.

An argument often mounted against registration is that, unlike nursing, teaching and law, in Australasia there are only nine primary police employers, it is therefore not necessary and the bureaucracy involved would outweigh any advantages gained. Those who argue for registration assert that such would increase community confidence in policing by providing certainty that a practitioner has met and continues to maintain the necessary standards. Registration would also facilitate professional mobility between police agencies; either permanent or temporary. There is little doubt however that broader mobility is becoming an increasing requirement of police. For example the increasing frequency of international deployment to countries such as East Timor, the Solomon Islands and Indonesia. Whilst the Australian Federal Police currently coordinate such, it is possible that in the future countries may wish to employ police directly. Registration would provide individuals seeking such work with accreditation (as to their education, skills and ability) to be employed in policing roles. Registration would confer eligibility for (rather than the right to) employment and it is envisaged that responsibility for discipline and integrity matters should continue to rest with the employer and relevant oversighting bodies.

Despite acknowledgment of the compatibility of their training (APPSC Project 4, 2006), other than at senior levels, Australasian police jurisdictions have tended to resist professional mobility between agencies – those who do manage to transfer at the lower levels are often required to undergo significant amounts of 'retraining', although this is slowly being recognised as inefficient. Registration through common practice standards might potentially alleviate the need for this to occur.

Uniform standards of fitness, medical and psychological health along with standards surrounding criminal and traffic history need to be agreed to and implemented. Identification of these standards is currently underway through APPSC Project 5 – Employment Requisites to the Policing Profession. Already some 212 professional practice standards for almost all policing functions exist and have been agreed to by police commissioners and are published upon the APPSC website.[2]

Perhaps a significant step towards mobility was taken between commissioners at the APPSC meeting on 20 April 2005, when they agreed that:

1. APPSC agrees in principle to participate in professional mobility between Australasian member jurisdictions in a time and manner appropriate to each jurisdiction.

2. Each participating member agrees to seek, where necessary, amendments to legislation, employee arrangements and policy mechanisms to facilitate professional mobility.

3. The Council agrees to the development of an Australasian Memorandum of Understanding on the formal exchange of relevant

---

2   See <www.appsc.com.au>.

information of the practitioners who may seek appointment to another agency.

As previously mentioned, Project 1c – Registration for the Policing Profession, initiated in January 2006, will 'investigate the implications of police registration (both mandatory and voluntary) and develop and recommend a model or models for implementation on a State and/or Australasian basis'. This project will explore the various issues surrounding registration and whilst registration is often closely linked to the concept of a professional body for policing, it is certainly possible to have one without the other therefore each of these needs to be considered somewhat separately.

6. Establishment of a professional body for policing

In their 1928 study of the transition of a number of diverse occupations towards professional status, Carr-Saunders and Wilson (1933, p 226) proposed that:

> professional associations are distinguished by the degree to which they seek to establish minimum qualifications for entrance into professional practice or activity, to enforce appropriate rules and norms of conduct among members of the professional group, and to raise the status of the professional group in the larger society.

Cioccarelli (2003) noted that whilst the industrial welfare of policing has been well-served by various police unions, an institution central and common to established professions had not yet been established in Australasia for policing. He asserts that such an institution would serve to protect the occupation whilst developing a culture based on shared social values and norms by its members and based upon other professional associations, one for policing would be 'instrumental in assuring the community as to the essential worth of the service that the profession extends to the community'. A policing professional body would aim to promote high standards and develop community involvement and understanding of policing and public safety issues. It is through this engagement that stronger links would be forged with communities, whilst the body could perform an independent advocacy role for policing.

Johnstone, Evans and Montague (1999), through lengthy consultation with policing, examined the various functions that a professional body could perform for policing and included, registration of practitioners; developing codes of ethics; developing professional practice standards; developing standards for university courses; advancing the profession in the eyes of the community and other professions; mandating and providing compulsory professional development; facilitating fellowship amongst members; publishing a professional journal and commissioning research.

In January 2006, APPSC initiated a project, 1b – A Professional Body for Policing, the aim of which is to recommend an appropriate model and implementation strategy for a professional policing body, including the roles and responsibilities that such a body should perform.

Whilst the outcomes of this project will be informative, as Johnstone, Evans and Montague (1999) agree, rarely are professional bodies formed as a result of government action. Perhaps then, rather than resting with the police commissioners, the establishment of a professional body might be a matter for police practitioners themselves, as ultimately the success of such a body will fall to the members.

To date, most of the discussion surrounding professionalisation of police has occurred at the executive level of the various police agencies with very little input or involvement from the practitioner level, in fact, as Darvall-Stevens (1994) discovered (in Victoria) that police, particularly the 'rank and file' were oblivious to the professionalisation movement. Similarly, the communities that we serve must be informed and engaged to support professionalisation of their police agencies as recognition as a profession 'cannot be requisitioned ... but must be bestowed' (Avery, 1991) and it is only through the acceptance of society that policing can ever claim full professional status.

Where there is a will ...

Sir David Phillips (2003) as the outgoing ACPO (Association of Chief of Police Officers) President correctly stated that in its visibility, policing is almost unmatched, and as enforcers of the law, police must been seen to represent the highest standards in society. The police role is not static, it is complex and diverse and has been evolving over the last century-and-a-half (Rohl 1994). There is no longer a role for the artisan practitioner who can not satisfactorily deal with the complex problems faced on a daily basis, the professional police practitioner needs to be fully equipped to meet the increasing demands and expectations of the community which necessitates higher order underpinning knowledge as delivered in the higher education sector. Etter (1992, p 51) asserts that '[I]f policing cannot deal with the more complex and intellectually demanding aspects of police work, then ... police may be left with only the routine and more mundane aspects of their present role'. Occupations that fail to lead the agenda in advancing their own professionalisation may well forfeit that role to other more influential agencies (WA Police News 1990) and policing might simply be relegated as the foot soldiers of the judicial system, rather than leaders in community policing.

Professionalisation of Australasian policing has been on the agenda since the 1980s with police ministers and commissioners in various forums confirming a commitment to achieving full professional status. Whilst significant progress has been made towards advancing professionalisation, an opportunity now exists to push onwards. It is time, and as Rohl (1990b) asserts, policing has to decide, it can retain the status of an occupation, albeit a very honourable occupation, or it can achieve full professional status. Such change cannot take place however, without excellent leadership, along with the involvement of community and practitioners. Whilst the 'six objectives' will undoubtedly progress professionalisation, it is suggested that perhaps a more strategic view needs to be taken, an embracement of the 'Klegon strategies' and even radical organisational reshaping of the current hierarchical militaristic structures is required to be truly considered a profession: and that is the challenge for the current and future police leadership in Australasia for where there is a will ...

9

LEADERSHIP DEVELOPMENT IN AUSTRALASIAN POLICING: THE ROLE OF EDUCATION

Stephen Pierce

The landscape of police leadership programs continues to change. A wide range of political, social, technological and competitive market pressures are rapidly altering the context in which policing operates. These pressures are leading to demands for substantially higher levels of performance and transparency in accountability, professional ethics, and effective resource use. Moreover, a large body of evidence from police corruption commissions and inquiries emphasises the criticality of police leadership programs (Lusher 1981; Fitzgerald 1989; Mollen 1994; Wood 1997; Murray 2000; Ferguson 2003; Kennedy 2004). Kennedy (2004, p 161) notes that:

> Previous corruption inquiries have identified a link between police corruption and poor management practices. In addition, the inappropriate culture of police services that allows corruption to develop is related to inadequacies in leadership and management.

Executive police leadership requirements are similar to those of the leaders of any large enterprise, but at the same time must also address the pivotal leadership role that police play in the community. Policing seeks to educate and prepare its leaders for challenges that include the maintenance of public trust, juggling of issues of independence and accountability, maintaining the balance between police powers and civil liberties in an increasingly challenging security environment, and the management of scarce resources at a time of increased demands. In the face of persistent pressures for change, policing requires leadership that provides clear guidance, innovative solutions and confident, assured direction. Many leadership programs in Australia and overseas are being planned and conducted both within jurisdictions and in partnership with external providers such as universities and commercial organisations (Lanyon, in this volume). Instead of leadership programs being directed only at the senior officers, they are also being applied at all levels of police organisations. In addition to formal education programs, jurisdictions are seeking ways to offer other learning experiences. Murray (2000, p 6), supporting the need for learning provided outside police organisations, argued that:

> Development of leaders entails not only formal training and education where necessary, but exposure to a range of experience that can eventually be used in leading and managing a police organisation ... Even with all this organisational knowledge and experience, however, future police leaders are handicapped unless they have had experience outside of their own organisations.

This chapter examines current initiatives in leadership education in Australasian policing, with particular emphasis on the work of the Australian Institute of Police Management.

Current police leadership education

All Australasian police jurisdictions undertake leadership and managerial training and development within strategic leadership frameworks across their organisations. The majority of police education departments have specific leadership and management divisions.

Police still tend to use the words 'training', 'education' and 'development' interchangeably, even though, in theory, training is 'vocationally-orientated education, or hands on skill development where skills are developed through practice, which is guided by formal structured means' (Woodall & Winstanley 1998, p 9), while education extends learning through undergraduate and postgraduate courses (Beardwell & Holden 2001). Development is particularly pertinent at senior management and executive level. It can be understood as the complex process of 'professional and personal growth, of acquiring and increasing knowledge, experience and skills, and of enabling personal qualities to mature' (Pierce 2001, p 96). In policing terms, the aim of training is to provide competencies to enable members to complete required tasks and to deal with prescribed and expected actions with a degree of certainty. Equally, the aim of education is to prepare leaders to deal with uncertainty where there is no prescribed action, and to acquire the skills and knowledge to become the best possible police leaders. Overall, innovative thinking and practices to enhance police services are the aim of education.

Australasian jurisdictions currently have formal links to 19 universities for the delivery of 49 tertiary courses, with 13 courses having leadership or management as core units of curricula (APPSC 2006b), and most jurisdictions have positioned, or are in the process of positioning, police training and education within the higher education sector. Leadership development in Australian policing is provided in many forms including work-based development, professional development opportunities via upgrading or out-placement, internal leadership courses, and specific external education courses via direct funding or scholarship. Coaching programs are being implemented in various areas and mentoring templates and tools are being developed with a particular emphasis on personal development support. Current internal courses are primarily aimed at Senior Management and Team Leader levels. The most noticeable change is the move from lengthy Academy-based leadership programs to a combination of short sharply focused courses combined with longer term tertiary education.

It appears, however, that leadership development concentrates mostly at middle level, with relatively fewer programs that focus on the lower ranks of the senior executive level. This means that the transactional leadership required of junior police in their daily operational roles is ignored, and may be based on a somewhat naïve assumption, that executive police leaders have achieved all that is possible in their self-development. At the same time, contemporary programs noticeably reflect the change in culture from a task-focused to a people-centred approach with regards to employee management.

In September 2006 the heads of Australian and New Zealand police human resources departments held a leadership development workshop at the Australian Institute of Police Management, located in Manly, New South Wales. The issues discussed included the advantages in having an appropriate leadership development framework, identification and examination of the drivers of leadership in policing, and the role of leadership in organisational culture development. In an effort to move towards common elements of leadership development the representatives initially agreed to identify and use shared principles for leadership development in their jurisdictions. Unfortunately they were only able to identify the gaps currently in leadership development rather than the desired future principles.

The Australian Institute of Police Management

This section will now review the role, function and future of the Australian Institute of Police Management. The Australian Institute of Police Management (AIPM) takes responsibility for providing police leadership courses. The AIPM has played a key role in the executive development of police for many years, both in its current form and in its earlier iterations as the Australian Police College (1960-1987) and the Australian Police Staff College (1987-1995). Since it was first established, more than 6,000 senior police officers from Australia, New Zealand and overseas have undertaken professional development programs, and other public safety and emergency service organisations also send staff to the programs. The AIPM is currently administered by the Australian Federal Police (AFP) and reports to a Board of Control comprised of all Police Commissioners in Australia and New Zealand.

The AIPM offers two core courses, the Graduate Diploma in Executive Leadership and the Graduate Certificate in Applied Management. The Graduate Diploma includes a two-week residential component, known as the Police Executive Leadership Program (PELP). It is designed to enhance the research and critical thinking skills of senior leaders. It is offered primarily for superintendents and more senior ranks. The Graduate Certificate includes a three-week residential component, known as the Police Management Development Program (PMDP). This is intended primarily for Inspectors and its focus is on critical and strategic thinking, action research, decision-making, problem solving, and practical leadership. A combination of personal study and mentoring is aimed at assisting participants in their current roles and in preparation for future executive responsibilities.

In summary, the two courses are based on the following themes:

- A strategic perspective of how internal and external processes, structure and resources operate together in organisations and the links between management, leadership and other organisational functions.
- A concern with self-management and career management to enhance career outcomes of participants.
- A strong leadership skills development focus based on enduring principles of leadership and management.
- An integration of theory and practice through the introduction of a well-developed body of literature, individual participant work experience, multiple assessment strategies and, vicariously, through introduction of leaders from diverse industries.
- A focus on the 'value-adding' and 'performance-related' aspect of leadership in policing and emergency services.
- A continuing reinforcement of the importance of issues including the framework of government in which policing and emergency services operate, global leadership trends in these industries, resource management as a leadership function, and corporate responsibility and accountability.
- A particular focus on how the external environment impacts on policing, and how contemporary issues in society (and future trends) should shape and determine police responses and processes.

The AIPM also conducts parallel executive development programs for the Australasian Fire Authorities Council (AFAC), as well as actively promoting the involvement and interaction of senior officers from all public safety and emergency services agencies in its police leadership programs. A recent example of this is the innovative Leadership in Criminal Intelligence Program designed to strengthen intelligence management within participating organisations by identifying, developing and implementing best practice in intelligence to support the work of Australian law enforcement bodies.

In addition to the core academic courses, the AIPM provides other services (for example, workshops on topics of priority interest to police) in response to specific requests from its policing customers. In 2006, the AIPM conducted the Leadership in Counter Terrorism Pacific Program in conjunction with the American Federal Bureau of Investigation, to provide leadership to organisations and communities to minimise the fear of terrorism in the face of current threat and to deal with the consequences of terrorism and global crime. These contemporary programs reflect the desire by Australian jurisdictions to remain informed and abreast of current practices in international policing.

The AIPM also provides a number of professional development programs under contract to the AFP. The Institute is currently assisting the AFP in re-building the Solomon Islands Police Force (SIPF). The AIPM is to provide a senior officer development program over the period 2006-2009 for SIPF officers, and to build capacity within the SIPF to conduct similar programs on an ongoing basis.

Future police leaders will require the capacity to operate within networks that extend well beyond their jurisdiction – networks with other law enforcement agencies within Australia and overseas, networks with other public safety organisations, and networks in the community. A distinctive feature of the AIPM is the multi-jurisdictional and international nature of its development programs. Course members are drawn from every jurisdiction in Australia and New Zealand, and include senior police officers from overseas.

Australian police jurisdictions supplement the AIPM teaching staff by providing Senior Police Fellows on 12-month secondments. In addition, the International Police Leadership Executive Consortium (IPLEC) was formed in 2004 to facilitate exchanges between the AIPM, the FBI, the London Metropolitan Police, the Central Police Training and Development Authority (Centrex) at Bramshill, the Scottish Police College (Tulliallan), the Canadian Police College and the US Drug Enforcement Agency (DEA), to further enhance course delivery and participant experience. Hong Kong Police and Singapore Police recently joined IPLEC. These agencies encourage senior officers to contribute to the teaching in leadership and management development programs, and to share course curricula, learning materials, post-course evaluation by exchange officers and relevant research. This diversity of experience brings an international dimension to AIPM courses, and results in senior Australasian police officers developing essential national and international professional networks.

The philosophical underpinning of AIPM courses is designed to produce accelerated results for participants. The courses strive to move beyond immediate industry concerns to introduce wider philosophical and theoretical considerations and better prepare participants for a rapidly changing industry environment. In essence, this philosophy demands a quality and rigorous process of blending current and emerging academic theories with industry best practice, and national and international schools of thought and professional practice. In keeping with industry demand for outcomes-based programs that do not commit senior managers to extended absences from high pressure positions, and having regard to adult learning principles, AIPM core programs combine supported distance education, short 'immersion' residential programs and industry based applied research.

The Australasian police jurisdictions require the AIPM to provide comprehensive evaluation of program delivery. In 2006 the AIPM completed a summary of evaluation surveys of all 2004-2005 programs (over 350 participants). Ninety six per cent agreed they were better prepared for their professional life (19 per cent agreed, 44.6 per cent strongly agreed and 35 per cent very strongly agreed). Ninety-seven per cent agreed they had been challenged to new levels during their program (15.4 per cent agreed, 40 per cent strongly agreed and 42.2 per cent very strongly agreed). However, to better define workplace benefits of AIPM programs, it has recently been recommended that the AIPM design a post-course evaluation model to survey participants in their workplace to provide for understanding and analysis over an extended period of time, of course benefit to individuals and to jurisdictions (AIPM 2006a).

Comparison of leadership education in Australasia with overseas

In 2005 the Australasian police jurisdictions, through the AIPM Board of Study, expressed the need to holistically identify Australasian and international police leadership requirements for the next decade and to build those requirements into a strategic framework of best practice programs, forums and leadership education. In response, the AIPM undertook the Academic Strategy Project (AIPM 2006a; 2006b; 2005a) which used a range of survey methods to ensure that a wide range of views were canvassed, and that recommendations were based on research and benchmarking.

The surveys and research, which included consultation with jurisdictional representatives and previous participants in AIPM programs, identified four strategic requirements for future police leadership development:

1. expand programs to ensure executive leaders are exposed to continued contemporary leadership learning and professional exchange;

2. ensure leadership studies are contextualised within the policing and broader emergency service and public safety environment;

3. enable continuous identification of emerging key issues;

4. design forums to provide professional learning for the continuous refinement of current programs with a focus on ethics, accountability, influencing and partnering.

The Academic Strategy Project also undertook comprehensive environmental scanning on contemporary leadership traits, both related to, and not directly related to, policing. It found that the 21st century is expected to be a period of discontinuous change requiring flexibility, efficiency, vision, creativity and intuition across all ranks and functions. Due to emerging trends in policing, adoption of the transformational leadership style will provide the necessary flexibility to deal with the increasingly networked, independent, and culturally diverse police force (Negus 2002). Transformational leadership is a process in which leaders take actions that seek to increase 'follower awareness' of what is important and right, to raise motivational maturity and to move followers beyond self interest by adopting organisational goals and developing a sense of organisational purpose.

In a context of rapid change, transformational leadership appears to be an approach that can succeed in vague and indistinct times. This leadership style, due to its emphasis on relationships, is aimed at building teams with common goals. However, we should recognise that while transformational leadership is a desired style for 21st century policing, it is not yet fully developed within the profession, but that police agencies and educational institutions are continuing to advance it through a range of development programs.

As part of the Academic Survey Project conducted by the AIPM, detailed interviews and surveys of key stakeholders from each Australian police jurisdiction and from policing overseas were conducted to determine what they, collectively, viewed as future trends and challenges in policing, and their expectations of leadership development in the next ten years to address those challenges. Table 9.1 (opposite) presents the key findings in regard to trends and challenges.

Table 9.2 (page 133) presents the key findings on the leadership development requirements over the next five to ten years, needed to address these trends and challenges.

Australasian and international jurisdictions listed influencing, negotiation skills, having a driving role in community capacity building and effective partnering and networking in multi-agency teams as critical to future successful leadership. The majority of jurisdictions spoke of the increasing politicisation of policing and the need for police to increase their skills in the area of political influence.

The project also undertook detailed web-based research and analysis of global delivery arrangements of institutions comparable to the AIPM. Institutions examined included Centrex (England/UK police leadership college), Tulliallan (Scotland), Federal Bureau of Investigation (US), Canadian Police College (Canada), Oxford College (UK), and Kennedy School of Management, Harvard University (US). In addition, the Senior Police Fellows at the AIPM provided a comprehensive report and analysis of international police institutions they had visited during 2005, based on experiential study, interview and research during their visits arranged under the International Police Leadership Executive Consortium. Only a few institutions provide the full range of leadership development programs from the entry level (Constable) to the Chief Executive level. However, emerging trends in policing indicate that leadership at the entry level will be more important for effective service delivery than has been thought in the past.

Table 9.1: Future trends and challenges facing Australian jurisdictions

Trends	Challenges
Development of leadership role in partnering/relationships with other agencies and community groups	Police leaders will need: • innovative networking and negotiation skills • greater understanding of the cultures and process of other agencies • to be more involved in informing and influencing the political scene through strong working relationships • to meet public expectations of their role of crisis leaders
Increased dependence on knowledge of how other jurisdictions act and operate	Police leaders will need: • increased capacity to adapt to different situations with efficiency and flexibility to deal with: terrorism, international crime, public order policing, emergency and major event management • to respond to increasing pressure for nationalisation of policing in order to address Australia-wide issues
Need for the better management of the business of policing at a high levels, including high level organisational, planning and administration skills	Leaders will need to respond to: • increasing external accountability • greater need for ethical frameworks and values that guide, influence and inspire leadership at both personal and organisational levels • the discretionary role of policing, associated with its power, authority and the ambiguity required in an environment that requires a high level of integrity, transparency and accountability in process, openness and dialogue within and beyond the organisation • increased exposure to major events with diminished resources, which will require more effective planning required

Source: AIPM 2006a

The main conclusions from the Academic Survey Project were:

- In comparison to other leadership development institutions, Australasian Police Services offer a narrow range of product, but to a broad and diverse range of stakeholders.
- Australian police development programs are generally competitive on a cost basis and avoid the commercialism factor of many international programs.
- A generation of new recruits in their late 20s, most with at least one degree and many with postgraduate degrees, have high career expectations and are highly ambitious, and so provide an important pool of talent ready to make an impact.
- Few institutions provide accelerated development programs, yet it is generally acknowledged that accelerated programs address the reality of modern police recruitment and arguably assist in retention of talented staff.
- All institutions examined offer programs for middle managers and those recently appointed to senior and executive levels. Some institutions offer a broader range of programs for candidates to select the educational elements that suit their needs.

All institutions appear conscious of the time constraints on leaders at the senior and executive levels and so the trend is to reduce the length of residential programs in favour of shorter programs with multiple residential components.

The review reported a number of themes:

- Leadership development is expensive in money and time.
- No leadership development program suits everyone.
- Leadership development should not be confined to senior management only.
- Leadership development is a whole-of-organisation requirement, especially for those public service organisations dealing with high levels of often conflicting public and government expectations.
- Effective leadership development requires participants continue a journey of individual reflection and change. For most, this journey barely commences within any residential program. Therefore the elements of flexibility, choice, and access become more important within the whole developmental process.
- Establishing the foundations of leadership development at earlier career levels is arguably more cost effective than commencing the process at the middle-management or executive level when an individual's style of leadership has been shaped.

On-site diagnostic work, team building and situation leadership programs are part of the trend away from long formal leadership development programs, and towards leadership development strategies that occur at or are aligned to the workplace and involve tangible benefits.

Table 9.2: Leadership development requirements in 5-10 years

Issue	Development Requirements
Safety and Security	• Policing must be contextualised in the political/social/ economic/security environment • Enhance critical event and incident management skills • Understand Australian and New Zealand governments' positions on external issues and matters relating to the region • Increase greater awareness of wider disciplines and greater connectivity with other criminal justice agencies • Increase global awareness and ability to swiftly deploy policing services to the diverse community needs
People Management	• Promote the need for supportive, values-driven leadership with dynamic and shifting patterns in human resource management • Improve diversity management, problem solving and analysis skills • Improve ability to be supportive of considered risk taking encourage entrepreneurial thinking • Enhance strategic capability – both capability and action by individuals • Create more adaptable police leaders, enhance their ability to maximise diminishing resources
Organisational Capacity Building	• Provide tertiary qualifications specific to policing and building on police leadership • Ensure organisations have the skills and capacity to ignite and drive areas across other national jurisdictions and our region • Increase influencing skills and negotiation levels at senior strategic levels, to take up the driving role in community capacity building • Build greater flexibility that looks at business approaches and differently • Enhance IT knowledge and understanding • Enhance the ability to be more attuned both nationally and internationally to policing trends

Source: AIPM 2006a

As David Garbutt, the former Scottish Police College director and member of the UK Executive Training Group notes, the crucial aspect of leadership development is that it must be delivered in a contextual framework of policing 'wrapped around the operational setting of policing' (Garbutt 2005). The research on overseas programs also revealed that senior executive level programs are more frequently conducted than in Australasian policing, which has a relative dearth of programs or opportunities at this level. Australasian officers can progress from Inspector to Commissioner without exposure to higher-policing-focused learning. In comparison, Centrex in England conduct a Chief Police Officer Development Program; the Royal Canadian Mounted Police (RCMP) conducts Senior Police Executive Workshops and the Irish *Garda* and Scottish Police College are currently developing Senior Executive Leadership Programs. It is suggested that newly appointed senior executive personnel should be exposed to policing professionals at a similar level to establish networks, liaison and support.

Finally, the research showed that integrity, ethics and accountability are critical elements in leadership programs. While the Australasian police provide good coverage of these elements, it is forecast that further examination of the manner, methods and opportunities for presenting these elements will be required to ensure police leadership is anchored within a solid ethical framework.

Not all overseas institutions award formal qualifications. Most rely upon the reputation of the institution and the program itself to provide recognition to the participant. The majority of institutions provide ongoing coaching and mentoring programs, directed mainly at leaders at the executive level. Several overseas police institutions have recently collaborated with universities to provide a Policing Masters – in the case of the Canadian Police College this is a Police MBA (offered in conjunction with Athabascau University). These programs have been designed to redirect police into tertiary studies directly related to policing activities and functions, and to recognise policing as a profession. Interestingly, the majority of international jurisdictions surveyed questioned the benefit of higher education that is unrelated to policing. Superintendent Francois Bidal, the Canadian Police College indicated that 'the RCMP foresaw the need for advanced tertiary study directly related to policing' (Pierce 2005b, p 2). While acknowledging the value of broad tertiary studies, Superintendent Bidal also stated 'the RCMP view was to add to the profession of policing and place policing as the critical aspect for their tertiary leadership studies'.

The AIPM has already articulated its current programs to higher education. The Police Management Development Program articulates to a Graduate Certificate and the Police Executive Leadership Program articulates to a Graduate Diploma, either through the accredited courses offered by the AIPM or through external universities. It is apparent there will be greater demand for awarding of a Masters Level program directly related to policing disciplines. Police should also consider academic Doctorates directly aligned to policing that further stretch and define the profession of policing. The AIPM has the advantage of its multi-jurisdictional format to enhance participant connections, as well as an understanding and recognition of the interdependencies between police agencies and between police and other government agencies. The AIPM also enables development of individual and collective capabilities to create shared meaning, to engage in inter-dependant work and to enact tasks of engaged, collaborative leadership beyond traditional boundaries.

Preparing for the changing leadership environment

A key function of the Australasian jurisdictions is to assist in making their officers effective in a range of leadership functions and processes. However, leadership development undertaken within jurisdictions cannot meet the challenges for future police, public safety and emergency service leaders without a critical understanding of the future environment. In preparing for the changing police leadership environment, a number of issues require consideration, including new social and leadership models; the increased need for international and multi-agency partnerships; an increase in community and workplace diversity; and new directions of higher education for police. Also requiring consideration are the new models of workplace engagement which have resulted in less distinction between roles, in personnel with narrower experiences because they remain in one stream of work, and increased demands of accountability. In discussing workplace engagement Woodruffe (2006) believes organisations must be attuned to the steps that make employees want to give their best to their work. His theories of employee engagement include increased education and training, potential for advancement, being treated civilly and with respect, supportive feedback and the opportunity to work on challenging tasks. Critically, he argues that engaging the more talented employees is the organisational challenge of the future. He supports the introduction and maintenance of a culture of talent retention with an increase in coaching and people management skills.

In examining the wealth of leadership development material available, Goldsmith and Walt (2005) have identified five key competencies needed for the 21st century leader, which can be equally applied to policing. These competencies are:

1. *Thinking globally*

In a world where financial crisis occurring in one country can dramatically influence the world, future leaders must understand the legal, political and economic implications of globalisation.

2. *Appreciating cultural diversity*

Future leaders will have to understand the attitudes, ideals and values of different cultures. As globalisation rapidly increases, joint ventures with different nationalities will increase. Leaders who can effectively understand, appreciate and motivate colleagues from different cultures are a major resource in any organisation.

3.   Technological know-how

Technological knowledge includes technological entrepreneurship where the leader will understand the use of technology in the organisation, and recruit, develop, and maintain a network of technologically sound professionals.

4.   Partnership building

Building partnerships is becoming more necessary as globalisation increases. As organised crime is becoming multi-national, anti-crime agencies must build trusting relations. Partnerships with private sector agencies are increasingly important.

5.   Sharing leadership

Leadership has changed from the old military philosophy to a more democratic style. Future leaders will rely on suggestions from their subordinates to increase productivity. This will also bring loyalty and a feeling of trust between managers and their staff.

The Academic Strategy Project (AIPM 2006a) identified that Australasian jurisdictions identify with these key competencies and in most cases are actively encouraging and modelling them in their leadership development programs. The difficulty appears to be the holistic application of these competencies and in particular the notion of shared leadership which has distinctively different levels of application across the jurisdictions.

Conclusion

This chapter has provided a synopsis of Australasian jurisdictional leadership requirements and comparative analysis of international police leadership education.

As leadership theory, education and practice continues to evolve, Australasian police are willingly seeking to undertake contemporary leadership education. The future strategic leadership education requirements of Australasian police include broadening of programs to ensure senior police leaders are exposed to further contemporary leadership learning and professional exchange; ensuring leadership studies are contextualised within the policing environment; identification of emerging key issues and the design of forums to provide for professional learning and exchange; and the refinement of current programs in topics of ethics and accountability, influencing and partnering.

Police leadership models have evolved from one of the charismatic and visionary leader at the head of an organisation, to the contemporary model of an enabling, engaging leader who values others and their input, at all levels of the organisation.

10

Leading for Integrity and Effective Accountability: A Challenge from Within

Colleen Lewis[1]

Evidence from commissions of inquiry in Australia and beyond clearly illus-trate that for many years corrupt, deceitful and brutal behaviour has been a feature of many police forces (Knapp 1972; Fitzgerald 1989; Mollen 1994; Wood 1997; Patten 1999; Kennedy 2004). The 'blue curtain of silence' made even stronger by the insular, 'them against us' attitude of police officers, coupled with the para-military nature of police organisations, and under-resourced, poorly designed and inappropriately staffed internal accounta-bility units led to structures, processes and a culture that demanded reform. But effective reform requires more than a change in behaviour by rank and file police. It also requires those in leadership positions to change their beha-viour, for the commission of inquiry referred to above also identified authoritarian, 'command and control', inward-looking leadership as contri-buting to the systemic nature of police malfeasance and the failure of pre-vious reform programs.

A definition of the term leadership/leader is required in context of this chapter. This is necessary because much has been written about the role, functions and attitudes of leaders vs managers (Casey and Mitchell, in this volume). While the debate is complex, far ranging and unresolved, it centres around whether leading and managing are two distinct roles and functions, which should be undertaken by different people: leaders and managers. This chapter is not about unpacking those debates. It adopts the position taken by John Kotter, a distinguished professor and author of several books on the subject, who argues that 'leadership and management are two distinctive and complementary systems of actions' (1990, p 103), 'management is about

---

1   The author would like to express her gratitude to Mr Glenn Ross and Dr David Baker for reading the penultimate draft of this chapter and for their valued suggestions.

coping with complexity ... leadership, by contrast, is about coping with change' (p 104).

The chapter explores the reaction of police leaders to change in the context of community demands for more effective accountability structures and processes. It argues that such demands pose particular challenges for police leaders as they require those in leadership positions (defined in this chapter as commissioned officer rank, inspector and above) to critically evaluate their response to externally generated reform and the message this conveys to rank and file police. The chapter draws primarily on Australian examples, in particular Queensland, New South Wales and Western Australia. These three police services[2] have been chosen because they are the only police organisations in Australia to be subjected to the forensic investigation of an independent, external commission of inquiry or royal commission in the past 20 years. (When used in a generic sense in this chapter, the term 'commission of inquiry' will include royal commission). As such, their culture, the effectiveness of accountability structures and processes and the attitude, actions and influence of their leaders have been independently scrutinised and evaluated. While Australian examples are cited the arguments raised are relevant to police services in democratic societies throughout the world.

Legacies

Institutional change does not take place on a blank canvas nor does it occur in a vacuum. The history of an organisation, its values and predominant culture are reflected in its rules, processes and daily routines (Fleming 2003; Schein 1999) and in its attitude to change. The para-military origins of policing coupled with the inordinately strong value placed on loyalty to fellow officers, and the insular nature of police organisations, have bred institutions that are resistant to change.

For much of their history Australian police services have adopted Peel's 1829 model of 'modern policing', which combines civilian police officers with 'a militaristic managerial philosophy and organisational design' (Murray 2002, p 3). Peel's legacy manifested itself in rigid hierarchical structures, inward-looking internal decision-making processes, an authoritative, 'command and control' leadership style and promotion by seniority accompanied by strong resistance to lateral entry or 'inter-service mobility' at senior levels (Etter & Palmer 1995, pp 281-283). The lack of exposure to different public and private sector strategies that has accompanied the isolationist approach to policing resulted in what ex-Commissioner of the Australian Federal Police, Mick Palmer described as 'much dead wood' at the top (Palmer 1994, p 85). For many years those in senior leadership positions, with some exceptions, focused on managing the status quo, not on leading innovative, meaningful reform (Etter 1995, p 283).

---

2   When the word 'service' is used, it also refers to police organisations that use the term 'force' to describe their organisation.

Leadership focus, as Schein (1985, p 225) points out, can facilitate or frustrate reform. For what leaders 'pay attention to, measure and control'; their 'reactions to critical incidents and organisational crises'; the examples they set; and how they determine and allocate 'rewards' reinforces organisational culture. The 'myopic, ethnocentric and defensive views' (Etter 1995, p 282) exhibited by those who have led police organisations in Australia, served to strengthen negative aspects of police culture by reinforcing the 'them against us' mentality and 'blue curtain of silence', both common features of police services throughout the world (Fitzgerald 1989; Wood 1997; Kennedy 2004). Chan (1999, p 126), drawing on examples from the New York Mollen Commission Report, comes to the same conclusion as Schein. She also points out how the attitude and actions of leaders 'are primarily responsible for contributing to the development and reinforcement of negative aspects of police culture'.

The following evidence of reform failure suggests that effective change not only necessitates a change in behaviour by rank and file police, it also requires police leaders to re-examine their approach to leadership, including the attitude and processes they employ when responding to external directions for reform.

Reform failure

Commissions of inquiry into Australian police organisations are replete with examples of those in leadership positions acting as competent or incompetent managers, but there is much less evidence of leadership designed to achieve meaningful and positive change. Indeed leaders have paid lip service to reform while continuing to support the status quo. On numerous occasions they have trotted out the discredited 'rotten apple' theory to explain misconduct, doggedly maintained an adversarial, punitive disciplinary system which relied on complaints to trigger action (Murray 2002), and clung to the traditional command and control, authoritarian leadership style. Often their response to reform has been characterised by 'glossy brochures' and motherhood statements which were not supported by appropriate action. This approach has repeatedly failed to deliver effective accountability or organisational values which have integrity at their core.

Commissions of inquiry into Australian police organisations have overwhelmingly exposed similar problems: police giving false evidence to courts, commissions and boards of inquiry; illegal assaults on citizens; police conspiring with other police to suppress evidence; unlawfully detaining and arresting people; and various forms of corruption ranging from accepting bribes for non-enforcement of the law to (more recently) active, illegal involvement in the drug trade (Beach Inquiry 1978; Lucas Inquiry 1977; Fitzgerald Inquiry 1989; Wood Royal Commission 1997 and Kennedy Royal Commission 2004). Inquiries also linked incompetent senior leadership to the failure to prevent corruption, misconduct and brutality within police organisations.

The 1976 Report of the Committee of Inquiry into the Enforcement of Criminal Law in Queensland (the Lucas Inquiry) was not established to examine allegations of corruption and malpractice. It was concerned with the enforcement of criminal law and the gathering of evidence by police officers. Nevertheless, the report was scathing about the extent of verballing in the Queensland Police Force. The practice was found to be so pervasive that it could not have occurred without the explicit or tacit support of those in leadership positions.

The 1978 Report of the Board of Inquiry into Allegations Against Members of the Victorian Police Force (the Beach Inquiry) documented evidence of 'unbridled sadism' which was not properly investigated by an inspector of police (p 49). The inspector's investigation was described in the report as a 'white wash' (p 106).

In one jurisdiction corruption was traced to the most senior leadership position. The 1989 Report of the Commission of Inquiry into Possible Illegal Activities and Associated Police Misconduct (The Fitzgerald Inquiry 1989) exposed the devastating effect corrupt leadership can have on the ethical wellbeing of a police force. Commissioner Terence Lewis was Commissioner of the Queensland Police Force from 1976 to 1987. His rapid promotion from inspector to commissioner was virtually unprecedented in Australian police history, as was the prison sentence he eventually received for corruption.[3] Lewis's legacy to the Queensland Police Force was an organisation 'debilitated by misconduct, inefficiency, incompetence and deficient leadership' (Fitzgerald 1989, p 200).

The Royal Commission into the New South Wales Police Force (Wood 1997) also exposed entrenched and systemic corruption within the service. Reasons for it are outlined in Volume One, Chapter 6 of the inquiry's report (Wood 1997, pp 189-203) and include:

- the code of silence;
- institutional pressure to protect the reputation of the service;
- the rigid nature of the disciplinary system;
- the punishment of internal informers;
- a plethora of regulations and instructions designed to apportion blame rather than change problematic behaviour;
- a management strategy driven by arrest rates which led to process corruption;
- institutional tolerance of brutality;
- the unnecessary retention of central decision-making; and
- a self-inflicted isolation of the service from outside ideas and influences.

---

3   For a more detailed account of Lewis's extraordinary promotion to Commissioner of Police see Phil Dickie (1989, pp 45-48) and Colleen Lewis (1999, pp 101-106).

Process corruption relates to a disregard for due process through the adoption of illegal and unethical means to achieve ends such as arrests, confessions and convictions.[4]

Explaining why the extent of systemic corruption had not been revealed previously, Wood (1997, p 193) cited, among other things, the institutionalised pressure to protect the reputation of the Service, which extended to 'denial of the obvious' by those in leadership positions. As he explained:

> The kind of defensive mentality was an inevitable recipe for collapse of command responsibility for the maintenance of integrity and for reinforcement of a 'them and us' attitude. It sent a very powerful message to the rank not only that the rhetoric to which they were exposed was empty, but that the opposite was what was truly expected (p 194).

The failure of leaders to deal with process corruption; the failure of senior command to match the integrity and accountability rhetoric with actions; and inadequate training of leaders in the identification of corruption risks also contributed to the institutional corruption uncovered by Wood.

The most recent commission of inquiry into policing in Australia, the Royal Commission into whether there has been Corrupt or Criminal Conduct by any Western Australian Police Officer (The Kennedy Royal Commission 2004) identified similar problems to those uncovered by Fitzgerald and Wood. The failure of leaders to ensure adequate and in some instances any supervision over detectives, was again noted as a particular problem, as was the link between deficient leadership and negative aspects of the police culture (Kennedy 2004, p 161).

In all three inquiries (Fitzgerald 1989, Wood 1987 and Kennedy 2004), police-controlled internal investigations units, theoretically established to improve accountability, came in for particular criticism.

Internal investigation units

Queensland

The Queensland Police Force's Internal Investigations Section (IIS), established by then Commissioner Lewis to address allegations of police misconduct was described by Fitzgerald (1989, p 181) as:

> a disastrous failure, inept, inefficient and grossly biased in favour of police officers. Over the years, some of the police officers by whom it has been staffed have been totally unsuitable for a wide variety of reasons, including personal involvement in corruption and other misconduct, prior involvement in criminal charges, and other unsuitable activities in the course of their career.

---

4   For a more detailed account of process corruption see the *Final Report of the Royal Commission into the New South Wales Police Service, 1997*, Volume One, Corruption, pp 36-38 (Wood 1997).

Some of the procedures adopted by the IIS were 'amazing' and included officers suspected of misconduct being given access to material before being interrogated. Often a police officer only had to deny involvement in mis-conduct or corrupt behaviour to be cleared of alleged misconduct. On the rare occasion when a departmental charge was laid (there was a 2 per cent substantiation rate from IIS investigations) the punishment overwhelmingly involved counselling, a caution, a reprimand or a reminder of their responsi-bilities as a police officer. Penalties, if applied, were in Fitzgerald's words 'ludicrous' (1989, p 81).

Lewis's corrupt conduct may explain in part the abject failure of the Internal Investigation Section. However, many of the problems uncovered by Fitzgerald were also found in police internal investigation units in New South Wales and Western Australia, yet in neither of these States was there any suggestion of corruption in the office of commissioner of police. The problems of police investigating their own is endemic to police services across the world, and are not confined to those that experience corruption at the top.

New South Wales

The Wood Royal Commission into the NSW Police Service revealed defi-ciencies in the internal investigation unit including its reactive, punitive ap-proach to misconduct and the inordinate amount of time taken to deal with minor matters. Investigations against police officers were not 'impartial' and investigations usually started from the premise that officers under investi-gation were innocent (Wood 1997, p 201). There was also a lack of security surrounding internal corruption investigations 'with information and war-nings being promptly passed on to police under investigation' (1996, p 201). Other examples of ineffective investigative techniques included 'the issue of directive memoranda calling for an explanation in writing which allowed groups of police under investigation to be forewarned of the inquiry, and to manufacture a watertight defence in collaboration' and of investigations which 'began and ended with the officer's denial of the allegations' (1996, p 201).

The result of such biased and deficient investigations was 'a general lack of trust on the part of potential informants (both internal and external) in the confidentiality of any information provided, and consequently in their own safety' (Wood 1997, p 201).

Western Australia

The Kennedy Report devoted a chapter to internal investigations. It began by saying that:

> The evidence led in nearly every segment of the hearings of the Royal Commission revealed a failure on the part of the Internal Affairs Unit ('IAU') of the Western Australia Police Service ('WAPS') to adequately

deal with allegations of corrupt conduct of officers under investigation (Kennedy 2004, p 235).

In Western Australia, a supported internal witness program – a 'Blueline' reporting system that provided a mechanism for officers to anonymously report suspected serious corruption to the Standards Development Unit; and a code of conduct for Western Australian Police officers, which made it the duty of officers to report possible corruption or unethical behaviour – failed to deliver effective accountability. This is not surprising given that police who reported corruption did not receive support including from those in senior leadership positions (Kennedy 2004, pp 254-270).

Police leaders who fail to support those who report corruption send a strong message to rank and file police: that accountability is not an organisational priority. The message is compounded when internal investigation units are widely known to be under-resourced. In New South Wales, Wood pointed out how the inadequately resourced Professional Responsibility Command contributed to institutionalised corruption. Kennedy in Western Australia noted that 'when asked to account for the failure of IAU (Internal Affairs Unit) to deal with officers whose conduct warranted investigation, a common explanation proffered was a lack of resources' (Kennedy 2004, p 235). While making the point that resources alone do not explain the ineffectiveness of the Unit, Kennedy did acknowledge that 'the claim seems to have some substance' (Kennedy 2004, p 235).

A defensive attitude by senior police to allegations of serious police misconduct and poor leadership in relation to complaints against police over many years resulted in the public not trusting police organisations and their leaders to deal openly, honestly and appropriately with alleged severe misconduct, brutality and corruption. Maguire (1991) argues that this lack of trust may well be permanent.

External, independent oversight

The inability of police organisations to effectively police the police led to the establishment of external, independent oversight agencies in all Australian States and in relation to the federal police. These agencies are becoming a feature of police accountability systems throughout the western world.

A criticism of these independent agencies is that responsibility for police behaviour is removed from police organisations and hence from police leaders (Freckelton 1991). This criticism is problematic as oversight bodies do not remove responsibility, rather they act as a check and balance on the effectiveness of the complaints process. All but the most serious complaints are returned to the police to investigate with the oversight body, if it wishes, maintaining a monitoring, review and/or auditing role over police investigations.

Independent oversight bodies are increasingly advocating a non-punitive approach for less serious misconduct matters, and in some instances for a broader managerial resolution of complaints. As Ede and Barnes (2002, p 129) explain, managerial resolution:

> asks managers and supervisors to take responsibility for staff perfor-
> mance, rather than assuming that responsibility for complaint resolution
> lies solely with an internal investigation unit or an external agency.

If this method is introduced an auditing system needs to be implemented, to ensure that officers who are the subject of repeat managerial
resolutions, are identified early so that steps can be taken to prevent a reoc-
currence of the behaviour that led to the need for managerial determinations.

Gloomy picture?

The above findings from the Kennedy report, the most recent commission of
inquiry into Australian police services, which span a 20-year-period, paint a
gloomy picture of police organisations, their internal investigation units and
the way in which they have been led for many years. They also suggest that
there has been little change in police organisations and police accountability
structures and processes. But that is not the case as many reforms have been
introduced into police services over the past two decades, including:

- lateral recruitment for senior leadership positions;
- flatter management structures;
- devolution of authority;
- promotion by merit;
- mandatory reporting of suspected misconduct;
- enforceable codes of conduct; and
- better-resourced internal investigation units.

As mentioned above, there has also been external change in relation to
police complaints which are now monitored, reviewed and/or investigated
by an external, independent agency.

These changes, which reflect in part New Public Management reforms
introduced into most public sector organisations in the 1970s and 1980s, may
have improved efficiency but it seems they have not greatly improved
accountability and integrity levels in Australian police services.

New public sector management practices for police

In an effort to try to change destructive elements of the police culture,
improve police leadership and operational performance, achieve efficiencies,
and expose police organisations to outside management practices, commissions of inquiry recommended, inter alia, the introduction of new public sector management techniques (Bayley 1994; Wood 1997; Fleming & Lafferty

2000).[5] Despite initial scepticism to 'new managerialism', which includes the requirement that leaders' performance be measured through key performance indicators, new public sector management is now a feature of Australian police organisations, including those referred to in this chapter.

Queensland

Fitzgerald identified the need for radical change in the Queensland Police Service. His reform program virtually turned the Service on its head, shook out draconian rules, regulations and routines and exposed the organisation to new management practices designed in part to improve integrity and accountability. Crucial to the successful implementation of the reform program was leadership. Fitzgerald made it clear that 'a new influential leadership must be established which is committed to excellent ethical performance' (1989, p 307). But he was careful not to confine leadership to the police. His model deliberately guarded against leaders reverting to an insular, reactive, defensive leadership style once the Inquiry was perceived as yesterday's news. Fitzgerald did this by giving ongoing carriage of the reform program to an external agency: the Criminal Justice Commission (now the Crime and Misconduct Commission). This, in effect, exposes the Queensland Police Service, including its leaders, to continual, independent external influence and oversight (Fleming & Lewis 2002). Fitzgerald took the added precaution of also making the appointment of Commissioner of Police subject to the approval of the independent Criminal Justice Commission (1989, p 387).

New South Wales

Unlike the Fitzgerald Inquiry, the Wood Royal Commission into the New South Wales Police Service was established after new public sector management techniques had been introduced into the NSW Police Service. But it appears that they did not generate meaningful, longer term change in leadership style or improve accountability.

There was a genuine attempt to reform the NSW Police Service during the 1980s which was led by Commissioner John Avery. It was largely based on the principles detailed in his book *Police Force or Service?* (Avery 1981), many of which were to become recommendations in the Lusher Report (1981). However after Avery resigned from the NSW Police Service, it began to demonstrate what Dixon (1999b, p 2) describes as a 'complacent face' accompanied by an air of 'self confidence'. He notes how the Service submitted an application for an Australian Quality Award which self-reported on what it described as its 10-year program to develop 'professional, accountable, responsible and innovative police officers'. Evidence from the Wood Royal Commission suggests that the goals of the program were not

---

5   See Appendix 31 of Volume III of the Final Report of the Wood Royal Commission for examples of these external management practices.

realised. While the Inquiry did reveal continued innovation, it often related to the corrupt practices of some police.

After Avery resigned, the new police commissioner, Tony Lauer, exhibited a more traditional, inward-looking leadership style. In the lead-up to the Wood Royal Commission, he responded to allegations of institutional corruption as a 'figment of the political imagination' (ABC 1996) and in evidence to the Inquiry, Lauer proclaimed that institutionalised corruption did not exist. Whilst not implicated in any corruption himself, Lauer's blinkered attitude to the problems exposed at the Commission of Inquiry led to his resignation (Kennedy 2004, p 42).

Western Australia

But New South Wales is not the only Australian police service to experience corruption, brutality and leadership problems after the introduction of new public sector management. Nearly 10 years before the establishment of the Kennedy Royal Commission in Western Australia, then Commissioner Brian Bull (1985-1994), in consultation with the Cabinet Subcommittee for Public Sector Reform, engaged an independent, external consulting firm to conduct a 'scoping review' of Western Australia Police (WAPol) with a view to providing a blueprint for reform. The report identified several problems within the Service including strong central control of decision-making, and an emphasis on a command and control, autocratic leadership style. The report formed the basis for the Delta Reform Program, implemented by Commissioner Robert Falconer (1994-1999) and the recipient of the Western Australian Premier's Award for Excellence in the Change Management Category. It was heralded as the 'engine of change that will take the Service from a centrally driven, functionally aligned and inward looking agency to a more accountable, open Service with local area management' (Premier's award for Change Management, 1996).[6]

Despite winning an award for effective change management it seems that reform may have been cosmetic, as evidence at the Kennedy Royal Commission suggests that it did little to inspire integrity, accountability and openness within WAPol.

While the Royal Commission was in progress, WAPol hired consultants to undertake a review of the award winning Delta Reform Program. The Bogan and Hicks report (2002), *Western Australia Police Service Qualitative and Strategic Reform – the Way Ahead*, identified five key strategies for overcoming what they called 'corporacy' and 'traction' deficiencies. Corporacy is defined as 'jointly developing and reliably practising a consistent set of values, plans and activities throughout the Service, and building on them through a strong and growing network of alliances'. Traction is defined as the practice of following through agreed plans and directions, ensuring that they are reliably put in place, with clear accountabilities and timelines, and that they

6   See <http://premiersawards.dpc.wa.gov.au>.

continue to be monitored and improved upon' (Bogan & Hicks cited in Kennedy 2004, p 26). The strategies were:

- reconfiguring the existing Police Service Command as a Police Strategic Executive;
- the establishment of a Police Advisory Council;
- an intensified emphasis on senior levels within the Service;
- an enhanced role for middle managers; and
- prioritising the reform of systems that were currently hampering outcomes delivery (Kennedy 2002, p 27).

The Kennedy Royal Commission accepted the Bogan and Hicks review as an accurate assessment of the situation within the Police Service and incorporated their recommendations into the commission's report. Western Australia has introduced many of the reforms that featured in the Queensland and New South Wales police reform program, but it is too early to evaluate if they have achieved their aims.

Early warning systems: an integrity tool for leaders

Integrity is an important aspect of the Australasian Police Ministers' Council strategy for 2005-2008, which is based on four 'Directions', with Direction 3 being 'Professionalism and Accountability'. This Direction aims to enhance 'individual and organisational integrity and the proper exercise of authority and discretion' (Australian Police Ministers' Council 2005, p 12). The ethical health and integrity of a police organisation is also a key performance indicator for police leaders. It is arguably one of the most difficult goals facing commissioners and other senior police. It can be described as the 'thorny' issue of leadership, for a successful outcome requires those who lead (what is still for many a para-military organisation with a long history of command and control leadership) to be open, transparent, consultative and proactive when dealing with integrity-related issues.

Use of early warning systems can provide a powerful proactive tool for leaders when attempting to implement the Police Ministers' Council Direction 3 and achieve one of their key performance indicators. Used in conjunction with other accountability and integrity policies, they can send a strong message to rank and file police that repeat misconduct will not be tolerated.

Analysis of civil litigations, reports of rule violations, incident reports emanating from inappropriate use of force incidents, managerial resolutions and other complaints against police data can provide police leaders with an early warning system that helps to identify officers who demonstrate ongoing behavioural problems. Leaders can then intervene before the conduct escalates into a more serious problem which results in a major scandal, a crisis between police and the community and/or civil action (Walker, Alpert & Kenney 2000, p 133; Bassett & Premolar 2002, p 132).

Early warning systems not only help leaders to keep those they are responsible for supervising accountable for their actions, they also have the potential to have a positive influence on a police organisation and its culture. Leaders who act quickly on the information provided by early warning systems convey a strong message that misconduct is being regularly monitored and that continued misconduct will not be ignored.

To be effective, indicators from early warning systems must be contextualised, as the type of work a police officer is assigned to (traffic duties as opposed to lecturing at the academy) can affect the number of complaints received. Bassett and Prenzler (2001, p 135) point out, that an appreciation of 'the different task environments needs to be built into the early warning system,' as does the nature of a complaint. Tallying up raw numbers only indicates the number of complaints or recorded incidents, not the severity of the complaint/incident (Bassett & Prenzler 2001, p 137).

Early warning systems have other limitations. They are not particularly effective in relation to identifying corruption which involves payment for non-enforcement of the law. Because this form of corruption is a secretive and consensual process, it is not usually the subject of a complaint. Indeed many police officers identified in various royal commissions as corrupt had never been the subject of a complaint. Some had received police awards and been considered highly effective investigators.

It is not being suggested that early warning systems are a panacea for police misconduct, brutality and corruption, but they can be an effective instrument for leaders who are serious about improving institutional integrity and accountability. The failure to use complaints data for early remedial intervention can, as the Wood Royal Commission found, lead to institutionalised corruption and entrenched integrity problems.

Conclusion

Commissions of inquiry in Australia and beyond demonstrate the degree to which systematic and serious misconduct coupled with deficient leadership have undermined the ethical health of police organisations. Part of the reason leadership has been found deficient relates to what Murray (2002, p 8) claims is a misunderstanding that lingers within policing in relation to the terms 'command' and 'leadership'. He argues that too often the terms are used interchangeably 'as if there is no difference'. While acknowledging that both styles can be required in policing, Murray, a former Deputy Commissioner of the Australian Federal Police, expresses concern about what he sees is a 'bias' toward the traditional command and control approach, which manifests itself in autocratic leadership being seen as 'the norm rather than the exception'.

Murray (2002) compares the traditional policing method of command and control with a contemporary model to which police services have been directed by various commissions of inquiry (Table 10.1, opposite):

Table 10.1: Traditional and Contemporary Models of Policing

Traditional	Contemporary
• Policing as a craft/trade	• Policing as a profession
• Authoritarian approach to policing	• Problem solving
• Quasi military management style	• Democratic management style
• Emphasis on physical attributes	• Emphasis on intelligence
• Insular and defensive culture	• Open and consultative culture

Source: Adapted from Murray 2002

New public sector management techniques, which include lateral recruitment for senior leadership positions, promotion based on merit, flatter management structures, mandatory reporting of suspected misconduct, enforceable codes of conduct, better-resourced internal investigation units, external independent oversight of complaints against police and key performance indicators for police leaders, are necessary to shift a police organisation along the continuum, from traditional to contemporary police services. But these reforms have not proved sufficient to deliver integrity and effective accountability. Achievement of these goals requires those in leadership positions to make the transition from manager of a traditional police force to leader of a contemporary police service. While leaders and the organisations they lead are heading in the right direction they should keep in mind one of the most important findings from the Mollen Inquiry into the New York Police Department (Mollen, 1994, p 1), that corruption and misconduct flourishes on secrecy and the encouragement of unquestioning loyalty to the police organisation. It is perpetuated and becomes entrenched when leaders 'fear the consequences of a corruption scandal more than corruption itself'.

11

POLICE OVERSIGHT: HELP OR HINDRANCE?

Glenn Ross

Anti-corruption agencies have a ... crucial weakness: the risk of cultural contamination. Over time, a 'watchdog' becomes familiar with those it guards and with whom it forms relationships, and may come to accommodate the values and practices of those it oversees (Rayner 2005).

In a democratic country such as Australia, police have a complex accountability structure that involves government, parliament, the courts, ombudsmen, academics, media, individuals who have been adversely affected, the community, and, as is the subject of this chapter, external civilian oversight agencies.

Given the propensity for corruption in the high-risk occupation of policing, there is little argument by non-police about the need for effective accountability mechanisms and oversight of the operations of police (Stone & Bobb 2002). There continues, however, to be debate over the effectiveness of various oversight models (Lewis 1999) and of the nature of the relationship between those who oversee and those who are over sighted. This is because police oversight agencies can take a number of forms. For example, they can perform in a reactive manner by simply monitoring the way in which complaints are managed by police – an Ombudsman-type model – or they can be more proactive by conducting their own investigations into police misconduct, such as the Police Integrity Commission in NSW. Additionally, they can also be proactive by undertaking research with police to understand the nature of a problem and how to prevent it from reoccurring. The Crime and Misconduct Commission in Queensland does this.

This chapter examines oversight agencies and other aspects of police accountability. Accountability is an interesting term in that, similar to the term democracy, it is capable of having different meanings for different people. Frequently, however, it is thought of and used in conjunction with terms such as ethical behaviour; the state of being accountable; answerability, liability to be called on to render an account; the acceptance of responsibility when untoward events occur; traceability of actions performed; and the obligation to bear the consequences for failure to perform as expected. A further major role for accountability is in ensuring that the institutions of government maintain the confidence of the citizens over whom they exercise authority.

The reason for the considerable interest in police accountability derives from the extensive powers that police have available to them and the capacity they have to use these powers in a way that impacts on the normal rights of citizens. This refers of course to the powers of arrest, search, seizure, etc and also to the capacity that these actions have to damage the reputations of citizens and deprive them of their freedom, no matter how unintended. There have been instances where persons have been able to control or influence police services in such a way as to make improper use of police powers. One need look no further than the Bjelke-Petersen government in Queensland for a lesson on how police powers can be misused (Prasser, Wear & Nethercote 1992; Hede, Prasser & Neylan 1992; see Lewis in this volume).

Interestingly, in exercising their powers and accountabilities, police differ from many other organisations in that, for most organisations power and authority is held at the top and delegated down, whereas each individual police officer exercises their own original powers and authority by virtue of the office of 'constable' and is personally accountable for their own actions (see *Enver v R* (1906)).[1] Hence, a police officer cannot be ordered to arrest someone or otherwise exercise their powers, they must do so on the basis of their own free will.

This ability to exercise their own powers and make decisions as to whether to arrest, whether to caution and whether to proceed with a matter places great responsibility on those who are generally the most junior officers in the police service – those who do 'beat' policing or otherwise interact with the public at street level. A difficulty can arise when officers misuse their powers and authority in a way that has negative consequences for innocent citizens. As a consequence of this capacity to cause harm or detriment, systems have been developed to make police increasingly accountable. Perhaps the greatest influence of this trend towards increased accountability has been from commissions of inquiry conducted within Australia and overseas into the operations and functions of police, and into police corruption. I speak here of the Commissions of Inquiry conducted by Fitzgerald (1989), Wood (1997) and Kennedy (2004), into the police services of Queensland, New South Wales and Western Australia respectively. Arguably the most significant recommendation of these inquiries was the establishment of permanent agencies to carry on their work – in effect, standing commissions of inquiry (Hall 2004, p 264).

---

1   *Enver v The King* (1906) 3 CLR 969.

Integrity and anti-corruption agencies

During the 1980s, the inability of traditional law enforcement bodies, using conventional law enforcement methods, to confront corruption within police services and the public sector lead to the establishment of a number of specialist agencies at the State level in Australia. This was in recognition of the difficulties that arise when police are left to police themselves. In Australia, the four most populous States now have such a specialist integrity agency, and the Commonwealth has committed to a similar oversight body:

Table 11.1: Australia's specialist oversight agencies

Queensland	Crime and Misconduct Commission
New South Wales	Police Integrity Commission
Victoria	Office of Police Integrity
Western Australia	Corruption and Crime Commission
Commonwealth	Australian Commission for Law Enforcement Integrity

Source: Author

Crime and Misconduct Commission (Queensland)

The Fitzgerald Commission of Inquiry (1989) into police corruption in Queensland recommended the establishment of a Criminal Justice Commission, which came into being in 1989. In 2002 it merged with the Queensland Crime Commission to form the Crime and Misconduct Commission (CMC). Like the Criminal Justice Commission, the CMC has both a misconduct function in relation to police and the public sector, and an organised crime function. In addition, the CMC also has a prevention function as detailed at s 5(3) of the *Crime and Misconduct Act 2001* (Qld) '[t]o help units of administration to deal effectively, and appropriately, with misconduct by increasing their capacity to do so'.

Police Integrity Commission (NSW)

Similar to the Criminal Justice Commission in Queensland, the Police Integrity Commission (PIC) was borne out of a commission of inquiry into police corruption – in the PIC's case; the recommendation came from the Wood Royal Commission. However, whereas the CJC was established with responsibility for the public sector including politicians, the PIC is confined to matters to do with NSW police.

In New South Wales there was already an existing integrity agency – the Independent Commission Against Corruption (ICAC), established in 1988 to investigate corruption in the public sector, including police. Wood was of the view, however, that, as ICAC had responsibility for the entirety of the public service, it lacked sufficient focus and resources to deal adequately with the specific issue of police corruption – hence the need for a specialist oversight body. The Ombudsman also maintains a police oversight role in NSW to deal with less serious issues than PIC.

Office of Police Integrity (Victoria)

The Office of Police Integrity (OPI) was established in November 2004 by the Victorian Government with a mandate to 'ensure that the highest ethical and professional standards are maintained in the Victoria Police Force and to ensure that Police corruption and serious misconduct is detected, investigated and prevented (OPI 2006)'. Before the establishment of OPI, police misconduct was the province of the Deputy Ombudsman (Police).

The OPI was established in response to a series of gang wars in which over 25 organised crime figures were murdered in 'tit for tat' killings in a short space of years. It was widely reported in the media that these murders were related to aspects of police corruption. The resultant outcry from the community, the media and the Opposition eventually resulted in the government creating a separate body to oversee police – the Office of Police Integrity. Although it is a separate statutory authority, the Director of the Office of Police Integrity is also the Ombudsman, and this has been severely criticised for the potential and real conflicts of interest it creates.

Similar to the PIC in New South Wales, OPI has no jurisdiction over the public sector, other than police, and has no organised crime function or specific role in corruption prevention.

Corruption and Crime Commission (Western Australia)

The Corruption and Crime Commission of Western Australia (CCC) is now over two years old, having been established in 2004 as a major recommendation of the commission of inquiry conducted into police corruption by Geoffrey Kennedy, AO QC (Kennedy 2004). The history of anti-corruption agencies in Western Australia predates the CCC and can be traced to the Official Corruption Commission (OCC), which was established in 1988. The OCC lacked its own investigative capacity and largely served as a 'post box' to receive complaints of corruption and forward them on to other agencies for investigation. Arising from considerable complaints and dissatisfaction about the ineffectiveness of the OCC and of corruption in the police service, in 1996 the OCC morphed into the Anti-Corruption Commission (ACC).

The ACC suffered in that its legislation placed heavy secrecy provisions such that it was unable to inform the public as to what it was doing, and was unable to defend itself in the face of criticism from the Police Union and others. The capabilities of the ACC were further restricted in that its extraordinary powers could only be used during preliminary inquiries and were not available to it during inquiries proper. These inabilities of the ACC were to lead to a serious loss of confidence by the public and as a result was replaced following the recommendation of the Kennedy Royal Commission.

Australian Commission for Law Enforcement Integrity (Commonwealth)

By way of a joint media release, the Attorney-General and the Minister for Justice and Customs announced on 16 June 2004 that the Australian Government was to set up an independent body that would be able to address corruption amongst law enforcement personnel at the national level. It is perhaps not coincidental that this media release on 16 June followed a 'Four Corners' television program on 14 June entitled 'Corruption Inc' wherein Peter Hastings QC commented:

> Well it seems strange that the Federal Government does not have any form of commission which oversights its own activities – whether it be police or public sector corruption. It has an Ombudsman, but as I think most of the States have now realised, the traditional process of the ombudsman is ineffective in terms of identifying and exposing corruption, and it seems to me that the Federal Government would be well served to appoint a commission which would oversight the Australian Federal Police and also provide a forum for public sector corruption investigations as well (ABC 2004).

The Australian Government Budget Papers 2005-2006 record that $9.5 million has been allocated over four years for the establishment of the Australian Commission for Law Enforcement Integrity (ACLEI) which began operations in December 2006. ACLEI is located within the Attorney General's portfolio with responsibilities for prevention, detection and investigation of corruption within the Australian Crime Commission and the Australian Federal Police. It is understood that there will be a potential to extend this coverage by regulation to include other agencies, such as the Australian Protective Services and possibly Australian Customs Services and the Department of Immigration, although this is unlikely to occur anytime soon.[2]

Comparison of models of integrity agencies

From Table 11.2 (opposite), it can be seen that there are broadly two models. Model 1 is that adopted by CMC and CCC whereby police are investigated as part of the overall public sector and where there is a strong focus on corruption prevention. Model 2 is that of PIC OPI and ACLEI where the agency exclusively oversights police activities and have a strong investigatory focus and at best a limited prevention function.

There are considerable benefits from having a diversified and specialist approach to police oversight. However, the quantity of scale argument and

---

2   See <www.aph.gov.au/senate/committee/legcon_ctte/aclei/index.htm> for further information.

Table 11.2: Comparison of police oversight agency functions

	CMC	PIC	OPI	CCC	ACLEI
Misconduct function – police	Yes	Yes	Yes	Yes	Yes
Misconduct function – public sector	Yes	No (1)	No	Yes	No
Prevention function	Yes	No (2)	No (3)	Yes	No
Organised Crime function	Yes	No (4)	No	Yes	No (5)
Independent agency	Yes	Yes	Yes	Yes	No (6)
Employee police from that jurisdiction	Yes	No	Yes	Yes	Yes

(1)   Misconduct in the NSW public sector is overseen by the Independent Commission Against Corruption (ICAC).

(2)   The prevention function for police is a responsibility of ICAC.

(3)   OPI have recognised the need for a corruption prevention function and are currently developing such.

(4)   Organised crime remains the province of the NSW Crime Commission.

(5)   Organised crime investigations are undertaken at Commonwealth level by the Australian Crime Commission.

(6)   ACLEI operates within the structure of the Federal Attorney General's Department.

Source: Author

economic realities saw Western Australia adopt a model similar to that of the Crime and Misconduct Commission in Queensland, which has the anti-corruption and the organised crime efforts located in the one agency. The Crime and Misconduct Commission is a product of the merge in January 2002 of the Criminal Justice Commission and the Queensland Crime Commission. As a result, and similar to the CMC, the Corruption and Crime Commission of WA has three major functions as described in its enabling legislation, the *Corruption and Crime Commission Act 2003* – these being the:

- prevention and education function;
- misconduct function; and
- organised crime function.

Carrying out all of these functions within the one agency has resulted in the CMC, CCC and their respective police agencies having a complex set of multifaceted relationships where at times they work cooperatively and at other times independently.

The New South Wales model makes for an interesting comparison with Queensland and Western Australia in that it has separate agencies undertaking different roles. New South Wales has:

- the NSW Crime Commission – cooperating on organised crime matters;
- the Police Integrity Commission – oversighting and investigating police corruption;

- the Independent Commission Against Corruption – retaining responsibility for corruption prevention and education within Police and for dealing with corruption in the remainder of the NSW public sector; and
- the Ombudsman.

Prevention and education function

It is argued here that it is important that oversight agencies have a prevention and education function that works in a proactive manner to improve integrity and to reduce misconduct. An example of the benefits of arose during 2005 when the Management Audit Unit of WA Police and the CCC undertook a review of the management of property by Police to identify system improvements and to reduce corruptogenic opportunities. This followed a number of incidents where evidence in the form of cash and drugs had been stolen whilst in police custody.[3]

This review was in addition to the individual investigation of the incidents of misconduct. This is an excellent example of a cooperative crime prevention relationship between police and the body that oversights the conduct of police.

It needs to be understood that working with police, as in the property management inquiry, does not mean excusing misconduct or lessening the rigour of inquiry and oversight. Systemic inquiries of this nature do, however, require that the perspective of the police be taken into account and that shortcomings in policy, practice and training are considered rather than simply determining the guilt or innocence of a misconduct offence.

Beyond the specific benefits of assisting police in this reform activity, it is held by Phillips & Trone (2002) that involvements of this nature also help the relationship between the oversight agency and police by providing a better understanding of the demands of police work and the concerns of officers.

Generally, oversight agencies also have a monitoring role, which involves aspects of 'marking of the report card' of police and this involves an independent relationship. At times this could lead to a potential conflict of interests should it be necessary to monitor an activity where the oversight agency has had direct involvement in assisting the police to identify the problem, pose solutions and assist with implementation.

Misconduct function

The misconduct function concerning police can be conceptualised as having two components: 1) complaints management, and 2) investigations. The volume of complaints and allegations received by oversight agencies means that there is little likelihood that they will have the resources or inclination

---

3   The full report of this inquiry can be found at <www.ccc.wa.gov.au/pdfs/WA%20Police%20Property%20Practices.pdf>.

to investigate them all. Rather, arrangements are entered into whereby the majority of complaints and allegations are investigated by the respective police service. Generally the more minor matters and a smaller number of the more serious matters are investigated by the oversight agency itself.

Complaints management is extremely important, as the way in which complaints are dealt with has come to be a de facto measure of police accountability and the progress of reform (Sossin 2004). Although there is much pragmatic cooperation in the negotiating of outcomes on a file by file basis, the work of complaints assessment and management can be categorised as an independent relationship.

Typically, the investigations units of the oversight agencies receive matters referred to it for investigation from a complaints management unit, but they also conduct investigations into matters on the basis of their own intelligence. In this way, the investigations unit works independently of police, although on occasions they will work on joint activities with police internal affairs. Thus, depending upon the nature of the activity, the Investigations Unit can be in either an independent relationship or in a joint relationship with Police. However, even when the two agencies work together, each is viewed separately in terms of their achievements and reporting requirements.

Investigation units of the oversight agencies referred to in this chapter all have the ability to undertake proactive investigations using integrity testing programs, telecommunications interceptions and electronic and physical surveillance. These investigations are valuable in gaining a further insight into police misconduct, and improve the understanding of police misconduct historically obtained from complaints investigations.

Organised crime function

The Commissions of Inquiry conducted by Fitzgerald (1989), Wood (1997) and Kennedy (2004) all gave some attention to organised crime and the involvement of police in either providing an environment to allow such crime to flourish or active involvement by some police in organised crime activities. There are arguments as to whether or not an agency overseeing police should also have an organised crime function. Kennedy (2002, pp 46-47) summarised these arguments as follows:

For the proposition

- An external oversight agency can assist police investigations by the use of its royal commission-type powers, which are not available to police, such as the ability to compel witnesses to give evidence and produce documents.
- There is a demonstrated link between organised crime and corrupt police officers that enables criminal activities to proceed unhindered.
- Cost savings should be achievable by co-locating these areas of crime investigation with royal commission-type powers in the one agency.

Against the proposition

- The police service is the principal law enforcement agency, and there is no argument to suggest that it has been deficient in the detection, investigation and prosecution of organised crime.
- Placing an organised crime function within the external oversight agency might lead to an erosion in the confidence placed in the police.
- Having the same agency exercise responsibilities for corruption and organised crime may lead to a loss of focus within the agency.
- The increased potential for the infiltration of corruption into the body that exercises both oversight and crime functions.
- The possibility of duplication of effort in the intelligence function.

Hall (2004, p 266) cites the argument that:

> Often, organised crime thrives because those involved are bribing or otherwise corrupting police officers or public officials. This means the effective dismantling of organised crime syndicates requires the investigatory agency to be able to probe the actions not only of members of organised crime syndicates, but also the conduct of corrupt public officials who protect and assist organised crime operations.

The relationship between those persons within the oversight agency working on organised crime investigations and their counterparts within police will require a high degree of cooperation and good will. The relationship thus created may become somewhat symbiotic where the success or failure of either party will reflect similarly on the other. Such a symbiotic relationship would be a distinct departure from the independent, cooperative and joint relationships described previously, and raises additional challenges.

Consequences for police management

The inception of these oversight bodies has, of course, an impact on the police agencies they oversee and on the management and leadership of these agencies. These oversight bodies do not look solely at individual instances of misconduct. Rather, they gather intelligence on and examine patterns of behaviour by individuals and cohorts of officers, linkages with organised crime, and the efficacy of policy and procedures, the outcomes of complaints and disciplinary processes, supervision arrangements of officers, adequacy of training and many other matters of systemic or thematic importance. In response, police managers need also to take a broader perspective on issues of police misconduct and accountability and establish systems and procedures accordingly. Anecdotal explanations for police management activities are no longer sufficient, and police management needs to be able to demonstrate, and at times justify, a clear connection between actions it has taken and the evidence it was based upon.

Furthermore, as the various commissions of inquiry have explored, there is an increasing emphasis placed on the vicarious responsibility of police supervisors and managers for the conduct of the officers under their control. It is not enough to explain poor instances of behaviour as being the sole responsibility of individual officers – their supervisors are also being held to account through these oversight agencies for both the applicability of policy and procedures, and for the way they have been carried out. On this point, Kennedy (2004, p 181) was to say:

> It may be the case that at some of the times when that conduct was carried out, the supervisors could claim that there was no indication that the corrupt conduct was taking place, particularly because many of the victims made no complaint at the time. However, any such claim is not valid. Failure to supervise properly cannot be tolerated. It is the duty of a supervisor to supervise. Failure to do so is a breach of duty. Appropriate sanctions should apply. Supervisors must be accountable for their failures.

Not all of the consequences of having an external oversight agency are negative from the police perspective. There are many occasions where an untoward event has occurred that places pressure on the police commissioner to explain what has happened and to make a response. Increasingly it can be seen that police commissioners are taking advantage of the presence of an oversight agency by advising the media, and hence the public, that the matter is being taken seriously and has been referred to the oversight agency for their attention. This has the effect of taking some of the pressure off the police commissioner and the police in general.

Walker (2001, pp 179-180) concludes that external oversight agencies interaction with police has the following elements:

- External oversight is a legitimate and necessary aspect of police accountability.
- When designed and implemented well, such oversight can make a positive contribution to enhancing police accountability.
- Importantly, the effectiveness of external oversight depends on the role it takes in the overall monitoring of police as it is particularly important to change police organisations and not just punish individual officers.
- There is little empirical evidence to demonstrate a relationship between the work of oversight agencies and the quality of day-to-day police work.
- Whilst it plays a role, external oversight is not the entire solution and is but one element of a mixed system of accountability.

Challenges in the oversight process

There is a real potential for external monitoring of police to be opposed by police at both executive and front-line level (Chevigny 1995). This has the capacity to result in a lack of cooperation, which would make it very difficult for the oversight agency to investigate matters and have policy recommendations adopted. It is necessary that an oversight agency neither be too timid in its dealings with police, nor to over-identify with either the police or the general community. At the extremes, police can either be viewed as the main mechanism of law enforcement, or as a major source of infringement on citizens' rights and due process, with pro-police and anti-police groups falling easily into the two camps (Sossin 2004).

Quinn (2004) identifies the critical issues for oversight agencies in striving for the middle ground and advocates for a balanced approach characterised as 'constructive tension' (see Table 11.3, below).

The community often has unrealistic expectations about what they can expect from an oversight agency, and care needs to be taken not to fuel these expectations further by blithely accepting complaints received as being totally factual. Staff from oversight agencies should remain balanced and unbiased in their appraisal of complaints received. This can be a major challenge in the oversight role as complaints received are inherently one-sided: innocent people who have been wrongly arrested or offenders who have received poor treatment may well complain, but criminals who have been mistakenly released rarely utter a word (Shi 2005, p 2). Oversight agency staff, who are mainly only confronted with tales of poor policing or police misconduct, could well form a picture of all police, as all bad. Care needs to be taken to guard against this occurring.

Another problem can arise with complaints management whereby an over-reliance on complaints by an oversight agency can act to induce police to avoid or under-police those areas that receive the greatest number of complaints. Brereton 2000 (in Goldsmith & Lewis 2000) argues against this and gives some statistics to back up his claim. As Shi posits, whilst careful policing may serve to reduce the number of complaints, less aggressive policing will certainly achieve this aim. This is an accusation that has been made re-

Table 11.3: Identification with police

Over-identification with community (complainants)	Constructive tension	Over-identification with police
Disrespectful, overheated rhetoric in discussions with police. Failure to learn the details sufficiently and know the legal issues clearly. Assume police did what they are accused of.	Respectful without assuming subordinate role. Unblinking attention to the issues. Assume that either version may be true, exaggerated or merely mistaken. We do not know until we examine the evidence.	Too cosy with police. Assume police are right. Assume military models apply to policing ('it's war', 'enemies'). Assume complainants have ulterior motives. Assume police 'could not have' done what they are accused of.

Source: Author based on Quinn 2004

cently regarding the NSW Police and their suspected failure to actively police Lebanese youth. Former Assistant Commissioner Schuberg is reported as saying 'Police had become so worried about facing official complaint or media scrutiny that they are often reluctant to arrest suspects, particularly those of ethnic backgrounds' (Higgins & Box 2006). Oversight agencies need to adopt a measured approach in their dealing with complaints. This is especially so in those areas where police can exercise discretion in using their powers, to ensure that the oversight activity doesn't serve to manipulate or corrupt the policing effort.

Many of the challenges in the relationship between police and their oversight agency have a greater consequence for the oversight agency than for the police themselves. This derives from the potential for employees of the oversight agency to be 'captured' by police.

Agency capture

Agency capture occurs when an agency established to oversight or regulate another organisation becomes acculturated to that organisation's interest, rather than serving unbiased public interest. Regulatory and oversight agencies generally tend to work in a cooperative way such that they try to bring about compliance through education and consultancy rather than through inspection and punishment. The concern with this approach, however, is that it is easy for the relationship to become too cosy and for staff of the oversight agency to over-identify with the regulated organisation and to become too lenient and overlook indiscretions.

Prenzler (2000) explains capture theory with reference to the methods used by organisations subject to regulation/oversight to subvert the impartiality and zealousness of the regulator/oversight agency. At its extreme, this can lead to 'conscious relationships of bribery or blackmail' (Prenzler 2000, p 662). More frequently, however, the capture of the oversight agency can occur unintentionally or with good intentions in mind through more subtle forms of inappropriate or undue influence.

A frequently cited source of undue influence surrounds the employment of staff from the organisation being overseen by the oversight agency. This can be in the form of permanent employment or temporary secondment. It is held that this interchange of personnel can result in the oversight agency coming to identify with the industry values of the organisation from which the staff members originated. Other than for limited circumstances, PIC is precluded from employing current or former members of the NSW Police by virtue of s 5 of the *Police Integrity Commission Act 1996*, which states 'Police officers and former police officers cannot be appointed to, employed or engaged by, or seconded to the service of, the Commission'. Former police of other jurisdictions are however eligible for employment.

A common method used to avoid capture, or to respond to it, is to limit the discretion and flexibility with which agency staff can deal with the regulated organisation. This can have the unfortunate outcome of the agency becoming overly harsh in its dealings through punishing organisations and their staff for trivial matters. The not unexpected consequence of this is resentment and animosity by the regulated organisation, and a pulling up of the 'draw-bridge', leading to a decline in the relationship. It is interesting to note that the PIC is the only oversight agency that has an embargo on the employment of police from their own jurisdiction.

An alternative is to have different staff carrying out the differing tasks of the oversight agency such as having separate persons fulfilling the education and assisting role, and another set of staff undertaking the regulatory, investigations and inspections activities – such as is the case with the CMC and CCC. Whilst this approach has significant appeal, it needs also needs to be recognised that it carries with it the risk or potential to create 'silos', where the exchange of information and views between the various areas can itself become problematic. The relationship between the sections of the oversight agency and the balance between sharing experiences and knowledge and the oft quoted 'need to know' basis for accessing information, is in some ways a reflection of the more macro relationship between the oversighter and the oversightee.

From a policing perspective, there is a further problem that can occur with oversight agencies whereby they will not engage in meaningful collaboration to solve problems for fear of capture. The outcome is an oversight body that will not say how to fix problems or advise police how to get it right, but will say that problems exist or advise police when they get it wrong. Police can then rightly complain that no matter what they do, they are criticised. The consequence can be that they stop trying to make changes at all.

Whilst there are benefits from having a range of relationships with police – prevention and education, misconduct investigation and organised crime – Prenzler (2000) warns that having an oversight agency assist in police management and with organised crime creates conditions favourable to a strategy of appeasement. Whereas traditional agency capture theory focuses on the regulated industry's control of an entire agency, the potential exists for such capture to occur with individuals or with particular groups within the oversight agency, such as a particular unit or directorate.

Relational distance

In examining the relationship between oversight agencies and police services account needs to be taken of 'relational distance' – the degree to which staff of the agency and police are involved with each other.[4] Relational distance can be expressed as occurring along four dimensions:

- frequency of contact;
- quality of contact;

---

4   See Black (1976) for a full discussion on relational distance.

- duration of the relationship; and
- degree of shared experiences.

A close relational distance can be described as one with high frequency and good quality of contact, extending over time and involving joint participation in activities leading to shared successes and/or failures. A relationship with a close relational distance is more likely than a remote relational distance to lead staff of oversight agencies to become over familiar with, and to over-identify with, the organisation being monitored. This over-familiarly can result in a loss of sense of differentiation and a co-adaptation of the values of the regulated organisation leading to a compromising of the independent judgment of the oversight agency and a positive bias in performance monitoring (Hood et al 2002).

Black (as cited in DeHart-Davis and Kingsley 2005) believed that relational distance gives rise to a number of hypotheses, which when applied to oversight agencies and police, would indicate that:

- Agency staff with more frequent contact with police both inside and outside the agency setting will perceive policing more favourably than those who have less frequent contact with Police.
- Agency staff with more years of experience working with police will perceive policing more favourably than those with less such experience.
- Agency staff that share a professional background in policing, will tend to perceive more positive compliance by police, and be less rule-bound and prosecutorial in their interactions with police.

There is, however, a contrary view, and it can be said that the best persons to identify and investigate corrupt police are those who themselves have a strong background in policing. The premise being that in order to be effective it is necessary to have an intricate and detailed understanding of the behaviours being examined.

The challenges to oversight processes, including the twin concepts of agency capture and relational distance, give rise to a need to adopt harm minimisation strategies to reduce the potential for capture.

Harm minimisation strategies

The development of strategies to properly manage police oversight agency relations and reduce the potential for agency capture commences with a realisation and appreciation that such potential exists. It is necessary for oversight agencies to consider these issues by instituting a formal acknowledgment of their existence and put in place dedicated strategies to avoid it. This is not to say that oversight agencies are totally exposed to agency capture as there are a variety of mechanisms that can be used to manage these relationships:

- The formation of an interagency consultative committee to set guidelines to regulate the relationship.
- The development of a Memorandum of Understanding can be a useful aid for the two organisations to express in some detail how the relationship between the parties is to work in practice.
- The creation of oversight agencies that accept complaints and allegations against all public sector agencies, rather than singling out the police for special scrutiny. This has the benefit of not viewing corruption as something that only police do; rather it is part of the broader social and political environment in which the public sector functions.
- Oversight agencies should employ staff from a wide range of investigatory type agencies – both policing and non-policing – with particular consideration to recruiting former police officers from interstate, together with a number of selectively recruited local police officers. This reduces the potential for undue influence that might arise based on pre-existing relationships of longstanding, but still allows for the benefit that is obtained from having investigators who have local knowledge.
- Having a legislated requirement for a prevention and education function mitigates against the development of an organisational culture that is dominated by what Prenzler (2000, p 673) describes as 'an unwieldy amalgam of traditional policing and legal cultures'.
- The compartmentalisation of the oversight agency – such that different teams work in the major interface areas of:
  o Prevention and education;
  o Organised crime;
  o Complaints assessment and investigation review; and
  o Investigations.

  This lessens the potential for the differing relationships to be carried over from one oversight activity to another, although not to the same extent as would be achieved through separate agencies.
- The prevention and education function ensures that, in addition to responding to individual allegations or complaints, the oversight agency is able to make practical recommendations for reforms arising from systemic reviews.
- Whereas police report to a specific minister, the oversight agency, as an independent agency, should report directly to parliament, and preferably through a Standing Parliament Committee. This avoids the oversight agency becoming subject to ministerial pressure which is a concern with the ACLEI.
- Oversight agencies need to be well-resourced so that there are no requirements to 'borrow' staff or other resources from the police for investigation or other purposes, thus mitigating against any sense of

obligation or over-identification with the 'police' view. The requirement to heavily rely on the resources of police was a feature of the
Ombudsman model in Victoria before the Office of Police Integrity
was established.

Future relationship requirements

In order for the oversight agencies to have appropriate relationships with
police in all its complexities, it is considered necessary that the oversight
agencies continue to strive to:

- attract a range of professionals from policing and non-policing backgrounds who are interested in, and expert in, corruption prevention
and investigation;
- achieve a relatively harmonious relationship with police where poor
performance is scrutinised and reported in order to pursue accountability, not simply to embarrass police;
- develop a culture within the oversight agencies that meets the association and affiliation needs of ex-police such that they have
stronger ties to their new oversight agency 'team' than their former
associates in Police;
- develop a range of mechanisms to undertake oversight activities,
rather than rely on a few formalistic scrutiny processes;
- be aware of the potential for capture, and be disciplined in avoiding
it by ensuring interested parties do not corrupt oversight agency
staff;
- accept that issues of capture, like many others, are dependent upon
personalities and the challenge is to develop ways of doing business
that eliminate or at least minimise the personality dynamic;
- engage with legislative processes so that scrutiny extends not only
to the police itself but also to the legislative environment in which it
functions; and
- remain sensitive to the need to refrain from compromising operational or judicial activity, without allowing these to block necessary
accountability processes (Adapted from Marinac & Curtis 2005).

Phillips and Trone (2002) refer to the continuous challenge in engaging
police in collaborative reform initiatives, while at the same time remaining
independent and impartial. They believe that the secret to success is to maintain sufficient relational distance from the police. In doing so, the oversight
agency is better able to preserve its clarity of purpose and objectivity and
keep the oversight process itself from being corrupted by the interests or
culture of the police. The relationship cannot however be at total 'arms
length' as an oversight agency's ability to investigate complaints and monitor police investigations depends on collaboration with the police, which can
become impossible if relationships are continually strained.

Conclusion

The relationship between an oversight agency and a police organisation that is subject to constant scrutiny and on-going monitoring requires careful attention. The oversight agencies need to be mindful of this lest it come to over-identify with complainants or over-identify with police. Vigilance is required to ensure that at both individual and agency levels there are mechanisms in place to regulate the relationship.

In the history of oversight agencies and police services across Australia, many oversight and complaints bodies have come and gone, yet all the police services remain. Whether oversight bodies have been captured in their relationship, and lost effectiveness as a consequence, or overzealous in their application of authority leading to animosity, the lesson to be drawn is the same. In its relationship with police, the oversight agencies must neither over-identify nor over-regulate. Police and oversight agencies have separate roles to perform, and while each must guard their sovereignty, they should do so while trying to achieve a balanced and constructive relationship.

12

DESIGNING PERFORMANCE MANAGEMENT SYSTEMS FOR AUSTRALIAN POLICING

John Gillespie, Allan Sicard and Scott Gardner

In this 21st century Australian policing organisations are facing increased accountability in their use of public resources and delivery of services to meet both government requirements and community expectations. Police leaders must now employ strategic management and performance reporting processes to maintain fit with a dynamic internal and external environment. As a result, police commissioners along with other public sector decision makers, must seek to balance politically determined government priorities with the provision of services to a more demanding and expanding range of stakeholders (Hoque, Arends & Alexander 2004; Fleming & Rhodes 2005; Jones 2003; Long 2003).

Since the early 1990s these dilemmas have been addressed within the broader New Public Management context in Australia and New Zealand. New Public Management has had a significant impact on policing juris-dictions in Westminster-style democracies notably the UK, Canada and New Zealand from the early 1990s, and in Australia, from the mid-1990s. The era of New Public Management was labelled the era of a 'new policing order' in which policing organisations had obligations and accountabilities to meet 'government desired outcomes' (Cope, Leishman & Starie 1997). More recently, the push for increased accountability through New Public Manage-ment combined with a focus on public sector corporate governance stan-dards and practices, has resulted in continuing reform in policing agencies (Hoque, Arends & Alexander 2004; Radnor & McGuire 2004; Long 2003; Jones 2003; Vickers & Kouzmin 2001). The recent push by the Australian federal and State governments towards citizen-centric governance frame-works and partnership structures, with greater attention to the diverse needs of a wide range of stakeholder groups, contrasts with the New Public Management focus on economic rationalisation, commercialisation, and the needs of the individual customer (Hartley 2005). The New Public Management themes of accountability and transparency remain but, according to Edwards, (2002, p 52) have been augmented with the other elements of good governance:

> Governance is best understood in terms of the key elements that are commonly seen to describe what is 'good governance' to assist performance: accountability, transparency, participation, relationship management and, depending on the context, efficiency and/or equity.

This combined legacy of New Public Management and governance, challenges police leaders to change their personal styles, management systems and for the working culture of the organisation to align with the changing face of government in Australia (Jones 2003; Wright 2002). Parallel shifts to 'joined up government' (Perri 2004), multi-agency partnerships, and the central provision of support services have added to the complexity of managing police organisations. These aspects which were designed to address the interface between government and civil society, have in turn blurred the boundaries between politically determined government desired outcomes and the traditional tasks, priorities, and operational domains of policing (Fleming & Rhodes 2005; Long 2003; Jones 2003; Collier, Edwards & Shaw 2004; Vickers & Kouzmin 2001). As noted by Jones (2003), police executives when establishing and maintaining a democratic framework for the provision of policing services, must negotiate the paradox of police governance. This involves both empowering and constraining their officers in their day-to-day duties, and accepting the limitations placed on their ability to 'influence policing in its own favour' (Jones 2003, p 606). This observation is particularly relevant when elections are imminent, with the attendant ripple effects of government change and popular public opinion leads to a reshuffling of monies and program priorities. Thus police strategy and allied performance management is always constrained by a duality of purpose, notably legitimising police, their functions and operations to the electorate, while encouraging and demonstrating efficient resource use.

With these considerations in mind this chapter explores the role and significance of a strategic and politically attuned approach to designing, implementing and maintaining agency, business unit or individual performance management. In doing so we aim to:

- discuss the political philosophy and historical reforms influencing performance management system design in contemporary public sector governance and New Public Management contexts;
- outline the links between Strategic Human Resource Management and performance management as a basis for compliance by the agency, capacity building, and staff development;
- highlight the key features and practical limitations of police performance management systems by drawing from relevant academic and professional literature and field research in Western Australia and New South Wales; and

- provide guidance on key design elements for police leaders and managers seeking to develop an effective performance management system that is aligned to agency and shifting government goals and priorities.

Reforms in Australian policing 1990-2006

Since the early 1990s most Australian policing jurisdictions have undergone reforms driven through either commissions of inquiry (notably the Fitzgerald Commission of Inquiry in Queensland (1987 to 1989), the Wood Royal Commission in New South Wales (1994 to 1997), and the Kennedy Royal Commission (2002 to 2004)) or the actions of police commissioners challenging traditional 'modus operandi'. As a result, State-level policing in Australia has undergone a shift towards a more transparent culture and modes of operation that are aligned to increasingly demanding compliance and performance regimes, and community expectations. In Western Australia, the Kennedy Royal Commission (2004) recommended a wide range of reform programs focused on cultural change, including recruiting and retaining a more diverse and gender-balanced workforce, embedding ethical practices and corruption prevention measures, and the introduction of improvements to performance reporting and management systems. As with the previous Royal Commissions in Queensland and New South Wales, particular emphasis was placed on the need for improved governance frameworks, leadership and supervision, and performance monitoring.

The impact of these reforms is particularly obvious in changes to the organisational and operational environments of Australian State policing in the post-2000 period. However it is arguable that the scope and impact of these changes is insufficient to stay in touch with the major demographic shifts impacting all Australian organisations. The ability to attract, retain and motivate Generation Y (individuals born between 1976 and 1996) (Cooper 2005), female, and non-Anglo Saxon origin officers remain major concerns for police leaders and managers across all Australian jurisdictions.

Performance management has also remained a difficult area with reference to the balance between compliance and the need to motivate both experienced and 'new generation' police officers. A wide range of views has been expressed in the business media and academic literature on the issues and challenges of workforce dynamics and management of performance across different generational and racial groups. In addition, the impact of Generation X and Generation Y values in the workplace and the challenges of managing this demographic group has been discussed in the literature (Cooper 2005), and their desire for feedback, recognition and reward, and a work/life balance. 'When properly engaged, Generation Y is the most creative, innovative and inspirational generation yet' (Sheahan, interviewed in Cooper 2005, p 20). Hubbard (2002, p 103) commenting on performance management in the Australian Defence Force suggests that Generation Y require '[a] coaching, mentoring approach with high emotional stimulation, partnering for performance and a climate where high performance fulfils individual aspirations and career satisfaction'. The debate on the implications of demographic change for future organisational design is of clear importance for police leaders and managers seeking to develop relevant and effective systems and practices to support organisational goals. However, the core ideas of diversity and relevance to the grass roots political and demographic issues impacting on contemporary Australian communities, is encompassed within the broader theme of how organisations can create a strategically aligned, contextually relevant and effective police performance management system in the era of governance imperatives and New Public Management.

Public accountability vs management of performance

Over the past decade, the language of New Public Management and managerialism provided a rational base for setting, measuring and benchmarking performance outcomes in Australian policing organisations. Such attempts by senior managers to impose performance management on their business units and portfolios have attracted cynicism and passive resistance, from the front-line and even officers in charge of the front-line. This effect can be compounded over time when local police stations, detectives, and traffic officers do not have the capacity to achieve targets imposed on them and have limited control over the process by which to achieve them. This is a longstanding criticism of New Public Management and public sector performance management that has been widely reported in the academic literature. (See Hoque, Arends & Alexander 2004; Long 2003; Wright 2002; and Cherrett, cited in Dadds & Scheide 2000.) To compound this, the New Public Management philosophy and the politics of goal setting, performance reporting and resource allocation, have not always been well understood by police executive teams and managers, when their primary focus has been on the practicalities of delivering effective policing services to the community.

While New Public Management spoke of reduced political interference and a shift from functional administration to autonomous management of services, traditional public sector compliance and accountability remain major constraints on the decisions and actions of police leaders (Hoque, Arends & Alexander 2004). By contrast, a recent study of preferred management cultures amongst 925 public servants, including 189 managers, in the Queensland public service found a shift towards a 'more flexible externally-oriented culture', compared with a traditional bureaucratic culture and 'internal process', model (Bradley & Parker 2006, p 96). Whether this is a significant departure from the traditional bureaucracy and control mechanisms in public sector agencies is debatable. In the era of New Public Management and new governance two points have become clear for police leaders and managers. First, they must continuously be seen to deliver public value through ethical, accountable and fiscally responsible use of resources. Secondly, to achieve effective service delivery and responsiveness to the needs of a disparate community, they must invest in systems to develop their internal capability and human capital. The need to combine these considerations within a broader public sector performance improvement framework is noted by Kim (2002, p 231 cited in Bradley & Parker 2006, p 96) who states '[o]ne of the leading challenges in public management has been implementing effective human capital strategies to enhance government performance and accountability'. With this in mind, effective performance management system design must encompass two agendas: the public accountability agenda of conforming and reporting at agency and business unit level; and the management agenda to motivate police officers towards achieving required targets and priorities.

A performance management system requires employees, line managers and senior managers to understand the importance of front-line employee motivation and how it can support achievement of desired business unit and organisational outcomes (Boice & Kleiner 1997; Kramer 1998; Nankervis & Leece 1997; McLean 1994). The need for a more strategic and effectively communicated approach to performance management was highlighted in both the Wood (1997) New South Wales Royal Commission and the Kennedy (2004) Western Australia Royal Commission, although individual motivation and culture change were not directly identified as aims of a performance management systems. The Wood Royal Commission for example, made the following recommendations:

- Development of performance management that supports the setting and agreeing of measures;
- Development of examples of acceptable measures at different levels explaining performance, quality and value for money;
- Documentation of an agreed process of performance management that is seen to have value in rendering obsolete autocratic and disciplinary processes;
- Development of an implementation and training plan and a pilot process;
- Assessment or real information needed to support the performance management process; and
- Feedback to systems development where gaps emerge. (Wood 1997, pp A249-A250)

The NSW Police have responded with several versions of performance appraisal systems, including the post-1997 Performance Management Scheme (PMS) targeting senior constables and senior sergeants (which met with little success), and the Career Management Plan (CMP) trialled in 2005-2006 with sergeants and commissioned officers in a few locations with the aim of aligning career development to local command and corporate goals.

The performance portfolio system was introduced from July 2006. Under this system, portfolios covering human resources, operations, systems, customer service and professional standards are issued to duty officers. Each contains specific performance requirements that are to be met for metropolitan and country local area commands (LACs), which each comprise three to five duty officers. If fully implemented, this system will represent a radical departure from previous police performance management regimes, with all superintendents and duty officers' performance reviewed and directly linked to pay increases, transfers, tenure, and promotions. While the career management plan and the portfolio system have the potential to shift the NSW Police beyond the process of performance appraisal towards strategic performance management, there is limited evidence that this has yet been achieved.

Western Australia Police have operated a two-tiered performance management system linking business unit and agency performance for some time. These link strategic planning key performance indicators with an Organisational Performance Review and localised Business Area Management Reviews. Since 2002, the Developing People for Success program has also been used to increase individual motivation and improve behavioural outcomes. However, according to Gillespie (2006, p 4) the process has 'inconsistencies and limited application within the current environment' that have led to employee dissatisfaction. These examples from New South Wales and Western Australia suggest concerted efforts towards a strategically aligned performance management system although with considerable gaps still to be filled.

Strategic approaches to human resource management and performance management system

We will now focus briefly on the link between Strategic Human Resource Management and PMS, before exploring the police PMS design framework derived from a recent two-year study conducted in Western Australia by two of the authors. Schuler and Jackson (1999, p 52) observed that strategic human resource management represents '[t]he pattern of planned human resource developments and activities intended to enable an organisation to achieve its goals'. This echoes Hamel and Prahalad's (1993) view that organisations should use human resource management as a means to build and configure internal capability to meet future conditions and market requirements. In the case of policing, strategic human resource management can be used to build future capacity to act in step with significant changes and unfolding future scenarios for police organisations and the communities in which they operate. To achieve this, police leaders must address both the compliance and future focused development agendas of their organisations by focusing staff skill, knowledge and expertise towards the achievement of current and longer term agency, business, and personal objectives (Furnham 2004; Radnor & Maguire 2004; De Waal 2004; O'Neill & Holsinger 2003; Weatherly 2004; Norman & Gregory 2003; Teo, Ahmad & Rodwell 2003; McLean 1994; Dunphy & Stace 1990). As such the theory of *strategic* human resource management suggests, as the social, economic, political and legal environment of policing change, so must their strategies, systems and culture. Leadership and management styles and approaches must evolve to fit the emerging culture through learning and feedback mechanisms such as performance management systems, and continually reconcile aspirational strategies and targets with resource constraints, and operational realities (Hoque, Arends & Alexander 2004; Fleming & Rhodes 2005; Dunphy & Stace 1996).

Performance management system design and knowledge

Progressive and flexible performance management system design is particularly important to maintain organisational assets such as human skills, knowledge, and the expertise gained over time. This intellectual capital should be managed to add useful capacity and support performance outcomes at all levels. This is particularly important in policing organisations, characterised as compliance-based bureaucracies with knowledge and intelligence networks that support evidence gathering and interpretation of data and information. These processes largely determine the crime investigation, harm reduction, and problem solving capability of police agencies and units. In view of the knowledge and intelligence-driven nature of policing, strategic human resource management and performance management systems could be combined to identify and develop human and organisational capability. Future performance management system design should therefore recognise and enhance the value of knowledge as an asset and as a process essential to the success of police operations and investigations across the complex activity that characterises police organisations. This can be a challenge for police leaders as it denotes a significant departure from the strong goal, task, and function orientation of traditional performance management and appraisal systems. Performance management systems based on intellectual capital focus on enabling knowledge accrual and sharing, as compared with controlling employee action.

Policing performance management system design: some recommendations

Drawing on our experience in policing and public sector management, our review of the literature, and our findings from field research conducted in WA Police and NSW Police, we propose that the following are required for effective strategically aligned PMS design:

1. All police officers need to understand what they have to achieve and how these actions will map against unit and agency goals or targets.
2. The setting of achievable goals through management allocation of human and capital resources to the right place, at the right time.
3. An integrated framework must be in place to monitor, measure and report on individual, unit and agency performance against

agreed Key Performance Indicators identified by system owners across all relevant levels and units in the organisation.

4. The process of monitoring, measuring and reporting should not become an end in itself. It should enhance rather than subvert the core relational aspects of policing notably knowledge sharing, intelligence gathering and positive collaboration across functional, agency, jurisdictional and network boundaries motivating staff and developing their potential as police officers and knowledge workers.

In policing, as with most government services, the desired outcome is effective and efficient service delivery achieved through clear expectations and responsibilities. However, in view of the mounting demographic pressure and community expectations impacting on contemporary Australian policing, these outcomes can only be maintained with considerable foresight and planning, and a demonstrated commitment to the future development of staff by police leaders. Performance management system design for policing should therefore incorporate both 'compliance based' and 'development focused,' elements, some with generic applications and others that are unique to specific policing contexts (Hoque, Arends & Alexander 2004). Tables 12.1 and 12.2 (opposite, and pages 176-177) have been developed from our review of relevant academic sources and field research. The primary source is a recent study of the performance management system objectives and relevant design elements conducted by the first author for the Western Australian police. Table 12.1 (opposite) outlines possible generic objectives for a strategic approach to police performance management, and Table 12.2 (pages 176-177) outlines corresponding elements to inform the design of a performance management system across Australian policing jurisdictions.

The objectives in Table 12.2 are consistent with a strategic PMS approach as identified by Coutts and Schneider (2004) and Vickers and Kouzmin (2001) and other authors in the SHRM field focused on the links between strategic planning, goal setting and training and development.

Table 12.1: Police performance management systems (objectives)

1.	Link to organisational strategy and objectives
2.	Influencing a culture of shared performance values
3.	Job definition
4.	Objective setting – assigning work efficiently
5.	Continuous communication – advising employees of work expectations
6.	Coaching and counselling/better working relationships
7.	Motivating employees/Improving work performance
8.	Public recognition – reward
9.	Identifying training needs/training and development
10.	Assisting in long-range planning
11.	Assessing employee potential/Helping employees set career goals
12.	Making promotion decisions
13.	Counselling employees for poor performance
14.	Making transfer decisions
15.	Making decisions about employment options
16.	Justifying other managerial actions

Source: Gillespie (2006, p 52)

Table 12.2: Design elements for a strategic policing PMS

Area of application	Conditions for successful application
Senior management support	PMS is a major compliance and culture change tool. Change will not be successful or sustainable in the absence of demonstrated and ongoing support by senior management.
Policy	Senior management support and commitment through good governance and policy-making can both facilitate and be enhanced by, effective PMS design and implementation. This forms the pathway for the organisation to develop a committed rather than a dysfunctional approach to PMS.
Strategic Human Resource Management	A strategic human resource management approach can help performance management system to focus staff capabilities on operational and strategic outcomes. Strategic human resource management incorporating effective PMS can bring about a change in culture and strategic direction. PMS is considered the key building block of an organisation's human resource management system.
Understanding and knowledge	After a policy has been established it is important to ensure understanding of the PMS approach and its linkage with SHRM and the organisational goals. Understanding should be addressed at the various business levels with particular focus on frontline employees and line management. Communication should be systemic and systematic. SHRM and PMS should maintain alignment with feedback and changes in internal systems.
Employee participation	A sound and grounded PMS methodological approach should be aimed at communicating the organisational strategic goals in conjunction with discussing relevant processes and measures with employees. Having ownership in the overall design of a PMS approach will enable a more committed and motivated approach to achieving organisational goals.
Competencies identification (Organisation-wide)	Organisational characteristics should be considered in identifying key competencies and job families across the organisation. This organisational competency building perspective should inform the design of the PMS.
Knowledge workers	Organisational information and knowledge capabilities enable an organisation to develop and maintain a strategic fit with its environment. Knowledge workers are the enablers of this organisational capacity. PMS process and rewards system should maximise their capabilities and maintain information and knowledge flows to support the core intelligence driven tasks of policing.

Competencies identification (Operational area)	PMS design elements may be different from one operating environment to another, including individual and team perspectives. The spread of business areas and functions, and geographical placements especially in policing are not uniform and require different competencies and measurement.
Link to promotion	Competencies are important to ensure that officers can undertake functions properly. Performance relating to individual competence and goal achievement should reflect behavioural attributes that will enable officers to demonstrate ability for promotion and succession planning opportunities. The PMS should be linked to the promotion process.
Operational area task link with organisational goals	The various tasks of each business/functional area all contribute to the overall organisational goals. It is important to recognise diversity and relevant attributes, and identify the activities that an area must focus effort on to ensure linkage with organisational outcomes. Tasks undertaken by employees must be aligned to that outcome to maintain consistency, focus and motivation. Individual and team task performance needs to rely on cognitive ability, skill and experience.
Training	Systemic training on PMS approaches is particularly important for supervisors and managers. This enables better understanding of the process and PMS application to overcome the traditional issues of managing poor performance and understanding of PMS measurement.
Frequent PMS reviews	The changing context of the policing environment is such that a PMS will require frequent review to ensure its continued relevance and strategic fit with the internal and external environment in which it operates. A system needs to be adaptable and flexible to meet emerging issues.

Source: Gillespie (2006, p 132)

Conclusion

The design of an effective performance management system is a task which has eluded many organisations in both the public and private sectors since 'Management By Objectives' first gained currency in the 1960s. It represents a particularly challenging proposition for police leaders and managers who juggle public accountability and good governance. Challenges are also presented by motivating a generation of police officers potentially more concerned with the 'here and now' than precedent and unquestioning compliance to rules and policy. Effective performance management system design should be sufficiently flexible to embrace demographic and social change, new rules of governance, the 'knowledge age', and the relational rather than the purely functional or task-oriented-basis of policing in 21st-century Australia.

13

It's Mine and You Can't Have It: Knowledge Sharing in Police Organisations

Vincent Hughes and Paul Jackson

One of the most important organizational factors hampering intelligence-led initiatives is that policing agencies and individual officers are notoriously loathe to share the information they collect. As information is often associated with owning a particular case, sharing such knowledge can dilute an officer's contributions to an investigation, increasing the likelihood that others might monopolize the glory and attendant career perks that can accompany a 'good pinch'. Longstanding inter (and intra) institutional animosities also reduce the willingness of officers to share information with other organizations which they frequently perceive as incompetent or suspect (Kruger & Haggerty 2006, p 88).

Policing can be described as mechanistic and reactive, requiring unthinking conformity and limited flexibility. Arguably, a change to more innovative problem solving depends on knowledge creation and sharing, assisted through the development of a knowledge support infrastructure within and between organisations. The term 'Learning Organisation' is used to describe one that is open, reflective and which learns from experience; a true learning organisation has as its foundation knowledge creation and sharing. To take this concept beyond rhetoric requires an understanding of the function of knowledge and its sharing and management. This chapter reviews some pivotal concepts and describes a recent case study of knowledge sharing in Western Australia Police.

Over the past decades, in large organisations such as policing, a concentration on information technology (IT) may have reduced the organisation's ability to create and share the tacit knowledge held by employees (Pawar et al 2001; Wilson 2002), and there is a strong interplay between technology, information and people (Kane 2003). Knowledge creation and sharing are, therefore, highly dependent upon the contributions of individuals and their willing participation (Boisot 1998; Iftikhar, Eriksson & Dixon 2003). Technical power is not a substitute for socialisation (Touskas & Vladimirou 2001). To foster knowledge creation and sharing using information technology, managers need to have an understanding of how information technology and people interface (Gardner & Ash 2003) and understand that the technical power available should be used intelligently and deliberately (Igbaria 1999). As Ruggles (1998) succinctly stated after studying the barriers to knowledge management in over 400 European organisations, 'If technology solves your problem, yours was not a knowledge management problem' (p 88).

As the quote at the start of this chapter illustrates, knowledge sharing in policing may be compromised by a range of work-practice, organisational and cultural characteristics. In a recent outstanding example of communication difficulties between the American Federal Bureau of Investigation (FBI) and Local Law Enforcement agencies, a Courts Subcommittee Hearing on communication problems found a chronic lack of communication and sharing of information (Senate Hearing 107, 2002). As has been commented upon frequently, a lack of knowledge sharing between emergency responders was a key finding of the report on the 2001 terrorist attacks on the United States (9/11 Commission 2004).

This chapter describes a case study of Western Australia Police (WAPol) which examined some of these issues within a real policing context amongst those with a crime management or intelligence-related background. But first some definitions of the terms used, and a brief summary of the limited research that has been conducted.

Knowledge

What is knowledge?

Although the terms *knowledge* and *information* are often used interchangeably, information is not knowledge (Sveiby 1997; Malhotra 2002). Some of this confusion may derive from technology companies marketing their products as 'knowledge management solutions' when they are simply information collection and managing tools (Duffy 2000; Broadbent 1998; Saint-Onge & Armstrong 2004). Information consists of facts and data that are organised to describe a particular situation or condition while knowledge can be explained as consisting of facts, truths, beliefs, perspectives, concepts, judgments, expectations methodologies and know-how (Wiig 1994). In other words, information presents a situation, and knowledge determines what that particular situation means. Knowledge is any process or practice of creating, acquiring, capturing, sharing and using information to enhance learning and performance in organisations (Quintas, Lefrere & Jones 1997). Others define it as 'a fluid mix of framed experiences, values, contextual information and expert insight' (Davenport & Prusak 1998, p 5). Knowledge can also be seen as representing a change from 'unreflective' to 'reflective' practice

(Touskas & Vladimirou 2001). Finally, knowledge has been described as 'know-how' and 'know why' (Gurteen 1998; Skyrme 1998; Davenport 1998) and includes *declarative* knowledge (which describes something); *procedural* knowledge (which concerns how something is done); and *causal* knowledge (which is about why something occurs) (Zack 1999). In the policing context we could describe it as the 'expertise' that is developed through specialist and general experience.

What is knowledge management?

Research on knowledge management has tended to concentrate on capturing and codifying information using information technology (IT), at the expense of research on the human social and psychological aspects of knowledge sharing (Malhotra 2002; Prusak 2001; Huber 2001). Knowledge management is not a stand-alone organisational procedure or a policy but an holistic attitude that demands total organisational commitment and cooperation to succeed (Burden 2000). Knowledge management can be thought of as a form of expertise-centred management that draws out people's tacit knowledge, making it accessible for specific purposes, to improve the performance of organisations (Broadbent 1998). It is therefore important in organisations to find out who has knowledge, how they get it and what they can do with it for the benefit of the organisation. In policing there is much loss of this organisational knowledge during their careers, and as they leave, officers who have been with the organisation for many years are sent off with a party rather than a set of detailed interviews on their highly valuable knowledge and experience.

What is knowledge sharing?

Little is known about knowledge sharing specifically in policing other than studies by Hoey 1998 and Hoey and Topping (1998) on knowledge sharing in police in Northern Ireland, and Collier (2001) and Collier, Edwards and Shaw (2004) on intellectual capacity in policing. What little research exists has tended to concentrate on the use of IT in the organisation, and the influence of IT on policing practices. Knowledge *sharing* is influenced by the attitudes, perceptions and behavioural traits of employees and so is more difficult to research and manage than data (Senge 1990). Knowledge sharing is the active process of communicating and consulting through social interaction or engaging with others to find out what they know. Taking time to do this is rare in police organisations. The Western Australia Police Academy has, however, recently commenced a series of regular 'Learning Events' intended to share knowledge amongst practitioners. At present these tend still to be in the format of an expert lecture rather than a discussion, but the format is developing and evolving.

A case study of knowledge sharing inhibitors in Western Australia Police
Western Australia Police (WAPol) was selected since it has invested significantly in information communication technology to collect and distribute information on crime investigation and intelligence analysis. WAPol has a

staff of approximately 4500 police officers and 2000 public servants employed in operations and administration. Research participants were drawn from general operations, specialists, public servants and managers and each was currently working in, or had, a crime-management or intelligence related background.

Data for this research were collected through individual interview with 40 sworn police officers and public servants. Focus groups were also used to facilitate the development of shared understandings between participants around the open question: *'What are your views on knowledge sharing in the Western Australia Police?'* This question was followed by further open questions relating to their experience and understanding of knowledge sharing inhibitors and facilitators in the organisation. As the research continued, dialogue about knowledge sharing was encouraged between participants during work projects and other related work duties. In many cases, these *ad hoc* conversations were an excellent medium through which to test the validity of data collected from more structured interviews. Through this open-ended method we found that knowledge sharing at work takes place in a highly complex environment and that it is difficult to examine matters in isolation.

Through the data gained from the interviews and conversations, we developed a list of *facilitators* or *inhibitors* to knowledge sharing. Table 13.1 (over the page) briefly summarises the seven inhibitors and one facilitator that emerged from our interviews.

We will now discuss the inhibitors and facilitator more fully, along with potential organisational solutions that may enhance knowledge sharing amongst employees. As we have indicated, the complexity of the knowledge generation and sharing environment within the organisation makes it impractical to think about each of these in isolation. Solutions would need to consider this environment in total.

Perceived inhibitors to knowledge sharing

The impact of the current promotion system producing a 'we to I' paradox

The most common inhibitor mentioned by participants relates to the promotion system. It was continually stated that an over-reliance on behavioural interviewing techniques, rather than exploring police officers' interaction in teams, encourages police to not share knowledge. Research into police promotion is limited and what little has been done has tended to concentrate on gender and cultural issues rather than on the impact of the content of the system, the characteristics of the applicant implicitly or explicitly being assessed and the style of interviewing. One study examining the potential relationship between the promotion system method and the likelihood of culture change within the organisation found an inhibiting effect. This, it was argued, was due to the focus on individual achievement, rather than

Table 13.1: Factors influencing knowledge sharing

Inhibitors	Description
Promotion system	Behavioural interviews concentrate on individual know-ledge rather than knowledge creation and sharing in teams.
Sworn vs unsworn	Integrated workforce of sworn officers and public sector staff not as yet achieved.
Suspicion and scepticism	Police officers sceptical of 'outsiders' which extends to public service staff. However, sharing can occur when police officers believe public service staff can value-add their outputs.
Qualifications	Qualified public service employees leave the service due to sworn police officers holding positions based solely on rank rather than skills and competencies. Police officers feel unrewarded for educational effort, and tend not to share knowledge.
Command and control management style	Police officers trained to be subservient to rank so inno-vation can be stifled. Socialising is not encouraged. Micro management style where knowledge sharing is reduced.
Managerialism	Managers forced to use frontline positions to cater for government reporting expectations. Takes officers away from the community so reducing intelligence gathering capacity. Decentralisation of districts promotes a 'patch mentality'. External organisation oversight leads to risk-adverse policies and practices.
IT drives business	IT has become omnipresent in the organisation and is described as 'conceptually elegant but functionally res-trictive', officers spend much time inputting data but find it difficult to access the information.
Facilitator	
Training courses	Allows staff to meet in informal settings and exchange knowledge.

Source: Authors

team effort (Bartels 2005). It appears from the current study that a component in current promotion interviewing and assessment practices needs to reflect the applicant's desire to share knowledge and their skill at doing so. Early in their career, police officers may be inclined to share knowledge but when exposed to the promotion system, knowledge sharing is reduced. Brunetto and Farr-Wharton (2003) found police officers' organisational commitment decreased as they moved from constable to sergeant ranks. The present study may contribute to understanding this observation by specifically identifying the influence of the specific type of promotion system on the arguably more morale building effect of sharing and valuing knowledge in a team.

We spoke to several managers to look at alternative methods of promotion. The use of 360 degree interview was suggested (Huggett 1998). The primary objective of such interviews is to pool feedback from several staff members including supervisors, peers and those lower in rank. It was suggested by interviewees in our study that such information could be used to identify candidates' strengths and weaknesses using a broader base of information, including candidates' willingness to share knowledge. Such techniques are almost universal among the Fortune 500 companies but are minimal among Australian companies (Stone 2002). A discussion with staff from the Human Resource department indicated that Australian Police agencies have attempted to implement 360 degree interviews, but not successfully in agencies characterised as autocratic or hierarchical. It is interesting to note that the 360 degree method is used to good effect in Scottish police agencies, although the specific relationship between that method and knowledge sharing has not been assessed. Future research will be needed to explore the reasons for the lack of success in implementing the 360 degree interviewing concept in an Australian policing environment and what accounts for its successful application in police organisations elsewhere. Having regard to the emphasis placed on behavioural interviewing as a means of promotion and the concerns raised in this research, the need for reflection on these practices is obvious.

The 'sworn' vs the 'unsworn' divide

A compelling inhibitor found in the current study is the perceived distinction between police officers and public service staff, even amongst those who carry out similar functions. In all police organisations, there are two types of employees: police officers and police staff. Police officers have taken an oath to enforce the law of the State and as such are colloquially referred to as 'sworn members'. On the other hand, police staff (public servants) do not take an oath and so do not have police powers of arrest. Colloquially, public servants are referred to as 'unsworn'. An example of the lack of knowledge sharing between these two groups was described by a public service crime analyst who conducts criminal profiles on specific offenders as a core duty as follows: whenever information was required but not available on the police computer, sworn police officers who were familiar with the case or the offender were contacted. However, on a number of occasions in making this contact, the 'unsworn' member was asked such questions as 'Are you a sworn officer?', 'What rank are you?', 'Why do you want it?', 'Have you got permission to have access to this data?' The fact that this public servant had 'Secret Level' security classification, which is a higher information access classification than the officers contacted, made no difference.

The sworn versus unsworn divide is not peculiar to the Western Australia Police. A similar state of affairs was found in the context of intelligence analysis in three British police forces where problems between public service intelligence analysts and police officers were evident. The problems were attributed mainly to low pay, the lack of a well-developed career and an ad-hoc promotion structure for intelligence analysts (John & Maguire 2004). It was also found that lack of standardisation of the intelligence products caused confusion among the operational officers who used these products. This in turn posed dangers of developing a vicious circle, where those who use the intelligence products lose respect for the efforts involved in developing the product while those who create the product lose the incentive to put energy into improving the quality. This research also complements the findings of Thomas and Davies (2002) relating to a police service in England which found that many police civilian managers resented the failure on the part of their senior officers and the senior uniformed ranks to recognise the value of their professional expertise. Further research is needed on this dichotomy to consider its origins, perpetuation and the impact that it has on more 'healthy' knowledge sharing within policing and strategies found to bridge the divide.

Suspicion, scepticism and mistrust

In our quest to explore the divide between public servants and police officers further, the findings were presented to senior detectives. This generated robust discussion and also unearthed other perspectives. For example, they pointed out that a core function of police officers is to investigate crime. One of the interviewees (a detective) said of this process and its potential impact on the desire to share knowledge:

> I suppose it is akin to a poker player who holds his cards close to his chest. Likewise, detectives or investigators hold their cards close to their chests and only disclose information that they feel will enhance the investigation. I suppose you could call it a type of survival. I am not sure if we are sceptical by nature or we become sceptical by experience – it is probably a combination of both. It is fair to say though, that this trait, no matter how insignificant it is at the beginning of our careers, becomes a learned behaviour over time and transports itself to other areas of the job. What is useful in one situation probably works against me in another situation. When I think about it, I even do that [adopt a sceptical and suspicious nature] at home. I am regularly accused my wife and kids of always acting as a police officer. Now I can see why those outside [non-police officers] have that perception of us.

Miller (1999) has discussed the advantages and disadvantages of police officers being sceptical or suspicious by nature and argues that while a character trait such as suspicion may be useful among police officers, it is not necessarily suitable in other professions. While a core role of policing is to investigate crime, many officers find themselves, especially in the later years of their careers, working in areas other than criminal investigation often alongside public servants. In these situations, the sharing of knowledge is necessary. This transition from working with sworn officers to working with public servants should not be difficult, but for some police officers it is since they do not have the same life experiences. As Harr (2001) argues, the culture and experiences of policing is a powerful force in shaping the attitudes and behavioural traits of officers. A 'working personality' develops out of the social and practice environment at work which may affect pre-existing personality traits (Albanese 1999).

This inhibitor to knowledge sharing raises a number of challenges for police managers since it can also be cultivated to act as a facilitator. If it is to be harnessed as an asset to knowledge sharing, public servants need to be encouraged to know that police officers will share knowledge if there is a belief that sharing knowledge will improve an operational outcome. Police officers may forget that other staff members have important but potentially less visible roles in investigations and that sharing knowledge with all staff may reduce the complexity of an investigation. If this concept is to be successful, it will not only involve a major shift in thinking by public servants it will also require innovative ways to change time consuming and potentially isolating work practices. Finally, in attempting to make change that will facilitate knowledge sharing, the question of 'what causes what?' needs to be explored: is scepticism and suspicion formed and perpetuated by the organisation through its practices, or does the behaviour of staff simply perpetuate these characteristics.

The qualification divide

Differences in skills and qualifications as an inhibitor to sharing knowledge was also raised by several police officers and public service employees. Public service employees believe that no matter what qualifications or skills they have, they will not be acknowledged by police officers, especially if those skills and qualifications relate to 'policing activities'. Their view is that they are considered to have crossed the boundary. Similarly, some police officers reported feeling disadvantaged by having qualifications. It was found that a number of police officers even felt they were penalised because of having educational qualifications and so may not draw attention to the knowledge gained from their studies. Such officers are generally self-starters and high achievers and tend to get involved early in applying for promotion or specialist positions. If unsuccessful and feel that their qualifications are not rewarded, in the current competitive law enforcement and security environment, they may leave the police service for other agencies resulting in a loss of expertise and knowledge.

This inhibitor to knowledge sharing is also reflected in other research (Kakar 1998). Kakar's study found that police officers with tertiary education believed they had an advantage over those who did not in the areas of taking responsibility, undertaking leadership roles and displaying initiative. However, they also found that police with tertiary qualifications were more cynical than those with no tertiary qualifications. This problem is not new, in fact Kakar (1998) quotes 30-year-old research by Regoli (1976) and Swanson (1977) who both found that university-educated officers felt unrewarded for their educational effort and were more likely to be dissatisfied with the job and under-stimulated by work. A sense of divide tended to inhibit knowledge sharing.

The influence of a command and control management style

The management style in police organisations typically emphasises a bureaucratic command and control approach. Findings from this research indicate that officers' subservience to the rank structure can inhibit knowledge sharing. Since police officers are trained to be subservient to higher-ranking officers, important knowledge sharing traits such as innovation and creativity can be stifled. On the basis of the current study, we would argue that there is a need for senior police officers to alter management and leadership styles to reduce the emphasis on command and control practices in order to encourage knowledge sharing. Reige (2005) also asserts that knowledge sharing is less likely to occur in highly structured multi-layered and hierarchical organisations.

The influence of the rank structure and the command and control philosophy on the working and behavioural practices of police officers is not a new finding. McCarrey (1993) argued that police managers in Western Australia received little training in the principles and techniques of management, and as such, base their style on their early training which emphasised a command and control philosophy. Similar comments were also made in the Western Australia Royal Commission (Kennedy 2004) which called for a more modern management approach with a reduced emphasis on command and control practices). Tangentially related to this inhibitor is that the high levels of oversight by external bodies, compared with other agencies may also impact on knowledge sharing.

Managerialism: New Public Management

New Public Management (NPM) when it was conceived reflected a greater concern for increased efficiency through measurable performance outcomes and decentralisation (Funnell 2001). The current study found that a management model introduced by governments over a decade ago to improve police effectiveness actually impedes knowledge sharing in WAPol. This move happened primarily during the 'Delta' reform program (Kennedy 2004), which was driven by New Public Management philosophies to improve organisational efficiencies and accountability. The concept embraced empowerment of district superintendents with control over resources and business processes (Western Australia Police 2001). In effect, superintendents were given the mandate to operate as local chiefs of police (Western Australia Police 2003a). While in theory, devolution and decentralisation had many benefits it also has a number of drawbacks especially in relation to knowledge sharing.

A number of interviewees in supervisory positions raised concerns about the increasing demands on them to collect data in relation to organisational inputs, outputs and outcomes at the expense (ie 'form filling'), as they saw it, of other activities such as creating intelligence documents. Comments were also made regarding the implementation of decentralisation and the devolution of centralised responsibility, which they saw as having created a 'patch mentality' where data, information and subsequent knowledge became 'District' property rather than an organisational asset shared appropriately across the organisation. A problem may be that the very functions that have been put in place to improve efficiency and accountability are to a degree inhibiting efficiency and inhibiting organisational development through knowledge sharing. The current study suggests that efficiency gains may be at the expense of reduced service delivery, poor staff morale, motivation and good will. The long-term impact and cost of the new managerialism has still to be ascertained (Loveday 1995). This research goes some way towards understanding the impact of managerialism on police services in relation to knowledge sharing.

IT driving business rather than business driving the IT

Some interviewees raised the issue of the information and communications technology as inhibiting knowledge sharing. They described the IT systems as being aesthetically pleasing but functionally restrictive. However, when they were questioned further about this matter, most officers acknowledged the need for IT to assist in police organisations' increasing accountability and compliance. Interviewees said that IT solutions were embraced by staff who believed that they would free hours for front-line police functions and assist in generating intelligence products, although who now believe that the current IT and information systems impede knowledge sharing. This finding is not peculiar to the Western Australia Police, in fact Chan et al (2001) found a similar situation in the Queensland Police. On a broader scale, research conducted by Ross and Weill (2002) found that 'most organisations are not generating the value from their IT investments that they should be' (p 85). While a number of factors impact this lack of return, the most important factor appears to be senior managers' role in the IT decision-making process. They found that when senior managers abdicate decision-making responsibility to IT executives 'disaster often ensues' (p 85).

It is acknowledged that advances in information and communication technology (ICT) can significantly influence the way in which organisations conduct their business and their overall competitiveness (Bai & Lee 2003). However, to fully realise these benefits, a degree of re-engineering needs to be undertaken, which may include a subtle shift in management style in the organisation (Hedelin & Allwood 2002; Irani & Love 2002).

Police managers should focus on developing a better understanding of the identification and application of ICT in policing environments. The need for such a focus is all the more important when it is considered that police support services have been utilising ICT to assist the 'fight against crime' for many years (Chan et al 2001), but that acquisitions have not been matched by improvements in police managers' ICT knowledge and skills (Ackroyd 1993; Enders 2001a). In fact almost 20 years ago when the ICT revolution was seen as an opportunity for police agencies, it was considered a crisis that very few high ranking police administrators were prepared to take advantage of the opportunity (Munro 1984, p 5). Munro argued in order for police managers to be in a position to meet future strategic challenges, three areas of police managers' professional development needed attention:

- Program budgeting;
- Strategic planning; and
- Information communication technology.

A casual review of police management educational courses nationally and internationally suggests the areas of strategic planning and to some degree financial budgeting have received attention. However, even though police agencies investments in ICT have increased significantly over the past 20 years, exposure to educational courses in information communication technology has not occurred. Accordingly, the situation as outlined by Munro (1984) some 20 years ago concerning police managers' understanding of technology still remains very much an issue that needs to be addressed if the full benefits for knowledge sharing are to be realised.

The perceived facilitator of knowledge sharing

Training courses

The only universally agreed *facilitator* of knowledge sharing is related to in-service training courses. Of particular relevance is our finding that the knowledge gained by attending the course was deemed less important than knowledge shared during breakout sessions and lunch breaks. If the networking is more important than the course, then the Western Australia Police needs to explore further ways of breaking down networking barriers and creating spaces for social interaction. For example, the spatial design of its offices may need to be reviewed. Another aspect of the review may include the adoption of communities of practice (Wenger 1998) and the tools to implement them. Our result is similar to Earl (2001) who found that networking was an important element for knowledge sharing and that this is more likely to be effective where there is a 'tradition of sociability and networking' (p 225).

Conclusion

It would be unfair to assert that police officers and staff have consciously created these inhibitors. Many have evolved unknowingly and often reflect the values of those who shaped the organisation and the senior managers who maintain it and enact initiatives. The literature shows that knowledge is more effectively shared when individuals are not simply presented with answers but are involved in discovering the solution (Leonard-Barton 1998). This involvement is best achieved in less hierarchical and bureaucratic organisations (Davenport & Prusak 1998) and therefore it seems impractical to try to implement such as approach in the current policing environment. Nevertheless, the suitability of the paramilitary, hierarchical structures and the associated authoritarian and bureaucratic command and control style of police management is being continually challenged and the need for police managers to adopt a more modern management style is becoming stronger (Stevens 2000; Etter 1996; Densten 2003).

When it is considered that the 'bread and butter' activities of intelligence analysts and investigators concern accessing, leveraging and sharing knowledge, this shift appears particularly necessary. Police managers need to recognise knowledge management as a holistic purposeful constructive management philosophy with multiple dimensions. Since it is an organisational philosophy, it is not owned by one group or business unit. It has been suggested that such a shift in management style can be achieved through the adoption and application of transformational leadership behaviours (Burns 1978; Bass 1998; Yukl 1998). It is argued that transformational leadership is appropriate to appeal to employees' higher ideals and values including emancipation, participation and equality and not to the more base emotions of fear, greed and jealousy.

Considering the entrenched stratified command and control structure in policing, such a move will not happen immediately. As a first step in this change process, the concept of diverting from the command and control paradigms may be achieved in small but well-designed increments. One solution suggested by Densten (2003) is to encourage employees to shift from continually focusing on their immediate operational environment to one that embraces and integrates other, external environments. Employees would be encouraged to develop 'conceptual maps' of their external environment to establish where their organisation links with that environment. But it is worthwhile repeating our earlier caveat that attempts to remove or ameliorate the impact of inhibitors to knowledge sharing need to consider the complexities and ramifications of the overall knowledge sharing ecology. This shift in focus can be achieved if employees are sufficiently intellectually stimulated which in turn depends on the organisation's commitment to critical reflection, learning and placing value on knowledge rather than solely on information. Ruggles (1998, p 88) endorses the importance of the human element in organisations in saying: 'if we have learned nothing else ... we have seen clearly the importance of getting approximately the 50:25:25 *people, process, and technology* balance right from the outset'.

14

STRESS AND DECISION-MAKING IN POLICE MANAGERS AND LEADERS

David Mutton

Police and stress

Research on police stress has almost become an industry in its own right. What lies behind this abiding interest in police stress? It is a common presumption that police officers work in an inherently stressful occupation although it can be equally asserted that stress is not only a part of most occupations, but is inherent to the human condition. This contention is supported by the finding that police officers perceive organisational factors as a greater source of stress than factors which are specific to policing (Collins & Gibbs 2003). It is precisely those factors that are pertinent to most occupations which police indicate produce the most distress.

The general cost of the impact of stress in occupational settings in both human and financial terms has been well documented in a number of research papers (Caulfield, Chang, Dollard & Elshaug 2004). However, some would contend that the police deserve special help in reducing the causes and consequences of stress, regardless of whether they are more stressed than other professional sectors, because of the singular role police officers play in society. Police officers engage in critical functions and society demands that police are effective in what they do – stress can potentially reduce the effectiveness and efficiency of police. Police officers who are under stress can, in certain situations, pose a real threat to the safety of fellow officers, offenders and the general public.

However, despite this plethora of research into the stress of front-line police, there has been limited research into occupational stress experienced by police leaders and managers. This chapter reviews the research and presents a series of case examples based on the author's experience as a police psychologist that illustrate many of the challenges facing those seeking to address issues of stress among police managers.

Case example 1

Police psychologists are often asked to assess front-line police officers regarding fitness for duty, especially following a major critical incident, or following a series of complaints or concerns about their behaviour or mental stability. It is assumed that the adverse impact that an 'out of control' police officer could create means that law enforcement agencies need to be sure that each officer is fit to undertake full duties, including the carrying and use of their firearms.

In stark contrast, it is rare that these psychologists are asked to address the mental wellbeing of the police managers, despite the fact that the are continually informed by the front-line police that the approach of many of their managers was the main cause for poor morale, absenteeism, turnover and low job satisfaction. One psychologist remarked that in an 11-year career with a major police agency, he was asked only once asked to assess the mental stability of one commander after a series of complaints and allegations of bullying and over-emotional interactions with subordinates.

Defining stress and related issues

Defining stress is a troublesome task. Occupational stress is usually viewed as a negative feature that is the 'harmful physical and emotional responses that occur, when the requirements of the job do not match the capabilities, resources, needs, or expectations of the worker' (Copes 2005, p 2). This of course is most evident when a police officer is required to contend with a critical incident. However, over 20 years ago Lazarus (1984) and colleagues hypothesised that it is not the dramatic critical incidents that (in the popular imagination at least) characterise police work, but rather the everyday hassles that are detrimental to the health of police. 'Hassles' are defined as daily interactions with the person's environment that are negative and, because of their chronic nature, could have a significant toll on health.

If a police officer is exposed to too much work, frequent frustrations and other chronic work hassles it can lead to a syndrome known as 'burnout'.

Case example 2

Police undertaking any stress management sessions rarely cite danger or other distressing critical incidents as major sources of stress. They were much more prone to allege poor management, lack of resources, excessive workloads, being let down by the legal system and other organisational issues as what wore them down in the work place. At times they had to be reminded that danger and critical incidents may even be considered possible causes of stress. But, for some, it was the danger and the excitement which motivated them to join the police in the first place.

Burnout is physical and emotional exhaustion and is an adverse work stress reaction with psychological, psycho-physiological and behavioural components (Stinchcomb 2004). Burnout seems to be a major factor in low worker morale, high absenteeism and job turnover rates, physical illness and distress, increased alcohol and drug use, marital and family conflict, and various psychological problems (Greenberg 2004). It has been found to be present among a number of people-focused professions including police (Stinchcomb 2004).

Previous research on senior police management and stress

In contrast to management positions in other organisations, most senior police rise through the ranks of the same organisation (see Casey and Mitchell in this volume). The personal characteristics of senior police are formed by the initial recruitment processes to an occupation that requires some physical competence, a willingness to place themselves in dangerous or distressing situations, moderate cognitive abilities, 'plus subsequent selection for administrative proficiency in a government service where a lack of mistakes is valued more than unusual initiative' (Kirkaldy, Shephard & Cooper 1993, p 73). The fact that they rise through the ranks ensures that senior officers have some credibility with the more junior staff that they manage, but it also limits the external perspective of police managers who, like their staff, may see the world through 'blue eyes'. There is a mindset that employees in a uniformed service develop which can become resistant to external influence or criticism.

Brown and Campbell (1994) show that frontline operational stressors decreasingly impact on high ranked officers, while management-generated stressors increase. This has the effect of placing police middle-managers (such as Local Area Commanders in NSW) at the point where operational and management stressors intersect, making this the rank where potentially the greatest number and variety of stressors impact.

Brown, Cooper, and Dudman (1992, cited in Brown & Campbell 1994) examined stress amongst superintendents or chief superintendents in the UK and Brown et al (1992), found that, when compared with private sector managers, the police superintendents were less likely to be subject to similar job stressors apart from those related to organisational climate and culture. The most frequently mentioned sources of stress were having too much work, staff shortages, insufficient finance and resources and lack of consultation and communication. In comparison, the private sector managers, to whom they were compared, were more likely to indicate sources of stress that were intrinsic to the job, for example, having too much work to do, keeping up with new techniques, career achievement-related stressors and home-work interface problems. Police superintendents also report greater stress associated with organisational structure or climate than their private sector counterparts. Similarly, Cacioppe and Mock (1985, cited in Brown &

Campbell 1994) reported on a study of Australian senior staff in a variety of public and private sector organisations. Senior police officers were found not to report stress symptoms at a greater rate than business managers who had amongst the lowest scores.

Different levels of senior mangers experience stress differently. Lower level police managers are usually highly motivated, success and career oriented in their newly acquired position, and the novel experience of senior management coupled with high personal satisfaction, may influence low stress levels. However, the middle period of an officer's career appears to be the most susceptible to stress (Violanti & Aron 1995). This may be a result of striving for promotion and the perception they are under close scrutiny and observation, and feelings of constantly being evaluated from superiors. For the top-grades of police management, overall job-related tension is lowest, presumably because they have achieved everything they can achieve, reaching the pinnacle of public sector management. Senior officers are most likely to report staff shortages, inadequate support and communication from their line managers, having to deal with police-public conflicts and responding to the media as sources of stress (Collins & Gibbs 2003).

Police officers and the senior officers who manage them, acquire a mindset that becomes entrenched and at times anachronistic. As a rule, the more senior the position, the more likelihood it will lead to survival within an organisation. In New South Wales' response to the Royal Commission into the New South Wales Police Service, there was an attempt to uproot the 'old guard' of police managers. This was achieved by restructuring the organisation, reducing the number of manager/commander positions, and requiring these commanders to apply for the limited number of positions. This was to ensure that the 'right thinking' commanders were put in positions to influence the future direction of policing, while the older style commanders were sidelined into positions of limited influence and power. A negative consequence of this approach was that, along with the disposal of the 'old style of thinking', went a lot of valuable policing experience; along with the 'new style of thinking' came commanders who were relatively unseasoned and not ready for the positions to which they were appointed.

Case example 3

> At one operational debrief after a major critical incident the senior police officer who was running it continually referred to the police involved in the incident as 'my men' and used male pronouns, despite the fact that two of his staff members who had been closely involved in the critical incident were females.

Differences between managers and front-line police

One psychological mechanism which may play an important part in how senior police differ to front-line police in their experience of stress is the concept of *emotional dissonance*. Emotional dissonance has been identified by many as a component of 'emotional labour' (Kruml & Geddes 2000; Morris & Feldman 1996; Steinberg & Figart 1999). Emotional dissonance may be defined as the conflict experienced by an individual between truly felt emotions and emotions required to be expressed by organisations during their working role. That is, emotional dissonance occurs when displayed emotions match with organisational norms and display rules, but clash with one's genuine feelings (Abraham 1999). It has been suggested that emotional dissonance is a form of person-role conflict, 'in which a person's response conflicts with role expectations of the desired level of emotion' (Abraham 1999, p 441).

This can be experienced by police officers if they are required to express emotions that they do not genuinely feel, which can result in feelings of hypocrisy. This may ultimately lead to lowered self-esteem and depression (Zapf 2002). Fox and Spector (2002) reported that emotional dissonance is negatively correlated with job satisfaction. However, reduced job satisfaction is not an equally distributed phenomenon amongst all serving police, but it is distributed differently amongst the different ranks of the organisation. Police officers are in the top six occupations experiencing the most stress and least job satisfaction. In comparison, senior police were found to be less stressed and more satisfied than their employees. It is not possible to ascertain why these differences are occurring but on the whole, lower ranking police officers will spend more time 'on the beat' and interacting with the public than senior police officers, who will spend at least a proportion of their time behind the scenes, suggests that the experience of emotional dissonance may prove to be salient.

Police managers spend proportionately more time in office and administrative duties than front-line police. Furthermore, senior police have a different experience by the mere fact of their relative success in progressing through the police hierarchy. As such, they are likely to identify more with police administrators and experience greater job satisfaction than front-line police. For example, senior police, having come up through the ranks, accept shift work as a normal part of the job. Shift plans are developed with major emphasis on what the military calls 'the needs of the service' and show little, if any, consideration for the social, psychological, and/or physiological impact on the officers.

Anecdotal reports suggest that managers appear to be more concerned with the welfare of the 'organisation' than with the welfare of the officers, and may be seen as having forgotten what it is like to work 'on the street'. Often those who are promoted to senior management are not on front-line duties immediately before promotion making them potentially further removed from the day-to-day experiences of patrol officers even before promotion.

In summary, the literature indicates that police managers (usually Superintendent and above) are more impacted by the non-operational and political stressors than officers on the front-line. There is a further contention that, as they rise through the ranks, police officers become detached from the front-line stressors (including the daily hassles) suffered by their officers, and an impression develops that they are more identified with the upper echelons of the organisation than with their officers.

Most of this literature indicates that it is the organisational issues that are the most pressing causes of stress for police in western policing services. However there are two other equally fundamental, but deeper, causes of stress. The first is that, in Australia, since most police leaders have 'risen through the ranks', they carry with them the stress and trauma that attach themselves to a long police career. The second cause of stress for senior police is the intense loyalties that develop amongst police officers, especially those forged on the front-line during early policing careers. Both of these may have profound effects upon the decision making of senior police officers, especially in relation to the management of their staff.

Stress and trauma

There is little doubt that for a police officer, there is the potential to be exposed to multiple traumas over their career. These range from multiple casualty incidents, attending scenes of death, serious harm to children, and potential life threatening danger to the officer. These are generally termed 'critical incidents', the management of which has caused a great deal of controversy over the past decade. Whether or not police receive debriefing or other psychological intervention post-incident, most police cope successfully with these challenges, and through this process they develop a level of psychological hardiness which offers some 'immunity' to subsequent critical incidents. However, this immunity can be developed at some psychological and personal cost to the individual police officer. This is evident in a 'hardening' process, which is most apparent to the friends and the family members of the police officer.

The higher the rank, the potentially harder and less sympathetic the officer may become to the emotional distress experienced by his or her staff having experienced stress and trauma in their earlier careers, and they cannot understand why many do not enjoy those challenges. Compounding this, many police officers deal with stress and trauma through the psychological defences of denial and suppression – that is, they suppress any notion that a particular experience has caused them any distress. This defence can be adaptive if it allows for a police officer to carry on working without being consumed by emotional reactions, which could affect their judgment or capacity to continue work. Many senior police officers have managed these reactions in this way. However, this practised disconnection with the psychological consequences that naturally follow critical incidents, may result in a limited capacity to function at an empathetic level. One outcome of this approach to trauma is that, if you cannot acknowledge emotional distress within yourself, it is difficult to recognise or respect emotional distress within others, especially your staff. This is compounded by the fact that the more senior the police officer, the less real contact he or she may have with front-line policing. Following critical incidents, subordinate officers are often looking for 'support' from their senior police officers – essentially empathetic acknowledgment. In the absence of this acknowledgment and empathy, many stressed police officers become further damaged in the aftermath of a critical incident.

Case example 4

The Psychology Section not only provides assistance to members of the police staff, but at times also to family members who are affected by the work that the serving officer performed. One spouse of a senior police officer stated that her husband had over the years become hard, un-feeling and intolerant towards the small misfortunes suffered by family members, resulting in a distant and unsympathetic relationship with his children. His wife also often felt that she was 'interrogated like a crimi-nal' during arguments, or that she felt she had to account for herself like a witness in a witness box. The result was that she and her children felt disconnected from her husband. This senior officer, who no doubt had dealt with real pain and trauma firsthand at many critical incidents, ex-pressed his philosophy of life to me: 'you're alive – so stop complaining'. Similar feelings of disconnection, in part, account for many of the relationship breakdowns experience by police officers.

Case example 5

A police psychologist was asked to provide a critical incident debrief to two front-line police officers, who put their lives at risk in pursuit and app-rehension of an armed offender. When she saw them the day after the incident, they were strongly affected by it, but only to the extent that one would expect after such a confrontation. They stated that after taking a couple of days of 'stress leave' they would be willing to return to normal duties in highway patrol. The psychologist had few concerns about the officers and believed quite smugly that the critical incident debrief was a job well done. Two days later she received infuriated telephone calls from the officers. The essence of their rage was that their commanding officer had directly stated to them that he wished that he could have a critical incident so that he could get a couple of days off work. Whether it was a ham-fisted attempt at humour or not, the two officers saw this as a complete disregard of their bravery and distress that they were experiencing. They promptly contacted the police union and decided to take a week off work rather than a couple of days. From there, the reper-cussion of the incident moved into damage control.

One of the roles that psychologists offer within policing organisations is providing education for staff on the effects of stress and trauma and how to manage them at a personal level. While the psychologists were attempting to create an awareness of the potentially negative effects of stress and trauma in policing, there was a suspicion by many senior police that the 'psychs' were in fact contributing to the stress epidemic within the police service. There was a notion by many senior officers, that by giving people the language by which to recognise and describe their emotional reactions, we were in fact creating these reactions. This apprehension may have accounted for a widespread reluctance by senior officers to utilise psychologists following critical incidents for fear that the influence of the psychologists may have on their staff. The NSW Police organisation is now paying dearly for this reluctance to provide suitable psychological assistance post critical incident, in defending (and often losing) claims of negligence in discharging its psychological duty of care to employees.

This inability to recognise psychological distress in others has had a profound impact on senior officers' attitudes towards their staff taking legitimate sick leave on account of psychological distress. They regarded these officers as 'shonks' as they believed that their sick leave and subsequent workers' compensation claims were indeed 'shonky'. In the mind of the senior officers, this had the effect of creating a perception of widespread malingering by staff, and denial of legitimate occupational stress concerns within the organisation. In the face of this apparent lack of support from some police managers, many officers used the workers compensation and sick leave systems as revenge against a supposedly uncaring system, which ultimately has become a great financial burden to the State.

Police loyalties

A further major source of stress in senior police officers arises from the intense loyalties that develop over a police officer's career. As in many service organisations, these loyalties are often forged through 'life and death' operational situations and are functional bonds essential to coping. Police officers assert that it is vital to be able to depend upon a colleague when confronting a critical incident. Officers are at pains to emphasise that they need to be able to act at these times with the full confidence that their colleagues will 'do the right thing' to guarantee their safety, and to ensure that the job was done properly.

These loyalties, however, can be forged at the cost of intolerance towards diversity. This is particularly evident in prejudice shown to those officers manifesting psychological vulnerability such as stress-related conditions. Such officers were often regarded as 'flaky' by their colleagues, who were reluctant to work with them. Their rationale was that they could no longer unquestioningly rely on their colleague's competence at critical moments. This further contributed to a culture of suppression and denial of psychological stress for fear of an individual officer being labelled 'flaky'.

A further effect of this loyalty becomes manifest in supporting one's colleagues regardless of their ethical conduct which can involve turning a blind eye to corruption and supporting those people you know will support you when *you* are called to account. This is not to suggest that all officers are prone to dishonesty. Rather it is a survival response in the face of a 'fault finding' system in which officers at all levels are held liable and punished for acts that many would regard simply as mistakes. In order to avoid the constraints of this punitive system, officers would support each other in the hope that the same favour will be extended to them when their time comes.

This quid pro quo is partly generated by fear. In times of physical danger, each officer wants to be certain that he or she will receive unquestioning, absolute and automatic support from his or her colleagues. They do not want this support to be conditional or diluted by resentment. Therefore this generalises to unquestioning loyalty and support at all times, whether the danger comes from an armed offender or the organisation. These loyalties are deep within the consciousness of senior police which have been forged over a long career and with a number of peers.

As senior officers attain higher and higher positions, the number of promoted positions becomes fewer and fewer. Consequently, they find themselves competing for them with the very people with whom they may have formed these loyalties during the earlier stages of their careers. This results in an interesting and dynamic tension. The very people who would be considered their peers, and with whom there may be strong loyalties, are the very people they feel constrained to discuss their issues with – especially any issues related to their vulnerability. They fear that disclosing vulnerability, such as a psychological distress, may be used against them in a future selection process by the person to whom they confided.

Case example 6

Since 1990, a large Australian police agency has developed a highly regarded peer support program which aims to formalise and facilitate some of the natural support systems that police provide to each other in times of distress. However, these peer support systems tend to focus more on the needs of the front-line police officers. Over this period, many of these peer support officers have assumed upper management positions. However, many senior police complained that, unlike their staff, they did not benefit from these peer support initiatives as they could not communicate distress to more junior peer support officers, especially in their own command. By the same account they were reluctant to discuss any of these issues with their real peers — that is, those officers like themselves who were also in senior management positions. As a result, many senior police officers felt isolated from the traditional support networks that would normally be provided by their fellow police officer peers. The agency battled with the issue of peer support for senior management for many years without a satisfactory resolution. In the end it gave up the idea of providing peer support to police managers. They were dealt with by referral to outsourced professional services if they confided that they were suffering from stress.

An additional outcome of this loyalty is the tendency for police organisations to become rife with 'cronyism'. These loyalties are difficult to disregard where management decisions involve promotion or other dispensation of favours. There is the tendency to confer these favours on to those who have shown loyalty in the past. This serves two purposes: the first is a protective function, in that the person favoured may be aware of past issues in the senior manager's occupational (or private life) which would be better kept undisclosed. The second purpose is that it acts as a reward for the past loyalty. It also ensures that upper management becomes a 'people like us club'.

Case example 7

> A new recruit joined the police, and was soon asked if he was a Catholic or a Mason. He said that he was neither. When he asked why, he was told that the organisation was split down these two lines, and that membership of either would be the only way that he could have a successful career in the organisation as it was at that time. He was strongly advised that, if he was not a Catholic, that he should join the Masons. Over the past 15 years the complexion of the organisation has changed; gone are the religious divides, only to be replaced by divides more aligned along party political lines – that is, Liberal or Labor.

Epilogue

When an author is required to write about occupational stress, the output is necessarily drafted in negative terms, such as 'adverse impacts', 'negative consequences', 'psychological harm' and so forth. This is the tone of the chapter. Accordingly, the picture painted above is not particularly flattering to senior police.

However, it is also possible to take an approach that looks at how the majority of police officers, whether they are junior or senior, cope under often adverse circumstances. In contrast to the plethora of studies into police stress which tends to paint a relatively negative portrait of police, there is also a movement looking at police *resilience* (Liberman et al 2002; Zhao, He & Lovrich 2002; Kelley 2005). This movement attempts to discover the individual personality characteristics, as well as the organisational structures, that allow people to cope under adversity. From an organisational perspective, this is ultimately a more productive pursuit than attempting to identify and eliminate all sources of occupational stress, which is ultimately futile. Identifying resilience factors has some important implications for the recruitment and selection of police. Understanding whether resilience is a body of techniques which can be taught, has great implications for police training. Lastly, research which can identify those managerial and supervisory styles that are likely to enhance resiliencies rather than extinguish it in subordinates will have a great bearing on the future selection and development of police leadership and management.

PART III

MANAGING RELATIONSHIPS IN POLICING

Having discussed police oversight in the previous section, the four chapters in this third and final section explore the many demands that are placed on police organisations from the external social and political environment. Stephen Jiggins explores the importance for police organisations of good management of the news media, and maintaining a positive interaction between the media and police. Jiggins concentrates mostly on the print news media since, as he argues, they are dominant in setting and influencing the daily news agenda. Jiggins also describes the resources that are put into managing the relationship with the media by police departments in order to generate positive publicity where possible and to deal with the inevitable crisis when it occurs. As well as managing external relations through the media, police jurisdictions also devote an enormous expenditure of individual officers' time into consulting with the community. In their chapter, Margaret Mitchell and John Casey provide a critique of some of the problems of consultation such as the representativeness of the 'community' and the explicit and implicit goals of consultation. This chapter is intended not only to provide a taxonomy of the types and forms of consultation but also to assist police managers to reflect on what community consultation is intended to do, and on their own consultation processes.

Police-work with specific Indigenous communities continues to be fraught with difficulties and the over-representation of Indigenous Australians in the justice system both as offenders and victims continues. Chris Cunneen argues in his chapter that policing in Indigenous communities is an important issue 'on any range of measures'. Positive policing in Indigenous communities in urban and rural parts of Australia presents an ongoing challenge to police leaders and local managers in this country. The book concludes, appropriately, with John Casey's chapter on international policing and the challenges associated with the deployment of police to a wide range of countries. The purposes of this deployment include a cooperative response to emerging transnational and international crime threats and peace operations and capacity building in post-conflict and transitional societies. The international deployment of police is only one of the direct, and some would say, positive effects of the new global security environment. We can see the reflection on practice which must occur – as police share and exchange practices – as an important element of new policing, and as having an impact on domestic police management practices far beyond the creation of international 'good practice'.

15

THE NEWS MEDIA

Stephen Jiggins

The media have a significant influence on community perceptions about crime and policing. Few members of the community have direct interaction with the criminal justice system and as a consequence draw their knowledge about such matters from the daily offerings of the print and electronic media and increasingly, online news services (Kirk 2006). The activities of police are heavily stereotyped in novels, television dramas, cartoons and cinema and each medium has its own formulaic and production conventions (Leishman & Mason 2003). Similarly, the news media also have identifiable characteristics associated with their coverage of crime and policing issues: crimes of violence are reported more frequently than crimes such as fraud; the more unusual the crime the more likely it is to be reported; and stories involving conflict tend to have high news value (Chappell & Wilson 1969; Grabosky & Wilson 1989; McGregor 1993; Surette 1992; Tulloch 1998; Reiner 1997).

Crime dominates the news agenda and there is widespread dissatisfaction with the way the media undertake the task of conveying information about this significant part of community life. Fear 'sells' and the media exploit this contributing to what some commentators (Cowdery 2001) have described as an irrational debate about law and order policy.

Police departments across the western world devote considerable resources to managing their relationship with the media in order to generate positive publicity where possible and to deal with the inevitable crisis when it occurs. This chapter explores the world of the print news and the interaction between the media and police. The selection of print media was made on the basis of their dominance in setting and influencing the daily news agenda (Bennett 1990; Kirk 2006).

What kind of dog?

The role of the media in western society has been conceptualised for over 160 years as that of a watchdog, monitoring arms of governance such as the police for the public good. Although it would seem few Australians now have faith in what they regard as 'a media too concentrated amongst a few corporate powerbrokers to check government power' (Denemark 2005, p 238). Implicit in the watchdog model is the assumption that the media are driven by the purest of motives and are not subject to external influences. There is now open questioning as to whether the watchdog metaphor is appropriate. The question '*What kind of dog?*' was posed by Donohue, Tichenor & Olien (1995) in order to try and achieve a better understanding of the contemporary functioning of the mass media. The authors identified three major perspectives of the mass media in the literature:

- the traditional 'fourth estate' role of independently powerful watchdog media;
- the lapdog view of media as largely submissive to status quo political and economic authority; and
- a view of media as neither watchdog nor lapdogs but as intrinsic to the maintenance of power by vested interests.

The authors observe that the ideology of the fourth estate as watchdog is well entrenched, going back to the 1840s, and reflected in US newspaper titles such as the *Sentinel, Monitor, Inquirer, Observer* and *Examiner*. Interestingly these themes are not typically reflected in the titles of major Australian newspapers. The essential elements of the fourth estate watchdog perspective include substantial autonomy for the media, their representation of the interests of the populace rather than dominant groups, and their independent power to challenge these dominant groups.

Donohue, Tichenor and Olien argue that the watchdog conceptualisation is fundamentally flawed because the media tend to be more concerned about the maintenance of power relationships than fundamental changes in social structures and are therefore constrained to commenting on the ideas and actions generated by these groups. Such a view is consistent with the position advanced by many other researchers who argue the conflicts generated by warring bureaucracies is what sets the news-agenda, not the media (Dahrendorf 1959; Altheide & Johnson 1980).

Australian researcher Julianne Schultz (1998) has adopted a more practical perspective and sees commercial pressures as contributing to the demise of the traditional watchdog role. Schultz argues the need to churn out 'product' and keep the ratings high makes it hard to sustain the type of substantial investigations that are associated with watchdog journalism. Peter Wilson, former deputy editor of *The Australian*, claims that investigative journalism in Australia represents less than 0.1 per cent of journalistic output (*The Australian* 2001). The reality is it is simply not cost effective to dedicate resources to long-term investigations that may, or may not, end up as a viable story. Journalism of the calibre of *The Moonlight State* by Chris Masters, that outlined the extent of police corruption in Queensland and contributed to the establishment of the Fitzgerald Inquiry, is becoming increasingly rare. Many commentators believe there is a crisis in western journalism and the basic tenets of the traditional role of the media have all but gone. As Eric

Beecher, former editor of the *Sydney Morning Herald*, has put it 'the horse has well and truly bolted' (Beecher 2001).

Media analysts (Tiffen 1999; Schultz 1998) have revised the watchdog model into something more akin to a 'lapdog'. Lapdog journalism may not be obvious to the average consumer as it is often reflected by omission, that is, what doesn't make the news and whose 'voice' is not reported. The Royal Commission into Aboriginal Deaths in Custody (RCIADIC) provides an insight into lapdog journalism. Studies undertaken for the Royal Commission into the coverage of Indigenous issues found there was a tendency to use non-Aboriginal spokespersons more frequently than Indigenous ones and for the media to focus on events that showed Aboriginal people in a negative light (RCIADIC 1991). Journalists involved in writing these stories may not even be aware of these practices as they are themselves embedded within the social structures on which they are reporting.

Tiffen (1999) has extended the canine metaphors of the media by adding *wolf* and *yapping pack* to the canine descriptions of the role of mass media. The wolf model questions the media's motives, their competence and the impact of news coverage. Media exposés are viewed as gimmicks used in an attempt to increase readers or viewers. While the media adopt a high moral posture on some issues they will, at the same time, titillate the audience with salacious details. Wolf journalism is driven largely by the media's own vested interests whether these be the commercial interests of proprietors or the career interests of journalists.

Tiffen's 'yapping pack' pictures the media as scavengers rather than hunters and reflects the tendency of the media to have a pack mentality 'they run when someone else sounds the hunt, and they chase small prey, their bark more apparent than their bite (1999, p 207). The emergence of the 'yapping pack' has resulted in elements of the media exercising a worrying degree of influence over what should be a broader and better informed debate about criminal justice issues

The transformation of the media from watchdog to yapping pack sounds an ominous warning about media standards. Schultz suggests that in the 1990s entertainment became the guiding principle of journalism in Australia with many long-held values being undermined. While the world was becoming more complex, much of the journalism that we see in Australia reduces issues to simple cardboard cut-outs, 'a shadow play of good and evil' (Schultz 1998, p 232). The view that the media take only the most superficial view of the issues they report is widely held in the literature on the mass media. This would seem particularly relevant to crime reporting where there appears little understanding of the problems confronting police and police executives.

Police-media relations

Historically, the media were probably too close to police to adopt an independent, critical, perspective. Veteran Australian police roundsman, Jack Darmody, describes the extraordinary levels of contact that used to exist between police, crime figures and the media (*The Australian* 2000). Police and reporters would eat together, drink together and share common work routines and practices, reflecting the commonalities between the business of journalism and the business of policing. Fitzgerald observed that this 'closeness' set up an unhealthy dynamic between police and media that potentially compromised the media's independence and their ability to report in a manner that best served the public interest (Fitzgerald 1989). As noted by Fitzgerald, and resonating in a number of contemporary debates (see Pilger 2004), the media can be used by politicians, police officers and public officials who wish to put out propaganda to advance their own interests and harm their enemies. A hunger for 'leaks' and 'scoops' (which sometimes precipitates the events which they predict) and some journalists' relationships with the sources that provide them with information can make it difficult for the media to maintain their independence and a critical stance (Fitzgerald 1989, p 141).

The practices associated with the Fitzgerald era are a far cry from what many see as the 'sanitised' world of today where increasingly junior reporters move from one round to another with limited understanding of the work of police or the fundamentals of the criminal justice system. Journalists are frequently interviewing police who they have never met about cases and issues about which they know little (Keelty 2006). Compounding this problem are police media policies that restrict contact between journalists and police, implemented often in response to the practices of wolf journalism, putting more strain on the police/media relationship. It could be said that the police and the media have gone from sleeping together to something more akin to an acrimonious divorce. Recent interviews with senior police and media contacts (Jiggins 2004) reflect generally high levels of mistrust and a lack of appreciation of each other's roles and problems.

Broader changes in the media environment have also contributed to this deterioration in relations. Competition from the electronic media has resulted in newspapers moving towards the editorial and opinion business and away from the reporting business (Weaver 2001). The electronic media has a natural advantage in covering breaking news and the print media accommodates this by trying to value-add to what has taken place by providing commentary and, ideally, context. Opinion pieces, both in the print and electronic media, are frequently superficial commentaries on the events of the day lacking in context and any real understanding of the issues. These are the simple 'black and white cardboard cut-outs' (Schultz 1998) and are particularly irksome to police struggling to balance competing priorities with community concerns over problems such as illicit drugs and terrorism.

Accompanying this trend is the move towards what Kovach and Rosenstiel (1999) label the 'journalism of assertion', which they see as replacing the traditional journalism of verification. The culture of assertion is one that is less interested in substantiating whether something is true and to one that is more interested in getting the issue into the public discussion. The implications for police are obvious and there are numerous examples in policing during the 1990s where assertions have proven to be without foundation and the officers involved have taken legal action against the newspapers concerned (see, for example, the *Sydney Morning Herald* 2001d).

As noted by Putnis (1996) the media and police have a symbiotic relationship and it is a critical one as most members of society have little direct contact with the criminal justice system. Information about crime, and the efforts of police to combat it, is obtained second-hand through fictional accounts from such vehicles as television dramas, and from the news media. As aptly described by Hall et al (1975), over thirty years ago, the media are the link between crime and the public. The police are therefore heavily reliant on the media to provide a balanced account of the array of issues surrounding the criminal justice system (Cowdery 2001). At its most fundamental, police require the support of the communities they serve in order to be effective, and the news media can have a major impact on perceptions about police performance (Keelty 2006; Reiner 1997; Surette 1992). As organisational entities, police need to compete with other bureaucracies for public funding, and the media are an essential tool in generating positive publicity about successful operations and policies. The media are, therefore, critical to the maintenance of positive relationships with the two most important stakeholders in the policing function: the community and the government.

The broader characteristics of media operations, discussed earlier, will also have a significant impact on the relationship. The emergence of 'wolf journalism' (Tiffen 1999, p 228) illustrates this point and the reader may recall the widely reported replacement of the police minister in New South Wales in 2002; the subsequent involvement of that minister in operational police matters (Williams 2002); and the departure of the State's police commissioner as a result of sustained media attack (ABC 2002b; Weatherburn 2002). A more recent example was claims that the Australian Federal Police (AFP) had been tipped off over the impending importation of drugs into Australia by the so-called 'Bali 9'. In the Bali 9 case, sections of the media repeatedly reported that the father of one of the drug 'mules' had alerted the AFP to the possibility of an importation in order to save his son. According to the AFP this was not the case: the journalist who filed the initial report had misread court documents, which indicated that the police officer who had been contacted by the family was from the Queensland Police not the AFP (Keelty 2006).

News media coverage of policing

A seminal commentary on the characteristics of print media coverage of policing issues compiled by McGregor (1993) resonates with contemporary research on the topic. McGregor noted: there are substantial discrepancies between official accounts of criminal activity and press reports of crime; the media tend to homogenise crime by concentrating on a limited range of crimes (mainly violent crime) and drawing facts from a limited range of sources (police/court reports); the media over-report serious crimes, especially murder and crimes with a sexual element; and, the press concentrates crime reportage on events rather than issues, so crime incidents and specific crimes form the bulk of crime news as opposed to analyses of the causes of crime or remedies, trends or issues. McQuail (1994, p 256) reminds us that assessing media performance on the basis of media content, measured against the extent to which content relates to reality, is open to question. He argues that there is no general answer to questions of meaning construction, but media research has pointed to several elements in a more general framework of social and personal meanings including clues as to what is more or less important, salient or relevant in many different contexts (1994, p 379).

One technique for examining news reports is through framing analysis (Reese, Gandy & Grant 2003). Framing analysis examines how journalists and editors 'package' information for their audiences and how that information is presented. Media frames can be viewed in a number of ways: they can reflect broader social processes as identified by Pilger (2004); they can reflect media views about audiences and what will sell newspapers; they can reflect power relations in terms of the sources that quoted and those that are marginalised; and they highlight the one view that is chosen to the exclusion of all others (Ansah 2000, p 31). As noted by Ansah (2000, p 32), it is this process of inclusion and exclusion, of emphasising or de-emphasising salience, that makes the identification of frames a practical mechanism for establishing predominant meanings and their potential impact in texts.

In print news, the headline is usually pivotal because it provides an instant summary of the story and at the same time locates it within certain reference points for the reader (such as the 'horse race' in the coverage of political matters). Cartoons, as illustrated by the cartoon in Figure 15.1, (opposite) are also indicators of what is at stake in news reports and point to the existence of particular types of media frames.

This particular cartoon provides commentary on the so called 'Keelty affair' when the AFP Commissioner, appearing on the television program 'Sunday', appeared to contradict federal government views about the likelihood of a terrorist attack in Australia ('Sunday' 2004). Commissioner Keelty subsequently issued a media statement (AFP 2004) clarifying his position on the issue but failing to retract his earlier claims. The media generally saw the statement as evidence that the police commissioner had been 'leant-on' by the government (*The Australian* 2004).

Surette (1992) has developed a model that illustrates how the media 'frame' their coverage of policing issues (see Figure 15.2, page 210). Under the model police are portrayed as sheepdogs, protecting the community (sheep) from predatory criminals (wolves). Media portrayals of violent crime reinforce the stereotype of the defenceless victim under attack by an unknown predator. Repeated portrayals in the media reinforce the stereotype and can create 'moral panics' about the level of crime (National Campaign Against Violence and Crime 1998). As noted earlier, the media's view of the world, driven by the news-values of fear, sex, violence and conflict, is not consistent with criminological data about the level and types of crime in our society. According to Surette the police have an impossible task of responding to media-generated crime waves based on isolated events being portrayed as the norm.

The cartoon (below) provides commentary on the so called 'Keelty affair' when the AFP Commissioner, appearing on the television program *Sunday* (Sunday 2004), appeared to contradict federal government views about the likelihood of a terrorist attack in Australia.

The diagram (Figure 15.2, over the page) shows the police protecting the public from predatory criminals. Media portrayals of violent crime reinforce the stereotype of the defenceless victim under attack by an unknown predator. Frequent portrayals reinforce the stereotype. The media's view of the world, reflected in the model, is not consistent with criminological data that show property crimes are more frequent than personal crime and, in terms of crimes against the person, the offender is frequently known by the victim.

Figure 15.1: Nicholson cartoon, *The Australian*

Source: The Australian (2004, p 12), reproduced with permission

Figure 15.2: The social ecology of crime in the entertainment media as proposed by Surette

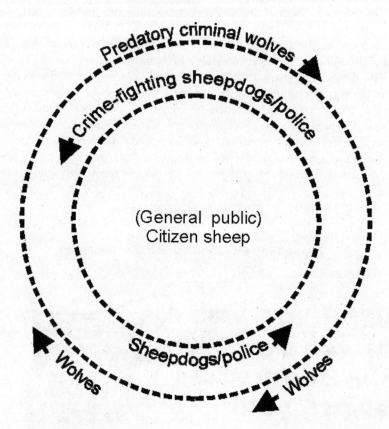

Source: Surette (1992, p 43)

Top Cops

As noted by AFP Commissioner, Mick Keelty (*The Australian* 2002, p 7), police commissioners are increasingly being seen as individually accountable for the delivery of an effective policing service. In an Australian context there is evidence (Jiggins 2004) to support the observation that senior police are high-profile public figures who are subject to increasing news media and public scrutiny. Two of Australia's most senior police officers: former AFP Commissioner, Mick Palmer, and former Victoria Police Chief Commissioner, Mr Neil Comrie, on their retirement both lamented the pressures of public office. In one of Commissioner Comrie's final media interviews he noted 'I have not enjoyed the fact that I am no longer anonymous' (*The Age* 2000, News Extra p 2). The journalist speculated that the media and public attention was one of the contributing factors that led to Commissioner

Comrie's decision to retire early. Commissioner Palmer, retiring AFP chief, also commented on the scrutiny associated with public office (Palmer 2001, p 2):

> Historically, police have regarded their activities as their own and inquiries from the media and elsewhere were met with a blunt 'this is private police business' response. Today, such an attitude would be untenable and quite frankly, I think the need for police to be more accountable for the expenditure of scarce public resources is a positive development.

Police chiefs, as noted by Palmer (2001, p 2), have emerged as significant public figures, reflecting, in part, government and public expectations about policing in the wake of police corruption, and, no doubt, the news media's tendency to personalise news:

> No one aspires to be a Police Commissioner simply to maintain the status quo. Quite rightly governments and the community are looking for innovative ideas and solutions to what some may see as intractable problems. For example, driving to work this morning, I heard a caller on Canberra radio station 2CN wanting more money to be spent on the 'drug problem'. The caller admitted that she did not have a solution to the problem, but thought that more needed to be done. The comment highlights the importance of listening to community concerns and explaining to the community why we do the things we do.

The problems of crime and corruption would seem to many in the community as insurmountable. The appointment in 1996 of NSW Police Commissioner, Mr Peter Ryan, was framed by the press as a new start towards addressing long standing problems:

- 'I'll clean force/New Commissioner's promise' (*Daily Telegraph* 1996a, p 1)
- 'Nowhere to hide for corrupt police' (*Daily Telegraph* 1996b, p 17)
- 'Ryan's new broom/Police chief to launch reform program' (*Daily Telegraph* 1996c, p 1).

Against this backdrop, in New South Wales at least, a person arrived who was described by the then NSW Premier as 'the world's greatest police chief' (*Sydney Morning Herald* 2001a). Commissioner Ryan had such a high profile that he was included in MacDowell's book *Inside Story* (2001) in which 'twenty famous Australians tell their story' – ironically Peter Ryan was more commonly associated with his British heritage and, as illustrated in the Warren cartoon at Figure 15.3 (over the page), was typically 'framed' as a London 'bobby' by Sydney cartoonists.

The cartoon depicts Commissioner Ryan as the iconic London 'bobby' with his plan for the day.

Within weeks of his departure from office, a biography, *Peter Ryan – The Inside Story* (Williams 2002), was in the bookshops. Williams (2002, p 336) concludes her biography by noting:

Figure 15.3: Warren cartoon, the *Daily Telegraph*

Source: Daily Telegraph (1998, p 10), reproduced with permission

Sure, he may have become the victim of his own celebrity. And maybe, just maybe, he could have looked down from his pedestal more carefully to see the warning signs.

The concept of a 'top cop' is not limited to high-profile police commissioners and it is frequently used by the media to frame their discourse about police leaders regardless of the profile of the person in the position. The 'top cop' is the figurehead for crime control policies and, as illustrated by the following quote (*Herald Sun* 2000, p 25), is expected to lead the community discourse about crime-control policy and be responsible for the actions of the police service:

> The state's top cop believes the drug is the single biggest scourge facing his force and society in general. But his solution to the problem would seem more in keeping with a liberal sociologist than a former frontline detective. He says the only way to beat heroin is with a multi-faceted approach with a heavy emphasis on identifying young people most vulnerable to drug addiction and getting them into education and treatment programs.

The report frames Victorian Police Commissioner Comrie as an opinion leader with a view 'more in keeping with a liberal sociologist than a former front-line detective'. The observation by the journalist reflects the changing nature of the role of police commissioner from conservative follower to radical reformer.

The police-media interface – where to from here?

Putnis (1996) notes it is a fact of life that police need the media and the media need the police. Occasionally these interests combine, often they don't, hence the uneasy marriage between the two. A senior police colleague described the situation this way: 'They are like a deranged dog: one minute they are the friendly family pet, the next minute they are at your throat' (Jiggins 2004, p 275). The media are of course both the family pet and the deranged beast depending on the issue and the circumstances at the time. The imperative for senior police is to recognise what type of dog they are dealing with.

Working with the media recognises the fact that today, journalists will tend to have less experience than their counterparts of a decade ago, and will probably be under greater pressure to produce stories quickly and to move on to covering something else (Keelty 2006). As a consequence stories about policing will tend to be 'lighter' and based on limited research. Editorial decisions will influence what issues are covered and how these issues are treated within the paper or bulletin (Pilger 2004). Police could benefit from a more realistic appraisal of where particular media are coming from and identify their general orientation. Knowing that journalists are under enormous pressure means that the packaged story, with relevant footage, spokespersons and background material, has a much higher probability of getting positive media coverage as illustrated through large drug seizures by federal law enforcement authorities. The sure-fire formulae of: file footage, live drugs and set press conference has delivered positive publicity for these agencies.

There is, of course, no such thing as 'the media' or 'the police'. In thinking about media/police relations we are looking at thousands of interactions that occur across a range of levels every day. In developing media strategies, police organisations should be more mindful of media frames than news values. With large drug seizures, for example, police can highlight the fact that such operations can lead to the dismantling of criminal syndicates – the media are more likely to focus on the amount of the drug and where it fits in to the hierarchy of 'record' seizures. Police could do a better job of identifying what is 'at stake' in police operations and frame their public comments accordingly.

Wilson (2001) reports on the outcomes arising from a UK conference on the aptly named theme 'Criminal Justice and the Media: an Uneasy Marriage?' Speakers at the conference observed that stories that arouse fear sell papers, and journalists exploit this, however, they also questioned whether this assumption couldn't be turned around and positive narratives, told in an interesting way, could also be used to sell papers. It was also noted that, although newspaper reporting of crime is often neither subtle nor sophisticated, television programs thrive on drama, which demands more of the viewer. Speakers questioned whether newspapers underestimate the curiosity and intelligence of the public and whether stories did need to be written to the lowest common denominator. This observation reinforces the call for media professionals to consider more carefully how they frame police-related stories.

Speakers at the conference also observed that the relationship between the criminal justice system and the media is often tense as they have to fulfil different roles, and hidden agendas may be operating, but it is still necessary to communicate effectively so as to identify 'win-win' situations.

In addition to the sort of paradigm change in how the print media frame police related stories, an area that obviously brings 'heat' into the relationship is the reliance on 'un-named' sources. Efforts by police to control contacts with the media have exacerbated this problem through media resorting to un-named sources for information, in the absence of more detailed information from official sources (Breen 1995). The UK conference recommended that police become less secretive and more proactive in providing information as a way around this problem (Wilson 2001).

The concept of 'public interest' is a defence invoked by the media to cover what might be seen as suspect journalist practices, and the term 'propriety interest' might be more appropriate (Christie 1998). A number of commentators (Altheide & Johnson 1980; Herman & Chomsky 1988; Pilger 2004; Rosen 1993; Schultz 1998) point to examples of news-stories based on leaks by sources that used the media to achieve a particular (hidden) objective. Chris Mitchell, Editor of the *Courier Mail* until 2002, suggests these practices may be changing:

> I think journalists were often more ready to accept feeds and leaks without questioning the motives of the leakers, simply to gain an exclusive. I think there's a much greater understanding across our profession now about the motives of people who leak the material to us, and I think, not just in Brisbane, but really across our business, people are conscious of not being used by their sources (ABC 2002a).

The fundamental ideal embedded in journalist codes of ethics is the objective reporting of events. However, we have seen in Australia over the past three decades, a more active media intent on pursuing a particular agenda. Examples include the anti-drugs campaign by the *Sun Herald* newspaper in New South Wales; and the *Daily Telegraph's* opposition to a heroin trial in the Australian Capital Territory, and campaign against Police Commissioner, Mr Peter Ryan.

Chartier and Gabler (2001) note that journalists are not educators, or at least, that is not their primary role. From this perspective, it is not surprising that media coverage seldom results in more than cursory coverage of an issue, contributing little if anything to the more complicated process of working through the problems. According to Yankelovich (1991), news coverage that presents positions as adversarial often actually retards progress towards dealing meaningfully with issues. The adversarial position rarely corresponds to the real views of most people but is a characteristic frame in news reports about policing in Australia (Jiggins 2004, p 346).

Chartier and Gabler (2001) also observe that drama seems to be the mainstay of media coverage. The media tend to highlight existing concerns, uncertainties and conflicts, rarely question the legitimacy of any source, and present all sources on an equal footing. Information is provided to the public with little or no analysis of its technical accuracy. This scenario presents major challenges for police in trying to communicate alternative, 'expert', views to the public. It is this aspect of the interface that is most troubling, as noted by Hall et al (1975) nearly 30 years ago, Surette (1992) over a decade ago, and most recently by Weatherburn (2002), Cowdery (2001) and Keelty (2006).

The UK conference report (Wilson 2001), contained some practical suggestions aimed at narrowing the gap between media and police constructions of reality. The report noted that the criminal justice system needs to take risks and let the media into its world, so that real communication can take place; and, that the media should be made more accountable and acknowledge they portray crime through a distorted world-view (Wilson 2001, p 15). The conference report called on police and the media to recognise that each has differing roles, and they needed to communicate more effectively. The police needed to be more open, transparent and accessible, and where possible, provide background briefings, taking into consideration the rights of individuals, victims and offenders; and to be more proactive in feeding good stories to the media and supporting these stories with statistics. An example of such an approach is by Keith Moor, Insight Editor for the *Herald Sun* newspaper on a range of major police operations (see excerpt of article, over the page, 'Dictator's drug ship', *Herald Sun* (2006)).

The article provides a detailed account of the events surrounding the importation, the subsequent trail and sentencing, and provides the reader with an understanding of the issues involved. Giving Moor access to the case officer facilitated a win-win situation for the paper and the law enforcement agencies involved. Police managers could read the report in full and to consider how they would have handled a request by the media to compile a similar report on any of their high profile operations.

Citizen media

The growth of personal weblogs or blogs, so called 'citizen media' warrants at least a brief mention. It is estimated that there are some 60 million blogs containing independent user-generated content on the Internet (Gordon 2006). *Technorati*, a web monitoring company claims there are over 175,000 new blogs every day with bloggers updating their blogs regularly to the tune of over 1.6 million posts per day, or over 18 updates a second (Gordon 2006).

Article: 'Dictator's drug ship' by Keith Moor

A North Korean official ordered the crew on the *Pong Su* heroin ship to stop and fight to avoid capture in Australia.

Radio messages seized by Australian Federal Police reveal the battle order was made as the *Pong Su was* being chased along the Victorian coast.

The *Pong Su sent* a message to North Korea saying: 'As a soldier for the greatest general we are determined to fight to the last man'.

It had just dropped 150 kg of heroin worth $165 million at Boggaley Creek near Lorne – resulting in Victoria's biggest heroin bust.

Source: Herald Sun (2006), reproduced with permission

The London bombings in July 2005 provide an insight into the world of the bloggers. *Technorati* put up a special page on its site to cover the events in London (Sifry 2005). There were just over 500,000 posts from Midnight – 11 am Pacific Time (the bombings took place at 12.51 am Pacific Time). *Technorati* is reported to have spotted the first cell phone pictures of the London bombings within minutes of the attacks, as images were posted on blogs (National Geographic News 2005). *Technorati* site founder David Sifry described the media's weaving of amateur phone images with professional footage as a 'seminal event'. Following the bombings, police appealed for video footage or phone images taken near the London bombing sites and established an email link for that purpose (<images@met.police.uk>).

Citizen media are likely to impact on both police and media operations.

Conclusion

The media environment has changed significantly over the past two decades. Competition from the electronic media has resulted in newspapers moving towards the editorial and opinion business and away from the reporting business. Some commentators argue this trend has also led to a dumbing down of media product and a move away from the journalism of verification to a journalism of assertion. Media organisations are also becoming more business orientated (Kirk 2006) and the search for profit has impacted on the more costly forms of journalism such as investigative reporting with a significant decline in this area. We are also witnessing the impact of the Internet as an information source and the emergence of other forms of information technology, like mobile phones, where images and voice 'grabs' can be captured by anyone, published on the Internet or sent to media outlets.

News values continue to impact on media reports about policing: there are substantial discrepancies between official accounts of criminal activity and press reports of crime; the media tend to homogenise crime by concentrating on a limited range of crimes (mainly violent crime) and drawing facts from a limited range of sources (police/court reports); the media over-report serious crimes, especially murder and crimes with a sexual element; and, the press concentrates crime reportage on events rather than issues, so crime incidents and specific crimes form the bulk of crime news as opposed to analyses of the causes of crime or remedies, trends or issues.

The world of the police has also changed. Following 11 September 2001 police are now more involved counter-terrorism and related issues. These issues go beyond traditional 'criminal' frameworks and cross into the realm of intelligence agencies, military assessments and foreign policy. Understandably these are very 'hot' topics on the public agenda and, as illustrated by the 'Keelty affair', governments are keenly sensitive to public perceptions about threat assessments how terrorist threats are being dealt with. Concerns about terrorism have also impacted on community perceptions about certain ethnic groups and this has impacted on the way the media report incidents involving these groups.

These changes to the media and policing environments highlight the increasingly complex environment facing police leaders and the intense public scrutiny they face. Recognising these changes is essential to building a more productive relationship with the media and the wider community. Police could do more to bring the media into their world, as AFP Commissioner Mick Keelty did with his address to the Australian Press Council, to explain the realities faced by police in their day to day operations. Police should also be more mindful of media frames and place more effort in identifying what is at stake in particular operations and incidents – if left to the media the result is likely to be a naïve analysis presented within well tried media frames: the 'record' drug bust, the 'most horrific car 'crash' and so on.

As identified in the report of the UK conference on police-media relations (Wilson 2001) all is not lost: working with the media is certainly more complex for police than it was a decade or two ago, but the potential for the news media to present a more informed view of the criminal justice system is significant.

16

COMMUNITY-POLICE CONSULTATION: WHAT IS IT AND WHAT IS IT INTENDED TO DO?

Margaret Mitchell and John Casey[1]

This chapter describes the practices and purposes of police consultation with the community. While community consultation has been a central policy in Australian and New Zealand police organisations for the past two decades, both 'community' and 'consultation' are understood to mean very different things depending on the cultural, political and pragmatic contexts of police activity. More recently, the interaction of police with the community has also changed due to an agenda of heightened security. This chapter is intended to assist police managers to reflect on what community consultation is intended to do, and on their own consultation processes. This will go some way to ensuring that the purpose of the various consultation structures is clear and that the outcomes are worth the enormous expenditure of time that community consultation requires. We will start by considering some key terms and concepts and then examine the mechanisms of community consultation and its desired outcomes. The practice and products of community consultation are rarely evaluated objectively, although Victoria Police is an exception. The main findings of the Victoria Police evaluations are presented as are the results of an audit of consultation structures conducted in NSW Police.

The theory of consultation

Community consultation implies input from individuals, advocacy groups and community organisations, although many consultation structures in-

---

1   The authors acknowledge the contribution of Delaine Trofymowych to the early stages of this research. The ideas and analyses in this chapter have previously appeared in conference papers by Casey and Trofymowych (1999), Mitchell (2003) and Casey and Mitchell (2005).

clude participation by other government departments, such as social services, education, health and public safety, and local government (Casey & Mitchell 2007). The term consultation tends to be used interchangeably with *engagement, participation,* and *involvement,* and encompasses a broad range of consultative structures and activities (Tilley & Bullock 2003; Myhill 2006). Consultation with communities is related to other movements in police practice such as *community policing,* and the notion of a police *service* (rather than *force*) (Casey & Mitchell 2007). Consultation underpins other contemporary police models and practices such as *problem-solving, proactive, cooperative, partnership, participation, reassurance and local priority policing* each of which imply dialogue with and some level of support by the communities and citizens policed (Findlay 2004). Policing strategies that are based on closer interaction and consultation with the community are also the basis of what Bayley and Shearing (2001) have described as the *multilateralisation* of policing strategies through social and preventive responses to crime and disorder. The rise of police-community consultation has coincided with broader public sector reforms and the emergence of *New Public Management* and *governance* processes which focus on accountability to stakeholders (Davis & Weller 2001).

The degree to which communities are truly consulted and can participate in decisions about police deployment, focus and priorities is a topic we will return to throughout the chapter. The degree of involvement by the community, and by other government departments, can be thought of as a continuum, from a public relations exercise in which the police simply inform the community about current and future activities, to a full partnership in which there is joint governance of projects or programs (Arnstein 1969; Davis & Bishop 2001; Casey & Mitchell 2007). Recently, there has been a shift in our understanding of law and justice with responsibility for managing crime increasingly being taken on by other agencies and stakeholders (Ransley & Mazerolle, in this volume). A decade ago, Garland (1996; 1997) proposed that the responsibility for safety and security is a community and individual responsibility – what he termed the 'responsibilisation' of crime control and prevention. The idea that police are not solely responsible for law and order is also reflected in ubiquitous 'whole of government' approaches in which agencies work together to mutually solve social, crime and health problems (Bayley & Shearing 2001; Fleming & Rhodes 2004).

Fundamentally, community consultation is intended to maintain positive relations between the police and the community with which it works. Consultation became enshrined in legislation in the United Kingdom through the *Police and Criminal Evidence Act 1984* (Pearse & Gudjonsson 1996), which created the legal responsibility for police to consult. This was confirmed more than a decade later through the 1998 *Crime and Disorder Act* which obliged local police authorities, in partnership with other agencies, to audit, evaluate and consult.

Since the late 1980s in Australia all jurisdictions have developed consultation structures, although there are no legislative requirements as there are in the UK. Consultative activities in Australian policing jurisdictions are based solely on internal management policies and guidelines. Maintaining good relations with the community and involving public opinion in police activities is seen as a central plank of greater openness which, in turn, is seen as an essential element of accountability and corruption resistance. Each royal commission into policing in Australia has recommended more consultation by police and involvement of external stakeholders, whether this is a particular group, such as Aboriginal communities, or consultation in general.

The commitment to consultation was re-affirmed in the recommendations of the Royal Commission into the New South Wales Police Service (Wood 1997) which emphasised the importance of the organisation being transparent in its activities, accountable in its service and not being isolated from the community. The Royal Commission specifically recommended that 'each patrol commander [now Local Area Commander] ... put into effect such form of Community Consultative groups or strategies for community feedback as best meet its needs', and 'that the effective establishment and use of community consultation be regarded as an important aspect in the ongoing assessment of the performance of patrol and regional commanders' (Wood 1997, p 368). Dixon (1999a) noted, however, that the Wood Royal Commission appeared to recreate the same flawed consultation structures that it had criticised in its review of the operations of past consultative committees.

Consultation in practice

Although there is a wide range of possible consultation techniques, including newly emerging processes such as citizen's juries, tele-voting and deliberative conferences police, almost all discourses on consultation quickly focus on the single technique of consultative committees. Community consultative committees – in all their possible manifestations such as *advisory groups*, *customer councils* or *local safety committees* – are the most common form of consultative structures (Ward 1995; Myhill et al 2003). New South Wales and Victoria provide good examples.

New South Wales

Mitchell and Urquhart (2002) conducted an audit of all means by which NSW Police was represented externally on committees, working parties and other consultation structures. This was conducted following the discovery that there was no corporate list of the plethora of public representation and consultation on which NSW Police officers served. Every Local Area Command and administrative unit in the organisation responded with detailed information. The request was deliberately kept simple and asked for the name of the consultation structure, the NSW Police officer who attended, who provides administrative support (ie who was responsible for the agenda, minutes and outcomes of the meetings), what was its general purpose and any other comments.

Over 2500 separate consultation and meeting structures in which sworn officers, primarily, and some civilian staff, regularly participated were reported. Given that the survey documented *all* structures, a small number of statutory committees attended by senior officers dealing with whole-of-government and inter-agency matters were reported. There were also working parties and groups set up to deal, usually in the shorter term, although once set up there seemed to be an inertia which prevented the group being disbanded. These working parties and groups dealt with a particular emergent or critical crime or legislation issue, the deliberations on which required external input and/or cooperation.

By far the majority of the consultation structures reported were the many specific-focus committees dealing with local youth, mental health, domestic violence, Aboriginal matters, drug issues or school liaison, for example, or matters to do with transport, traffic, housing, rural crime matters, police input into community planning, relationships with gay and lesbian groups, or particular ethnic groups. Of these, the greatest number of committees and consultation exercises were concerned with mental health issues and matters concerning youth. Included also were meetings on programs of long standing such as Neighbourhood Watch, most of which were attended by one or more police representatives, and which could take place as frequently as bi-monthly.

Each geographical area also had its own structures dealing with the broad range of community crime and safety matters, including small businesses and representatives from the chamber of commerce. This was particularly the case in more remote areas of the State.

It was also found that, perhaps not surprisingly, a different person often attended to represent the police. This was explained by the fact of shift work, pressure of more urgent police work, the frequent changes in responsibility and location which characterises much of police work, illness, vacations and other reasons why a delegate or new representative would be sent. The occasions when this did not occur were when community consultation was part of the officer's job, such as the Aboriginal Community Liaison Officers, Youth Liaison Officers, and Crime Prevention Officers. Even here there was movement when new staff were appointed to these posts. This when added to the fluidity in representation from the community, the problems of discontinuity are obvious. Often, other than at high-level peak meetings attended by senior government officials and senior police commanders where resolutions and agreements could be reached, and committed to, the police representatives attending the meetings often did not have the necessary decision-making authority. Discontinuity and an inability to commit to decisions clearly hampered the productiveness of the consultation process.

Each meeting of such groups require research, review and preparation and often yielded recommendations and outcomes that needed to be acted upon. Despite this there was no over-arching system to centrally manage problems and solutions as they emerged, to incorporate information about inter-agency projects and programs, to share good practice from other law enforcement agencies, or to provide consistent guidance on corporate issues. The first steps towards such an over-arching system was afforded by the implementation by NSW Police of the new Police and Community Teams (PACTs) in 2002 under the then Minister for Police, Michael Costa. The PACT process included a structure through which information could be centrally collected using a pro-forma communicated electronically through the NSW Police intranet. In the case of the PACT reports this information was available on the NSW Police website to be perused by interested parties both within and outside the organisation. There is an obvious benefit to this open informed communication for the public image of the police. Maintaining such a process, however, requires a substantial commitment both organisationally, and by individuals, and it is understood that the PACTs continue only in certain areas, and central reporting of the results of community consultation is no longer a requirement.

In the survey of consultation structures a degree of duplication of effort was also found, suggesting that rationalisation of the number of community consultation structures might be advisable. However, these structures were considered important to the participants and, in general, both community and police members felt that to amalgamate one process with another, or to disband it, would result in a loss of 'voice' by the community. It is evident that consultation with the community and the community's engagement with the police are both seen as an important component of civic engagement. It was also evident that NSW Police is fulfilling its commitment to consultation with the community and that, as a result, an enormous amount of police time was spent on these necessary consultative groups.

The large number of committees could have been further categorised to obtain an overall picture of consultation by NSW police. Casey and Mitchell (2007) have developed such a taxonomy characterising the differences between consultative committees according to the following dimensions:

- **Ownership/Control.** This describes the power in the consultation represented not only by who makes the decisions (following appropriate consultation) but also who initiates, chairs, hosts, and provides administrative support. In Australia, local governments have an increasing role in crime prevention and may initiate consultation between police and the wider community.

- **Coverage.** This describes the main focus of the committee in geographical terms, whether a local government area, a neighbourhood, a single shopping street or mall, or in terms of a subset of the community such as youth or an ethnic group.

- **Appointment/selection of members.** This describes how members are appointed whether by authorities or through a range of processes akin to an election or nomination.

- **Open versus closed participation**. This describes specifically who may attend and who has a voice and a vote at the meetings can be restricted to appointed/selected members or open to the public.
- **Relationship to other processes**. This describes how the committee interacts with other structures with common interests (eg Neighbourhood Watch with other crime prevention programs) or stands alone.
- **Focus or purpose of activities.** This describes what the committee is intended to do such as information exchange, development of local safety strategies, or the management of public safety and crime prevention programs.

Such taxonomies are useful to both managers and participants in fully understanding the function, purpose and potential outcomes of consultative committees in which they are involved and as a basis for their performance management.

Victoria[2]

Victoria is the Australian police jurisdiction that has made consultation most central to its operating philosophy. In 1998 Victoria Police embarked on a major strategic realignment known as Local Priority Policing, which sought to ensure that the local community became an active participant in shaping policing priorities (Victoria Police 1999). Victoria Police aligned operational boundaries to coincide with local government boundaries, gave local managers more control over specialist services, and created a range of processes to promote community input (Victoria Police 2003).

Each District Inspector was responsible for the establishment of a Local Safety Committee (LSC) as the key local-level component of the Local Priority Policing strategy. The LSCs were implemented against the background of the prior existence of the Police Community Involvement Program, first established in 1981; Neighbourhood Watch, established in 1983; and Police Community Consultation Committees (PCCCs), which were first launched in 1991 as the consultation mechanism for a range of crime prevention initiatives such as the Safer Cities and Shires program. There was also a wide array of previously established community safety committees and other community-based crime prevention programs that had been instituted by other public organisations such as local governments, social service agencies and non-government organisations.

The membership of LSCs comprises a range of appointed representatives from local government, from local offices of State-wide agencies and non-government organisations, and some community representatives. The committees were not intended as forums for grassroots community representation; instead they are seen more as 'management committees' for local

---

2   The following section on Victoria Police is based on cited evaluations and a series of confidential interviews with key stakeholders.

crime prevention and community safety activities (Victoria Police 2003, p 17). District Inspectors were given flexibility to implement the new committees according to local conditions and local experiences with previous consultation. As a result, in some Districts pre-existing consultation structures took on LSC responsibilities and a range of different linkages were created with existing PCCCs and Neighbourhood Watch.

In recent years, there have been four separate evaluations of police consultation and the community governance of community safety programs in Victoria:

1. an internal evaluation by Victoria Police of the LSCs (CMRD 2004);

2. an evaluation of PCCCs done by a consultant under contract to Crime Prevention Victoria;

3. a division of the Victoria Department of Justice (Martin Bonato and Associates 2003); and

4. two evaluations of the governance of local crime prevention structures done in partnership between Crime Prevention Victoria and local universities. (Totikidis, Armstrong & Francis 2005; Sutton, Dussuyer & Cherney 2003)

The combined findings of these four evaluations give a comprehensive picture of the operation of community consultation in Victoria.

The LSC and PCCC evaluations highlighted the considerable variation in how local structures operate and how they interact with other consultation mechanisms. As a result of these variations, the committees were able to respond to local conditions and generally garner positive reviews. The PCCCs were regarded as groundbreaking initiatives at the forefront of the shift to a community policing philosophy. The LSCs, established almost a decade later, were seen as being able to able to fulfil a commitment to extend the existing community consultation by building on the past experiences. The two reports found that both committee structures had significantly enhanced relationships with other government departments, local government and organisations within the community.

But both reports also indicate that, despite the successes, there is widespread concern about the functioning of consultation. The conclusion of the PCCC report was that many committees had not achieved sustained, effective consultation and information exchange with broad representation from local citizens. Many PCCCs had limited reach into the community due to lack of time and resources, and the skills and knowledge on how to approach the wider community were sometimes lacking on committees. The subsequent introduction of LSCs somewhat complicated the situation. The evaluation of PCCCs found that their role was 'severely challenged' as many of the stated aims and objectives of the two types of committees remain the same or similar, despite the theoretical division between the more grassroots focus of PCCCs and the interagency focus of the LSCs. At the time of the evaluations the PCCCs and the LSCs were operating through different units within Victoria Police and there was only limited coordination between the two structures.

The evaluations found that the consultation structures were also hampered by structural difficulties as there were few mechanisms to link consultation with other operational processes. Victoria Polices' internal cultures, and current management processes such as COMPSTAT[3], continued to tie reward and recognition more to reactive crime-fighting approaches than to preventive approaches and to the pursuing of cross-agency synergies. There continued to be operational staff, particularly District Inspectors who still had not embraced community consultation and/or did not have the skills or commitment to promote successful processes. Many senior police acknowledge the value of the interactions on committees and relationships built, but the impacts are generally not considered substantial in terms of their own operational targets.

The two evaluations done in partnership between Crime Prevention Victoria and universities also served to highlight the variations in structures that have been created at local levels to ensure consultation with and participation by a range of stakeholders in crime prevention. Somewhat curiously, one of the reports notes in the Introduction that LSCs were launched by the Police Minister and Chief Commissioner in 2000, but then makes almost no other mention or analysis of the role of Victoria Police or of the Local Priority Policing approach and the 'ownership' of the LSCs is attributed more to local councils than to Victoria Police (Totikidis, Armstrong & Francis 2005). While this is not inconsistent with the flexibility accorded to by Victoria Police to District Inspectors, it also probably reflects the intensity of 'turf wars' in local community safety projects. Leaving aside any debates about ownership, it can be concluded from these evaluations that consultation structures have been effective in generating networks of people, they have had significant input into local safety plans, and they are able to bring diverse resources together to successfully tackle local issues.

All the evaluations identified key elements for successful consultation. The most successful outcomes were observed where there were long established forum that responded to pressing issues, such as drug problems or youth violence. Where such triggers did not exist there appeared to be less incentive to maintain the structures. Success of community consultation was also dependent on the commitment and capacities of key 'local champions'; a clear direction and a sense of purpose; representative membership and continuing attendance; effective chairing of meetings; the availability of resources to support the committees work, and a strong sense of having achieved results individuals.

The reports highlighted the need for local flexibility in the design of consultative structures, and the need for a clear definition of purpose, principles, goals, objectives and performance measures. All the reports called for

---

3   The accountability process based on the New York Police Department model of the same name.

greater coordination between the diverse consultation processes, for the greater dissemination of information about consultative process and good practices, and for skills training for those involve with consultation. Finally, while the reports reaffirmed the primacy of consultation through committee structures, they also called for the use of a greater variety of consultation processes, such as surveys, focus groups, and online feedback.

Criticisms of the process of community consultation

Casey and Trofymowych (1999) have identified structural, operational and ideological criticisms of police-community consultation. Probably the most cutting criticism of the process is a concern about who is representing the community – which community, or community interests do the participants represent, and is this what those recommending that police consult with their communities intended? Those with the time and the inclination to participate in community consultation tend to be older and middle class. While their voice is as legitimate as any other member of the community, ('they may not be *the* community but it is *a* community', Squires 1998, p 171), the challenge is to reach the more marginalised, with whom the police need to engage but who are also the more difficult to engage (Hughes 1994; O'Malley 1997; Squires 1998; Jones & Newburn 2001). Self-evidently, in contemporary Australia where diversity defines the community, there is no one community and so the pursuit of consensus and consistent support for police programs and activities is elusive, as is a common view of the most serious or significant crimes, and the priorities for crime fighting. Consultation can be dominated by organisations such as local councils or business groups or self-selected influential sections of the population, who are likely to be biased towards majority and elite interests. While critics argue that effective responses to broader social needs cannot be achieved with this bias, others argue that the changing equilibria in social relations and service delivery are creating pluralist and multilateral approaches to the challenges of policing and public security (Bayley & Shearing 2001). And despite any elite biases, any well-organised consultative partners are capable of far more than relatively passive acceptance of the police line (Squires 1998). The uneven power relationships inherent in any consultation process can undermine community involvement. There is always the danger that instead of consulting, the police control the agendas, paying only lip-service to other inputs. Carson has said:

> What currently passes for consultation and involvement is mere window dressing. Paraphrasing Beck (1994), can we really scrutinise our programs in crime prevention … and say that the citizens who participate know that the decisions in question are truly open and not just being publicly legitimised? Are communal groups actively involved in decision-*making*, or are their views merely listened to and taken back, even if indeed to be 'taken into account', by a traditionally hierarchical decision-making structure? (Carson 2004b, p 204)

This need to control agendas is attributed to both the ideological imperative of maintaining existing power relationships and demonstrating police expertise in crime fighting and to the organisational imperative of determining priorities by other means which may not coincide with those that emerge from consultation. Hughes (1994) also sees the potential token-ism of consultation as serving only to break down community dissent and distract people from other possibly more conflictive agendas. He believes that this enhances the articulation of traditional, patriarchal values of secu-rity, property and privacy, while allowing issues such as sexual and racial harassment and domestic violence to slip from the agenda.

Finally, the pragmatic argument that 'it [community consultation] doesn't reduce crime' is reinforced by managerialist discourses about per-formance indicators and measurement, arguing that if a quantifiable reduc-tion in crime cannot be attributed to a particular strategy it should not be continued (Bayley 1999; Murray 1999). Evaluations of community policing and consultation processes often find a short-term increase in reported crime usually attributed to the increased confidence that residents have in repor-ting crime to the local police now seen as more accessible (Collins 1996). The stress on crime fighting and social controls which reject consultation-related strategies, call for a return to 'traditional' reactive policing. Note that a wide range of policing philosophies lay claim to 'tradition'. Here, tradition refers to motorised, reactive policing, but others would argue that traditional poli-cing is based on the Peelian notion of the 'beat police' and that 'the people are the police and the police are the people'. While this dialogue also takes place in external social debates over law and order policies, it is most often characterised as part of an internal clash between 'hard' or 'real' and 'soft' policing. Participation by officers in consultation activities is also often not fully compensated under overtime provisions or in performance and promo-tion criteria. Officers can also see consultation and community relations work as undervalued by their peers, being derided as the 'meet and greet cops'. In 1999, Sarre and Tomaino observed that:

> what is conceptualized in theory, however, many not translate well into practice. Asking police to become problem-solvers and expecting them to be constantly engaged in widespread community consultation involves a fundamental challenge to police leadership and culture. Given the current culture, reward structure and community expectations, translating rhe-toric into reality has proved to be a formidable task (p 103).

While progress continues to be slow, there is also widespread evidence of a substantial shift in how the police themselves view their relationship to the communities they serve. A recent example is the US Department of Justice project *Hiring in the Spirit of Service* (Scrivner 2006) which seeks to re-brand US police departments in order to attract new recruits who see service to the community as much an integral part of policing as adventure and law enforcement. While the main emphasis of the project is on recruitment it also

works with police departments to incorporate community-oriented competencies into staff appraisals and performance management processes.

Local intelligence gathering

In addition to being consulted, according to current heightened security
initiatives, communities are also being watched. Perhaps the biggest challenge to consultation efforts over the next few years is how to reconcile these
two operational imperatives Evolving strategies of intelligence-based policing, combined with the current climate of heightened security alert, means
that police seek to engage with the community not only to get their input
into possible policy directions, but also as a valuable source of information
and intelligence and, in the case of certain ethnic communities, as the objects
of heightened scrutiny. In a recent interview with an Australian senior police
commander (Mitchell 2006), it was his view that an important counter-terro-
rist strategy for front-line police was 'to get closer to the communities that
we are policing ... especially to the multi-cultural groups in Australia'.

The current move to strengthen intelligence-driven policing seeks to
combine the 'objective' data generated by centralised crime mapping with
the community intelligence provided by local input, and the possible information flow from consultation processes can be a key to achieving this input
(Maguire & John 2006). Most crimes are solved through information
gathered in the community by cooperative citizens and informants (Findlay
2004; Dixon 2005). Augmenting the hard data generated in intelligence-led
policing with the 'soft data' information provided by local community members renders the data more meaningful, and capable of being acted upon.

Since the terrorist attacks in New York, Madrid and London, rhetoric in
policing is that front-line police officers are in a good position to be the 'eyes
and ears', watching and listening for indicators of, or precursors to, potential
terrorist activity. But how is this to be done? If front-line police are the 'eyes
and ears', what is it that they are to watch and listen for? In addition, 'home-
grown' terrorism has added a further layer of uncertainty about what should
be considered a 'sign' of terrorism. Working closely with communities, while
at the same time observing members of these communities as potential
objects of suspicion, arguably produces dissonance on the part of frontline
police. The suspicion cuts both ways. The Member of Parliament from the
northern England area where the London suicide bombers lived acknowledged that the community was highly suspicious and mistrustful of the
police (BBC News 2006).

Lyons (2002, p 530) argues that 'until we learn to police in ways that
build trusting relationships with those communities where criminals or
terrorists can more easily live lives insulated from observation – no amount
of additional funding or legal authority, consistent with living in a free
society, will increase the capacity of our police forces to gather the crime and
terror-related information we need'. Lyons further argues that police lack

the skills and capability to work in 'genuinely reciprocal citizen partner-ships'. with 'new' socially isolated or immigrant communities who do not traditionally partner with police. 'Community-police partnerships work best' declares Lyons, 'when they are structured to encourage information sharing, [and are] composed of citizens from those communities often least willing to assist police' (2002).

Conclusion

From the case studies on New South Wales and Victoria, it can be concluded that, despite any shortcomings, community consultation continues to have some success as a process that creates dialogue and interchange on local crime and disorder issues and serves to assist police in meeting local accoun-tability and oversight imperatives. While the link to crime reduction of these outcomes may be hard to measure, they are an important value in them-selves. As Casey and Tofymowych (1999) noted, consultation establishes legitimacy with key stakeholder communities such as business and com-munity elites, local activists, and specific ethnic and racial communities, and it continues to be an integral part of the New Public Management and gover-nance frameworks applied to policing.

Consultation processes continue to be essential for mobilising support for police (Squires 1998) and for responding to the consumerist rhetoric of an ethos of effective service and responsiveness to clients. Despite its flaws, consultation continues to reinforce the current agenda of *serving* the com-munity and provides the basis for intelligence-led and problem solving approaches to policing. Consultation is a lynch pin of both operational effec-tiveness and public accountability; it continues to enjoy widespread support, both from within policing and from external oversight bodies and it is an integral part of a wider public movement of public sector reform and citizen participation.

Consultation itself has become entrenched as part of operation philo-sophies over the past fifteen years; Terms like 'partnership' and 'community ownership' have become part of the stock in trade of many crime prevention policies (Carson 2004a, p 2). But are face-to-face committee meetings – the most common form of consultation – the best way to achieve that goal? In other words can 'local policing solutions for local crime problems' actually be achieved through a committee? Further analysis of the different structures – for example, as gained from the reviews of New South Wales and Victoria consultation structures – would be informative as to the value in organi-sational and strategic terms of the large expenditure of time involved in these activities. In both States there is still some frustration about whether the time spent in consultation is productive. While there is a clear and energetic commitment to consultation by managers and commanders, they continue to explore more efficient and effective ways to achieve its purposes. Efforts need to continue not only to find more efficient and effective ways to consult but also to address some ideological issues to ensure that consultation is not seen as a 'soft' option that takes time from real policing. Whatever forms consultation take, each needs to demonstrate that it is capable of measuring the 'pulse' of public safety and crime concerns in its community.[4]

---

4   Practical advice on how to conduct community consultation can be found from the International Association for Public Participation (*IAP2 – Public Participation Toolbox 2000-2004*) or from Carson and Gelber (2001), *Ideas for Community Consultation, Department of Urban Affairs and Planning, New South Wales.*

17

POLICING IN INDIGENOUS COMMUNITIES

Chris Cunneen

Policing in Indigenous communities is a vast topic to summarise, analyse and discuss in just one chapter. It is an important issue on any range of measures. For example, recently some members in the Indigenous community of Palm Island were so impassioned after a death in police custody, they burnt a police station to the ground. This alone should give us pause for reflection that even when Aboriginal-police relations appear stable there can be an underlying volatility. In 2005 the fourth national police custody survey was released by the Australian Institute of Criminology. The survey showed that 26.3 per cent of police custodies in Australia involved Indigenous people. The rate of Indigenous custody was 2028.7 per 100,000 of the Indigenous population. Indigenous people were 17 times more likely to be held in custody than non-Indigenous people in Australia (Taylor & Bareja 2005, pp 22-23). Conversely, Indigenous victimisation rates are also high. The Steering Committee for the Report of Government Service Provision (SCROGSP) noted that, nationally, twice the proportion of Indigenous males and more than two and a half times the proportion of Indigenous females reported being victims of physical or threatened violence than their non-Indigenous counterparts (SCROGSP 2005, Table 3A.11.2). Clearly a great deal of police work involves working with Aboriginal people as both offenders and victims of crime.

Policing in Indigenous communities is an issue that demands attention to a range of broad political, socio-economic, cultural and historical contexts, as well as the more mundane matters of police operational concern. The political context requires us to understand the parameters in which Indigenous communities operate including the nature of Indigenous political demands and the key organisations that articulate those demands. It also requires us to understand the State and Federal policy framework which governments have applied to working with Indigenous communities. The socio-economic context requires us to have knowledge about the position of Indigenous people in Australian society, in particular the consequences which arise from the profound level of disadvantage which many communities face and the impact that has on the relationship with the criminal justice system. The cultural context requires some knowledge about the nature of social relationships and cultural concerns in communities. This might include local aspects of customary law that are important, or local mechanisms for dealing with disputes such as the use of elders. Finally, the historical context is probably more important for police than any other government organisation delivering a service in Aboriginal communities, because police were an important arm in implementing government policy for Indigenous people in many parts of Australia during the much of the 20th century.

Given the complexity of the topic, this chapter will be selective and, from necessity, concentrate relatively briefly on a few key themes. They include the following:

- The background to the contemporary relationship between police and Indigenous people.
- A discussion of some of the key drivers for reform including the Royal Commission into Aboriginal Deaths in Custody (RCIADIC), and more recently Aboriginal Justice Advisory Councils (AJACs) and the development of Aboriginal Justice Agreements.
- A discussion of some of the key policing approaches specific to Indigenous communities such as Aboriginal liaison officers and Aboriginal community police.
- A discussion of some of the key interface issues between police and community including the development of Indigenous community justice mechanisms.

Background

The fundamental contextual issue in the historical relationship between Indigenous people and the police is the fact that Australia was a continent colonised by the British and at the expense of the original inhabitants. The various Indigenous peoples and nations spread throughout the land before the arrival of the British were systematically and extensively removed from their land and generally denied recognition of legal rights to that land and the social and political structures which had governed their lives. This colonising 'project' did not occur in a single instance but can be seen as a long historical process over several centuries.

The legal order which police came to enforce was very much the law of a colonial State which excluded Aboriginal people and sought their control. The defining features of colonial policing in relation to Indigenous people in Australia included the following. First, Indigenous people were subject to paramilitary policing units in a way which was largely outside the experience of other people in Australia. These included groups such as mounted police and native police forces. Secondly, much of the policing which occurred in the 19th century was in the context of military-style operations which

232

at many times resembled far more a state of war, than the type of policing expected in rural and urban communities where there was a degree of political and social consensus. The war-like police operations which existed were influenced by the level of Indigenous resistance, which at times could appear to threaten the general prosperity of the colony (Reynolds 1987, p 27). Policing was an important component in the expansion of British de facto jurisdiction in Australia.

Thirdly, policing was contextualised within the legal ambiguity which surrounded the position of Indigenous people within the colonies. While on the one hand they were seen to be British subjects, Indigenous people were afforded little protection by the law. During the 19th century summary executions and mass murder by police and settlers showed how clearly Indigenous people were beyond the boundaries of legal protection.[1] A characterisation of the early colonial period was the suspension of the rule of law in relation to Indigenous people: the murder of Indigenous people could be overlooked.

In the later 'protection' period of the first half of the 20th century police also played a fundamental role in many States in ensuring government policy was implemented. Police were involved in enforcing work relations and prohibiting movement, in controlling day-to-day lives of Indigenous people, in the removal of children in some parts of Australia, and in policing particular moral and social standards (Johnston 1991, Vol 2, p 21). The protection period was a time in Australia's history when common law protections ensuring basic rights and freedoms could be cast aside and when basic citizenship rights were denied.[2]

As a result, the rule of law as a constraint on arbitrary power and as a guarantee of equality before the law was suspended in relation to Aboriginal people from the time of first colonisation in the late 18th century until firmer legal commitments to the equality before the law came into play in the 1970s, such as the introduction of the *Racial Discrimination Act 1975* (Cth). In the long term, police legitimacy itself relies on the rule of law; on the impartial application of rules, the protection of individual rights and procedural fairness. In this sense, police legitimacy has not existed in Indigenous communities. Historically, Aboriginal and Torres Strait Islander communities have not been policed by consent in Australia.

Finally, the suspension of the rule of law and the use of violence against Indigenous people was also contextualised and legitimated within racialised constructions of Aboriginal people as inferior, lesser human beings. There is no doubt that these racialised constructions of Aboriginality changed during the 19th and 20th centuries from notions of primitive bar-

---

1   See Kercher (1995, pp 7-9) for a discussion on the use of the term 'mass murder' in this context.

2   See the *Bringing Them Home* report for a discussion of the loss of common law and international human rights protections (NISATSIC 1997, pp 247-276); see Chesterman and Galligan (1997) for an extensive discussion on citizenship rights and Indigenous people in Australia.

barism to views about a race 'doomed' to extinction, and indeed competing views about race were often prevalent at the same time (McGregor 1997). However, what is important in the context of policing is that racialised constructions of Aboriginality inevitably facilitated discriminatory intervention. Such institutionalised and legalised discrimination reached its peak during the protection period when police were authorised to exercise extensive control over the lives of Indigenous people.

The impetus for reform

The key driver to reform the relationship between Indigenous people and the police over the last several decades has been the Royal Commission into Aboriginal Deaths in Custody (RCIADIC) and the range of initiatives that were connected to the recommendations from the inquiry, including the development of Aboriginal Justice Advisory Councils (AJACs), the national Indigenous and Ministerial Summits on Deaths In Custody (1997) and the subsequent development of Aboriginal Justice Agreements.

The Royal Commission into Aboriginal Deaths in Custody

The Royal Commission into Aboriginal Deaths in Custody (RCIADIC) was established in 1987 and reported to the Federal Parliament some four years later. It was generated by the activism from Aboriginal organisations including the Committee to Defend Black Rights and Aboriginal Legal Services, the families of those who had died in custody and their supporters. From the early 1980s there had been a number of deaths in police and prison custody which caused serious alarm among Aboriginal communities across the country. In the end the RCIADIC investigated 99 deaths, of which nearly two-thirds (63) occurred in police custody.

The Royal Commission found that the high number of Aboriginal deaths in custody was directly relative to the over-representation of Aboriginal people in custody. The RCIADIC did not find that the deaths were the result of deliberate violence or brutality by police or prison officers. However, failure by custodial authorities to exercise a proper duty of care was also exposed by the Royal Commission (Johnston 1991, Vol 1). The Commission found that there was little understanding of the duty of care owed by custodial authorities (including police) and there were many system defects in relation to exercising care. There were many failures to exercise proper care. In some cases, the failure to offer proper care directly contributed to or caused the death in custody (Wootten 1991; Cunneen 2001, pp 124-125).

The Royal Commission found that there were two ways of tackling the problem of the disproportionate number of Aboriginal people in custody. The first was to reform the criminal justice system; the second approach was to address the problem of the more fundamental factors which bring Indigenous people into contact with the criminal justice system – the underlying issues relating to over-representation. The Commission argued that the principle of Indigenous self-determination must underlie both areas of reform. In particular the resolution of Aboriginal disadvantage could only be achieved through empowerment and self-determination.

The Royal Commission made 339 recommendations to achieve the ends of reducing custody levels, remedying social disadvantage and assuring self-determination. All Australian Governments committed themselves to implementing the majority of recommendations.

The Royal Commission clearly prioritised the need to address the 'underlying issues' affecting Indigenous contact with the criminal justice system:

> Changes to the operation of the criminal justice system alone will not have a significant impact on the number of persons entering into custody or the number of those who die in custody; the social and economic circumstances which both predispose Aboriginal people to offend and which explain why the criminal justice system focuses upon them are much more significant factors in over-representation (Johnston 1991, Vol 4, p 1).

However, the Royal Commission also found that there was much potential to reform the criminal justice system, including both increased diversion from the system and reforms for minimising deaths in custody. This overall focus is reflected in the recommendations from the Royal Commission. The 339 recommendations can be broadly grouped as follows:

- 126 recommendations dealing with underlying issues;
- 106 recommendations dealing with over-representation in the criminal justice system;
- 107 recommendations dealing with deaths in custody (Victorian Implementation Review Team 2004, p 18).

Thus more than a third of recommendations dealt with underlying issues (including education, health, housing, employment and land issues), and slightly less than a third dealt with the changing of the criminal justice system to minimise over-representation (law reform and changes to law, policies and procedures) and another third with deaths in custody issues (including reforming the coronial system and improving custodial health and safety).

Many of the recommendations dealt with diversion from police custody and this is not surprising given that two-thirds of all the deaths which were investigated occurred in police custody rather than prison. Furthermore, most Aboriginal people at the time of the Royal Commission were in police custody for public drunkenness and, to a lesser extent, street offences (Johnston 1991, Vol 1, pp 12-13). The focus of recommendations in this regard was to decriminalise public drunkenness, provide sobering-up shelters, change practice and procedures relating to arrest and bail (particularly for minor offences) and to provide alternatives to the use of police custody. Changes to police practice and legislation to enhance diversion from police custody are called for in Recommendations 60-61, 79-91 and 214-233 (Johnston 1991, Vol 5).

While there were many recommendations made in relation to specific issues like arrest and bail, it is the broader policy-oriented recommendations that are of interest to us in the context of this chapter. Many of the recommendations addressing underlying issues and reform of the criminal justice system implicitly or explicitly referred to the need for negotiation with Indigenous people and organisations. In other words, self-determination is a principle that runs through all the recommendations. It is encapsulated in Recommendation 188 that:

> governments negotiate with appropriate Aboriginal organisations and communities to determine guidelines as to the procedures and processes which should be followed to ensure that the self-determination principle is applied in the design and implementation of any policy or program or the substantial modification of any policy or program which will particularly affect Aboriginal people (Johnston 1991, Vol 5, p 111).

Self-determination was the broad context in which the process of change was to occur.

Aboriginal Justice Advisory Councils

As part of establishing a framework for negotiating with Aboriginal communities, the Royal Commission recommended that independent Aboriginal Justice Advisory Councils (AJACs) be established to provide advice to government on justice-related matters, as well as monitoring the implementation of the Royal Commission recommendations.

In the years immediately following the RCIADIC, all Australian States and Territories established AJACs. Table 17.1 (opposite) summarises the relevant organisations that were originally formed (ATSIC 1997, pp 6-14). In the subsequent years many of the AJACs have been either abolished or allowed to collapse by government. However, New South Wales and Victoria provide examples where the Advisory Committees have flourished and are an important contemporary voice for Indigenous people in relation to criminal justice issues.

When AJACs have failed to operate, police management has often found it necessary to develop a State-wide advisory structure (for example, Queensland Indigenous and Police Service Review and Reference Group).

Indigenous and Ministerial Summits on Deaths in Custody 1997

In 1997 AJACs, ATSIC and other key Indigenous organisations met in Canberra to discuss the outcomes of the Royal Commission into Aboriginal Deaths in Custody and the continuing issue of deaths in custody and high incarceration rates.

Table 17.1: AJACs originally formed in the States and Territories

State/Territory	Date
South Australia	AJAC established in 1990.
Western Australia	An interim AJAC was formed in 1992, followed by the Aboriginal Justice Committee (AJC) in 1994. Later disbanded by the government.
New South Wales	An AJAC was established by the New South Wales Attorney-General in 1993. Still operating today.
Victoria	An AJAC was established in 1993. Still operating today.
Queensland	An AJAC was formed in 1993. In 1997 it was combined with the Aboriginal and Torres Strait Islander Overview Committee and reformed as the Indigenous Advisory Board. Disbanded by the government in 2002.
Australian Capital Territory	An Aboriginal and Torres Strait Islander Consultative Council was appointed by the ACT Government in 1995.
Northern Territory	An AJAC was established in 1996. It is unfunded and only partially functioning.
Tasmania	An interim AJAC was established in September 1997.

Source: ATSIC 1977

The Indigenous Summit recommended the development of Justice Agreements for each State and Territory as a way of improving the delivery of justice programs. It was recommended that Commonwealth, State and Territory Governments develop bilateral agreements on justice issues, and they negotiate with AJACs and other relevant Aboriginal organisations in the development of the agreements. It was recommended that the framework provided by the National Commitment to Improved Outcomes in the Delivery of Programs and Services for Aboriginal and Torres Strait Islander People be utilised in the development of the Justice Agreements, particularly given that this was a Council of Australian Governments endorsed process, and one that had established precedents in health and education during the early part of the 1990s.

The National Commitment had placed a strong emphasis on developing a framework which respected Indigenous self-determination and it was seen as appropriate that this emphasis be included in the development of Justice Agreements. The guiding principles for Justice Agreements as developed at the Indigenous Summit included empowerment, self-determination and self-management by Aboriginal and Torres Strait Islander people. The need to negotiate with and maximise participation by Indigenous people through their representative bodies in the formulation of justice policies which affect them was held to be a central requirement (Ministerial Summit 1997, p 221).

The Indigenous Summit noted best-practice examples of Aboriginal community justice initiatives and established three key principles for the development of Justice Agreements in regard to policing issues. These were:

- the full implementation of the recommendations from the Royal Commission into Aboriginal Deaths in Custody in relation to police and Aboriginal community relations would result in a significant decline in Aboriginal contact with the criminal justice system;
- Aboriginal communities had made significant efforts through community justice programs to address the level of contact between Aboriginal people and the police; and
- locally devised community justice strategies were generally a voluntary effort which required greater government commitment for their development and expansion (Ministerial Summit 1997, p 228).

These community justice initiatives include the Kowanyama and Palm Island Community Justice Groups in Queensland, the Community Justice Panels in Victoria, and various night patrols in Western Australia and also Murri Watch (Queensland), and Tangentyere (Northern Territory). See Cunneen (2001, pp 93-201) for further discussion of these programs.

In July 1997 some 20 Commonwealth, State and Territory ministers responsible for various criminal justice portfolios met with Indigenous representatives from ATSIC, the Aboriginal and Torres Strait Islander Social Justice Commission and AJACs. The Summit resolved to develop justice agreements between Government and Indigenous peoples relating to justice issues. These agreements would address social, economic and cultural issues; justice issues; customary law; law reform and Government funding levels for programs. The agreements would include targets for reducing the rate of Indigenous over-representation in the criminal justice system; planning mechanisms; methods of service delivery; and monitoring and evaluation (Dodson 1997, p 153).

Indigenous justice agreements

Queensland, Western Australia, Victoria and New South Wales have negotiated and signed Justice Agreements with Indigenous people (as represented through AJACs). These agreements vary between jurisdictions but can be seen to contain commonalities, and certainly set the policy framework within each State in relation to criminal justice issues.

The Queensland Justice Agreement can be used as an example. The long-term aim of the Agreement is to reduce Indigenous contact with the criminal justice system to parity with the non-Indigenous rate. A specific goal was to reduce by 50 per cent the rate of Aboriginal and Torres Strait Islander peoples incarcerated in the Queensland criminal justice system by 2011. It will achieve this goal through a range of twenty supporting outcomes and initiatives. Justice agencies, including police, have been required to report against these initiatives and outcomes. There is not space here to discuss each of these twenty initiatives however they include such matters as:

- effective early intervention for Indigenous young people at risk of criminal justice intervention;
- effective diversionary strategies;
- safety and security for Indigenous people in custody;
- criminal justice policies, procedures and practices that are appropriate for Aboriginal and Torres Strait Islander people; and
- increased participation by Aboriginal and Torres Strait Islander in the administration of justice including the development of own solutions.

A recent evaluation of the Justice Agreement in Queensland found that there had been progress in meeting the aims of the Agreement. However, there was a need to resource and expand current initiatives. While the police service had introduced some innovative programs (like the Indigenous Licensing Program) one of the main failings was to ensure alternatives to arrest are used more equitably for Indigenous juveniles and adults (Cunneen 2005).

Agency-specific Indigenous strategic plans

In many States and Territories, police services have developed their own strategic plans for working with or responding to Indigenous clients. Some have been aimed at reducing over-representation, while others have focused on more effective service delivery. These should be distinguished from Justice Agreements because they are not negotiated agreements, although their aims may be similar to the agreements.

An example of this type of plan is the New South Wales Police Service Aboriginal Strategic Direction 2003-2006. The plan sets out six objectives with a range of strategies designed to meet those objectives. The six objectives are:

1. Strengthen communication and understanding between Police and Aboriginal people.

2. Improve community safety by reducing crime and violence within the Aboriginal community.
3. Reduce Aboriginal people's contact with the criminal justice system.
4. Increase Aboriginal cultural awareness throughout NSW Police.
5. Divert Aboriginal youth from crime and anti-social behaviour.
6. Target Aboriginal family violence and sexual abuse.

The plan was audited by the NSW Ombudsman in 2005. In general the Ombudsman found that 'there appears to be an historic shift in the willingness of many Aboriginal communities and leaders to work with police on achieving better outcomes' and that local area commanders 'are now much more conscious of their obligations under the Aboriginal Strategic Direction' (NSW Ombudsman 2005, p 27).

Indigenous people in policing roles

Indigenous people can have a number of roles in policing. The most obvious role is as a fully sworn police officer. Other roles include community police, Aboriginal police–community liaison officers, or as 'special' police such as the pilot Queensland Aboriginal and Torres Strait Islander Police (QATSIP) program.

Aboriginal police–community liaison officers have been in existence for several decades. It appears that in more recent years there has been an improvement in training, employment conditions, and utilisation, at least in some States (Cunneen 2005). However, there are also ongoing endemic problems including the basic difficulty of the role in providing a bridge between police and the community. Some issues recently identified in New South Wales include the failure to fill vacant positions promptly, the lack of females in the position and the lack of an obvious career path (NSW Ombudsman 2005, pp 4-15).

Indigenous community police emerged on the former reserves, and in general exercise powers conferred on them through legislation which enables community councils to pass by-laws for the maintenance of peace and good order. The problems associated with the role and functions of the community police in Queensland for example, have been identified in reports by the Royal Commission into Aboriginal Deaths in Custody, and a number of coronial inquiries into Indigenous deaths in custody. The most recent inquiry was the Coronial Findings in the Death of a Hope Vale Man in an Aboriginal Community Police Van.[3]

The main issues which have been identified are the very limited powers of arrest. Supervision by State police has been consistently found to be inadequate. There are also a range of problems similar to those identified with community liaison officers including employment conditions and training.

---

3   See <www.justice.qld.gov.au/courts/coroner/findings/HopeVale.pdf>.

In an attempt to resolve the problems with Indigenous community police, the Queensland Government piloted the transfer of management and control of Aboriginal and Islander community police to the Queensland Police Service (QPS). Officers were sworn is as 'special constables' and completed the accredited training course designed for Aboriginal community police, as well as additional POST (Police Operational Skills and Tactics) training and training in the use of QPS information technology. An evaluation of the trial on Yarrabah, Woorabinda and Badu Island found at each of the sites, despite contextual differences, that the trial had been successful. However, it was most successful where there was an effective community justice system operating in the community concerned, and a local court to hear charges under the community by-laws (See Cunneen 2005, pp 183-186).

Contemporary issues at the interface with police and Indigenous communities

Community and problem-solving policing

Much of the change in policing in recent decades was brought about within the broad policy framework of community and problem-solving policing. Community policing has been a powerful influence on policing developments even if its adoption has been uneven and contradictory. Problem-solving policing can also lead to contradictory results for the policing of Indigenous people – particularly if it reinforces a particular 'zero tolerance' towards specific types of offenders or offences (for example, repeat offenders or street offences).

The policy initiatives involved in community policing (particularly those aimed at improving Aboriginal-police relations) can sit uncomfortably with the issue of 'over-policing' which has often been associated with policing in Indigenous communities (Cunneen 2001). In townships with a large Indigenous population and with a large police presence it is difficult to see how community policing can be matched with the feeling among the Aboriginal community that they are the object of constant and adverse police attention. Indeed, the 'local problems' which community policing might be called upon to resolve are complex social divisions generated by racism, marginalisation and the history of colonisation. Although the problems of racial tension and poor Aboriginal-police relations manifest themselves at the local level, the root cause of these issues lies more deeply in the specific history of colonial relations in Australia. Understanding and discussing these issues does not mean that community policing is bound to fail, but it does mean we must be aware of the constant constraints and tensions in which particular policies operate.

Community justice mechanisms

Rather than seeing community policing in narrow terms, police managers would do well to think of community policing in the context of its potential relationship to the community justice mechanisms that have developed as initiatives by Indigenous people. Thinking about these potential linkages between community policing and community justice mechanisms allows police managers to consider how they might reposition or realign their interests in developing better relations with Indigenous communities to the interests of Indigenous communities in developing programs and initiatives that reflect an Indigenous response to crime.

Over the past two decades there have been significant development in Indigenous community justice and there are many initiatives in Aboriginal communities that have shown positive results or are promising in their potential impact. When we are looking at successful programs such as those relating to drug and alcohol or to family violence there are a number of themes that re-emerge in relation to ensuring success.

In relation to drug and alcohol programs there appears to be consensus that culturally appropriate and community-based programs that utilise multiple modes of intervention and involve the family and community in treatment are most successful. Harm reduction, treatment and supply control should not be seen as mutually exclusive approaches – for example coordinated approaches between night patrols, sobering-up shelters and treatment facilities might bridge all three approaches (Cunneen & AJAC 2002).

The common themes in evaluations of Indigenous family violence programs include the need for holistic approaches, the utilisation of community development models which emphasise self determination and community ownership, the provision of culturally sensitive treatment which respects traditional law and customs and involves existing structures of authority such as elders, including women (Blagg 2000).

Evaluations of night patrols, community justice groups and Aboriginal courts (or circle sentencing) have been promising (Blagg & Valuri 2004; Harris 2004; Marchetti & Daly 2004; Potas et al 2003). Several of these programs, in particular the community justice groups, have the potential to operate as effective primary crime prevention programs, and to address issues such as:

- Working with Aboriginal young people to keep them connected with their school and actively engaged in learning and/or other pursuits
- Helping Aboriginal communities strengthen their families and communities to better address issues such as early learning difficulties and protection from child abuse and neglect
- Helping Aboriginal people enhance their social and economic wellbeing; and

- Building on the cultural strength of Aboriginal people and Aboriginal communities.

Involvement of Aboriginal courts and community justice groups in sentencing Aboriginal offenders can have a powerful effect on reducing recidivism and assisting rehabilitation. For these types of Indigenous initiatives to work they need the active cooperation and assistance of police at both local and State levels. The type of practical assistance that is required by police can be covered in protocols, guidelines and referral processes.

More generally, police can also play a role as active supporters and advocates for Indigenous run projects. This provides a real opportunity for police to support Indigenous people, to engage with the community and develop a type of community policing that has its starting point in the aspirations of Indigenous people. In this vision of community policing, the building of better Aboriginal-police relations starts with support for local initiatives that derive from Indigenous community aspirations.

18

INTERNATIONAL POLICING

John Casey

Until relatively recently, policing operated primarily in a local dimension. While there were always exceptions, crime tended to be generated from within a limited area; most police officers almost never came into contact with colleagues from distant jurisdictions; and knowledge about policing was generally based on local experiences. Now, the average police officer's operating environment encompasses much broader horizons: crime threats are increasingly global and so police routinely deal with transnational and international issues such as terrorism, e-crime, and human trafficking; officers occasionally find themselves operating on foreign soil, either as part of international investigations, or assigned to one of the increasing number of police contingents working abroad; and police agencies are now measured by international standards of good practice, as knowledge about policing flows freely between countries. Law enforcement has witnessed the same compression of space and time that the current wave of globalisation has imposed on other aspects of society.

For the management of Australian police agencies, this globalisation implies a number of key consequences. Officers at all levels must become conversant with wider realities. They need to understand how policing operates in jurisdictions they are likely to have contact with, and also how shifts in the global political, social and economic landscape are likely to impact on policing in their jurisdiction. This chapter briefly examines the new global security environment and then explores three key areas of the international dimension of policing:

- comparative policing and the creation of international 'good practice';
- cooperative efforts to respond to emerging transnational and international crime threats; and
- peace operations and capacity building in post-conflict and transitional societies.

These themes are examined against the backdrop of the changing imperatives for police managers and leaders to build the organisational capacity needed to operate in a global environment.

Globalisation, crime and policing

Since the late 1980s the world has experienced a new wave of globalisation resulting from a combination of economic and political integration, the widespread use of new communication technologies and cheaper means of transportation. Whether the current globalisation is in fact unprecedented in its level of economic integration, and what its impact will ultimately be is still widely debated. While some authors claim that the new globalisation signals the death knell for nations, others note that nations have survived earlier globalisation processes and that they continue to be the strongest political entities (Firth 2005). National authority may be under siege from global market forces and supranational structures, but it has also been enhanced by concerns for control over sovereignty, the continued strength of national identities, and the failure to produce global institutions that can deliver the same effectiveness, decisiveness and accountability as national-level governments (Bislev 2004; Loader 2004). Similarly, there are competing claims regarding any economic benefits for nations, regions and even individuals.

Notwithstanding such debates about political and economic impacts, there is little doubt that the current wave of globalisation has resulted in new cross-border flows and networks, some of which have had criminogenic consequences that have generated new security concerns (Loader 2004). The mobility of people, money, ideas and commodities has provided new opportunity for crime and any benefits gained by legal economies are also matched by those in illegal economies, criminal enterprises, and terrorist networks, as the world is moving towards a 'single market' for crime and disorder. Sovereign States are finding that their capacity to deliver order and security is increasingly undermined by global forces (Grabosky 1998; Loader 2004).

In western industrialised democracies, the new security environment has developed concurrently with pressures to reduce the size of the State and to pluralise service delivery. Globalisation has facilitated the spread of ideas such as New Public Management and Integrated Governance which have lead to the profound transformation of how governments conduct all public services, at the same time that aspirations for greater private security have transformed how important sectors of society are policed (Bislev 2004). Industrialised democracies were characterised in the post-Second World War period as 'welfare States' that sought to secure the wellbeing of their citizens, but increasingly they are now also conceptualised through a framework of 'risk'. Wellbeing in itself is no longer sufficient, and the governments of these nations must now also guarantee security for their citizens and protect against external threats. An integral part of the reduction of the

State has been the increasing privatisation of public goods and services and in policing there has been an explosion in the use of private security, both locally and on the international scene.

Nation-States are ceding their authority over policing both upward and downward as policing is being restructured by multilateralisation within countries and supranationalisation among countries (Bayley & Shearing 2001). National law enforcement agencies strengthen relations with their counterparts in other countries, undertake joint operations, exchange information, and share facilities through police-specific institutions such as Interpol, at the same time as international institutions such as the European Union and the United Nations are assuming continually greater policing responsibilities. Moreover, development and funding agencies such as the World Bank, the International Monetary Fund and the United Nations Development Program now require recipient nations to reform policing as a condition for receiving assistance. The need to construct security at more encompassing levels is driving the move to create supranational structures for policing for much the same reasons that existing nation-States were created out of previously sovereign principalities, estates, kingdoms, cities, and small countries (Bayley & Shearing 2001).

Comparative policing

The structure and style of policing is the outcome of specific political, legal and cultural histories, and there are considerable differences between countries in how policing responsibilities are structured and how they are distributed between public and private institutions (Pakes 2004; Mawby 2003; Reichel 1999). The mandate and operational framework of any particular police agency may be significantly different from that of its 'equivalent' in another country and such differences extend to the structuring of relationships between the public and private entities with responsibilities for crime prevention, security and public safety.

There are also significant differences in the use of key operational concepts, which are then complicated even further when they are translated from one language to another. In English-speaking industrialised countries, community policing has been a core operating principle for the last two decades. The equivalent term in French is *police de proximité* (similar terms are used in most Latin-based languages), which translates back into English as 'proximity' or 'close' policing. What impact does such a linguistic difference have when English-speaking police compare notes with their colleagues in French, Portuguese or Spanish-speaking countries? (What, for example, happens to all the English-language debates about 'what is community'?) Moreover, there are real questions of how such strategies are applied in countries where community may be defined primarily by social class or ethnic affiliation, or where there is significant lack of *proximité* – social and physical – between the police and the population.

While globalisation is leading to a certain convergence in policing structures and styles, the reality remains that anyone seeking to understand global law enforcement structures must begin with a base of understanding of different policing models. The major dimensions of those differences are the following.

Military vs civilian models

In Britain, Sir Robert Peel established modern policing in 1829 as a purposely civilian organisation, separated from the government under the Westminster system. In contrast, policing authority in many countries is derived more exclusively from the State – the police are servants of the State and not of the people – and tend to be associated more with the military function of government. Militarised police operate with military rank structures (General, Lieutenant, Private, etc) and adhere to strict chains of command, while more civilian police use civilian rank structures (Superintendents, Inspector, Constable and Agent, etc) and have governance structures and practices more along the lines of other public services. In some instances, militarised police may act in a repressive manner and are regarded by the population almost as an occupying force, but there is also a misconception that militarised policing is by definition undemocratic. Authoritarian regimes do rely on militarised policing, but militarised police services are also present in democracies such as Italy and France, where the *Carabinieri* and the *Gendarmerie* are under the Ministry of Defence.

Centralised vs decentralised structured

In highly centralised systems there is only one police agency, which usually has some form of regional management structure that gives only limited independence to the regions. Decentralised systems have multiple police agencies, which may be the result of horizontal decentralisation (parallel agencies at the same level) or vertical (based on regions or levels of government). While Australia is decentralised as a result of the federal system, each State is highly centralised with only one single agency operating throughout the State. In contrast many countries have a number of parallel agencies at each level of government. Italy has six national police forces that operate throughout the country – two with general duties (*Carabinieri* and *Polizia di Stato*) and four with specific duties (including *Guardia di Finanza* that polices fiscal crimes and smuggling) – and there are also provincial and municipal police. The US has a highly decentralised system with more than 20,000 law enforcement agencies around the country operating at the federal, State, county, city and township level, as well as in special districts such as parks and universities.

The reasons for having multiple police agencies vary. They may be a result of the historic independence of different political divisions, or the perceived need for specialisation in policing. Multiple agencies may also be considered necessary to have 'checks and balances' between law enforcement agencies.

Division of responsibilities between criminal justice and public safety agencies

The powers conferred on a police agency and the role that the police play in the broader criminal justice system varies under different legal traditions. In Australia, the police carry out the investigation of an offence and the public prosecutor only acts on finalised investigations; in contrast, the Swedish police share the initiative of the investigation with the prosecutor, while in France and Spain, a third party, the investigative judge, has a key role in preparing a case for court. There are also considerable variations in the division of responsibilities with other public safety and regulatory agencies, such as fire departments, emergency response, and public health.

Level of economic development

The level of economical development of a country will also define the level of service offered to the community as there are considerable costs associated with ensuring a 24-hour, 7-day response capability. In countries where this beyond the means of the economy, some alternatives might exist to fill the void, through either traditional community arrangements or through private security for those who can afford it, but often policing is simply absent. The level of economic development is also reflected in the education levels of the recruits, the training they receive, the wages police earn (with consequent impact on discipline, morale and exposure to corruption) as well as in the availability of sufficient equipment, technology and support services. It may also be reflected in the role of women in policing, with women tending to be marginalised in all but the most developed countries.

'Cultural' differences

The sum total of the above aspects of policing, along with a range other historical, political and social factors, is often translated into an approach that looks at the 'cultural' differences between police agencies (note that the word culture here refers as much to police culture as to the broader cultural aspects of society). The following four broad groupings can be identified (based on the work of Mawby 2003, Reichel 1999 and others):

- **Democratic 'Anglo-Peelian'.** Citizen-focused policing that combines crime control and crime prevention with a welfare and service role. The US version of the model is highly fragmented, leading to significant variations in operational approaches and relations with the communities served.
- **Democratic 'Continental'.** Legitimacy tied more to government and law than to citizens. Policing structures tend more towards centrali-

sation and military models. Multiple agencies may exist to provide 'checks and balances'.

- **Developing nations.** Policing operates with considerable economic constraints, with low-paid police and often without the resources to fully enforce the rule of law or control police corruption. In the most extremes cases, the national government no longer controls internal security, which is largely in the hands of private, and often rival, militias.

- **Authoritarian.** Policing is centralised and militarised, with legitimacy based on government force. Significant focus on controlling dissent which is often repressed brutally, including through torture and extra-judicial killings. Some authoritarian regimes have a religious basis and seek to strictly impose religious law.

Formal structures may be further mediated by other cultural norms and by evolving political and social contexts. Some authors speak of an 'Asian' approach to policing in which a centralised and militarised policing style is complemented by cultural norms that put greater emphasis on social order than on individual rights (Asian Human Rights Commission 2001). The capacity of the police to respond to the needs of citizens, as opposed to only enforcing the power of the State, depends on the rule of law being widely established and on citizen oversight over police conduct.

Globalisation has lead to a significant increase in the international flow of information about policing, as well as the increase in visits of police officers between countries and in assistance and capacity building programs for developing countries. One result is that there is greater dialogue about 'what works' and about good practice in policing and this has resulted in a certain convergence in approaches to policing as police agencies around the world seek to adopt the best of what they see happening in other countries. This convergence has also been promoted through the simultaneous development of responses to emerging international and transnational threats, and by increasing joint international regulation through multilateral agreements and supranational entities. The circulation of good practice has been greatly facilitated by the Internet[1], but often new ideas are imposed without allowing for the impact of traditional practices, indigenous cultures, or adapting them to local conditions.

Responding to transnational and international crime

Transnational crimes are 'offences, the inception and effects of which involve more than one country', while international crimes are 'by their very nature crimes of a global calibre' (Pakes 2004, p 141). While Pakes makes this distinction, other authors use the two terms interchangeably, or use alternate

---

1   See for example the websites of the UN Office of Drugs and Crime and the UN Crime and Justice Research Institute.

terms such as global and cross-border crime. Whichever term is used, they all reflect the reality that criminals and political extremists are using the tools and consequences of globalisation to extend their reach and to create new forms of crime. New international relations have generated a greater mandate to pursue human rights violations, corruption and environmental crime, but they have also generated new political-criminal connections that corrupt governments and imperil attempts to break cycles of poverty and underdevelopment. A final dimension of transnational and international crime is the new impetus for countries to prosecute their citizens who engage in criminal activities abroad or to pursue foreigners who commit crimes from abroad against their citizens.

A small number of entirely new crimes have emerged that use the unique capabilities of information technologies, but the foremost effect of globalisation has been to provide additional means and impetus to existing cross-border criminal activities such as drug smuggling and people trafficking, and to facilitate the commission of an array of previously more 'domestic' activities. As political and economic impediments to travel and international transactions have been minimised, crimes such as fraud, forgery, money laundering, identity theft and commerce in illegal materials have now taken on transnational dimensions, where their prosecution is made more difficult by geographical and jurisdictional limitations and by their sheer scale (Grabosky 1998; Edwards 2004). If a paedophilia website has thousands of subscribers around the world, vast resources and complex international negotiations are needed to investigate and prosecute all those involved, particularly if the website is located in a nation that does not have the means nor will to pursue the crime.

As with all crime, the probability of victimisation as a result of international or transnational crime are filtered through the lens of the public's fear of these crimes and the political capital associated with debates about them. Australia has been fortunate to have not yet suffered a direct terrorist attack, and the probability of being the victim of any of the new crimes is no more likely than other more traditional forms of crime. Yet, given the political salience of threats such as terrorism or the novelty of online crimes such as phishing (stealing bank passwords by creating false websites), and subsequent media focus on them, considerable resources are being allocated to addressing them. There is a real danger of budgets being skewed to focus on new issues while more traditional crime issues are neglected, but transnational and international crime inescapably imply more work for law enforcement agencies in Australia and they require new levels of international cooperation.

Police agencies have options to respond through domestic means, through strengthening existing networks and structures, and through the establishment of new cooperative structures and new supranational structures. Table 18.1 (opposite) lists a range of responses available to Australian law enforcement agencies.

Table 18.1: Operational responses to transnational and international crime

Category of response	Possible responses
Domestic	Increase operational capacity by strengthening: • internal expertise and access to new technologies • cooperation with other Australian police agencies and other security and regulative agencies • cooperation with foreign policy and international relations agencies.
Existing international networks	• Increase cooperation with foreign police and security organisations. • Strengthen links with aid programs to assist potential source countries to increase policing capacity.
New intergovernmental cooperation	• Extend bilateral and multilateral agreements on operational cooperation, extradition, etc • Create joint data bases and mutual access to intelligence • Synchronise legislation
New supranational structures	• Create new structures for international exchange of best-practice and training. • Confer investigative and prosecutorial authority to supranational entities

Source: Author

Not all these responses are within the remit of police agencies, as they may depend more on foreign policy and international law initiatives. Therefore, to operate effectively in international and transnational spheres, police agencies must cooperate more closely with the governmental structures that handle international relations and understand how their task interfaces with related issues such as regional and global security. Currently Australia has dozens of law enforcement and security mutual assistance agreements with nations throughout the world and is a signatory to a number of supranational arrangements and UN conventions. The growing nexus between security issues and foreign aid has become cause for concern by many in the development field (Howell 2006), but from a policing perspective, it provides considerable opportunities for building relations with foreign law enforcement agencies.

Private security is also very much a growing part of transnational and international policing (Walker 2003). New 'professional service' and 'risk management' firms, that eschew the earlier models of clandestine mercenary outfits, now work openly and are awarded large UN-, government- and private contracts to work in quasi-military and civilian policing roles in international deployments and Aid programs. UN peacekeepers and UN CIVPOL (civilian police) officers are hired by, or trained by, private firms such as DynCorp, Civilian Police International Inc, Wakenhut and AEGIS. These firms also work in 'white collar' areas such as commercial fraud, industrial espionage and security of transnational corporations, as well as in areas previously considered to be exclusive to the public policing domain such as security of diplomatic staff, detention of irregular immigrants, and even drug enforcement and peacekeeping operations.

While international relations and cross-agency work is essential, effective responses begin at home, and the capacity of any single police agency to respond to transnational and international crime depends foremost on its internal expertise and its relations with other domestic agencies. While terrorism is an international crime, it is the State police agencies in Australia that must work with the new powers conferred on them. State police marshal the resources to monitor possible suspects and work with other State police agencies and the Australian Federal Police when suspected criminal activities are discovered.

The rise in international and transnational crime has resulted in the considerable strengthening of the role of the Australian Federal Police (AFP). Until the late 1990s the AFP was considered to be a relatively minor player in policing in Australia. But a combination of the need to develop operational capacity against transnational and international crime, to protect Australia against possible terrorist attacks, and to increase Australia's capacity to send police on overseas deployments has meant that significant resources have been given to the AFP. The creation of the AFP's Australian High Tech Crime Centre in 2003 and the International Deployment Group in 2004 are just two examples of the new AFP operations, as are its more visible presence in initiatives related to Australia's foreign policy and aid interests. It is the AFP who represents Australian police internationally, through its networks of 86 international liaison officers posted in 26 countries, through its participation in international cooperation structures such Interpol and regional structures such as the Pacific Islands Chiefs of Police Committee, and through its supervision of overseas policing deployments. This representational role is reinforced externally, given that many partner countries have single national police agencies and so seek a single national intermediary when working with the Australian law enforcement community.

While the post-2001 security environment has created a renewed focus on global threats and on law enforcement cooperation, there have been long standing processes of international law enforcement cooperation. At the beginning of the 20th century it was already being declared that 'police cooperation is more prompt and thorough throughout the world than ever before' (Sylvester 1905 cited in Deflem 2002, p 226) and organisations such as the International Association of Chiefs of Police and Interpol were created in 1901 and 1923 respectively. The current wave of globalisation has given new impetus to this cooperation, both directly in response to transnational and international crime, but also as a globalisation dynamic in itself. Currently supranational policing organisations such as Interpol and the UN Office of Drugs and Crime restrict themselves to gathering and disseminating intelligence about criminal activities, working to harmonise laws and policies on criminal behaviour, providing documentation and training on comparative policing and on evaluating good practice. In contrast, Europol, established in 1992, has provided a model in which police cooperation increasingly goes beyond information exchange and joint operations by vesting operational capacity to a supranational entity. Calls for the establishment of a global police service date to well before the events of 11 September 2001 (Smolen 1995).

However, as Das and Kratcoski (2001, pp 12-25) note, there are also considerable challenges for police agencies in sustaining international cooperation. These include:

- Cooperation requires the full support of politicians and other officials who determine diplomatic relationships between countries. If political barriers are not eliminated cooperation is not possible.

- While there have been efforts to harmonise laws and procedures, nations continue to have different legal traditions, political structures and value systems. If the differences between countries are great, cooperation can be difficult.

- The amount of resources needed to maintain the cooperative agreements is in itself a considerable challenge. Maintaining an effective network of liaison officers or simply assuring the smooth operation of numerous bilateral and multilateral arrangements can be extremely costly.

- Language barriers and lack of knowledge of other countries' customs and cultures are often cited as major factors that inhibit the effectiveness of agreements. Complaints are often voiced about the lack of understanding and sensitivity of visiting officers.

- Distrust because of suspected corruption is a major inhibitor of co-operation. If a country is known for being corrupt, it is unlikely that agreements will be seriously explored with its police organisations, or if such agreements already exist at a diplomatic level there is little chance of them being operationalised.

- Incompatible situations – whether differences in economic development or political stability – are likely to reduce the effectiveness of cooperation. More prosperous countries are generally seen as donors and less prosperous countries are seen as recipients and this imbalance may hinder true cooperation.

- A reluctance to share information continues to be a major barrier, as does the incompatibility of information systems.

Peace operations

In July 2006 Australian police agencies sent 150 officers to East Timor to help re-establish policing functions there after military intervention had quelled the violence that had broken out in May of that year. The Australian police were sent to work with an international policing contingent that included 40 New Zealand officers, 250 officers from the Royal Malaysian Police and some 120 officers from the Portuguese Republican National Guard, a paramilitary force under the Portuguese Ministry of Defence. Among the Australian contingent were 10 officers from Western Australia, the first overseas deployment from that State since it had withdrawn from a previous operation in South-East Asia because of staff shortages. The work of the foreign contingent was made even more difficult by the fact that the sectors of the East Timor police had been implicated in the May violence. A Human Rights Watch report published only a month before the outbreak of violence had warned that the East Timorese government needed to urgently address the problem of police torture and ill-treatment of detainees (Human Rights Watch 2006).

This East Timor example contains all the elements of the challenges currently facing Australian police in regard to peace operations. Australian police are increasingly being called on to participate in international deployments to re-establish functional civilian policing after military interventions have restored immediate calm, and such deployments are considerably taxing the resources of the individual agencies. Once on these deployments, Australian officers are required to work in multinational teams with officers from different policing traditions and to achieve positive outcomes they must address endemic structural problems in the existing local police, many of whom may have been implicated in the violence that lead to the crisis. As they do their job, they are often acutely aware that they earn more in one day than their local counterparts earn in a month.

The East Timor deployment falls under the rubric of 'peace operations', the term used to describe a range of military and police interventions that seek to restore order and create a sustainable society after a period of war or violent civil unrest. These operations include peacekeeping, peace enforcement and capacity building, with these terms focusing on the three typical phases of peace operations – pacification, stabilisation, and institutionalisation (Bayley 2001). During the first phase, public security is provided by the international military; in the second, it is provided either by an international police force or by an interim local police force; and in the third, it is provided by a reconstituted local police force supported through external technical, and perhaps financial, assistance. Once the initial operation has contained the worst of the violence through military intervention, the general rule is that police agencies then take the responsibility of maintaining order. In the final phase, the policing function is transferred back to the newly functioning State.

Although this chapter focuses on policing, it should also be recognised that the role of the military is changing as a result of its increased participation in peace operations and humanitarian aid. The military forces of many countries are transitioning from armed forces focused primarily on war-fighting to forces capable of also conducting a wide range of non-combat functions. The military is important not only because it is capable of wielding deadly force but also because it is equipped with disciplined personnel who can oversee peacemaking and provide humanitarian aid in difficult situations. Bayley (2001) notes that in countries where effective government has ceased to exist, the division between military and police during peace operations will be blurred. A security gap will inevitably emerge unless the military involved in the initial intervention is willing to serve as police until the international community provides a non-military alternative or competent local police are created. Despite the blurring of functions, most international entities still seek to maintain the separation, both operational and symbolic, between military operations and civilian policing.

The ultimate goal of peace operations is to fully return policing responsibility to the newly established State. One of the major challenges is how to recruit police officers, when those employed under old regimes may be compromised. Experts agree that those with records of human rights abuses must be excluded from newly formed local police, as re-established policing can quickly become discredited by association with discredited officers and old behaviour patterns may be passed on to new recruits (Bayley 2001). At the same time, former police, military and militia personnel may be the only ones who have the training needed, and if they are recruited to the new organisations they may have no other employment opportunities and will be a possible source of future criminal activity. This situation also applies to demobilised fighters who formed part of anti-government forces in the previous conflict. The temptation is to attempt to covert these forces into civilian policing organisations, but as Jackson and Lyon (2002) demonstrate through the example of Kosovo (a region of the former Yugoslavia), this can be a dangerous strategy. The armed Albanian ethnic faction in Kosovo agreed to demobilise and it eventually was transformed into the 5000-member civilian-based Kosovo Protection Corps (KPC). The international community envisioned an administrative role for the KPC as fire fighters and civil servants, while the commander of the KPC declared that they would be 'one part police force, one part civil administration and one part Army of Kosovo'. Instead, the KPC soon remobilised its clandestine capabilities and began organising retaliatory violence against ethnic Serbians that returned to the region. To avoid such outcomes, it is essential to establish a fair and transparent vetting process that clearly distinguishes between those with records of abuse from others who may have simply worked for the old regimes.

Another challenge is how to effectively transfer policing expertise. Many foreign experts only have experience from their own country and try to apply that wherever they go, even though advising on police reform requires broad knowledge of alternative models and respect for and adaptation to local culture, social conventions and political realities. The Spanish *Guardia Civil*, a militarised force that polices rural areas in Spain, was selected to serve as the main foreign support for the transformation of the Guatemalan security forces into a National Civilian Police. While the Spanish experts had the advantage of speaking the national language of Guatemala, subsequent evaluations of the reform project strongly criticised its over-reliance on the military model, and recommended a more democratic policing structure be established (International Peace Academy 2003). Reform programs should build on the positive policing and justice traditions that exist locally and take local ownership seriously. At the same time, reform by its very nature presumes that the systems and processes currently in use are inadequate and require modification, but changes must respond to local limitations (Mobekk 2005).

The violence in East Timor has not been the only major challenge facing Australian police deployments in recent years. In 2006 there also was civil unrest in the Solomon Islands, and in 2005 the policing component of the Enhanced Cooperation Program with Papua New Guinea (PNG) was suspended as a result of a PNG court ruling that declared the immunity of Australian police contingent to be unconstitutional. There had also been other tensions between the Australian and PNG police that culminated in a meeting of 300 local officers calling for the expulsion of the Australians. While the difficulties faced in East Timor, Solomon Islands and PNG cannot in any way be blamed solely on the actions of the foreign police deployed in these countries, they do serve as salutary lessons in the challenges inherent in peace operations.

Conclusion: building organisational capacity in global policing

As this chapter has detailed, the last decades have seen significant growth in the international dimension of policing. For Australian police officers this has meant new responsibilities which require a much greater understanding of global contexts and international cooperative structures as well as advanced skills in working in a range of cultural and linguistic settings. It has also put created new organisational pressures as agencies' resources are stretched to meet new commitments and as individual officers are tempted away by new careers in international security and aid programs.

So what can Australian police agencies do? To respond effectively, individual police agencies must build the organisational capacity through a range of human resource responses. Police agencies can incorporate approaches such as productive diversity and cultural competence in order to build this capability needed to work in cross-cultural settings. These approaches have been used by Australian police agencies in the domestic context to ensure stronger relationships with ethnic communities (NPEAB

2000), and their application can be extended to the international context. In operations related to transnational and international crime that are carried out on home soil, there is evident overlap with the domestic use of these approaches, but similar approaches applied to a broader global context can be used to ensure that officers have the cultural knowledge, language skills and networks to work with foreign police and on overseas deployments. The knowledge, behaviours and attitudes needed to effectively work in international settings should be part of the core capacities required of officers assigned to these tasks.

There has been an assumption that police from industrialised countries are able to conduct international operations because they are well-equipped and relatively well-trained. However, as Mobekk (2005, p 24) notes, 'conducting policing within domestic territories is very different from doing so internationally'. Police should receive in-depth training in foreign policing systems, the cultural contexts in which they will work, the lessons learnt from past deployments, and the cross-cultural skills needed for creating trust and obtaining support in international operations. Mobekk (2005) cites the pre-deployment training offered in Australia by the AFP as an example of good practice, but there continues to be a need for coordination between police jurisdictions and with other government and private organisations to ensure that a collective organisational capacity for working in the international arena is continually developed. This capacity is built through education and training, through appropriate recruitments, but also through the management of the human resources needed to effectively deploy officers to transnational and international duties, to provide the necessary logistical and social support to them and their families, and then to re-integrate the officers into other duties when then they complete such service.

References

ABC (Australian Broadcasting Corporation) (1996) A figment of the political imagination, 'Background briefing', Radio National, 24 March, viewed 30 April 2007 <www.abc.net.au/rn/backgroundbriefing/stories/1996/10773.htm>.

ABC (2001) Four Corners celebrates 40 years: interview with Chris Masters, 'Four Corners', 21 August, viewed 14 April 2006 <http://abc.net.au/4corners/4c40/interviews/masters.htm>.

ABC (2002a) Queensland media – beautiful one day, on trial the next, 'The media report', 20 June, viewed 14 April 2006 <www.abc.net.au/rn/talks/8.30/mediarpt/stories/s584866.htm>.

ABC (2002b) A dangerous set of numbers, 'AM program', 1 August, viewed 14 April 2006 <www.abc.net.au/rn/talks/8.30/mediarpt/stories/s635135.htm>.

ABC (2004) Corruption Inc, 'Four Corners' 14 June (Chris Masters), viewed 28 November 2006 <www.abc.net.au/4corners/content/2004/s1131829.htm>.

Abraham, R (1999) 'Emotional dissonance in organisations: conceptualising the roles of self-esteem and job induced tension', *Leadership & Organisation Development Journal*, Vol 20, No 1, p 18.

Achieving Professionalisation of Australasian Policing (2006), PCC/APMC Review – Developing the Future of Policing, unpublished paper presented to Police Commissioners Conference in Melbourne May 2006, to which Ian Lanyon contributed.

Ackroyd, S (1993) 'A case of arrested development? Some consequences of inadequate management in the British Police', *International Journal of Public Sector Management*, Vol 6, No 2, pp 5-12.

ACPO (2003) *Association of Chiefs of Police Officers Investigative Interviewing Strategy*, National Crime and Operations Faculty, England.

Adams, K and Beck, K (2001) 'Critical behaviours for good police managers', *Australasian Centre for Policing Research*, Publication No 139.1, viewed 7 May 2006 <www.acpr.gov.au/pdf/ACPR139_1.pdf>.

Adlam, R and Villiers, P (2003) *Police Leadership in the Twenty-First Century, Philosophy, Doctrine and Developments*, Waterside Press, London.

AFP (Australian Federal Police) (2004) Media Statement from Commissioner Keelty, AFP, Canberra, 16 March.

The Age, (2000) 'A policeman's unhappy lot', News Extra Section, p 2, 9 December.

Albanese, JS (1999) *Criminal Justice*, Allyn and Bacon, Needham Heights, MA.

Alderson, K (2002) 'Powers and responsibilities: reforming NSW criminal investigation law', PhD thesis, University of New South Wales.

Allen, K (1991) 'In pursuit of professional dominance: Australian accounting 1953-1985', *Accounting, Auditing & Accountability Journal*, Vol 4, No 1, pp 51-67.

Allio, R (2005) 'Leadership development: teaching versus learning', *Management Decision*, Vol 43, Issue 7/8.

AIC (Australian Institute of Criminology) (2004) 'Why local government has a major role in crime prevention', No 19, *Crime Reduction Matters*, Australian Institute of Criminology, Canberra.

AIC (2006) 'Crime and criminal justice statistics', viewed 7 May 2006 <www.aic.gov.au/stats/#cjs>.

AIPM (Australian Institute of Police Management) (2005a) *Academic Strategy Project, Stakeholder Interviews*, AIPM, Sydney.

AIPM (2005b) *Annual Report 2004/05*, AIPM, Sydney.

AIPM (2006a) *Academic Strategy Project, Final Report*, AIPM (unpublished report).

AIPM (2006b) *Evaluation Survey Results – All Programs 2004-2005*, AIPM, Sydney.

AIPM (2006c) *Leadership in Counter Terrorism*, AIPM, May, Sydney.

ALRC (Australian Law Reform Commission) (1975) *Criminal Investigation: Interim Report, Australian Law Reform Commission Report #2*, Australian Government Publishing Service, Sydney.

Altheide, D and Johnson, J (1980) *Bureaucratic Propaganda*, Allyn and Bacon, Needham Heights, MA.

An Garda Siochana (2004) 'Programme proposal for consideration by Garda Commissioners', *Garda Executive Leadership Program*, An Garda Siochana (Ireland National Police Service), Dublin, unpublished.

Ansah, K (2000) 'Framing armed conflicts: an analysis of Australian press reporting on the Bougainville Civil War', unpublished PhD thesis, Charles Sturt University.

APMC (Australian Police Ministers Council) (1998) 16th Meeting, Minutes of Proceedings, Gold Coast, 25 November.

APMC (1990) 18th Meeting, Minutes of Proceedings, Darwin, 8 March.

APMC (2005) *Directions in Australasian Policing: 2005-2008*, Australasian Police Ministers' Council, electronic version viewed 30 April 2007 <www.acpr.gov.au/pdf /Directions05-08.pdf>.

APPSC (Australian Police Professional Standards Council Inc) (2001) *Review Report*, 20 July.

APPSC Meeting (2005) Minutes of Proceedings and Resolutions, Cairns, 20 April.

APPSC (2006a) 'Australasian police vacancies', viewed 7 May 2006 <www.appsc. com.au/jobs/search.php>.

APPSC (2006b) 'Police links to universities for degrees', viewed 30 April 2007 <www.appsc.com.au/dbs/tafeunicourses/new_search.php>.

APPSC (2006c) *Project Initiation, Project 1a – Defining the Australasian Policing Profession*, Melbourne, 16 January.

APPSC (2006d) *Project 2*, viewed 7 May 2006 <www.appsc.com.au/programs/project 2.php>.

APPSC (2006e) *Project 4 Final Report*, Resolution by Council, Adelaide, 4 May 2006.

APSC (Australian Police Staff College) (1991a) Board of Control Meeting, Minutes of Proceedings, Canberra, 10 April.

APSC (1991b) Board of Control Meeting, Minutes of Proceedings, Sydney, 10 October.

Arnstein, SR (1969) 'A ladder of citizen participation', *Journal of the American Institute of Planners*, Vol 35, No 4, pp 216-224.

Arsenualt, PM (2004) 'Validating generational differences: a legitimate diversity and leadership issue', *The Leadership & Organisational Development Journal*, Vol 25, No 2, pp 124-141.

Ashworth, A (1994) *The Criminal Process*, Clarendon Press, Oxford.

Ashworth, R, Boyne, G and Walker, R (2002) 'Regulatory problems in the public sector: theories and cases', *Policy and Politics*, Vol 30, No 2, pp 195-211.

Asian Human Rights Commission (2001) 'An overview of the police and rule of law in Asia', viewed 7 May 2006 <www.ahrchk.net/pub/mainfile.php/hrviolations /45/>.

ATSIC (1997) 'Five years on, implementation of the Commonwealth Government responses to the recommendations of the Royal Commission into Aboriginal Deaths in Custody', *Annual/Five Year Report 1996-97*, ATSIC, Canberra.

Australasian Police Education Standards Council Meeting (2001) Minutes of Proceedings, Canberra, 17 May.

Australia, Parliament (1987a) *Higher Education: A Policy Discussion Paper*, [also known as the Dawkins Green Paper] circulated by the Hon J S Dawkins MP, Minister for

Employment, Education and Training, December 1987, Canberra, Government Printer.

Australia, Parliament (1987b) *Higher Education: A Policy Statement*, [also known as the Dawkins White Paper] circulated by the Hon J S Dawkins MP, Minister for Employment, Education and Training, July 1998, Canberra, Government Printer.

The Australian (2000) 'Cops, robbers and reporters', p T14, 20 January.

The Australian (2001) 'And a Walkley goes to?', Media Supplement, p 3, 29 November.

The Australian (2002) 'Police and politics a dangerous blend', p 7, 20 April.

The Australian (2004) 'PM sought Keelty backdown', p 1, 18 March.

Australian Competition and Consumer Commission (ACCC) (2006) *Definition of a Profession*, viewed 2 June 2006 <www.accc.gov.au/content/index.phtml/itemId/277 772>.

Australian Government (2007) City of Gosnells STR8 Talking Community Safety Project, 2007-2010, National Community Crime Prevention Programme, Canberra.

Australian Productivity Commission (2006) *Report on Government Services 2006*, Australian Government, viewed 7 May 2006 <www.pc.gov.au/gsp/reports/rogs/2006 /justice/index.html>.

Australian Public Service Commission (2006) *The Integrated Leadership System*, The Australian Public Service Commission, viewed 7 May 2006 <www.apsc.gov. au/ils/ils.pdf>.

Avery, J (1981) *Police Force or Service?*, Butterworths, Sydney.

Avery, J (1989) 'Professional responsibility in Australian policing', *Police Studies (USA)*, Vol 12, No 4, pp 160-164.

Avery, J (1991) 'Whence cometh professionalism?', *Platypus*, Vol 31, pp 9-12.

Avolio, B, Waldman, D and Yammarino, F (1996) 'Leading without authority: an examination of the impact of transformational leadership cooperative extension work groups and teams', *Journal of Extension*, October.

Bai, RJ and Lee, GG (2003) 'Organizational factors influencing the quality of the IS/IT strategic planning process', *Industrial Management & Data Systems*, Vol 103, No 8, pp 622-32.

Baldwin, J (1992) 'Video-taping of police interviews with suspects – an evaluation', *Police Research Series: Paper No 1*, Home Office, London.

Baldwin, J (1993) 'Police interview techniques – establishing truth or proof?' *British Journal of Criminology*, Vol 33, No 3, pp 325-351.

Barak, G (1994) 'Media society and criminology' in G Barak (ed) *Media Process and the Social Construction of Crime*, Garland Publishing, New York.

Barber, B (1963) 'Some problems in the sociology of professions', *Daedalus*, Vol 92, No 4, pp 669-688.

Bartels, EC and Silverman EB (2005) 'An exploratory study of the New York City Civilian Complaint Review Board mediation program' *Policing: An International Journal of Police Strategies & Management*, Vol 28, No 4, pp 619-630.

Bartels, S (2005) 'Promotion in the WA Police Service: an investigation into the influence of system perceptions on candidate behaviour and initiative traction', unpublished masters thesis, Charles Sturt University.

Bass, BM (1998) *Transformational Leadership: Industrial, Military and Educational Impact*, Lawrence Erlbaum, New Jersey.

Bassett, M and Prenzler, T (2002) 'Complaint profiling and early warning systems' in T Prenzler and J Ransley (eds) *Police Reform: Building Integrity*, Hawkins Press, Sydney.

Bayley, D (1994) *Police for the Future*, Oxford University Press, New York.

Bayley, D (1997) *What Works in Policing?* Oxford University Press, New York.

Bayley, DH (1999) 'Capacity-building in law enforcement', *Trends and Issues in Crime and Criminal Justice Series*, No 123, Australian Institute of Criminology, Canberra, viewed 30 April 2007 <www.aic.gov.au/publications/tandi/tandi123.html>.

Bayley, D and Shearing, C (2001) *The New Structure of Policing: Description, Conceptualisation and Research Agenda*, National Institute of Justice, Washington DC, viewed 8 May 2006 <www.ncjrs.gov/pdffiles1/nij/187083.pdf>.

Bayley, DH (2001) 'Democratizing the police abroad: what to do and how to do it', *National Institute of Justice, Series: Issues in International Crime*, viewed 7 May 2006 <www.ncjrs.org/pdffiles1/nij/188742.pdf>.

BBC News (1989) 'Guildford Four released after 15 years', 19 October, BBC News Report viewed 14 December 2006 <http://news.bbc.co.uk/onthisday/hi/dates/stories/october/19/newsid_2490000/2490039.stm>.

BBC News (2006) 'Bombers' community may hold clues', 11 May, BBC News Report, viewed 12 December 2006 <http://news.bbc.co.uk/go/pr/fr/-/2/hi/uk_news/england/west_yorkshire/4761745.stm>.

Beach, B (1978) *Report of the Board of Inquiry into Allegations Against Members of the Victoria Police Force* (The Beach Report), Government Printer, Melbourne.

Beardwell, I and Holden, L (2001) *Human Resource Management: A Contemporary Approach*, Prentice Hall, Harlow.

Beecher, E (2001) Andrew Olle Media Lecture, viewed 14 April 2006 <www.abc.net.au/specials/olle>.

Bennett, W (1990) 'Toward a theory of press-state relations in the United States', *Journal of Communication*, Spring.

Bimbauer, B (2000) 'The story behind fatal care', Online Journal *The Fifth Estate*, viewed 31 January 2002 <http://fifth.estate.rmit.edu.au/August/bill.htm>.

Biro, F, Campbell, P, McKenna, P and Murray, T (2001) 'Police executives under Pressure', Police Futures Group: Ottawa viewed 7 May 2006 <http://crpr.icaap.org/issues/issue1/tmurray.html>.

Bislev, S (2004) 'Globalization, state transformation and public security', *International Political Science Review*, Vol 25, No 3, pp 281-296.

Black, D (1976) *Behavior of Law*, Academic Press, New York.

Blagg, H and Valuri, G (2004) 'Self-policing and community safety: the work of Aboriginal community patrols in Australia', *Current Issues in Criminal Justice*, Vol 15, pp 1-15.

Blagg, H (2000) 'Crisis intervention in Aboriginal family violence', *Summary Report, Partnerships Against Domestic Violence*, Commonwealth of Australia, Canberra.

Blagg, H and Valuri, G (2004) 'Self-policing and community safety: the work of Aboriginal community patrols in Australia', *Current Issues in Criminal Justice*, Vol 15, No 3, pp 205-219.

Blair, I (2003) 'Leading towards the future', A speech for the Future of Policing Conference, UK, October.

Bogan, R and Hicks, S (2002) *Western Australia Police Service Qualitative and Strategic Review of Reform: The Way Ahead*, Western Australian Police Service, Perth.

Boice, DF and Kleiner, BH (1997) 'Designing effective performance appraisal systems', *Work Study Journal*, Vol 46, No 6, pp 197-201.

Boisot, MH (1998) *Knowledge Assets: Securing Competitive Advantage in the Information Economy*, University Press, Oxford.

Bolden, R, Gosling, J, Marturano, A and Dennison, P (2003) 'Review of police leadership theory and competency frameworks', University of Exeter: Centre for Leadership Studies.

Bradley, L and Parker, R (2006) 'Do Australian public sector employees have the type of culture they want in the era of new public management?', *Australian Journal of Public Administration*, Vol 65, No 1, pp 88-99, March.

Bratton, W and Knobler, P (1998) *Turnaround: How America's Top Cop Reversed the Crime Epidemic*, Random House, New York.

Breen, M (1995) 'Pedagogical correctness in journalism education: using the guest lecturer to advantage', *Australian Journalism Review*, Vol 17, No 1, pp 140-147.

Brereton, D (2000) 'Evaluating the performance of external oversight bodies', in A Goldsmith and C Lewis (eds) *Civilian Oversight of Policing: Governance, Democracy and Human Rights*, Hart Publishing, Oxford.

Brereton, D (2002) 'Monitoring integrity' in T Prenzler and J Ransley (eds) *Police Reform: Building Integrity*, Hawkins Press, Sydney.

Broadbent, M (1998) 'The phenomenon of knowledge management: what does it mean to the information profession?' *Information Outlook*, viewed 14 December 2006 <www.contentdigital.com.br/biblioteca/gestao_conhecimento/broadbent.pdf>.

Brock, P, Fisher, RP and Cutler, BL (1999) 'Examining the cognitive interview in a double-test paradigm', *Psychology, Crime and Law*, Vol 5, pp 29-45.

Brown, J and Campbell, E (1994) *Stress and Policing*, John Wiley & Sons, Brisbane.

Brown, MK (1988) *Working the Street – Police Discretion and the Dilemmas of Reform*, Russell Sage Foundation, New York.

Brunetto, Y and Farr-Wharton, R (2003) 'The commitment and satisfaction of lower ranked police officers: lessons for management', *Policing: International Journal of Police Strategies & Management*, Vol 26, No 1, pp 43-63.

Brunetto, Y and Farr-Wharton, R (2005) 'The role of management post-NPM in the implementation of new policies affecting police officers' practices' *Policing: An International Journal of Police Strategies & Management*, Vol 28, No 2, pp 221-241.

Bull, R (2006) Plenary Session, Paper presented at the Second International Investigative Interviewing Conference, University of Portsmouth, Portsmouth, England, 5-7 July.

Burbeck, J (2001) New Association of Chiefs of Police Officers Investigative Interviewing Strategy, unpublished Warwickshire Police Document.

Burbeck, J (2003) *Standard Entry for Association of Chiefs of Police Officers Manuals on Investigative Interviewing*, ACPO, unpublished, London.

Burden, P (2000) *Knowledge Management: The Bibliography*, American society for information science and technology, New Jersey.

Burns, JM (1978) *Leadership*, Harper & Row, New York.

Cacioppe, R (1998) 'Leaders developing leaders: an effective way to enhance leadership development programs', *Leadership & Organization Development Journal*, Vol 19, No 4, pp 194-98.

Campbell, E and Whitmore, H (1966) *Freedom in Australia*, Sydney University Press.

Carr-Saunders, AM and Wilson, PA, 1933, *The Professions*, Clarendon Press, Oxford.

Carson, WG (2004a) 'Is communalism dead? Reflections on the present and future practice of crime prevention: part one', *The Australian and New Zealand Journal of Criminology*, Vol 37, No 1, pp 1-21.

Carson, WG (2004b) 'Is communalism dead? Reflections on the present and future practice of crime prevention: part two', *The Australian and New Zealand Journal of Criminology*, Vol 37, No 2, pp 192-210.

Carson, L and Gelber, K (2001) Ideas for Community Consultation: a discussion on principles and procedures for making consultation work, a report prepared for the NSW Department of Urban Affairs and Planning.

Casey, J and Trofymowych, D (1999) Twenty Years of Community Consultative Committees: is it Possible to Solve the Conundrum? Paper presented at the History of Crime, Policing and Punishment Conference, Australian Institute of Criminology, Canberra, 9-10 December, viewed 14 December 2006 <www.aic.gov. au/conferences/hcpp/caseytro.html>.

Casey, J and Mitchell, M (2005) Twenty Years of Community Consultation: trying to Solve the Conundrum, Paper presented at the Australian and New Zealand Society of Criminology Conference, New Zealand, 9-11 February.

Casey, J and Mitchell, M (2007) 'Police-community consultation in Australia: working with a conundrum', In J Ruiz and D Hummer (eds) *Handbook of Police Administration*, CRC Press, (Taylor & Francis), New York.

Caulfield, N, Chang, D, Dollard, M and Elshaug, C (2004) 'A review of occupational stress interventions in Australia', *International Journal of Stress Management*, Vol 11, No 2, p 149.

Centrex (Central Police Training and Development Authority) (2006) 'Leading for those we serve, the police leadership qualities framework', Centrex, Bramshill, viewed 5 May 2007 <www.npia.police.uk/en/docs/PLQFLeadingForThoseWe Serve.pdf>.

Chan, J, Brererton, D, Legosz, M and Doran, S (2001) *E-policing: The Impact of Information Technology on Police Practices*, Criminal Justice Commission, Queensland, pp 1-128.

Chan, J (1995) 'Systematically distorted communication? Criminal knowledge, media representation and public policy', *Australian and New Zealand Journal of Criminology, Special Supplementary Issue*, pp 23-30.

Chan, J (1999) *A Culture of Corruption: Changing an Australian Police Service*, Hawkins Press, Sydney.

Chan, J, Devery, C and Doran, S (2003) *Fair Cop: Learning the Art of Policing*, University of Toronto Press, Toronto.

Chan, J (ed) (2005) *Reshaping Juvenile Justice*, Sydney Institute of Criminology.

Chappell, D and Wilson, P (1969) *The Police and the Public in Australia and New Zealand*, University of Queensland Press, Queensland.

Chappell, D and Wilson, P (1996) *Australian Policing: Contemporary Issues*, Butterworths, Sydney.

Charlesworth, H, Chiam, M, Hovell, D and Williams, G (2003) 'Deep anxieties: Australia and the international legal order', *Sydney Law Review*, Vol 25, pp 423-465.

Chartier, J and Gabler, S (2001) 'Risk communication and government: theory and application for the Canadian food inspection agency', viewed 5 April 2006 <www.inspection.gc.ca/english/corpaffr/publications/riscomm/riscomme.shtml>.

Chermak, S (1995) 'Image control: how police affect the presentation of crime news', *American Journal of Police*, Vol XIV, No 2, pp 21-43.

Chesterman, J and Galligan, B (1997) *Citizens Without Rights*, Cambridge University Press, Melbourne.

Chevigny, P (1995) *Edge of the Knife: Police Violence in the Americas*, The New Press, New York.

Chilvers, M and Weatherburn, D (2004) 'The NSW "COMPSTAT" process: its impact on crime', *The Australian and New Zealand Journal of Criminology*, Vol 37, No 1, pp 22-48.

Christie, S (1998) 'Trial by media: politics, policy and public opinion, the case of the ACT heroin trial', *Current Issues in Criminal Justice*, Vol 10, No 1, July, pp 37-51.

Cioccarelli, P (2003) 'The quest for professional status in policing', *New South Wales Police News*, Vol 83, No 11, p 27-35, November.

Clarke, C and Milne, R (2001) 'National evaluation of the PEACE investigative interviewing course', *Police Research Award Scheme, Report No PRAS/149*, Institute of Criminal Justice Studies, University of Portsmouth, viewed 15 March 2007 <http://scienceandresearch.homeoffice.gov.uk/hosdb2/pdfs/peaceinterviewcourse.pdf?view=binary>

Clarke, RV (1992) *Situational Crime Prevention: Successful Case Studies*, Harrow and Heston, New York.

CMRD (Corporate Management Review Division, Victoria Police) (2004) 'Evaluation of local priority policing phase three – the community consultation model, Victoria police corporate management review division' (unpublished confidential paper), Melbourne.

Cohen, S (1972) *Folk Devils and Moral Panics*, Paladin, St Albans.

Collier, PM (2001) 'Valuing intellectual capacity in the police', *Accounting, Auditing & Accountability Journal*, Vol 14, No 4, pp 437-455.

Collier, PM, Edwards, JS and Shaw, D (2004) 'Communicating knowledge about police performance', *International Journal of Productivity and Performance Management*, Vol 53, pp 458-467.

Collins, D (1996) Community Policing in Australia: evaluation of significant police developments in Australian policing – Policing in the ACT, Paper presented to Fourth Annual Crime Prevention Conference: Problem Oriented Policing and Crime Prevention – Towards Best Practice, 11-12 June, Griffith University, Brisbane.

Collins, P and Gibbs, A (2003) 'Stress in police officers: a study of the origins, prevalence and severity of stress-related symptoms within a county police force', *Occupational Medicine*, Vol 53, No 4, p 256.

Commonwealth of Australia (2006) *Report of the Security Legislation Review Committee*, Commonwealth of Australia, Canberra, Australia.

Conference of Commissioners of Police of Australasia and the South West Pacific Region (PCC) (1991a) Minutes of Proceedings, Adelaide, March.

Conference of Commissioners of Police of Australasia and the South West Pacific Region (PCC) (1991b) Minutes of Proceedings, Sydney, 11 October.

Conference of Commissioners of Police of Australasia and the South West Pacific Region (PCC) (2005) Minutes of Proceedings, Resolution 13, Brisbane, March.

Cooper, C (2005) 'Working with Generation Y', *Management Today*, pp 18-21, June.

Cope, N (2003) 'Crime analysis: principles and practice', in T Newburn (ed) *Handbook of Policing*, Willan Publishing, Devon.

Cope, N (2004) 'Intelligence led policing or policing led intelligence?' *British Journal of Criminology*, Vol 44, pp 188-203.

Cope, S, Leishman, F and Starie, P (1997) 'Globalization, new public order and the enabling state', *International Journal of Public Sector Management*, Vol 10, No 6, pp 444-460.

Copes, H (2005) *Policing and Stress*, Pearson Education, New Jersey.

Cordner, GW (1979) 'Police patrol work load studies: a review and critique', *Police Studies*, Vol 2, No 4, pp 50-60.

Cornish, D and Clarke, R (1987) 'Understanding crime displacement: an application of rational choice theory', *Criminology*, Vol 25, pp 933-947.

Corruption and Crime Commission (2005) *Report to the Joint Standing Committee on the Corruption and Crime Commission with Regard to the Commission's Organised Crime Function and Contempt Power*, State Law Publisher, Perth.

Costigan, F (1984) Royal Commission into the Activities of the Federated Ship Painters and Dockers Union, AGPS, Canberra.

Coutts, LM and Schneider, FW (2004) 'Police officer performance appraisal systems: how good are they?' *Policing: An International Journal of Police Strategies and Management*, Vol 27, No 1, pp 67-81.

Cowdery, N (2001) Whose sentences: the judges', the public's or Alan Jones'?, paper presented to the Plenary Session, Conference of the Australian Academy of Forensic Sciences, 7 November, viewed 30 April 2007 <www.odpp.nsw.gov.au/speec hes/AAFS%20-%20meeting%207.11.01.htm>.

Cunneen, C (2001) *Conflict, Politics and Crime*, Allen & Unwin, Sydney.

Cunneen, C (2005) Evaluation of the Queensland Aboriginal and Torres Strait Islander Justice Agreement, Report to the Justice Agencies CEOs (unpublished), Brisbane.

Cunneen, C and AJAC (Aboriginal Justice Advisory Council) (2002) *New South Wales Aboriginal Justice Plan Discussion Paper*, AJAC, Sydney.

Dadds, V and Scheide, T (2000) *Police Performance and Activity Measurement*, Australian Institute of Criminology, No 180.

Dahrendorf, R (1959) *Class and Class Conflict in Industrial Society*, Stanford University Press, Stanford.

Daily Telegraph (1998) 'Today's strategy', Warren cartoon, p 10, 10 February.

Daily Telegraph (1996a) 'I'll clean force/new Commissioner's promise', p 1, 12 August.

Daily Telegraph (1996b) 'Nowhere to hide for corrupt police', p 17, 13 August.

Daily Telegraph (1996c) 'Ryan's new broom: police chief to launch reform program', p 1, 28 August.

Dale, A (1994) 'Professionalism and the police', *The Police Journal*, Vol 67, No 3, pp 209-218, July-September.

Darvall-Stevens, R (1994) 'An analysis of the professionalisation of policing in Australia: perspectives from Victoria', unpublished Masters thesis, University of Melbourne.

Das, DK and Kratcoski PC (2001) 'International police cooperation: a world perspective', in DJ Koenig and DK Das (eds) *International Police Cooperation: A World Perspective*, Lexington Books, Lanham.

Davenport, TH (1998) 'Putting the enterprise into the enterprise system', *Harvard Business Review*, July-August, pp 121-131.

Davenport, TH and Prusak, L (1998) *Working Knowledge: How Organizations Manage What They Know*, Harvard Business School Press, Boston.

Davies, H, Nutley, S and Walter, I (2005) Assessing the impact of social science research: conceptual methodological and practical issues, A background discussion paper for the ESRC Symposium on Assessing Non-Academic Impact of Research, May 2005, RURU, University of St Andrews, viewed 1 May 2006 <www.st-and.ac.uk/~ruru>.

Davis, G and Bishop, P (2001) 'Developing consent: consultation, participation and governance', in G Davis and P Weller (eds) *Are You Being Served? State, Citizens and Governance*, Allen & Unwin, Sydney.

Davis, G and Weller, P (eds) (2001) *Are You Being Served? State Citizens and Governance*, Allen & Unwin, Sydney.

Davis, O and Cebron, MJ (2005) 'Trends now shaping the future: technological, workplace, management and institutional tends', *The Futurist*, May-June pp 37-54.

Dawkins Green Paper – *see Australia, Parliament (1987a)*.

Dawkins White Paper – *see Australia, Parliament (1987b)*.

De Waal, AA (2004) 'Stimulating performance-driven behaviour to obtain better results', *International Journal of Productivity and Performance Management*, Vol 53, No 4, pp 301-316.

Deflem, M (2002) *Policing World Society: Historical Foundations of International Police Cooperation*, Oxford University Press, Oxford.

DeHart-Davis, L and Kingsley, G (2005) 'Managerial perceptions of privatization: evidence from a state department of transportation', *State and Local Government Review*, Vol 37, No 3, pp 228-241.

Denemark, D (2005) 'Mass media and media power in Australia', in S Wilson, G Meagher, R Gibson, D Denemark and M Western (eds) *Australian Social Attitudes, The First Report*, University of New South Wales Press, Sydney.

Dennison, S, Stewart, A and Hurren, E (2006) 'Police cautioning in Queensland: the impact on juvenile offending pathways', *Trends and Issues in Crime and Criminal Justice*, Report No 306, Australian Institute of Criminology, Canberra.

Densten, IL (1999) 'Senior Australian law enforcement leadership under examination', *Policing: An International Journal of Police Strategies & Management*, Vol 22, No 1, pp 45-57.

Densten, IL (2003) 'Senior police leadership: does rank matter?' *Policing: An International Journal of Police Strategies and Management*, Vol 26, No 3, pp 400-418.

DHS (Department of Homeland Security) (2003) *Preparedness Guidelines for Homeland Security*, US Department of Homeland Security, Office for Domestic Preparedness, Washington DC.

Dickie, P (1989) *The Road to Fitzgerald and Beyond*, University of Queensland Press, Brisbane.

Dingwall, R (1976) 'Accomplishing profession', *The Sociological Review*, Vol 24, No 2, pp 331-349.

Dixon, D (1997) *Law in Policing: Legal Regulation and Police Practices*, Oxford University Press.

Dixon, D (1999a) *A Culture of Corruption: Changing an Australian Police Service*, Hawkins Press, Sydney.

Dixon, D (1999b) 'Issues in the legal regulation of policing', in D Dixon (ed) *A Culture of Corruption: Changing an Australian Police Service*, Hawkins Press, Sydney, pp 36-68.

Dixon, D (1999c) 'Reform, regression and the Royal Commission into the NSW Police Service', in D Dixon (ed) *A Culture of Corruption: Changing an Australian Police Service*, Hawkins Press, Sydney, pp 138-179.

Dixon, D (2005) 'Why don't the police stop crime?', *Australian and New Zealand Journal of Criminology*, Vol 38, No 1, pp 4-24.

Dodson, M (1997) *Aboriginal and Torres Strait Islander Social Justice Commissioner Fifth Annual Report*, HREOC, Sydney.

Donaghue, S (2001) *Royal Commissions and Permanent Commissions of Inquiry*, Butterworths, Sydney.

Donohue, G, Tichenor, P and Olien, C (1995) 'A guard dog perspective on the role of media', *Journal of Communication*, Spring.

Duffy, J (2000) 'Knowledge exchange at GlaxoWelcome', *Information Management Journal*, Vol 34, pp 64-67.

Dunphy, D and Stace, D (1990) *Under New Management: Australian Organizations in Transition*, Reprinted 1995, McGraw-Hill, Sydney.

Dupont, B (2006) 'Power struggles in the field of security: implications for democratic transformation', in J Wood and B Dupont (eds) *Democracy, Society and the Governance of Security*, Cambridge University Press, Cambridge.

Dworkin, R (2003) 'Terror and the attack on civil liberties', *New York Review of Books*, 6 November 2003, p 37.

Earl, M (2001) 'Knowledge management strategies: toward a taxonomy', *Journal of Management Information Systems*, Vol 18, pp 215-233.

Eck, J and Spelman, W (1987) 'Problem-solving: problem orientated policing in New-port', *Police Executive Research Forum and National Institute of Justice*, US Dept of Justice.

Eck, J and Wardell, J (1998) 'Improving the management of rental properties with drug problems: a randomised experiment', in L Mazerolle and J Roehl (eds) *Civil Remedies and Crime Prevention, Crime Prevention Studies* Vol 9, pp 161-183, Criminal Justice Press.

Ede, A and Barnes, M (2002) 'Alternative strategies for resolving complaints' in T Prenzler and J Ransley (eds) *Police Reform: Building Integrity*, Hawkins Press, Sydney.

Edwards, C (2004) *Changing Policing Theories for 21st Century Societies*, 2nd Edition, Federation Press, Sydney.

Edwards, M (2002) 'Public sector governance – future issues for Australia', *Australian Journal of Public Administration*, Vol 61, No 2, pp 51-61.

Edwards, M (2004) *Social Science Research and Public Policy: Narrowing the Divide, Occasional paper, Policy Paper 2*, Academy of the Social Sciences in Australia, Canberra.

Enders, M (2001a) 'Australian policing in context', in M Enders and B Dupont (eds) *Policing the Lucky Country*, Hawkins Press, Sydney.

Enders, M (2001b) 'The social construction of crime and policing', in M Enders and B Dupont (eds) *Policing the Lucky Country*, Hawkins Press, Sydney.

Ericson, R and Haggerty, K (1997) *Policing in the Risk Society*, University of Toronto Press, Toronto.

Etter, B (1992) Future Direction of Policing in Australia, paper presented to the 8th Annual Conference of the Australian and New Zealand Society of Criminology Conference, Melbourne 1992, reproduced in *Australian Police Journal*, Vol 47, No 1, pp 43-54, 1993.

Etter, B (1995) 'Mastering innovation and change in police agencies', in B Etter and M Palmer (eds) *Police Leadership in Australasia*, Federation Press, Sydney.

Etter, B (1996) Where to from here?, Paper presented at Australian Institute of Criminology Conference: First Australasian Women Police Conference, Sydney, 29-31 July, pp 1-13.

Etter, B and Palmer, M (eds) (1995) *Police Leadership in Australasia*, Federation Press, Sydney.

Feeley, M and Simon J (1994) 'Actuarial justice: the emerging new criminal law', in D Nelken (ed) *The Futures of Criminology*, Sage Publications Inc, London.

Ferguson, G (2003) *Review and Recommendations Concerning Various Aspects of Police Misconduct*, Toronto Police Service, Toronto.

Findlay, M (2004) 'Globalisation of crime: terror in a contracting globe' in V George and RM Page (eds) *Global Social Problems*, Polity Press, Cambridge.

Findlay, M (2004) *Introducing Policing: Challenges for Police and Australian Communities*, Oxford University Press, Melbourne.

Finn, P and Hylton, MO (1994) *Using Civil Remedies for Criminal Behaviour: Rationale, Case Studies and Constitutional Issues*, National Institute of Justice, US Dept of Justice.

Firth, S (2005) *Australia in International Politics: An Introduction to Australian Foreign Policy*, Allen & Unwin, Sydney.

Fitzgerald, G (1989) *Report of a Commission of Inquiry into Police Illegal Activities and Associated Police Misconduct*, Government Printer, Brisbane, viewed 10 May 2007, <www.cmc.qld.gov.au/data/portal/00000005/content/81350001131406907822.pdf>.

Fleming, J (2003) 'Changing institutions: pluralism, traditions and the contradictions of reform' in I Holland and J Fleming (eds) *Government Reformed: Values and New Political Institutions*, Ashgate, Aldershot.

Fleming, J and Lafferty, G (2000) 'New management techniques and restructuring in police organisations', *Policing: An International Journal of Policing Strategy and Management,* Vol 23, No 2, pp 154-168.

Fleming, J and Lewis, C (2002) 'The politicisation of police reform', in T Prenzler and J Ransley (eds) *Police Reform: Building Integrity,* Hawkins Press, Sydney.

Fleming, J and Rhodes, R (2004) It's situational: the dilemmas of police governance in the 21st century, Refereed paper presented to the Australasian Political Studies Association Conference University of Adelaide, viewed 7 May 2006 <www.adelai de.edu.au/apsa/docs_papers/Pub%20Pol/Fleming%20%20Rhodes.pdf>.

Fleming, J and Rhodes, RAW (2005) 'Bureaucracy, contract and networks: the unholy trinity and the police', *Australian and New Zealand Journal of Criminology,* Vol 38, No 2, pp 192-205.

Fletcher, RM (2001) 'Civilian oversight of police behaviour' in M Palmiotto (ed) *Police Misconduct: A Reader for the 21st Century,* Prentice Hall, New Jersey.

Flood, P (2004) *Report of the Inquiry into Australian Intelligence Agencies,* Commonwealth of Australia, Canberra, Australia.

Forst, B and Manning, P (1999) *The Privatization of Policing: Two Views,* Georgetown University Press, Washington DC.

Foster, J (2003) 'Police culture', in T Newburn (ed) *Handbook of Policing,* Willan Publishing, Devon.

Fox, S and Spector, PE (2002) 'Emotions in the workplace: The neglected side of organizational life', *Human Resource Management Review,* Vol 12, No 2, pp 167-171.

Freckelton, I (1991) 'Shooting the messenger: the trial and execution of the Victorian police complaints authority', in A Goldsmith (ed) *Complaints Against the Police: The Trend to External Review,* Clarendon Press, Oxford.

Fredman, S (2006) 'From deference to democracy: the role of equality under the Human Rights Act 1998', *Law Quarterly Review,* Vol 122, pp 53-81.

Funnell, W (2001) *Government by Fiat: The Retreat From Responsibility,* University of New South Wales Press, Sydney.

Furnham, A (2004) 'Performance management systems', *European Business Journal,* Vol 16, No 2, pp 83-94.

Garbutt, D (2005) *Personal Communication with Stephen Pierce,* 22 September.

Gardner, S and Ash, C (2003) 'ICT-enabled organisations: a model for change management', *Logistics Information Management,* Vol 16, No 1, pp 18-24.

Garland, D (1996) 'The limits of the sovereign state', *British Journal of Criminology,* Vol 36, pp 445-471.

Garland, D (1997) 'Governmentality and the problem of crime: Foucault, criminology, sociology', *Theoretical Criminology,* Vol 1, No 2, pp 173-214.

Garland, D (2001) *The Culture of Control,* Oxford University Press.

Gennaro, V, Walsh, F, William F and Kunselman, JC (2005) 'Community policing: the middle manager's perspective', *Police Quarterly,* Vol 8, No 4, pp 490-511.

George, R (2004) 'Fixing the problem of analytical mindsets: alternative analysis,' *International Journal of Intelligence and CounterIntelligence,* Vol 17, No 3, pp 385-404.

Gibson, A and Villiers, P (2005) *Leading for those we serve, The Police Leadership Qualities Framework* Central Police Training and Development Authority, Bramshill.

Gillespie, J (2006) 'Policing performance management systems: identifying key design elements within a New Public Management context', Masters by Research thesis, Edith Cowan University, Perth.

Gilligan, G (2002) 'Royal Commissions of Inquiry', *The Australian & New Zealand Journal of Criminology,* Vol 35, No 3, pp 289-307.

Gimenez-Salinas, A (2004) 'New approaches regarding private/public security', *Policing and Society,* Vol 14, No 2, pp 158-174.

Goldsmith, A (1996) 'Taking police culture seriously: police discretion and the limits of the law' in R Reiner (ed) *Policing, Vol II – Controlling the Controllers: Police Discretion and Accountability*, Dartmouth Publishing, Aldershot.

Goldsmith, M and Walt, C (2005) 'The global leader of the future: new competencies for a new era' *Leader Values*, June.

Goldstein, H (1990) *Problem Orientated Policing*, McGraw-Hill, Sydney.

Golsby, M and O'Brien, R (1996) *A Co-operative Approach to Crime Prevention: Police and Security Working Together*, Australian Institute of Security and Applied Technology, Edith Cowan University, Perth.

Goode, WJ (1960) 'Encroachment, charlatanism and the emerging profession', *American Sociological Review*, Vol 25, pp 902-14.

Gordon, D (2006) 'About technorati', viewed 22 November 2006 <http://technorati.com/about/>.

Grabosky, P and Wilson, P (1989) *Journalism and Justice: How Crime is Reported*, Pluto Press, Sydney.

Grabosky, PN (1998) 'Crime in a shrinking world', *Trends and Issues in Crime and Criminal Justice*, No 83, Australian Institute of Criminology, viewed 2 May 2007 <www.aic.gov.au/publications/tandi/ti83.pdf>.

Green, L (1996) *Policing Places with Drug Problems*, Sage Publications Inc, California.

Greenberg, J (2004) *Comprehensive Stress Management*, 8th Edition, McGraw-Hill, New York.

Greene, J and Grant, A (2003) 'Solution focused coaching', *Managing People in a Complex World*, Pearson Education, London.

Greenwood, E (1957) 'Attributes of a profession', *Social Work*, Vol 2 (July), pp 45-55.

Griffiths, A, Retford, S and Milne, R (2006) Is all training good training? A comparison study of two different witness interview training programmes, Paper presented at the Paper presented at the Second International Investigative Interviewing Conference, University of Portsmouth, Portsmouth, 5-7 July.

Gudjonsson, G (1992) *The Psychology of Interrogations, Confessions and Testimony*, Wiley, Chichester.

Gudjonsson, G (1994) 'Psychological vulnerability: suspects at risk', in D Morgan and G Stephenson (eds) (1994) *Suspicion and Silence: The right to silence in criminal investigations*, Blackstone, London.

Gudjonsson, G (2003) *The Psychology of Interrogations and Confessions: A Handbook*, Chichester, Wiley, Chichester.

Gurteen, D (1998) 'Knowledge, creativity and innovation', *Journal of Knowledge Management*, Vol 2, pp 5-13.

Haberfeld, MR (2006) *Police Leadership*, Prentice Hall, New Jersey.

Hall, P (2004) *Investigating Corruption and Misconduct in Public Office: Commissions of Inquiry – Powers and Procedures*, Thomson, Sydney.

Hall, S, Clarke, J, Crichter, C, Jefferson, T and Roberts, B (1975) Newsmaking and crime, paper presented to NACRO conference on Crime and the Media, January, Birmingham.

Hallett, L (1982) *Royal Commissions and Boards of Inquiry: Some Legal and Procedural Aspects*, The Law Book Co, Sydney.

Hamel, G and Prahalad, CK (1993) *Competing for the Future: Breakthrough Strategies for Seizing Control of your Industry and Creating the Markets of Tomorrow*, Harvard Business School Press, Boston.

Harr, RN (2001) 'The making of a community policing officer: the impact of basic training and occupational socialization on police recruits', *Police Quarterly*, Vol 4, No 4, pp 402-33.

Harris, M (2004) 'From Australian courts to Aboriginal courts in Australia – bridging the gap', *Current Issues in Criminal Justice*, Vol 16, No 1, pp 26-35.

Hartley, J (2005) Changing paradigms in public governance, Conference presentation, viewed 2 May 2007 <www.dan-eurashe.dk/pages/index/JH-Prague.ppt>.

Heaton-Armstrong, A (1995) 'Recording and disclosing statements by witnesses – law and practice', *Medicine, Science and the Law*, Vol 35, No 2, pp 36-143.

Heaton-Armstrong, A and Wolchover, D (1992) 'Recording witness statements', *Criminal Law Review*, pp 160-172.

Hede, A, Prasser, S and Neylan, M (1992) *Keeping Them Honest: Democratic Reform in Queensland*, University of Queensland Press, Queensland.

Hedelin, L and Allwood, CM (2002) 'IT and strategic decision making', *Industrial Management & Data Systems*, Vol 102, No 3/4, pp 125-139.

Herald Sun (2000) 'Top cop draws bead on heroin', p 25, 25 March.

Herald Sun (2006) 'Dictator's drug ship, 6 March, viewed 15 April 2006 <www.heraldsun.news.com.au/common/story_page/0,5478,18357710%255E661,00.html>.

Herman, E and Chomsky, N (1988) *Manufacturing Consent: The Political Economy of the Mass Media*, Pantheon Books, New York.

Herman, M (1996) *Intelligence Power in Peace and War*, Royal Institute of International Affairs and Cambridge University, Cambridge University Press, Cambridge, UK.

Heur, R (1999) *The Psychology of Intelligence Analysis*, Centre for the Study of Intelligence, CIA, Washington DC.

Higgins, E and Box, D (2006) 'Police nervous to act on Lebanese', *The Australian*, p 5, 27 January.

Higgins, O (2004) 'Rising to the collection challenge', in J Ratcliffe (ed) *Strategic Thinking in Criminal Intelligence*, Federation Press, Sydney.

Hillyard, P (1994) 'The normalization of special powers', in N Lacey (ed) *Criminal Justice*, Oxford University Press, pp 63-102.

Hoey, A (1998) 'Inside the RUC: information technology and policing in Northern Ireland', *International Review of Law, Computers & Technology*, Vol 12, No 1, pp 15-26.

Hoey, A and Topping, A (1998) 'Policing the new Europe – the information debate', *International Review of Law, Computers & Technology*, Vol 12, No 3, pp 501-511.

Hogg, R (1995) 'Law and order and the fallibility of the justice system', in Brown et al (eds) *Criminal Laws* (1996) Federation Press, Sydney, pp 309-315.

Home Office Circular No 22 (1992) *Principles of Investigative Interviewing*, The Home Office, London.

Home Office (2001) *Policing a New Century – A Blueprint for Reform*, viewed 7 May 2006 <www.archive.officialdocuments.co.uk/document/cm53/5326/cm5326.htm>, Home Office, London.

Home Office (2003) *Getting the Best Leaders to Take on the Most Demanding Challenges*, Home Office, London.

Home Office (2004) *Building Communities, Beating Crime: A Better Police Service for the 21st Century*, Home Office, London.

Home Office/Cabinet Office (2002) *PACE Review*, Home Office, London.

Hood, C, Scott, C, James, O, Jones, G and Travers, T (1999) *Regulation Inside Government*, Oxford University Press, New York.

Hoque, Z, Arends, S and Alexander, R (2004) 'Policing the police service: a case study of the rise of "new public management" within an Australian police service', *Accounting, Auditing and Accountability Journal*, Vol 17, No 1, pp 59-84.

Howell, JP and Costley, DL (2006) *Understanding Behaviours for Effective Leadership*, Pearson Prentice Hall, New Jersey.

Howell, J (2006) 'The global war on terror, development and civil society', *Journal of International Development*, Vol 18, pp 121-135.

Howitt, D (1998) *Crime, the Media and the Law*, Wiley, Chichester.

Hoyle, C and Young, R (2003) 'Restorative justice, victims and the police', in T Newburn (ed) *Handbook of Policing*, Willan Publishing, Devon, pp 680-706.

Hubbard, G (2002) *The First XI, Winning Organisations in Australia*, John Wiley & Sons, Camberwell, p 147.

Huber, GP (2001) 'Transfer of knowledge in knowledge management systems: unexplored issues and suggested studies', *European Journal of Information Systems*, Vol 10, No 2, pp 72-79.

Huggett, M (1998) '360-degree feedback: great expectations?', *Industrial and Commercial Training*, Vol 30, No 4, pp 128-130.

Hughes, G (1994) 'Talking cop shop? A case-study of police community consultative groups', *Transition, Policing and Society*, Vol 4, pp 253-270.

Human Rights Watch (2006) 'East Timor: torture and mistreatment by police', viewed 7 May 2006 <http://hrw.org/english/docs/2006/04/19/eastti13223.htm>.

Huptman, B J 2000 'Ethical leadership' in W Doerner and ML Dantzker (eds) *Contemporary Police Organisation and Management: Issues and Trends*, Butterworth-Heinemann, Woburn MA.

Iftikhar, Z, Eriksson, I and Dickson, GW (2003) 'Developing an instrument for knowledge management project evaluation', *Electronic Journal of Knowledge Management*, Vol 1, No 1, pp 55-62.

Igbaria, M (1999) 'The driving forces in the virtual society: examining the factors propelling the evolution to a virtual workplace and the arrangements being used to implement these changes in a societal context', *Communications of the ACM*, Vol 42, No 12, pp 64-70.

International Peace Academy (2003) *Challenges in Police Reform: Promoting Effectiveness and Accountability*, International Peace Academy, viewed 7 May 2006 <www.ip academy.org/PDF_Reports/CHALLENGES_IN_POLICE.pdf>.

Irani, Z and Love, PED (2002) 'Developing a frame of reference for ex-ante IT/IS investment evaluation', *European Journal of Information Systems*, Vol 11, pp 74-82.

Jackson, A and Lyon, A (2002) 'Policing after ethnic conflict', *Policing: An International Journal of Police Strategies and Management*, Vol 25, No 2, pp 221-241.

Jennett, C, Elliot, G and Robinson, P (2003) Developing Practitioner Researchers for Policing and Related Professions, Paper presented at Continuing Professional Education Conference, Australian National University, Canberra.

Jiggins, SG (2004) 'An examination of the nature and impact of print media news reporting on selected police organisations in Australia', Unpublished PhD thesis, University of Canberra.

John, T and Maguire, M (2004) 'The national intelligence model: early implementation experience in three police force areas', in *Working Paper Number 50*, Cardiff University and Home Office, London, pp 1-63.

Johnson, S, Cooper, C, Cartwright, S, Donald, I, Taylor, P and Millet, C (2005) 'The experience of work-related stress across occupations', *Journal of Managerial Psychology*, Vol 20, No 2, p 178.

Johnson, TJ (1972) *Professions and Power*, Macmillan, London.

Johnston, E (1991) *National Report*, 5 Vols, Royal Commission into Aboriginal Deaths in Custody, AGPS, Canberra.

Johnston, L (1992) *The Rebirth of Private Policing*, Routledge, London.

Johnstone, I, Evans, G and Montague, A (1999) *Advancing Police Professionalisation: Through Standards Based Education and Training*, Centre for Training, Assessment and Development, Canberra Institute of Technology.

Jones, T and Newburn, T (2001) 'Widening access: improving police relations with hard to reach groups', *Home Office Police Research Series Paper 138*, viewed 11 November 2005 <www.homeoffice.gov.uk/rds/prgpdfs/prs138.pdf>.

Jones, T (2003) 'The governance and accountability of policing', in T Newburn (ed) *Handbook of Policing*, pp 625-658, Willan Publishing, Devon.

Kakar, S (1998) 'Self evaluations of police performance: an analysis of the relationship between police officers', *Policing: An International Journal of Police Strategies & Management*, Vol 21, pp 632-647.

Kane, HC (2003) 'Reframing the knowledge debate, with a little help from the Greeks', *Electronic Journal of Knowledge Management*, Vol 1, No 1, pp 33-38.

Kassin, S M and Gudjonsson, G (2004) 'The psychology of confessions', *Psychological Science in the Public Interest*, Vol 5, No 2, pp 33-67.

Kebell, MR and Milne, R (1998) 'Police officers' perceptions of eyewitness performance in forensic investigations', *The Journal of Social Psychology*, Vol 3, pp 323-330.

Keelty, M (2004) Can intelligence always be right?, paper given by Commissioner Mick Keelty at the 13th Annual Conference of the Australian Institute of Professional Intelligence Officers, Melbourne, 20 October.

Keelty, M (2006) 'Between the lines: new powers and accountability for police and the media', *Australian Press Council Annual Address*, 23 March, viewed 2 May 2007 <www.presscouncil.org.au/pcsite/activities/a_address/keelty.html>.

Kelley, T (2005) 'Mental health and prospective police professionals', *Policing: An International Journal of Strategies and Management*, Vol 28, No 1, pp 6-29.

Kennedy, G (2004) *Final Report of the Royal Commission into whether there has been Corrupt or Criminal Conduct by any Western Australian Police Officer*, conducted by Commissioner The Hon G Kennedy AO QC, State Law Publisher, Perth, viewed 7 May 2006 <www.ccc.wa.gov.au/publications.php>.

Kennedy, L (1989) Europe v England: the advantages of the Adversary System of Criminal Justice System, Lecture given by Sir Ludvic Kennedy to the Howard League for Penal Reform, 15 November, viewed 15 November 2006 <http://flac.htmlplanet.com/news/kennedy89.htm>.

Kercher, B (1995) *An Unruly Child*, Allen & Unwin, Sydney.

King, M and Prenzler, T (2003) 'Private inquiry agents: ethical challenges and accountability', *Security Journal*, Vol 16, No 2, pp 7-17.

Kintsch, W (1974) *The Representation of Meaning in Memory*, Lawrence Erlbaum, New Jersey.

Kirk, D (2006) How Fairfax is Repositioning Itself in the New Media Landscape, National Press Club address, Canberra, 24 October.

Kirkaldy, B, Shephard, R and Cooper, C (1993) 'Relationships between Type A Behaviour, work and leisure', *Journal of Personality and Individual Differences*, Vol 15, p 69.

Klegon, D (1978) 'The sociology of professions: an emerging perspective', *Sociology of Work and Occupations*, Vol 5, No 3, pp 259-283.

Klockars, C (1985) *The Idea of Police*, Sage Publications Inc, California.

Knapp, W (1972) *The Knapp Commission Report on Police Corruption*, New York.

Kotter, John, P (1990) 'What leaders really do', *Harvard Business Review*, May-June.

Kovach, B and Rosensteil, T (1999) *Warp Speed: America in the Age of Mixed Media*, Century Foundation Press, USA.

Kramer, M (1998) 'Designing an individualised performance evaluation system', *FBI Law Enforcement Bulletin* pp 20-26.

Krimmel, JT and Lindenmuth, P (2001) 'Police Chief performance and leadership styles', *Police Quarterly*, Vol 4, No 4, pp 469-483.

Kruger, E and Haggerty, KD (2006) 'Review essay: intelligence exchange in policing and security', *Policing & Society*, Vol 16, No 1, pp 86-91.

Kruml, S and Geddes, D (2000) 'Exploring the dimensions of emotional labour: the heart of Hochschild's work', *Management Communication Quarterly*, Vol 14, p 8.

Law Commission of Canada (2002) *In Search of Security: The Roles of Public Police and Private Agencies*, Government of Canada, Ottawa.

Laycock, G (2001) 'Research for police: who needs it?', *Trends and Issues in Criminal Justice*, No 211, Australian Institute of Criminology, Canberra.

Lazarus, R (1984) 'Puzzles in the study of daily hassles', *Journal of Behavioral Medicine*, Vol 7, No 4, p:375.

Lee, M and Punch, M (2004) 'Policing by degrees: police officers' experience of university education', *Policing & Society*, Vol 14, No 3, pp 233-249.

Leishman, F and Mason, P (2003) *Policing and the Media: Facts, Fictions and Factions*, Willan Publishing, Devon.

Leo, R (1992) 'From coercion to deception: the changing nature of police interrogation in America', *Crime Law and Social Change*, Vol 18, No 1-2, pp 35-59.

Leonard-Barton, D (1998) *Wellsprings of Knowledge: Building and Sustaining the Sources of Knowledge*, Harvard Business School Press, Boston.

Lewis, C (1999) *Complaints against Police: the Politics of Reform*, Hawkins Press, Sydney.

Liberman, A, Best, S, Metzler, T, Fagan, J, Weiss, D and Marmar, C (2002) 'Routine occupational stress and psychological distress in police', *Policing: An International Journal of Strategies and Management*, Vol 25, No 2, pp 421-439.

Loader, I (2000) 'Plural policing and democratic governance', *Social and Legal Studies*, Vol 9, No 3, pp 323-345.

Loader, I (2004) 'Policing securitisation and democratisation in Europe', in T Newburn and R Sparks (eds) *Criminal Justice and Political Cultures: National and International Dimensions of Crime Control*, Willan Publishing, Devon.

Long, M (2003) 'Leadership and performance management', in T Newburn (ed) *Handbook of Policing*, Willan Publishing, Devon, pp 625-658.

Loveday, B (1995) 'Contemporary challenges to police management, developing strategies for improving the delivery of police service', *Policing and Society*, Vol 5, pp 281-302.

Loveday, B (2005) Police Staff and Service Modernisation: A Reform Too Far? *Working Paper 14*, Faculty of Law Humanities and Social Science, UCE Birmingham, viewed 7 May 2006 <www.uce.ac.uk/lhss/research/pdfs/paper14.pdf>.

Lucas G (1977) *Report of the Committee of Inquiry into the Enforcement of Criminal Law in Queensland* (The Lucas Report), Government Printer, Brisbane.

Lusher, E (1981) *Report of the Commission to Inquire into the New South Wales Police Administration*, NSW State Government, Sydney.

Lutz, BJ, Lutz, JM and Ulmschneider, GW (2002) 'British trials of Irish Nationalist defendants: the quality of justice strained', *Studies in Conflict & Terrorism*, Vol 25, pp 227-244.

Lutz, BJ, Ulmschneider, GW and Lutz, JM (2002) 'The trial of the Guildford Four: government error or government persecution?' *Terrorism and Political Violence*, Vol 14, No 4, pp 113-130.

Lynch, J and Tuckey, M (2004) *Understanding Voluntary Turnover: An Examination of Resignations in the Australasian Police Organisations,* Australasian Centre for Policing Research, Report Series No 143.1, South Australia.

Lyons, W (2002) 'Partnerships, information and public safety: community policing in a time of terror', *Policing: An International Journal of Police Strategies and Management,* Vol 25, No 3, pp 530-542.

Macdonald, R (1995) 'Skills and qualities required of police leaders, now and in the future', in B Etter and M Palmer (eds) *Police Leadership in Australasia,* Federation Press, Sydney.

MacDowell, R (2001) *Inside Story,* Hobson Dell Publishing, Victoria.

MacPherson, W (1999) *The Stephen Lawrence Inquiry,* Report of an inquiry by Sir William MacPherson of Cluny, viewed 14 December 2006 from: <www.archive .official-documents.co.uk/document/cm42/4262/4262.htm>

McBarnet, DJ (1981) *Conviction,* Macmillan, London.

McCarrey, LE (1993) *Report of the Independent Commission to Review Public Sector Finances: Agenda for Reform Vol 1,* Independent Commission to Review Government Finances, Perth.

McCulloch, J and Palmer, D (2005) *Civil Litigation by Citizens Against Australian Police between 1994-2002,* Criminology Research Council, Canberra.

McDonnell, D (2001) 'Committee and commissions of inquiry into criminal justice agencies: a history repeating itself', in M Enders and B Dupont (eds) *Policing the Lucky Country,* Federation Press, Sydney.

McGregor, J (1993) *Crime News As Prime News,* Legal Research Foundation Publication No 36, New Zealand.

McGregor, R (1997) *Imagined Destinies, Aboriginal Australians and the Doomed Race Theory, 1880-1939,* Melbourne University Press, Carlton South.

McLean, J (1994) 'Performance management that works', *Workplace Reform Monitor,* Vol 9, para 1.1-1.11.

McQuail, D (1994) *Mass Communication Theory,* Sage Publications Inc, London.

Maguire M (1991) 'Complaints against police: the British experience', in A Goldsmith (ed) *Complaints Against the Police: The Trend to External Review,* Clarendon, Oxford.

Maguire, M (2003) 'Criminal investigation and crime control', in T Newburn (ed) *Handbook of Policing,* Willan Publishing, Devon.

Maguire, M and John, T (2006) 'Intelligence-led policing, managerialism and community engagement: competing priorities and the role of the National Intelligence Model in the UK,' *Policing and Society,* Vol 16, No 1, pp 67-85.

Malhotra, Y (2002) 'Why knowledge management systems fail: enablers and constraints of knowledge management in human enterprises', in CW Holsapple (ed) *Handbook on Knowledge Management 1: Knowledge Matters,* Springer-Verlag, Heidelberg, pp 577-599.

Malton, J (2001) 'Fictionalising the police', in S Wilson (ed) *Criminal Justice and the Media: An Uneasy Marriage?,* St Catherine's Conference Report, The King George VI and Queen Elizabeth Foundation of St Catherine's Cumberland Lodge, Berkshire.

Maravelias, C (2003) 'Post-bureaucracy – control through professional freedom', *Journal of Organizational Change Management,* Vol 16, No 5, pp 547-566.

Marchetti, E and Daly, K (2004) 'Indigenous courts and justice practices in Australia', *Trends and Issues No 277,* Australian Institute of Criminology, Canberra.

Marinac, A and Curtis, J (2005) The scrutiny of government agencies by parliamentary joint committees, Paper presented at the 2005 ASPG Conference, 7-8 October viewed 28 November 2006 <www.aspg.org.au/events/conferences>.

Martin Bonato and Associates (2003) Report from Review of Police Community Consultative Committees, Crime Prevention Victoria, (unpublished confidential paper).

Mawby, RI (2003) 'Models of policing', in T Newburn (ed) *Handbook of Policing*, Willan Publishing, Devon.

Mayhew, P (2003) 'Counting the costs of crime in Australia', *Trends and Issues in Crime and Criminal Justice*, Vol 247, pp 1-8.

Mazerolle, L and Prenzler, T (2004) 'Third party policing: considering the ethical challenges', in JR Greene, AR Piquero and MM Hickman (eds) *Police Integrity and Ethics*, Wadsworth, Belmont.

Mazerolle, L and Ransley, J (2004) 'Third Party policing: prospects, challenges and implications for regulators,' in N Taylor, R Johnstone and R Sarre (eds) *Current Issues in Regulation: Enforcement and Compliance*, Australian Institute of Criminology, Research and Public Policy Series.

Mazerolle, L and Ransley, J (2006a) *Third Party Policing*, Cambridge University Press, Cambridge.

Mazerolle, L and Ransley, J (2006b) 'Third party policing', in D Weisburd and A Braga (eds) *Prospects and Problems in an Era of Police Innovation*, Cambridge University Press, Cambridge.

Mazerolle, L, Roehl, J and Kadleck, C (1998) 'Controlling social disorder using civil remedies: results from a randomised field experiment in Oakland', in L Mazerolle and J Roehl (eds) *Civil Remedies and Crime Prevention, Crime Prevention Studies* Vol 9, Criminal Justice Press.

Mazerolle, L, Rombouts, S and McBroom, J (2006) 'The impact of operational performance reviews on reported crime in Queensland', *Trends and Issues in Crime & Criminal Justice*, No 313, pp 1-6, Australian Institute of Criminology, Canberra.

Mazerolle, L, Soole, D and Rombouts, S (2006) 'Street-level drug law enforcement: a meta-analytic review', *Journal of Experimental Criminology 2*, p 409-435.

Menzies, DC (2004) 'An investigation of transformational leadership in the Scottish police service', *Police Leadership and Management University of Leicester*, February.

Miller, J, Quinton, P and Bland, N (2000) *Police Stops and Searches: Lessons from a Programme of Research*, Home Office, London.

Miller, L (2004) 'Good cop – bad cop: problem officers, law enforcement culture and strategies for success', *Journal of Police and Criminal Psychology*, Vol 19, No 2, pp 30-48.

Miller, S (1999) 'Private and professional character in policing', *Perspectives on the Professions*, Vol 18, No 2, viewed 1 February 2006 <www.iit.edu/departments/csep/perspective/pers18_2spr99_3.html>.

Milne, R and Bull, R (1999) *Investigative Interviewing: Psychology and Practice*, Wiley, Chichester.

Milne, R and Shaw, G (1999) 'Obtaining witness statements: the psychology, best practice and proposals for innovation', *Medicine, Science and the Law*, Vol 39, No 2, pp 127-137.

Ministerial Summit on Indigenous Deaths in Custody (1997) *Speeches and Papers from the Ministerial Summit*, ATSIC, Canberra.

Mintzberg, H (1994) *The Rise and Fall of Strategic Planning*, Prentice Hall, New York.

Mitchell, M (2003) Perceptions of Crime and Community Responsiveness, Paper presented at the Australian and New Zealand Society of Criminology Conference, Sydney, 1-3 October.

Mitchell, M (2006) Interview with senior State police commander, 15 June.

Mitchell, M and Jennett, C (2007) 'Research literacy in police organisations: a luxury that we can afford', in J Ruiz and D Hummer (eds) *Handbook of Police Administration*, CRC Press, (Taylor & Francis), New York.

Mitchell, M, Munro, A, Thomson, D and Jackson, J (1997) *Exposing Police Probationers to Incidents of Sudden Death*, Home Office Police Policy Directorate, London.

Mitchell, M and Urquhart, JD (2002) 'Representation of NSW Police on meetings, committees, working parties, councils and other bodies', *Operational Policy and Programs*, NSW Police, Sydney (unpublished).

Mobekk, E (2005) 'Identifying lessons in United Nations international policing missions', Geneva Centre for the Democratic Control of Armed Forces (DCAF), viewed 7 May 2006 <www.dcaf.ch/_docs/pp09_united-nations-international_policing.pdf#search=%22capacity%20building%20for%20international%20policing%22>.

Moffatt, S, Goh, D and Poynton, S (2005) *New South Wales Recorded Crime Statistics 2005*, NSW Bureau of Crime Statistics and Research, Sydney.

Mollen, M (1994) *Report of the Commission to Investigate Allegations of Police Corruption and the Anti-corruption Procedures of the Police Department*, Mollen Commission, City of New York.

Moore, D, Krizan, L and Moore, E (2005) 'Evaluating intelligence: a competency based model,' *International Journal of Intelligence and CounterIntelligence*, Vol 18, No 2, pp 204-220.

Moore, WE (1976) *The Professions: Roles and Rules*, Russell Sage Foundation, New York.

Morgan, D and Stephenson, G (1994) *Suspicion and Silence: The Right to Silence in Criminal Investigations*, Blackstone, London.

Morreale, S and Ortmeier, J (2005) 'Preparing leaders for law enforcement', *The Police Chief*, December.

Morris, A and Feldman, D (1996) 'The dimensions, antecedents and consequences of emotional labour', *The Academy of Management Review*, Vol 21, p 986.

Munro, JL (1984) 'Criminal justice management: towards the year 2000', Second Justice Administration Public Oration, 13 September 1984, South Australian Institute of Justice Studies, South Australian Institute of Technology, pp 1-28.

Murray, J (1999) *Challenges Facing Police Leadership in the Future*, Australian Graduate School of Police Management, Charles Sturt University (unpublished discussion paper).

Murray, J (2002) Leadership and Integrity in Policing: The March Away from Militarism, presentation at the Third Police Leadership Conference, Managing Change Through Principled Leadership, Vancouver, 10-12 April, viewed 7 May 2006 <www.afp.gov.au/__data/assets/pdf_file/4016/leadershipcanada02.pdf>.

Murray, T (2000) 'Police and the challenge of the 21st Century: managing change in police organisations', *Royal Canadian Mounted Police Gazette*, Vol 62, No 1, pp 6-18.

Myhill, A (2006) 'Community engagement in policing, lessons from the literature', Home Office, London, viewed 2 May 2007 <http://police.homeoffice.gov.uk/news-and-publications/publication/communitypolicing/Community_engagement_lit_rev.pdf>.

Myhill, A, Yarrow, S, Dalgleish, D and Docking, M (2003) 'The role of police authorities in public engagement', *Home Office Online Report 37/03*, London, viewed 12 November 2005 <www.homeoffice.gov.uk/rds/pdfs2/rdsolr3703.pdf>.

Nankervis, A and Leece, P (1997) 'Performance appraisal: two steps forward, one step back?', *Asia Pacific Journal of Human Resources*, Vol 35, No 2, pp 80-92.

Napier, M (2005) 'The need for higher education', *Law and Order*, September.

National Campaign Against Violence and Crime (1998) *Fear of Crime Vol 1 and Vol 2*, Commonwealth of Australia, Canberra.

National Commission on Terrorist Attacks upon the United States (2004) *The 9/11 Commission Report*, viewed 14 December 2006 <www.9-11commission.gov/report/911Report.pdf>.

National Geographic News (2005) 'London bombing pictures mark new role for camera phones', viewed 22 November 2006 <http://news.nationalgeographic.com/news/2005/07/0711_050711_londoncell_2.html>.

National Institute for Governance (2003) *Public Service Leadership: Emerging Issues: A Report for the Australian Public Service Commission*, viewed 7 May 2006 < www.apsc.gov.au/leadership/emergingissues.pdf>.

Negus, T (2002) 'Leadership in the year 2010 – implications for policing', *Platypus Magazine*, No 74, pp 7-44.

Nethercote, JR (2003) 'Australian public administration in perspective' in *The Australian Public Sector Reform*, Australian Public Service Commission, Commonwealth of Australia.

Newburn, T (1999) 'Understanding and preventing police corruption: lessons from the literature', *Police Research Series Paper 110*, Home Office, London.

Neyroud, P and Beckley, A (2001) *Policing, Ethics and Human Rights*, Willan Publishing, Devon.

Neyroud, P (2003) 'Policing and ethics', in T Newburn (ed) *Handbook of Policing*, Willan Publishing, Devon, pp 578-602.

Nicholl, J (2004) 'Task definition', in J Ratcliffe (ed) *Strategic Thinking in Criminal Intelligence*, Federation Press, Sydney.

NIJ (National Institute of Justice) (2005) *Engaging the Private Sector to Promote Homeland Security: Law Enforcement-Private Security Partnerships*, US Department of Justice, Washington DC.

9/11 Commission Report (2004) *The 9/11 Commission Report: The Final Report of the National Commission on the Terrorist Attacks upon the United States*, WW Norton & Company, New York.

NISATSIC (National Inquiry into the Separation of Aboriginal and Torres Strait Islander Children) (1997) *Bringing Them Home, Report of the National Inquiry into the Separation of Aboriginal and Torres Strait Islander Children from Their Families*, HREOC, Sydney.

Norman, R and Gregory, R (2003) 'Paradoxes and pendulum swings: performance management in New Zealand's public sector', *Australian Journal of Public Administration*, Vol 62, No 4, pp 35-49.

NPEAB (National Police Ethnic Advisory Bureau) (2000) *Culturally Competent Police Organisations: National Recruitment and Retention Strategic Framework*, NPEAB, viewed 7 May 2006 <www.apmab.gov.au/pubs/reports/Strategic_Framework.pdf#search=%22cultural%20competence%20police%22>.

NSW Ombudsman (2005) *Working with Local Aboriginal Communities*, NSW Ombudsman, Sydney.

Nutley, S (2003) Bridging the policy/research divide: Reflections and lessons from the UK, Presentation to the National Institute of Governance Conference, Canberra.

Nutley, S, Walter, I and Davies, H (2002) *From Knowing to Doing: A Framework for Understanding the Evidence-Into-Practice Agenda, Discussions Paper 1*, Research Unit for Research Utilization, University of St Andrews, Scotland.

O'Malley, P (1997) 'The politics of crime prevention' in P O'Malley and A Sutton (eds) *Crime Prevention in Australia*, Federation Press, Sydney.

O'Neill, C and Holsinger, L (2003) 'Effective performance management systems', *World at Work Journal*, World at Work, Arizona, Vol 12, No 2, pp 61-67.

Ord, B and Shaw, G (1999) *Investigative Interviewing Explained: The Operational Guide to Practical Interviewing Skills*, The New Police Bookshop, Surrey.

Ord, B, Shaw, G and Green, T (2004) *Investigative Interviewing Explained*, LexisNexis Butterworths, Sydney.

Orr-Munro, T (2005) 'May the force be with you', *Police: The Voice of the Service*, January, pp 19-21.

Packer, H (1968) *The Limits of the Criminal Sanction*, Stanford University Press, Stanford.

Pakes, F (2004) *Comparative Criminal Justice*, Willan Publishing, Devon.

Palmer, M (1994) 'Managing a hierarchical para-military organisation', in K Bryett and C Lewis (eds) *Un-peeling Tradition: Contemporary Policing*, Macmillan, Sydney.

Palmer, M (2001) 'Today's AFP has not evolved by chance', *Platypus Magazine*, (Journal of the Australian Federal Police), Australian Federal Police, Canberra, No 70, pp 2-5.

Pan, Z and Kosicki, G (2001) 'Framing as strategic action in public deliberation', in S Reese, O Gandy and A Grant (eds) 2003, *Framing Public Life: Perspectives on Media and our Understanding of the Social World*, Lawrence Erlbaum, New Jersey.

Parry, N and Parry, J (1976) *The Rise of the Medical Profession*, Croom Helm, London.

Pastor, J (2003) *The Privatization of Police in America*, McFarland & Company, Jefferson.

Patten, C (1999) *A New Beginning: Policing in Northern Ireland*, Report of the Independent Commission on Policing for Northern Ireland, Ireland.

Pawar, KS, Horton, AR, Gupta, A, Wunram, M, Barson, RJ, Weber, F (2001) Inter-organisational knowledge management: Focus on human barriers in the telecommunications industry, Paper presented at the 28 July-1 August 2001, 8th ISPE International Conference on Concurrent Engineering: Research and Applications, West Coast Anaheim Hotel, California, USA, s 271-278.

Pawson R (2006) *Evidence Based Policy: A Realist Perspective*, Sage Publications Inc., London.

PCC – *See Conference of Commissioners of Police of Australasia and the South West Pacific Region*.

Pearse, J and Gudjonsson, G H (1996) 'A review of the role of the legal adviser in police stations', *Criminal Behaviour and Mental Health*, Vol 6, pp 231-239.

Perri 6 (2004) 'Joined-up government in the Western world in comparative perspective: a preliminary literature review and exploration', *Journal of Public Administration Research and Theory*, Vol 14, No 1, pp 103-138.

Petersen, F (2004) 'Enlist private security to bolster defences: Police', *Sydney Morning Herald*, p 11, 15 March.

Petit, A and Haines, V (1994) 'Three performance appraisal instruments', *Gestion*, pp 59-68.

Phillips, D (2003) 'The route to professionalism', *Policing Today*, Vol 9, No 1, pp 5-6.

Phillips, E and Trone, J (2002) *Building Public Confidence in Police through Civilian Oversight*, Vera Institute of Justice, New York.

Pierce, C (2001) *The Effective Director*, Kogan Page, London.

Pierce, S (2005a) *AIPM Academic Strategy Project*, 'Visiting fellow focus group', 11 July, Australian Institute of Police Management.

Pierce, S (2005b) *AIPM Academic Strategy Project*, 'International survey', 22 September, Australian Institute of Police Management.

Pilger, J (2004) *Tell Me No Lies*, Vintage, Great Britain.

Police Professional (2005) 'Looking for leadership' *Police Professional Online*, viewed 7 May 2006, <www.policeprofessional.com/news.aspx?id=1334>.

Potas, I, Smart, J, Bignell, G, Lawrie, R and Thomas, B (2003) *Circle Sentencing in New South Wales, A Review and Evaluation*, New South Wales Judicial Commission and Aboriginal Justice Advisory Committee, Sydney.

Prasser, S, Wear, R and Nethercote, J (1992) *Corruption and Reform: The Fitzgerald vision*, University of Queensland Press, Queensland.

Prenzler, T and King, M (2002) 'The role of private investigators and commercial agents in law enforcement', *Trends and Issues in Crime and Criminal Justice*, No 234, Australian Institute of Criminology.

Prenzler, T (2000) 'Civilian oversight of police: A test of capture theory' *British Journal of Criminology*, Vol 40, No 4, pp 659-674.

Prenzler, T (2000) 'The privatisation of policing' in R Sarre and J Tomaino (eds) *Considering Crime and Justice: Realities and Responses*, Crawford House Publishing.

Prenzler, T (2004) Security Industry Report Card, Paper presented at the National Security Industry Forum, Australian Security industry Association Limited, Melbourne, 20 April.

Prenzler, T (2005) 'Mapping the Australian security industry' *Security Journal*, Vol 18, No 4, pp 51-64.

Prenzler, T (2006) Growth, Scandal and Reform in the Australian Security Industry, Paper presented at the Sixth Australasian Security Research Symposium, Brisbane, 20-21 April.

Presser, B (2001) 'Public policy, police interest: a re-evaluation of the judicial discretion to exclude improperly or illegally obtained evidence', *Melbourne University Law Review*, Vol 25, pp 757-85.

Private Security Advisory Council (1977) *Law Enforcement and Private Security: Sources and Areas of Conflict and Strategies for Conflict Resolution*, Department of Justice, Washington DC.

Prusak, L (2001) 'Where did knowledge management come from?' IBM *Systems Journal*, Vol 40, No 4, pp 1002-1007.

Putnis, P (1996) 'Police-media relations: issues and trends', in D Chappell and P Wilson (eds) *Australian Policing: Contemporary Issues*, Butterworths, Sydney.

Quinn, S (2004) 'Varieties of civilian oversight: similarities, differences and expectations', viewed 28 November 2006, from www.nacole.org/ModelsCivOversight_1204.pdf.

Quintas, P, Lefrere, P and Jones, G (1997) 'Knowledge management: a strategic agenda', *Long Range Planning*, Vol 30, pp 385-391.

Radnor, Z and McGuire, M (2004) 'Performance management in the public sector: fact or fiction?' *International Journal of Productivity and Performance Management*, Vol 53, No 3, pp 245-260.

Ratcliffe, J (2002) 'Intelligence-led policing and the problems of turning rhetoric into practice', *Policing and Society*, Vol 12, No 1, pp 53-66.

Ratcliffe, J (2003) 'Intelligence-led policing', *Trends and Issues in Crime and Criminal Justice*, No 248, Australian Institute of Criminology, Canberra.

Rawlings, P (1995) 'The idea of policing: a history', *Policing and Society*, No 5, pp 129-149.

Rayner, M (2005) 'A nose for the rottenness in the bulkhead', *New Matilda*, viewed 17 August 2005 <www.newmatilda.com/home/articledetailmagazine.asp?ArticleID=848&CategoryID=-1>.

RCIADIC (Royal Commission into Aboriginal Deaths in Custody) (1991) *National Report Vol 2*, Australian Government Publishing Service, Canberra.

RCCJ (Royal Commission on Criminal Justice) (1993) *Report of the Royal Commission on Criminal Justice*, Cm 2263, HMSO.

RCCP (Royal Commission on Criminal Procedure) (1981) *Report of the Royal Commission on Criminal Procedure*, Cmnd 8092, HMSO.

RCPPP (Royal Commission on Police Powers and Procedure) (1929) *Report of the Royal Commission on Police Powers and Procedure*, Cmd 3297, HMSO.

Reese, SD, Gandy, Jr OH and Grant, AE (2003) *Framing Public Life*, Lawrence Erlbaum, New Jersey.

Reichel, P (1999) *Comparative Criminal Justice Systems: A Topical Approach*, Prentice Hall, Upper Saddle River.

Reige, A (2005) 'Three-dozen knowledge-sharing barriers managers must consider', *Journal of Knowledge Management*, Vol 9, No 3, pp 18-35.

Reiner, R (2000) *The Politics of the Police*, Oxford University Press, New York.

Reiner, R (1997) 'Media made criminality', in M Maquire, R Morgan and R Reiner (eds) *The Oxford Handbook of Criminality*, 2nd Edition, Oxford University Press, Oxford.

Reiner, R (2000) *The Politics of the Police*, Oxford University Press.

Reuss-Ianni, E and Ianni, F (2005) 'Street cops and management cops: the two cultures of policing', in T Newburn (ed) *Policing: Key Readings*, Willan Publishing, Devon, pp 297-314, (originally published 1983).

Reynolds, H (1987) *Frontier, Aborigines, Settlers and Land*, Allen & Unwin, Sydney.

Robbins, S, Bergman, R, Stags I and Coulter, M (2006) *Management*, Prentice-Hall, Sydney.

Robson, C (2002) *Real World Research*, 2nd Edition, Blackwell Publishing, Oxford.

Rock, F (2001) 'The genesis of a witness statement', *Forensic Linguistics*, Vol 8, No 2, pp 44-72.

Rohl, T (1990a) 'Moving to a professional status', *Police Journal* (South Australia), Vol 71, No 6, pp 6-9.

Rohl, T (1990b) 'Moving to a professional status', *Police News* (Western Australia), July, pp 16-18.

ROHL, T (1994) 'The professional police practitioner in the twenty-first century', in D Moore and R Wettinghall (eds) *Keeping the Peace: Police Accountability and Oversight*, University of Canberra and The Royal Institute of Public Administration Australia, Canberra.

Rosen, J (1993) 'Getting the connections right: public journalism and the troubles in the press', viewed 21 May 1997 <www.cpn.org/topics/communication/getting 1.html>.

Ross, L and Weill, P (2002) 'Six IT decisions your IT people shouldn't make', *Harvard Business Review*, November 2002.

Roth, JA (1974) 'Professionalism: the sociologist's decoy', *Sociology of Work and Occupations*, Vol 1, No 1, pp 6-23.

Rowe, M (2006) 'Following the leader: front line narratives on police leadership', *Policing: An International Journal of Police Strategies & Management*, Vol 29, No 4, pp 757-767.

Ruggles, R (1998) 'The state of the notion: knowledge management in practice', *California Management Review*, Vol 40, No 3, pp 80-89.

Saint-Onge, H and Armstrong, C (2004) *The Conductive Organization: Building Beyond Sustainability*, Elsevier Butterworth-Heinemann, Oxford.

Saks, M (1983) 'Removing the blinkers? A critique of recent contributions to the sociology of professions', *The Sociological Review*, February, pp 1-21.

Sallybanks, J (2005) 'Monitoring injuries in police custody: a feasibility and utility study, technical and background paper', *Report No 15*, Australian Institute of Criminology, Canberra.

Sarre, R and Prenzler, T (2000) 'The relationship between police and private security: models and future directions', *International Journal of Comparative and Applied Criminal Justice*, Vol 24, No 1, pp 92-113.

Sarre, R and Prenzler, T (2005) *The Law of Private Security in Australia*, Thomson Lawbook Co, Sydney.

Sarre, R and Tomaino, J (1999) *Exploring Criminal Justice: Contemporary Australian Themes*, South Australian Institute of Justice Studies, Adelaide.

Sarre, T and Prenzler, T (2005) *The Law of Private Security in Australia*, Thomson Lawbook.

Scarman, Lord L (1981) *The Brixton Disorders*, Cmd 8427, HMSO.

Schein, E (1985) *Organizational Culture and Leadership*, Jossey-Bass, San Francisco.

Schein, EH (1999) *The Corporate Culture Survival Guide: Sense and Nonsense about Cultural Change*, Josey-Bass Publishers, San Francisco.

Schollum, M (2005) *Investigative Interviewing: The Literature*, Office of the Commissioner of Police, Wellington, New Zealand Police, viewed 12 December 2006 <www.police.govt.nz/resources/2005/investigative-interviewing>.

Schuler, RS and Jackson, SE (1999) *Strategic Human Resource Management*, Blackwell Publishers, Malden.

Schultz, J (1998) *Reviving the Fourth Estate*, Cambridge University Press, Cambridge.

Shuy, RW (1998) *The Language of Confession, Interrogation and Deception*, Sage Publications Inc, California.

Scrivner, E (2006) *Innovations in Police Recruitment and Hiring: Hiring in the Spirit of Service*, US Department of Justice: Office of Community Oriented Policing Service.

SCROGSP (2005) *Overcoming Indigenous Disadvantage – Key Indicators 2005*, Productivity Commission, Melbourne.

Seltmann, H (2005) 'Police in a democratic society: from "force" to "service"', viewed 7 May 2006 <www.coe.int/T/E/Human_Rights/Police/9._Network_Conference /05_speechHartmann.asp#TopOfPage>.

Senge, P (2003) *The Fifth Discipline; The Art and Practice of the Learning Organisation*, Doubleday, New York.

Senge, PM (1990) 'The leader's new work: building learning organizations', *Sloan Management Review*, Vol 32, No 1, pp 7-23.

Shaw, G (2001) 'Current state of force interview training', in J Burbeck (ed) (2001) *New ACPO Investigative Interviewing Strategy*, unpublished Warwickshire Police Document.

Shaw, G (2002) 'The management and supervision of interviews', *Management Briefing Note*, Vol 3, 20 October, 2002, Centrex, Bramshill, (unpublished).

Shaw, G (2003) *Training Curriculum for Tier 4 of the ACPO Investigative Interviewing Strategy*, Centrex, Bramshill, (unpublished).

Shearing, C (1992) 'The relation between public and private security', in M Tonry and N Morris (eds) *Modern Policing: An Annual Review of Research*, Chicago University Press, Chicago.

Shearing, C, Stenning, P and Addario, S (1985) 'Police perceptions of private security', *Canadian Police College Journal*, Vol 9, No 2, pp 127-154.

Shepherd, E (1991) 'Ethical interviewing', *Policing*. Vol 7, No 1, pp 42-60.

Shepherd, E (ed) (1993) 'Aspects of police interviewing', *Issues in Criminological and Legal Psychology*, The British Psychological Society, Leicester.

Sheptycki, J (2004) 'Review of the influence of strategic intelligence on organised crime policy and practice,' *Special Interest Series Paper, No 14*, Research, Development and Statistics Directorate, Home Office, London.

Shergold, P (2003) New Challenges for the Australian Federal Police, speech given at the Australian Federal Police College, by the Secretary Department of the Prime Minister and Cabinet, viewed 7 May 2006 <www.dpmc.gov.au/speeches/sher gold/afp_challenges_2003-11-19.cfm>.

Sherman, L (1978) 'Scandal and reform', cited in J Chan (1997) *Changing Police Culture: Policing a Multicultural Society*, Cambridge University Press, Cambridge.

Sherman, L (1998) *Evidence Based Policing*, Washington DC Police Foundation, Washington DC.

Shi, L (2005) 'Does oversight reduce policing? Evidence from the Cincinnati police department after the April 2001 riot', viewed 28 November 2006 <www. aeaweb.org/annual_mtg_papers/2006/0106_0800_0903.pdf>.

SIA (Security Industry Authority) (2004) *SIA Annual Report 2003/4*, Security Industry Authority, London.

Sifry, D (2005) 'An update on the blogosphere's reactions (and resources) to the London bombings, 7 July 2005' <www.sifry.com/alerts/archives/2005_07.html>, viewed 22 November 2006.

Skelley, BD (2002) 'The ambiguity of results: assessments of the New Public Management', *Public Administration & Management: An Interactive Journal*, Vol 7, No 2, pp 168-187.

Skogan, W (2004) 'Preface', *The Annals of the American Academy of Political and Social Science*, Vol 593, pp 6-14.

Skogan, W and Frydl, K (eds) (2004) *Fairness and Effectiveness in Policing: The Evidence*, National Academies Press, Washington DC.

Skyrme, D (1998) 'Know-why know-how', *Information Age*, September, pp 8-9.

Smith, D and Gray, J (1985) *Police and People in London*, Gower Publishing, Aldershot.

Smolen, Z (1995) 'A global police service is the inevitable consequence of rising international crime: discuss', *The Police Journal*, Vol 68, No 1, pp 7-16.

Sossin, L (2004) 'The oversight of executive police relations in Canada: the constitution, the courts, administrative processes and democratic governance', viewed 28 November 2006 <www.ipperwashinquiry.ca/policy_part/pdf/Sossin.pdf>.

Squires, P (1998) 'Cops and customers: consumerism and the demand for police services, is the customer always right?' *Policing and Society*, Vol 8, No 2, pp 169-188.

Stacey, H and Mullan, B (1997) 'Cognitive interviewing', *Policing Issues and Practice Journal* (July 1997), pp 36-41.

Steinberg, R and Figart, D (1999) 'Emotional demands at work: a job content analysis', *Annals of the American Academy of Political and Social Science*, Vol 561, p 177-191.

Stevens, DJ (2000) 'Improving community policing', *Law and Order*, Vol 48, No 10, pp 197-204.

Stinchcomb, JB (2004) 'Searching for stress in all the wrong places: combating chronic organizational stressors in policing', *Police Practice and Research*, Vol 5, No 3, pp 259-277.

Stockdale, JE (1993) *Management and Supervision of Police Interviews*, Police Research Group, Home Office, London.

Stone, C and Bobb, M (2002) 'Civilian oversight of the police in democratic societies: global meeting on civilian oversight of police', Los Angeles, 5-8 May, viewed 28 November 2006 <www.safereturn.info/publication_pdf/179_325.pdf>.

Stone, RJ (2002) *Human Resource Management*, John Wiley & Sons, Brisbane.

Stubbs, M (1983) *Discourse Analysis: The Sociolinguistic Analysis of Natural Language*, Basil Blackwell, Oxford.

'Sunday' (2004) Interview with Mick Keelty, 14 March, viewed 14 April 2006 <http://sunday.ninemsn.com.au/sunday/political_transcripts/article_1506.asp>.

Surette, R (1992) *Media, Crime and Criminal Justice*, Brooks/Cole Publishing Company, Pacific Grove.

Sutton, A, Dussuyer, I and Cherney, A (2003) Assessment of Local Community Safety and Crime Prevention Roles in Victoria, Crime Prevention Victoria and Department of Criminology, University of Melbourne (unpublished paper).

Sveiby, KE (1997) *The New Organizational Wealth: Managing & Measuring Knowledge-Based Assets*, Berret-Koechler Publishers Inc, San Francisco.

Sydney Morning Herald (2001a) 'Now the watchdogs will deal the cards', Features, p 8, 3 January.

Sydney Morning Herald (2001b) 'Herald apologises to Mr Jeff Jarratt', p 2, 22 June.

Sydney Morning Herald (2001c) 'I've been terminated: Deputy Jarratt's exit', p 1, 6 September.

Sydney Morning Herald (2001d) 'Ousted Jarratt weighs up whether to take legal action', p 15, 8 September.

Sydney Morning Herald (2006) 'The Force is with the police again', viewed 5 May 2006 <www.smh.com.au/news/national/the-force-is-with-the-police-again/2006/05/05/1146335911486.html>.

Taylor, N and Bareja, M (2005) *2002 National Police Custody Survey, Technical and Background Paper No 13*, Australian Institute of Criminology, Canberra.

Teo, ST Ahmad, T and Rodwell, JJ (2003) *HR Role Effectiveness and Organisational Culture in Australian Local Government*, Asia Pacific Journal of Human Resources, Vol 41, No 3, pp 298-315.

Thomas, RT and Davies, A (2002) 'Restructuring the "old bill": policing identities and commitment', *Women in Management Review*, Vol 17, No 3/4, pp 180-89.

Tiffen, R (1999) *Scandals: Media, Politics and Corruption in Contemporary Australia*, University of New South Wales Press, Sydney.

Tilley, N (2003) 'Community policing, problem-oriented policing and intelligence-led policing', in T Newburn (ed) *Handbook of Policing*, Willan Publishing, Devon.

Tilley, N and Bullock (2003) *Crime Reduction and Problem Oriented Policing*, Willan Publishing, Devon.

Totikidis, V, Armstrong, A and Francis, R (2005) Local Safety Committees and the Community Governance of Crime Prevention and Community Safety, Paper presented to the Beyond Fragmented Government: Governance in the Public Sector conference, Victoria University, Melbourne, 15-17 August 2005, viewed 3 May 2007 <www.businessandlaw.vu.edu.au/conferences/psc_proceedings/Totikidis_VUREF.pdf>.

Touskas, H and Vladimirou, E (2001) 'What is organizational knowledge?' *Journal of Management Studies*, Vol 38, No 7, pp 973-993.

Tulloch, J (1998) 'Fear of crime and the media socio cultural theories of risk', in *National Campaign Against Violence and Crime, Fear of Crime Vol 1 and Vol 2*, Commonwealth of Australia, Canberra.

Tyler, T (1989) 'The psychology of procedural justice: a test of the group-value model', *Journal of Personality and Social Psychology*, Vol 57, No 5, pp 830-838.

Tyler, T and Fagan, J (2005) *Legitimacy and Cooperation: Why Do People help the Police fight Crime in their Communities?*, Columbia Law School Public Law and Legal Theory Working Paper 06-99.

US Department of Justice (2005) 'Intelligence led policing: the new intelligence architecture', in *New Realities: Law Enforcement in the post 9/11 Era*, Bureau of Justice Assistance, Washington DC.

Vander Beken, T (2004) 'Risky business: a risk based methodology to measure organised crime', *Crime Law and Social Change*, Vol 41, pp 471-516.

Vickers, M H and Kouzmin, A (2001) 'New managerialism and Australian police organizations: a cautionary note', *The International Journal of Public Sector Management*, Vol 14, No 1, pp 7-26.

Victoria Police (2005a) *Annual Report 2004/2005*, viewed 19 March 2007 <www.police.vic.gov.au/retrievemedia.asp?Media_ID=1838>.

Victoria Police (2005b) *Code of Ethics 2005*, viewed 19 March 2007 <www.police.vic.gov.au/content.asp?Document_ID=676>.

Victoria Police (1999) Strategic Development Department, *Continuous Improvement Handbook*, Victoria Police.

Victoria Police (2003) *The Way Ahead: Strategic Plan 2003-2008*, Victoria Police, Melbourne viewed 8 November 2005 <www.police.vic.gov.au/files/documents/352_The-Way-Ahead-Strategic-Plan-2003-2008.pdf>.

Victorian Implementation Review Team (2004) *Discussion Paper, Review of the Recommendations from the Royal Commission into Aboriginal Deaths in Custody*, Melbourne.

Violanti, JM and Aron, F (1994) 'Ranking police stressors', *Psychological Reports*, Vol 75, pp 824-826.

WA Police News (1990) 'Policing – is it an occupation in transition', *WA Police News*, July, pp 13-18.

Wah, L (1999) 'Is "knowledge management" an oxymoron?' *Management Review*, April, pp 18-26.

Walker, N (2003) 'The pattern of transnational policing', in T Newburn (ed) *Handbook of Policing*, Willan Publishing, Devon.

Walker, S (2001) *Police Accountability: The Role of Citizen Oversight*, Wadsworth, Belmont.

Walker, S, Alpert, GP and Kenney, D (2000) 'Early warning systems for police: concept, history and issues' *Police Quarterly*, Vol 3, No 2, pp 132-152.

Walsh, P and Ratcliffe, J (2005) 'Strategic criminal intelligence education: a collaborative approach,' *IALEIA Journal*, Vol 16, No 2, pp 152-166.

Walsh, P (2005) Intelligence-led policing: evolving Australian perspectives, paper presented to the International Forum on Intelligence-led policing, Hangzhou, China, 17-19 June.

Walsh, W and Vito, G (2004) 'The meaning of COMPSTAT; analysis and response', *Journal of Contemporary Criminal Justice*, Vol 20, No 1, pp 51-69.

Walsh, WF (2001) 'COMPSTAT: an analysis of an emerging police managerial paradigm', *Policing: An International Journal of Police Strategies & Management*, Vol 24 (3), pp 347-362.

Ward, J (1995) *Facilitative Police Management*, Partnership Press, Melbourne.

Warren, I (1998) 'Patron cultures, policing and security: trends from two Australian sport sites', *Security Journal*, Vol 10, No 2, pp 111-119.

Weatherburn, D (2002) Does Australia have a law and order problem?, a public lecture delivered in the Tyree Room at The Scienta, in the University of New South Wales 21 May at 5.00 p.m. under the auspices of the School of Social Sciences and

Policy, viewed 15 July 2002 <www.arts.unsw.edu.au/ssp/donweatherburn lecture.pdf>.

Weatherly, LA (2004) 'Performance management: getting it right from the start', *HR Magazine*, Alexandria, Vol 49, No 3, pp 1-11.

Weaver, B (2001) 'The fewer the facts, the stronger the opinion? Problems with comment in Australian newspapers', cited in *Ejournalist*, Vol 1, No 1, viewed 31 January 2006 <www.ejournalism.au.com/ejournalist/facts.pdf>.

Weisburd, D and Eck, JE (2004) 'What can police do to reduce crime, disorder and fear?' *The Annals of the American Academy of Political and Social Science*, Vol 593, pp 43-65.

Wenger, E (1998) *Communities of Practice: Learning, Meaning and Identity*, Cambridge University Press, Cambridge.

Western Australia Police (2001) *Central Areas Review*, Management Audit Unit, p 78, Perth.

Western Australia Police (2002) *Managing Staff Performance: Recommended Approach for the WAP*, Final report, Human Resources Directorate (Advance), Perth.

Western Australia Police (2003a) *Devolution/Decentralisation*, Strategic Reform Program, Perth.

Western Australia Police (2003b) *Doing It Right, A Review of Supervision*, Final report, Management Audit Unit, Perth.

Western Australia Police (2003c) 'Intelligence-led policing in the Western Australia Police Service – proposed framework', *Strategic Reform Program*, Perth.

Western Australia Police (2005) *2004-05 Annual Business Plan*, viewed 28 July 2007 <www.police.wa.gov.au/AboutUs/pdf/waps_abp0405.pdf>.

Wheeler, J (2005) *An Independent Review of Airport Security and Policing for the Government of Australia*, Commonwealth of Australia, Canberra.

White, R (1998) 'Curtailing youth: a critique of coercive crime prevention', *Crime Prevention Studies*, No 9, pp 93-113.

Wiig, KM (1994) *Knowledge Management: The Central Management Focus for Intelligent-Acting Organizations*, Schema Press, Arlington.

Williams, S (2002) *Peter Ryan – the Inside Story*, Penguin Books, Australia.

Wilson, D and Sutton, A (2003) *Open-Street CCTV in Australia*, Criminology Research Council, Canberra.

Wilson, S (2001) 'Criminal justice and the media: an uneasy marriage?', *St Catherine's Conference Report*, The King George VI and Queen Elizabeth Foundation of St Catherine's Cumberland Lodge, Berkshire, UK.

Wilson, TD (2002) 'The nonsense of "knowledge management"', *Information Research*, Vol 8, No 1, viewed 14 December 2006 <http://informationr.net/ir/8-1/paper144.html>.

Winzler, HR and Lanyon, IJ (2006) 'Professionalisation of policing in Australasia; and the evolution of the Australasian Police Professional Standards Council – a short history', viewed 12 June 2006 <www.appsc.com.au/docs/History_of_APPSC_Jan_2006.pdf>.

Witham, DC (1985) *The American Law Enforcement Chief Executive: A Management Profile*, Police Executive Research Forum, Washington DC.

Wood, J (1997) *Final Report of the Royal Commission into the New South Wales Police Service*, Government Printer, Sydney, viewed 11 November 2006 <www.pic.nsw.gov.au/Reports_List.asp?type=Royal>.

Wood, J and Dupont, B (eds) (2006) *Democracy, Society and the Governance of Security*, Cambridge University Press, Cambridge.

Woodall, J and Winstanley, D (1998) *Management Development: Strategy and Practice*, Blackwell Business, Malden.

Woodruffe, C (2006) 'The crucial importance of employee engagement', *Human Resource Management International Digest*, Vol 14, No 1.

Wootten, H (1991) 99 Reasons, 'The Royal Commission into Black Deaths in Custody', *Polemic*, Vol 2, No 3, pp 124-128.

Wright, A (2002) *Policing: An Introduction to Concepts and Practice*, Willan Publishing, Devon.

Yankelovich, D (1991) *Coming to Public Judgement: Making Democracy Work in a Complex World*, Syracuse University Press, Syracuse.

Yeschke, CL (2003) *The Art of Investigative Interviewing – A Human Approach to Testimonial Evidence*, Second edition, Butterworth-Heineman, Boston.

Yukl, GA (1998) *Leadership in Organisations*, Prentice Hall, London.

Zack, MH (1999) 'Managing codified knowledge', *Sloan Management Review*, Vol 40, No 4, pp 45-58.

Zapf, D (2002) 'Emotion work and psychological well-being: a review of the literature and some conceptual considerations', *Human Resource Management Review*, Vol 12, No 2, pp 237-268.

Zedner, L (2005a) 'Securing liberty in the face of terror', *Journal of Law and Society*, Vol 32, No 4, pp 507-533.

Zedner, L (2005b) *Criminal Justice*, Oxford University Press.

Zhao, JS, He, N and Lovrich, N (2002) 'Predicting five dimensions of police officer stress: looking into organizational settings for sources of police stress', *Police Quarterly*, Vol 5, No 1, pp 43-62.

Index